Network Security
first-step

Tom Thomas

Cisco Press
800 East 96th Street
Indianapolis, IN 46240

Network Security
first-step

Tom Thomas

Published by:
Cisco Press
800 East 96th Street
Indianapolis, IN 46240 USA

Printed in the United States of America 1 2 3 4 5 6 7 8 9 0

First Printing May 2004

Library of Congress Cataloging-in-Publication Number:
2003107987

ISBN: 1-58720-099-6

Warning and Disclaimer

This book is designed to provide information about network security. Every effort has been made to make this book as complete and as accurate as possible, but no warranty or fitness is implied.

The information is provided on an "as is" basis. The authors, Cisco Press, and Cisco Systems, Inc. shall have neither liability nor responsibility to any person or entity with respect to any loss or damages arising from the information contained in this book or from the use of the discs or programs that may accompany it.

The opinions expressed in this book belong to the author and are not necessarily those of Cisco Systems, Inc.

Publisher
John Wait

Editor-in-Chief
John Kane

Cisco Representative
Anthony Wolfenden

Cisco Press Program Manager
Nannette M. Noble

Production Manager
Patrick Kanouse

Senior Development Editor
Christopher Cleveland

Project Editor
San Dee Phillips

Copy Editor
Bridget Collins

Technical Editors
Matt Birkner
Amos Brown
Cary Riddock
Mark Zimmerman

Team Coordinator
Tammi Barnett

Book and Cover Designer
Louisa Adair

Compositor
Mark Shirar

Indexer
Tim Wright

Trademark Acknowledgments

All terms mentioned in this book that are known to be trademarks or service marks have been appropriately capitalized. Cisco Press or Cisco Systems, Inc. cannot attest to the accuracy of this information. Use of a term in this book should not be regarded as affecting the validity of any trademark or service mark.

Corporate and Government Sales

Cisco Press offers excellent discounts on this book when ordered in quantity for bulk purchases or special sales.

For more information please contact: U.S. Corporate and Government Sales 1-800-382-3419 corpsales@pearsontechgroup.com

For sales outside the U.S. please contact: International Sales international@pearsoned.com

Feedback Information

At Cisco Press, our goal is to create in-depth technical books of the highest quality and value. Each book is crafted with care and precision, undergoing rigorous development that involves the unique expertise of members from the professional technical community.

Readers' feedback is a natural continuation of this process. If you have any comments regarding how we could improve the quality of this book or otherwise alter it to better suit your needs, you can contact us through e-mail at feedback@ciscopress.com. Please make sure to include the book title and ISBN in your message.

We greatly appreciate your assistance.

CISCO SYSTEMS

Corporate Headquarters
Cisco Systems, Inc.
170 West Tasman Drive
San Jose, CA 95134-1706
USA
www.cisco.com
Tel: 408 526-4000
    800 553-NETS (6387)
Fax: 408 526-4100

European Headquarters
Cisco Systems International BV
Haarlerbergpark
Haarlerbergweg 13-19
1101 CH Amsterdam
The Netherlands
www-europe.cisco.com
Tel: 31 0 20 357 1000
Fax: 31 0 20 357 1100

Americas Headquarters
Cisco Systems, Inc.
170 West Tasman Drive
San Jose, CA 95134-1706
USA
www.cisco.com
Tel: 408 526-7660
Fax: 408 527-0883

Asia Pacific Headquarters
Cisco Systems, Inc.
Capital Tower
168 Robinson Road
#22-01 to #29-01
Singapore 068912
www.cisco.com
Tel: +65 6317 7777
Fax: +65 6317 7799

Cisco Systems has more than 200 offices in the following countries and regions. Addresses, phone numbers, and fax numbers are listed on the
Cisco.com Web site at www.cisco.com/go/offices.

Argentina • Australia • Austria • Belgium • Brazil • Bulgaria • Canada • Chile • China PRC • Colombia • Costa Rica • Croatia • Czech Republic
Denmark • Dubai, UAE • Finland • France • Germany • Greece • Hong Kong SAR • Hungary • India • Indonesia • Ireland • Israel • Italy
Japan • Korea • Luxembourg • Malaysia • Mexico • The Netherlands • New Zealand • Norway • Peru • Philippines • Poland • Portugal
Puerto Rico • Romania • Russia • Saudi Arabia • Scotland • Singapore • Slovakia • Slovenia • South Africa • Spain • Sweden
Switzerland • Taiwan • Thailand • Turkey • Ukraine • United Kingdom • United States • Venezuela • Vietnam • Zimbabwe

About the Author

Tom Thomas claims he never works because he loves what he does. When you meet him, you will agree!

Throughout his many years in the networking industry, Tom has taught thousands of people how networking works. Tom is the author or coauthor of 17 books on networking, including the acclaimed *OSPF Network Design Solutions*, published by Cisco Press. Beyond his many books, Tom also has taught computer and networking skills through his roles as an instructor and training-course developer.

Tom holds the Cisco Certified Internetwork Expert (CCIE No. 9360) certification—the pinnacle of networking certifications. Tom also holds Cisco CCNP, CCDA, and CCNA certifications and is a certified Cisco Systems instructor. These certifications support his industry-proven, problem-solving skills through technical leadership with demonstrated persistence and the ability to positively assist businesses in leveraging their IT resources.

Tom was the founder of NetCerts.com (now CCPrep.com) and is currently the principal owner and founder of Granite Systems, Inc. (www.GraniteSystems.net), a managed IT service provider for medium-sized businesses, where he is responsible for the corporate infrastructure, security implementations, and new product service development such as its ground-breaking IP Telephony Management System a.k.a. Bedrock. He was previously an instructor for Chesapeake Computer Consultants, Inc. (CCCI) and a course developer for Cisco Systems.

About the Technical Reviewers

Matthew H. Birkner, CCIE No. 3719, is a technical advisor at Cisco Systems, where he specializes in IP, MPLS, and QoS network design. He has influenced many large carrier and enterprise network designs worldwide. Matt has spoken at Cisco Networkers on MPLS in both the U.S. and EMEA over the past few years. A double CCIE, he wrote *Cisco Internetwork Design*, published by Cisco Press. Matt holds a BSEE from Tufts University, where he majored in electrical engineering.

Amos Brown is a Cisco Certified IPT Design engineer and co-founder of Granite Systems, Inc. in the RTP. He has worked with the Cisco AVVID solution for four years in various settings, ranging from small- to mid-sized businesses to campus deployments. Amos has created several web-based management and monitoring tools for Cisco IPT as an added offering for Cisco clients. He still finds time for his hobby, network security and Open Source security tools.

Cary Riddock, MCSE, CCDA, CCNP, is the principal and senior engineer for the Aegis Security Group LLC, headquartered in Florida. Cary has more than 16 years of experience as an IT professional, including years of specialization as a network engineer and security specialist. He has extensive experience in the vulnerability analysis and remediation of sensitive information networks, including both government and medical systems. Under Cary's leadership, Aegis is currently providing IT security consulting services for several federal agencies in the Washington, D.C., area. Cary is a contributing author and technical editor for Cisco Press and other IT security publications.

Mark Zimmerman, CCIE No. 11312, is a U.S. channels systems engineer for Cisco Systems outside field office in Research Triangle Park, NC. He is responsible for Cisco partner support and development. This role encompasses partner product training and technical help on solutions.

Mark works closely with the enterprise services organization and many other Cisco groups to grow and develop sales. He has worked with Cisco for three years. Before Cisco, Mark was a senior systems engineer for the State of Virginia building and gained valuable hands-on experience by supporting the community college systems networks. He worked for the state for eight years. Before this, Mark spent three years as an engineering consultant in Ohio, where he designed some of the first LANs using Arcnet. He earned his Bachelor of Science degree from Kent State University in electrical engineering technology.

Dedication

How do you put into words the importance someone has in your life? Love and time strengthens the emotions until they are so powerful and deep that the act of holding hands expresses them in such a fundamental way that words cannot. My wife, Rose, knows her importance to my life. Without her love and support, I never would have become the husband, father, Christian, and man that I am today. Rose, you are my partner, foundation, and sharer of dreams, and I dedicate this book to you. Thank you for your support, love, faith, questions, and our two wonderful children (Rebekah and Daniel). We are truly blessed as a family.

Acknowledgments

Special acknowledgments go to my good friend and the best editor, Chris Cleveland. His insight, abilities, and editorial comments take a rough manuscript and give it life beyond what a simple nerd was able to envision. I also want to thank John Kane for always listening.

Amy Moss, whom I have had the privilege and joy of knowing, is a great friend. Her understanding and friendship has been a joy to my family and I over the years. Amy helped me start this book and has been involved in every book I have written for Cisco Press, of which this was the last. Best of luck in the future, Amy; you will be missed!

As always, I would like to thank my technical editors, Matt, Amos, Cary, and Mark, for their friendship, insight, and awesome comments. Your knowledge helped to fine-tune my thoughts. I know that this book will help many people, and that was the goal. Thank you.

Contents at a Glance

Contents

Icons Used in This Book

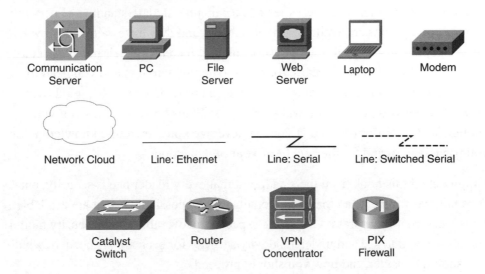

Communication Server | PC | File Server | Web Server | Laptop | Modem

Network Cloud | Line: Ethernet | Line: Serial | Line: Switched Serial

Catalyst Switch | Router | VPN Concentrator | PIX Firewall

Command Syntax Conventions

The conventions used to present command syntax in this book are the same conventions used in the IOS Command Reference. The Command Reference describes these conventions as follows:

- **Boldface** indicates commands and keywords that are entered literally, as shown. In actual configuration examples and output (not general command syntax), boldface indicates commands that are manually input by the user (such as a **show** command).

- *Italics* indicate arguments for which you supply actual values.

- Vertical bars (|) separate alternative, mutually exclusive elements.

- Square brackets [ ] indicate optional elements.

- Braces { } indicate a required choice.

- Braces within brackets [{ }] indicate a required choice within an optional element.

Introduction

This book was written to address the need for increased understanding of network security. Many texts are available on the subject, and they have value. However, many people and companies are now considering increasing their network security. Where do you start? Perhaps you want to deploy wireless and you need to ensure that it is secure. What single resource can provide you with a good overview of wireless security or firewalls, and so on? This book provides you with enough security information that you can leverage your newfound knowledge for your own benefit and for the benefit of your organization.

I approached this book from the standpoint that every reader needs security, but does not really understand the risks, techniques, and possibilities that are available. Thus, each chapter addresses a specific aspect of an overall layered security model and allows you to see and understand why security for each area is needed, what you should consider, and how you should proceed.

Goals and Methods

The goal of this book is provide a resource for every person concerned with security. Readers do not have to be networking professionals or CIOs to benefit from this book, although they can as well. It is my hope that all readers, from students to professionals, all readers will benefit from this book.

My method was to take each component of the network and verify how it can be deployed securely. When complex security technologies or concepts are encountered, they are explained with real-world examples and practical analogies. This book covers serious topics, but it should also be fun and easy to read. I have endeavored to meet this goal.

Who Should Read This Book?

This book was written with a broad audience in mind. Consider students who are hearing all about the importance of network security and considering focusing on this area. This book helps them by providing an understanding of all the major components of securing a network. Perhaps you are a networking professional with in-depth expertise in routing and switching, and now you have been asked to deploy wireless (securely). This book provides a solid foundation upon which to explore the subject matter in more depth, while understanding the different components necessary for accomplishing your goals. You might even be a CIO who has been tasked with determining whether you should invest in an Intrusion Detection
System (IDS). Perhaps you need to understand why they are needed, how they work, and when/where to use them.

Regardless of your expertise or role in the IT industry, this book has a place for you; it takes concepts and simplifies them to give you a solid foundation of understanding. What you do with that knowledge is up to you. This book might give you what you need, or it might be the first step in your journey.

How This Book Is Organized

Although you could read this book cover-to-cover, it is designed to be flexible and allow you to easily move between chapters and sections of chapters to cover only the material you need. If you do intend to read them all, the order in which they are presented is an excellent sequence.

Chapters 1 through 10 cover the following topics:

- **Chapter 1, "Here There Be Hackers!"** —This chapter provides a glimpse into the mind and motivation of the individuals who are attacking your systems. This chapter covers tools, techniques, and attacks.

- **Chapter 2, "Security Policies and Responses"** —This chapter starts the layered defense concept with the foundation of securing your network,

which is the security policy being discussed. When you finish this chapter, you will understand the role that policies play and one of the ways to prepare/respond to an incident.

- **Chapter 3, "Overview of Security Technologies"** — This chapter discusses the nuts and bolts of how to use security technologies — from the most basic access control lists available in every router to global solutions such as PKI. Many of these technologies are used today without your need to fully understand when or where they are operating. After reading this chapter, you will understand the benefits of these technologies, where they operate, and some of the risks associated with them.

- **Chapter 4, "Security Protocols"** — This chapter looks at security and the encryption protocols that are being used to secure your network. In addition, it considers the limitations of each security protocol that is covered, because nothing is perfect.

- **Chapter 5, "Firewalls"** — This chapter covers firewalls and how they operate. It examines who needs a firewall and why they are an essential part of your network's defense.

- **Chapter 6, "Router Security"** — If you have a network, you have a router; they have evolved over the years and are now capable of being effective security devices. This chapter discusses the expanded security capabilities of routers.

- **Chapter 7, "IPSec Virtual Private Networks (VPNs)"** — This chapter discusses the role of VPNs and how they are reshaping the public Internet, encrypting all information that flows across the Internet. This includes the functional characteristics and operational parameters.

- **Chapter 8, "Wireless Security"** — This chapter discusses the hottest technology, wireless, and explains that all is not well in this IT nirvana. Hackers have also come here, and they bring a full compliment of tools. Many think that wireless is safe and easy; this chapter ensures that those people become security conscious.

- **Chapter 9, "Intrusion Detection and Honeypots"**—This chapter discusses how you can detect a hacker's attempt to gain access into your network by using an IDS. In addition, it discusses one of the ways to confuse a hacker—through a honey pot—so the reader will understand the role of each device.

- **Chapter 10, "Tools of the Trade"**—This chapter discusses the security tools used by hackers so readers can understand what they are up against. This chapter then examines the available tools for identifying weaknesses in your network, and the anatomy of a security audit, which is a crucial piece for ensuring that a network is secure.

What You Will Learn

By the end of this chapter, you should know and be able to explain the following:

- ✔ What is the difference between a target of opportunity and a target of choice?

- ✔ What are the six major components of an attack and the purpose of each?

- ✔ Where are the online security organizations and how can they assist you?

What are the breadth and scope of possible attacks and exploits that are available to attackers? Being able to answer these key questions will allow you to understand the overall characteristics and importance of network security. By the time you finish this book, you will have a solid appreciation for network security and understand its issues, how it works, and why it is important.

CHAPTER 1

Here There Be Hackers!

When the ancient mapmakers reached the edge of the world they said,
"There Be Dragons Here!" — Anonymous

In today's interconnected world, this ancient representation of the world beyond a person's knowledge holds true. When you connect your home or corporate network to the Internet, everything beyond your network is literally the edge of the world and the beginning of the World Wide Web, wherein the hackers are looking to take advantage of the unwary.

In a book about understanding network security, the obvious first step is to introduce and review what a *hacker* is and some of the methods a hacker employs to threaten your network.

From finding the right target to executing the attack, this chapter provides an overview of a hacker attack's anatomy. You will learn some of the factors and footprints of hackers that will allow you to understand the threat that is present beyond the edge of your network.

Essentials First: Looking for a Target

There are only several billion possible public IP addresses on the Internet, so how hard can it be to find a suitable target? This is probably the first aspect of security on which people concentrate. Certainly your network's presence on the Internet is a way for hackers to find you; as a result, you should consider the security of your network from attackers. You have purchased the best security technology to protect your PC, and you constantly ensure that it is up-to-date with the latest security

patches. This includes your firewall, screening router, VPNs, antivirus software, proxy server, biometrics, and all the best security technologies that money can buy. You have done this, right?

It is natural to think that security technology can protect you from the malicious threats of hacker technology. In this case, however, you might have been yearning for a sense of security but forgotten about the weakest security link: the human factor.

Consider for a moment whether your employees are trained in security. Would they know what to do if someone tried to fool them into giving away potentially sensitive information? How many sets of keys to the building exist? What are the cleaning people doing when you are not there? Are they disposing of your trash properly, or are they bagging and dropping it into the dumpster? Could an intruder break a window or pick a lock to enter your building undetected? Now how does that awesome firewall completely protect you?

You might be thinking that you have a great IT staff or even a team dedicated to network security, which is a good thing. Security professionals are expected to have a high level of technical competence and, for the most part, this is true. However, these same professionals often do not expect the same to be true of those attackers and intruders from whom they defend their sites. Many do not take heed of the axiom that *"There's always someone out there smarter, more knowledgeable, or better-equipped than you."* Having an engineer who thinks that he is the smartest person in the company is a recipe for disaster.

Consider a popular term known as ***dumpster diving***. You have probably heard the stories where people become obsessed with a movie star or popular television personality and go through their trash. In reality, this practice began with people trying to hack into the AT&T phone system; of course, they were called phone phreaks, not hackers. The point is that, to a social engineer, even the garbage a company places in the dumpster is not safe.

If you want a better understanding of the actual benefits of dumpster diving, rent the hacker movie, *Sneakers*. Not only is it an entertaining movie, but it also provides insight into many of the topics discussed in this section and the next.

Security is often simply an illusion that is facilitated and made more believable by the ignorance or naiveté of everyone in an organization. Do not place all your trust in security products; if you do, you are settling for the illusion of security. Any security process must be implemented—that is, both "technology" *and* rules. (Specifically, all people in an organization must hold to these stated rules.) In addition, you must perform random audits to determine whether certain people in the company, such as the CEO who does not heed all the rules, bypass any rules. The CEO usually has access to secrets and is a first target for a hacker. Letting the CEO bypass security policies is a sure way to weaken a security policy.

In summary, "true" security is more than a product; it is a series of processes that encompass products and personnel across an organization. The following section covers the importance of having company personnel be aware of the security process.

Hacking Innocent Information

Considering the introduction to this chapter, this discussion begins with hacking innocent information, which is also known as *social engineering*. Hacking innocent information from a person via social engineering is much easier than bypassing a firewall.

Fundamentally, people want to trust and help others, so they are more vulnerable to social engineering; combating this most basic hacking can be one of the biggest challenges to those who are responsible for security.

Although you might not think innocent information is worth protecting, it can be crucial to a social engineer attacker. When an attacker is armed with this information, he can use it to present himself as believable. In reality, this is where the hacker usually begins penetrating a company by obtaining some document that might seem innocent and commonplace; be careful, however, because it could be useful to others.

Consider the following scenario, which I used once while performing a Network Assessment. To see what people would be willing to give up to someone who "sounded" official, I called the senior IT engineer, Daniel:

> "Hello, this is Tom from WindWing Travel. Your tickets to San Jose are ready; would you like us to deliver them or arrange for you to pick them up as e-tickets at the airport? "

> "San Jose?" Daniel says, "I do not have any travel plans there."

> "Is this Daniel Thomas?" I asked.

> "Yes, but I do not have any trips scheduled until AppleCon in Las Vegas, later this year."

> "Well," I chuckle, "are you sure you do not want to go check out San Jose?"

> Daniel chuckles as well, responding to a humorous situation and a break in his normal routine by saying, "Sure, I'd be happy to go if you can convince my boss…."

> "Sounds like another computer glitch," I say and, while chuckling, I remark, "I thought computers were supposed to make our lives easier."

> Daniel laughs too.

> "In our travel system, we track travel arrangements under your employee number. Perhaps someone used the wrong number when booking the flight. What is your employee number?"

Daniel knows that several groups within his company have his employee number: security, human resources, his boss, and obviously finance, so why wouldn't the travel company use a way to identify him that would fit with his company. There is no danger here, is there?

A competent hacker working on social engineering can take this simple piece of information and use it with some rather easily obtained data to take his hack to the next level. Imagine what access he might gain if he had an employee's number, full name, telephone extension, department, work location, e-mail address, and even his manager's information. This information is innocent when viewed in pieces, but it paints a scary picture when gathered together.

Clearly, innocent information should be protected and employees should be made aware that mishandling information that should never be released to the public could truly endanger both the company and, more importantly, the employee. For example, consider the following example:

> "Daniel, I can't find you by employee number. Let me try this another way. What is your social security number?"

A good rule of thumb is that all company data should be considered sensitive in nature and not released unless explicitly stated in a Data Classification Policy.

note

For additional information on social engineering and how hackers gather information without ever alerting your network engineers, refer to the following text: *The Art of Deception: Controlling the Human Element of Security*, by Kevin Mitnick and William Simon.

This text also describes techniques and policies that can be used to defend against these types of attacks. I strongly recommend this enjoyable and well-written book.

Targets of Opportunity

I cannot keep track of the number of times I have been with a customer who discusses their network and its security only to hear the following:

> "We are a <Non-IT business> and there is nothing on our network that a hacker would want. Why should we be worried?"

Wow! What a statement. It astounds me every time I hear it. There are many ways to reply to such a statement—some of which are politically correct, and some of which are not. Usually the person making this statement is a customer, so the focus here should be on the correct response.

This belief is also known as *Security Through Obscurity*. In this book, you will see that when it comes to security, relying on obscurity is dangerous regardless of the company's size or business.

Perhaps the company in question might not be a bank, but its network certainly contains servers, hard drive space, bandwidth to the Internet, and personal employee information. Believing that this information is unimportant to a hacker can be fatal. Consider what a hacker could do with such information:

- **Servers**—Hack a server and you get a slave device that could potentially be used remotely to attack other, more important targets. Can you envision getting a call from men in dark suits who have no sense of humor regarding what your server might be doing?

- **Hard drive space**—Every network has unused disk space. What if you were hacked and files of a questionable or perhaps even illegal nature were placed on them? Consider what the lawyers enforcing copyright laws might think. Perhaps, the files might contain pornography or terrorist material. In addition, most server hard drives today are of the hundred gigabyte variety or larger, the capacity of which is attractive to someone who needs to park a recently bootlegged movie for a few hours or even days.

- **Bandwidth**—A hacker can always use extra bandwidth and alternative means of connecting to other companies to hack into them.

- **Personal employee information**—Armed with all the information an employer might need to verify employment and even pay its employees, a hacker could engage in identity theft.

These hacker activities could place IT personnel, management, or even the entire company in danger with legal or criminal ramifications, not to mention the bad press associated with being hacked to this degree.

The more important question is not, "Why would someone hack us?" but, "Am I vulnerable enough to be selected as a target?"

Targets of opportunity are clearly the easiest for a hacker to penetrate because something has happened or not happened that allows him to easily identify and gain access to a corporate network that *has nothing valuable*.

Are You a Target of Opportunity?

In many cases, hackers prowl the Internet using a variety of tools (covered later in this book) and usually have an agenda in mind when they discover a potential target. In addition to hackers, there are a variety of individuals known as *script kiddies*:

note

A script kiddie (sometimes spelled "kiddy") is a derogative term, originated by the more sophisticated hackers of computer security systems for the more immature, but unfortunately often just as dangerous, exploiter of Internet security lapses. The typical script kiddie uses existing and frequently well-known and easy-to-find techniques and programs or scripts to search for and exploit weaknesses in other computers on the Internet—often randomly and with little regard or perhaps even understanding the potentially harmful consequences. Hackers view script kiddies with alarm and contempt because they do nothing to advance the "art" of hacking, except sometimes unleashing the wrath of authority on the entire hacker community.

While a hacker takes pride in the quality of an attack—leaving no trace of an intrusion, for example—a script kiddie might aim at quantity, seeing the number of attacks that can be mounted as a means of obtaining attention and notoriety. Script kiddies are sometimes portrayed in the media as bored, lonely teenagers seeking recognition from their peers (http://www.searchsecurity.com). Script kiddies usually hack for the challenge and not for financial gain; although, that can be a motivator. As novices, script kiddies often do not know what they are doing and can inadvertently cause a Denial of Service (DoS.) The word is that, in most cases, expert hackers were script kiddies at one time.

Determining whether you are a target of opportunity depends on your security infrastructure. A good rule of thumb is that if you do not have a firewall in place or your firewall has not been updated in a while, you are likely to be a target of opportunity. Because they employ automated tools that look for vulnerabilities in your security, script kiddies are the most common threats to networks that are tar-

gets of opportunities. One of the easiest ways to ensure that you do not become a target of opportunity is to update your infrastructure with the latest patches. Do not let yourself get lulled into a false sense of security by patching only a server or two. You might not be a target of opportunity, but a target of the hacker's choice.

Targets of Choice

Hackers often have a goal in mind when selecting a target. Consider the role the media has played in setting our internal vision of what a hacker is. Many people think that a hacker possesses the following characteristics:

- Disgruntled, negative, and angry at the world

- Bitter, with few friends and low self-esteem

- Extremely smart, yet not able to focus on traditional careers

- Has trouble maintaining relationships, friendship, or romance

- Disrespects authority; a social misfit

- Young and inept with women

- Enjoys junk food and pizza, ensuring the presence of pimples

- Writes with numb3r5 in th3r3 w0rd5 to be kewl

These stereotypes are true in some cases; regardless, a subculture of hacking exists, and some hackers revel in it. However, believing that all the security threats against your network come from individuals like these would be a mistake.

Are You a Target of Choice?

The following scenarios can help you understand that your company—or perhaps even *you*—might be a target of choice by a hacker:

- Perhaps your company has a new product that is going to revolutionize your area of business. What if it is a breakthrough?

- Perhaps you are engaged in a bitter dispute with a family member and you have information that the other party wants.

- Perhaps you have upset someone who knows a hacker.

- Perhaps you have a good credit rating, making your identity very attractive.

- Perhaps your company is in a business that, if disrupted, would allow people with an agenda to make a point?

- Perhaps your company has information on another company that is important to someone.

- Perhaps an employee has become disgruntled and wants to make a point.

- Perhaps you are trying to hide something from a lawyer during a bitter divorce. (Smile if you want, but it does happen.)

- Perhaps your company is doing business in a part of the world that is in the middle of social or political upheaval—even hackers have geopolitical consciences nowadays.

In these cases and perhaps many others, you are now officially a target of choice. Certainly the hacker could fit within the subculture described earlier, but perhaps he is not something out of a Hollywood movie. What about private investigators and lawyers—might they not be interested in information that you or your company might have?

As people wanting to know all sorts of things hire them, private investigators are learning new skills; therefore, to be successful, they could have turned to the Internet to find this information about you. What about the ex-military or those trained by the government as security specialists? It is highly doubtful that they fit the Hollywood hacker stereotype. What about a spurned lover or spouse who has some computer skills, or an employee who knows all your partnering companies. These groups do not fit the hackers we see on Hollywood's silver screen, but they can certainly be viewed as a threat to your network.

Understand, as well, that a hacker might not do all the work himself, and it might not be electronic. For example, do you recall the dumpster diving discussion?

Dumpster diving is legal and is an easy means of acquiring all kinds information that could be helpful to a hacker.

The following section covers how an attack begins, and the process an attacker takes to begin compromising the target system.

The Process of an Attack

There are many ways that an attacker can attempt to gain access to or exploit a system. This system can be as simple as a home computer connected to the Internet through a DSL connection, or a complex corporate network. Regardless of the kind of system an attacker is targeting, they typically employ the same fundamental steps:

1. Reconnaissance and footprinting

2. Scanning

3. Enumeration

4. Gaining access

5. Escalating

6. Creating backdoors and covering tracks

The following sections discuss these steps in detail. It is important to understand the concepts of what an attacker might be doing in each step, and her goal.

Reconnaissance and Footprinting (a.k.a. Casing the Joint)

"Intelligence preparation of the battlefield" is a military term used to define the methodology employed to reduce uncertainties concerning the enemy, environment, and terrain for all types of military operations. During military actions, this concept has been clearly demonstrated through the use of drone aircraft that allowed military commanders to "see" the battlefield and thus pick when and, more importantly, *how* they engaged the enemy. Understanding the battlefield and subsequently having the ability to choose *how* you engage the target is analogous to the choices hackers make.

Hackers conduct intelligence preparation operations against your company and network. It is a continuous process that is used throughout all planned and executed operations. The networked environment that security professionals are tasked with securing is analogous to a battlefield. The myriad of attackers and intruders from the void are the aggressors who are constantly on the offense. The security professionals are the defenders, entrusted to preserve the confidentiality and integrity of data against these intruders.

In network security terms, this intelligence preparation is known as reconnaissance and footprinting; in Hollywood movies, it is referred to as "casing the joint." In the real world, many criminals perform this step, but they probably have not named it. For example, a criminal might review the security of a convenience store so he can understand what the security is, where the money is kept, the location of security cameras, possible exits, and any other items that might help them succeed in his crime. As shown in Table 1-1, hackers look to gain information during this phase.

Table 1-1   Goals of Reconnaissance and Footprinting

Technology	What is Learned
Internet Presence	Ideally, a target would be connected to the Internet; an attacker would therefore want to learn the following: • The target's domain names and DNS servers. Assigned blocks of public IP addresses. • Which specific IP addresses (of those assigned) are accessible from the Internet. • Of the IP addresses found to be accessible from the Internet, what services (www, ftp, e-mail, and so on) are viable targets? • Of the services found, what kind of computers—both hardware and operating system (including version/build so potential vulnerabilities can be known)—are they running on? For example, Windows, Linux, Sun, UNIX, and so on. Each of these has different vulnerabilities. • Are there any mechanisms in place that control access to the network? • What kind of firewall, Intrusion Detection Systems are present? • System enumeration allows for the specific identification of a system and some of the data available on it (user and group names, system banners, routing tables, and SNMP information). • Where are these devices and systems physically located? • Network protocols (routed and routing) that are in use—for example IPX, IP, OSPF, or RIP. • Construct a simple network map with all of the previous information, plus which company provides the target internet access. • Develop any information that might make it easier to conduct "social engineering." • Information on individuals associated with the systems: name, phone #, position, address, what do they know, and so on.
Intranet Characteristics	Network engineers understand that hackers try and gain access to the Internet; thus, many networks have duplicate infrastructure inside and outside their firewalls. As a result, the thorough hacker repeats the footprinting steps he conducted from the Internet against the targets' intranet.

Table 1-1   Goals of Reconnaissance and Footprinting (continued)

Remote Access	Many companies not only have normal Internet access through Frame Relay or Broadband, but they will also have dialup access. This is yet another way for an attacker to enter the network, so a thorough hacker footprints these as well:
	• What type of remote access is available?
	• Where does the remote access connect, and what is the connection's destination?
	• How is access to the network controlled? (RADIUS, TACACS, and so on)

There are certainly a lot of steps a hacker can take to learn about your network without your knowledge. Consider what simply looking at what Domain Name System (DNS) can reveal about your network through the use of a simple command known as **nslookup**. (See Example 1-1.)

Example 1-1   Using DNS for Passive Reconnaissance

```
[AppleKick:~] topkick% nslookup
Default Server:  [192.168.254.69]
Address:  192.168.254.69

> www.cisco.com
Server:  [192.168.254.69]
Address:  192.168.254.69

Non-authoritative answer:
Name:    www.cisco.com
Address:  198.133.219.25




> set querytype=mx (mx means mail servers)
> cisco.com
Server:  [192.168.254.69]
Address:  192.168.254.69

Non-authoritative answer:
cisco.com       preference = 20, mail exchanger = proxy6.cisco.com
cisco.com       preference = 20, mail exchanger = proxy9.cisco.com
cisco.com       preference = 20, mail exchanger = proxy1.cisco.com
cisco.com       preference = 20, mail exchanger = proxy2.cisco.com
cisco.com       preference = 20, mail exchanger = proxy3.cisco.com
cisco.com       preference = 10, mail exchanger = proxy0.cisco.com
```

continues

Example 1-1 Using DNS for Passive Reconnaissance

```
cisco.com          preference = 20, mail exchanger = proxy5.cisco.com

Authoritative answers can be found from:
cisco.com          nameserver = ns1.cisco.com
cisco.com          nameserver = ns2.cisco.com
proxy6.cisco.com        internet address = 203.41.198.245
proxy9.cisco.com        internet address = 192.135.250.71
proxy1.cisco.com        internet address = 128.107.241.179
proxy2.cisco.com        internet address = 128.107.241.180
proxy3.cisco.com        internet address = 128.107.241.181
proxy0.cisco.com        internet address = 128.107.241.178
proxy5.cisco.com        internet address = 64.103.36.137
ns1.cisco.com   internet address = 128.107.241.185
ns2.cisco.com   internet address = 192.135.250.69
>
```

Consider that through using just DNS tools, the attacker can reveal the public IP address of the Cisco website and that of its DNS and e-mail servers; in addition, it looks like the attacker is using proxy servers. Whois is a tool that is again freely available in many applications and on the Internet at the following locations. Try it out on your domain:

> http://www.networksolutions.com/—whois web interface
>
> http://www.arin.net/—ARIN Whois
>
> http://whois.ripe.net/—European Whois
>
> http://whois.apnic.net/—Asia Pacific IP Address Allocations
>
> http://whois.nic.mil/—U.S. Military
>
> http://whois.nic.gov/—U.S. Government

Cisco.com is queried all the time and is, therefore, not alarmed by *passive reconnaissance*. Do not forget the information available on a company's website and how useful it is to know the address, main phone number, fax number, mergers, press releases, and members (with bios) of the company's management team. A target's corporate website has become a well of useful information from which an attacker can learn quite a lot. The hacker could use this knowledge for social engineering, identity of network systems, system administrators, and so forth. USENET and WEB searches on the system administrators and technical contacts are found when running host queries. By taking the time to track down this information, the attacker might be able to gain greater insight into the target network.

If you were a hacker, however, you could begin a more ***active reconnaissance*** to determine what services you could see on these servers through their public IP address.

Unfortunately, most companies are not prepared to detect these types of scans or probes. It is not that they do not have some of the basic tools; it is simply that the target devices most likely are not logging what is going on–or, if they are, no one is looking at the logs. Consider that one of the next steps could be a simple ping scan using any number of freely available tools on the Internet. Refer to Figure 1-1, in which you can see the results of a ping scan on a class subnet using WhatRoute. (A very neat tool; check it out at http://www.whatroute.net.)

Figure 1-1   Ping Scan of a Class C Subnet

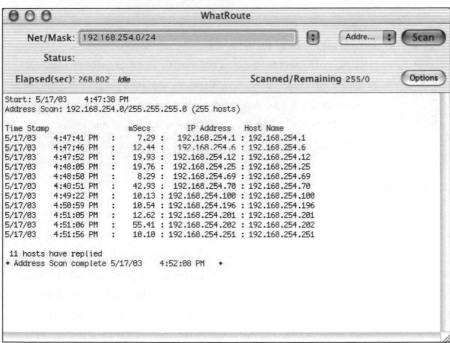

Attackers know this and also understand that the more active they are, the more likely their activities will be noticed. An attacker will, therefore, start active reconnaissance and allow it to continue until he has learned enough information to launch an exploit against that system. If the exploit succeeds, the attacker moves onto the next step; if not, he goes back and gathers more information.

During this phase of an attack, the methods employed involve nonintrusive and standoff methods that hopefully will not allow the attacker's efforts to be detected. The attacker wants to determine the type of network with which he is dealing, and with whom he is dealing: system, network, and security administrators. Again, the intent is to develop a network map that uses information gathered during footprinting; he then figures out which devices are routers and firewalls and places them on the map, and identifies key systems such as mail servers, domain name servers, file servers and so on. The attacker also wants to know where the target gets its Internet access in case he needs to try and access the target through its ISP.

note
Do a Google search on the words, "Welcome to IIS 4.0," and you will see how many IIS servers exist in the world. The fact that there are any responses to these search terms speaks volumes for how hastily web servers are set up and deployed—not to mention that a hacker now has an "all-night buffet" of servers from which to choose and enjoy.

Scanning

At this point, the attacker has a good idea of the machines on the network, their operating systems, who the system administrators are, any discussions posted to newsgroups, their office locations, and who their upstream Intrusion Prevention System (IPS) is. The attacker also knows that, from this point forward, everything he does might be logged; at a minimum, he should assume that it is. The attacker has a map of the network and devices and is ready to move on to identifying listening services and open ports. The attacker will also determine the acceptable risk. Can he afford to be logged during scanning? Is compromise acceptable during the latter stages of the attack? Is concealment of the originating attack location necessary? What about exposure of the sponsor if he is working on behalf of another entity?

There is a lot going on in the attacker's mind. Some attackers sketch things out, and others internalize these considerations as they move from step to step.

In Example 1-2, the attacker has initiated a more active set of scans against a target using *NMAP* (www.insecure.org), a free tool that both hackers and ethical hackers (good guys) commonly use. Because it is free, you will not find a script kiddie without it!

Example 1-2   Active Port Scan Results

```
[AppleKick:/Users/topkick] topkick# nmap -sS -O 192.168.254.69

Starting nmap V. 3.00 ( www.insecure.org/nmap/ )
Interesting ports on  (192.168.254.69):
(The 1579 ports scanned but not shown below are in state: closed)
Port       State       Service
7/tcp      open        echo
9/tcp      open        discard
13/tcp     open        daytime
17/tcp     open        qotd
19/tcp     open        chargen
25/tcp     open        smtp
42/tcp     open        nameserver
53/tcp     open        domain
80/tcp     open        http
119/tcp    open        nntp
135/tcp    open        loc-srv
139/tcp    open        netbios-ssn
443/tcp    open        https
445/tcp    open        microsoft-ds
563/tcp    open        snews
1025/tcp   open        NFS-or-IIS
1027/tcp   open        IIS
1031/tcp   open        iad2
1033/tcp   open        netinfo
3372/tcp   open        msdtc
3389/tcp   open        ms-term-serv
Remote operating system guess: Windows 2000/XP/ME

Nmap run completed -- 1 IP address (1 host up) scanned in 5 seconds
[AppleKick:/Users/topkick] topkick#
```

If you refer back to Figure 1-1, you will see that the ping scan revealed an active host at 192.168.254.69 and that the more detailed scan with NMAP, shown in Example 1-2, provided additional information. You might be wondering how accurate NMAP is. The answer is *very accurate*; specifically, the device scanned was, in fact, a Win2k server.

For example, Figure 1-2 uses TigerSuite (http://www.tigertools.net) to see the other services that are accessible on the server. The figure shows that the server is readily identified, as are some extraneous services that are easily exploitable: SMTP, NTP, and FTP. Also notice that the scan revealed the server's name and domain, which is very helpful to users and hackers in a Windows network!

Figure 1-2 Server Query Scan

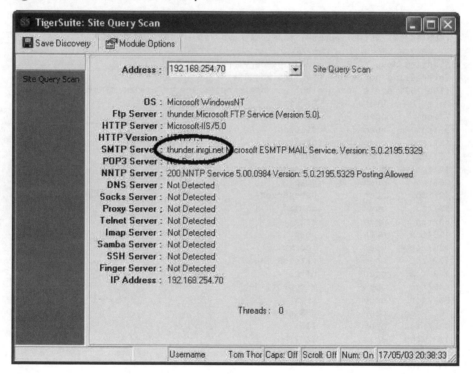

Being somewhat concerned about these services, I immediately shut them off and disabled them from starting again. This is a relatively new server, and I was more concerned about getting it functioning for my users than securing it. In their hearts, most OS vendors felt the desire to be helpful and reduce the number of expensive (for them) technical support phone calls turning on every single service and function from the beginning. Clearly, they were not thinking of security in this decision—only money. Apparently, they want their CEO to be the richest man in the world. Regardless of their irresponsible motives, Figure 1-3 shows that it does not take the IT professional long to correct this situation.

Figure 1-3   Secured Server Scan Results

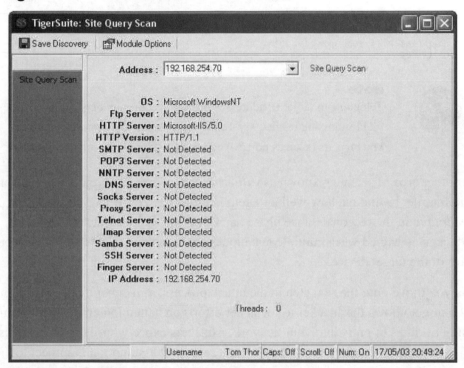

You can Telnet to an open port 80 and do a simple **get** command. The result should be a "banner," which identifies web server type (IIS, Apache, and so on) and other interesting facts, as shown in Example 1-3.

Example 1-3   Telnet to Port 80 to ID a Server

```
[AppleKick:~] topkick% telnet 192.168.254.69  80
Trying 192.168.254.69...
Connected to 192.168.254.69.
Escape character is '^]'.

get

HTTP/1.1 400 Bad Request
```

continues

Example 1-3   Telnet to Port 80 to ID a Server (continued)

```
Server: Microsoft-IIS/5.0
Date: Tue, 20 May 2003 00:43:14 GMT
Content-Type: text/html
Content-Length: 87

<html><head><title>Error</title></head><body>The parameter is incorrect. </
body></html>Connection closed by foreign host.
[AppleKick:~] topkick%
```

note

Telnetting to target IP addresses on various port numbers can sometimes yield surprising results. Try Telnetting to some of the more commonly known ports (such as port 80) and see what kind of results you get.

Another type of scanning known as *vulnerability scanning* is typically done from the Internet to find out how well a system is protected. As you have seen, each *technique* in the reconnaissance phase has value, but the true value (for the attacker) is gained when multiple techniques are combined to gain a complete picture of the target device.

As you move onto the next step in the attack process, remember that the scanning of a target allows the attacker to focus her efforts and attention on the most promising avenues of entry into your network. Attackers expect your IT professionals to be watching, but they doubt they will be seen; that assumption is subject to change, however.

Enumeration

Defining the network environment involves footprinting, scanning, and enumeration. Footprinting allows the attacker to limit the scope of her activities to those systems that are potentially the most promising targets to vulnerabilities she plans on running against the server. Scanning told the attacker what ports are open and what services are running.

Enumeration is the extraction of valid account information and exported resources. The key difference between the preceding scanning and footprinting techniques is that enumeration involves active connections to specific systems and directed requests to connect to these specific systems, too.

note
The previous section concluded by saying that attackers expect to be seen, but ignored while they are footprinting. However, when enumeration begins, the attackers attempts must be stopped or, at the very minimum, logged and *acted upon!*

Like all steps in the attack, pulling the activities together makes the difference in the success of the attack. Following are the four main categories within a network:

- Network resources and shares

- Users and group

- Applications

- Device banners

As you can tell, the presence of each of these categories differs on every operating system. Consider that every major operating system allows for shares, but each—MAC OS, Windows, Linux, and Novell—handles them in a different way. This means that, from an attacker's perspective, each operating system must be handled differently.

The earlier example of a layered approach becomes apparent here because, through the use of NMAP, you have a good idea of what operating systems you are trying to attack.

Enumerating Windows

As the industry leader in computer operating systems, Microsoft Windows is perhaps the most widely discussed; therefore, it makes sense to spend some time on it first. Windows operating systems still depends heavily on the use of NetBios (UDP Port 137), and many of the tools an attacker might use to learn more about a

Windows-based network are built into the operating system itself as you will see in the text that follows.

Example 1-4 shows the results of issuing a **net view** command from the command line of a Windows machine. In this case, the domain was known, so including it in the command revealed all the machines in that domain. Had the domain been omitted, all the LAN's domains would have been displayed.

Example 1-4   Using Windows Net View

```
C:\>net view /domain:inrgi

Server Name            Remark
-------------------------------------------------
\\APPLEKICK            Toms MAC
\\LIGHTNING
\\ROSE-LAPTOP
\\THUNDER
\\TOPKICK

The command completed successfully.

C:\>
```

This enumeration technique is even more useful when you combine it with the results of the earlier ping scan. IP addresses and NetBIOS names can be used interchangeably so for example with NetBIOS, you might access another computer using \\COMPUTER-NAME. You can also use \\192.168.254.69. Attackers know this and modify their systems so that their machines "automatically" cache the NetBIOS names.

Another great built-in Windows tool is **nbtstat**, which allows you to query another computer for its NetBIOS name table. What this means is an attacker can query a server for its table, as shown in Example 1-5.

Example 1-5   Query via **nbtstat**

```
C:\>nbtstat -A 192.168.254.70

Local Area Connection:

Node IpAddress: [192.168.254.69] Scope Id: []

          NetBIOS Remote Machine Name Table
```

Example 1-5   Query via **nbtstat**

```
    Name                 Type        Status
    ---------------------------------------------
    THUNDER        <00>  UNIQUE      Registered
    THUNDER        <20>  UNIQUE      Registered
    INRGI          <00>  GROUP       Registered
    INet~Services  <1C>  GROUP       Registered
    IS~THUNDER.....<00>  UNIQUE      Registered
    INRGI          <1E>  GROUP       Registered
    INRGI          <1D>  UNIQUE      Registered
    .._MSBROWSE__.<01>   GROUP       Registered
    MAC Address = 00-C0-9F-20-E4-F0

C:\>
```

And if you do not know the IP address of the machine you have your sights set on, you can issue the command **nbtstat –c**; you will then be provided with a listing of the NetBIOS names (in your cache) and their corresponding IP addresses. Don't you just love friendly operating systems?

Example 1-6   Using **nbtstat –c** to Display NetBIOS Names

```
E:\>nbtstat -c
Local Area Connection:
Node IpAddress: [192.168.1.101] Scope Id: []
                 NetBIOS Remote Cache Name Table
Name         Type    Host      Address          Life [sec]
PRO200       <20>    UNIQUE    192.168.1.100     587
PRO200       <00>    UNIQUE    192.168.1.100     95
```

The best way to stop an attacker from learning this kind of information from your network is to ensure that your router and firewall are blocking the entry *and* exit of NetBIOS packets. Block at both points in order to prevent a layered approach to security. Specifically, block the following:

- TCP and UDP on ports 135 through 139

- TCP and UDP 445 for Windows 2000

Blocking these ports does not stop NetBIOS; it simply prevents it from entering your network. There are ways to disable NetBIOS on a Windows PC; however,

this might not be an option. Table 1-2 shows some of the common tasks and tools that attackers use.

Table 1-2   Attacker Tasks, Tools, and Techniques

Attacker Tasks	Tools and Techniques
List file shares	Being onsite
List user names	NetBIOS and NetBUI
Identify applications	Using Telnet to see default banners
Identify operating systems	Null sessions

As discussed at the beginning of this section, each operating system has associated techniques that enumerate against it. You have looked at a couple techniques that are just for Windows, and there are many more. Later in this chapter, you will see some recommended titles that discuss more about the other enumeration possibilities.

Gaining Access

Many people mistakenly believe that an attacker wants to "take control" of a target device and that is the ultimate goal an attack. This is not entirely true. What is more likely is that an attacker want to gain access to a target PC. After enumeration identifies promising avenues of entry, more intrusive probing can begin as valid user accounts and poorly protected resource shares are exploited to gain access.

Ultimately, the attacker must gain access to a system through some aspect of that system. There are typically four major types of exploits that reflect different aspects of a system that attackers target:

- Operating system attacks

- Application attacks

- Misconfiguration attacks

- Script attacks

Within these different aspects of an attack, two ways in which an attacker can proceed follow:

- **Automated attacks**—These types of attacks target one or more aspects of the target and are usually opportunistic by their design. Automated attacks are opportunistic in the sense that they scan an entire block of IP addresses to look for vulnerability. For example, an automated attack might scan every IP address in a Class C block on port 80 looking for a known vulnerability that affects web servers. If the scan is successful, the attack proceeds; if not, the scan continues looking.

- **Targeted attacks**—These types of attacks are more dangerous than automated attacks because your organization has been singled out for an attack. In other words, an attacker knows that you have something he wants, or that by succeeding in his attack on you, he can achieve a goal. Increasingly, the later force drives attacks by using politics or social agenda as a rational for an attack. Fortunately, targeted attacks seem to make up the minority of Internet activity. However, the bad news is that if you are targeted, the more skilled the attacker, the less likely you are to "see" or detect the attack.

Remember these two ways an attack might occur as you consider how an attack can affect the different aspects of a system.

Operating System Attacks

An operating system is designed to support what a user would like to accomplish and, in the context of this discussion, the operating system must enable networking to some degree. The more networking that is enabled on a system, the more services are activated to support these needs. This results in more open ports and active services being available and visible. Therefore, attackers have more opportunities to select an attack, thereby resulting in the access they want.

In addition, users and administrators often think that the job is finished when a server has its OS installed and its services configured. Alas, this is a mistake that results in a perfect target for attackers. Consider being a hacker and finding a server that has the original operating system installed without patches and with all default services activated. That server will be compromised within the hour!

Application Attacks

I once worked in a business unit that wrote networking software for one of its products. The company was a large, international company with a strong history in telecommunications. I explain this background because, with all the software being written these days, you would think that this company would take advantage of its understanding of the technology and security.

Alas, that was not the case; software programmers were under amazingly tight deadlines and were always asked for new features. I knew many of them— they inherently wanted to do the right thing, but outside factors drove their activities in many ways. Essentially, software was not being tested as it should have been. Add in its increasing level of functionality, and you have opportunities for attackers. This is all terrible, but consumers did not care about security several years ago— only whether the software had the features they wanted. Perhaps, if consumers change what they spend money on, secure software will become more of a pressing issue.

Misconfiguration Attacks

Sometimes, system administrators work on the system when trying to secure a system or ensure that it provides the functionality users need. Usually, this means turning on several options, and the desired feature starts working when you hit the right option.

Did you clean up those options after yourself? Likely not. The problem is that the system administrator does not go back and research what fixed her issue and deactivate the unneeded options. This is perplexing because verifying that a system is not misconfigured is an easy precaution to ensure that your system is functioning correctly. A good rule of thumb is to turn unnecessary services off and concentrate on correctly securing and configuring those that are needed.

Keep a written record of what services and options you enable or disable; in the heat of the moment (especially when it is 3:00 a.m. and you are wondering what you did to deserve being hacked), the written record will help you reverse what you might have done earlier.

Another issue that fits under the misconfiguration umbrella is deploying a device and not changing the default administrator username and password that was programmed into the device. If you are wondering what I am referring to, look at the manual that came with your shiny new firewall device that has all the blinky lights and whiz-bang security features. Have you looked at the "quick startup" section that almost all manuals have nowadays? Somewhere among those pages is a section about logging in for the first time and setting up the device. Most security devices either have no password, or the username/password combination is something like "admin/admin." Guess what? Hackers read manuals too, and they are aware that default passwords are still active on routers, firewalls, and other Internet toys.

Script Attacks

UNIX and Linux are undoubtedly the systems for which attackers will find scripts susceptible to their activities. Many of these operating systems come with sample scripts and programs that are available for use. These are a blessing in disguise and, if left activated or unchecked, they can result in successful attacks against your system.

Attackers try to execute some of the following attacks against your system during this phase of the attack:

- **Buffer memory overflows**—The information has to go somewhere, and the attacker can direct it to compromise a system. When the BIQ (Buffer In Question) blows, the OS might do things that the developer never intended.

- **Brute force guess passwords**—The attacker starts a program that tries every word in a dictionary. Webster's is fine, but it could also be a dictionary of names, movies, or sports teams/lingo, and so on.

- **Try and sniff a password**—Everyone has to log in and, if the attacker can "see" a user's password, he is in! Can you imagine the number of captured passwords that could be seen in the morning when everyone is logging in to your network?

- **Capture the password flag**—In this case, the attacker will want to capture the password file, which can then be decrypted and cracked at the attacker's leisure and most likely *not* on the system that was compromised. In other words, the attacker copies this file and cracks it at his leisure (that is, sleeping or at his day job) so the information it contains is useful.

The techniques, tools, and procedures vary according to the attacker's level of expertise and ability to code custom scripts and programs. Either way, a plethora of free open source tools are available for use; the attacker will more than likely make use of some, if not all of the following:

- NMAP—http://www.insecure.org/

- STROBE—http://www.deter.com/unix/index.html

- NESSUS—http://www.nessus.org

- SATAN—http://www.cerias.purdue.edu/coast/satan.html

- WinScan, Sam Spade, and others, if using a Windows box

Do not discount the fact that commercial products such as CyberCop Scanner and Internet Security Scanner (ISS) might also be used because these are available for sale on the open market. The following section discusses how an attacker works on escalating how much he is allowed to do (that is, privilege) after accessing a system.

Escalating Privilege

At this point in a hack, an attacker might have gained access to a system. Perhaps the attacker learned/guessed/hacked a user's password because it was something simple, like the user's favorite sports team or movie. A regular user, however, might not have the privileges the attacker needs for his goal. Thus, in this phase of the hack, the attacker must begin escalating his privilege level. He now understands the system a bit more, so he will likely look for the following:

- Being "in" the system, the attacker can run the appropriate exploit code against the system to gain more privileges.

- Try to crack passwords using the many freely available password crack tools.

- Look for passwords that are not encrypted (that is, clear text).

- Evaluate the trusts that exist between the hacked system and others within the network. Perhaps there is another opportunity?

- Perhaps file or share permissions are set incorrectly.

These are the types of steps an attacker will take after he has gained rudimentary access. He would not likely go through all the risk and trouble to stop without ensuring that he can do whatever it is he intended to do.

If all else fails, or if the attacker wants to implement a denial of service (DoS) attack, he uses specialized tools called *exploit code* to disable a system. The use of these exploits is operating system-specific and can also depend on the patch level of the system state. Specifically, this means that system X is vulnerable to exploit 666, but if it has been patched with service patch 5, it is not vulnerable. Some of the exploits that could be used are SYN flood, ICMP techniques, overlapping fragments/offset bugs, and out of buffer. Again, the effectiveness largely depends on the system's patch level. The attacker knows that, when an exploit becomes public, he can quickly become useless against systems where the system administrators stay on top of things; however, an attacker also knows that new exploits are found daily, and that research and experimentation is required to find the most effective tools and techniques.

The remaining steps are rather straightforward and obvious. After the hacker has gained Administrator/Root access (that is, ownership), he completes the reason behind the attack, begins concealing his activities, and perhaps leaves a way for them to get back into the system.

Covering Tracks

After the attackers accomplish ownership of the target system, they must hide this fact from the system administrator. This is one of the most fundamental rules of hacking; however, it is also one of the hardest for the attacker to accomplish. For Windows-based systems, event log and registry entries are cleared/cleaned. For a

UNIX-based system, the attacker clears the history file and executes a log wiper to clean entries from UTMP, WTMP, and Lastlog.

note

Note that the attacker *clears* the logs—not deleted. When log files are deleted or cleared, a notification occurs that might draw attention to the fact that the system was compromised.

If the attackers want to maintain access to the system after achieving initial access, they create backdoors for future access. The methodology, tools, and techniques are system-dependent, but the intent is to create accounts, schedule batch/cron jobs, infect startup files, enable remote control services/software, and replace legitimate applications and services with Trojans. Possible tools include the following:

- **Netcat**—A simple UNIX utility that uses TCP or UDP protocol to read and write data across network connections.

- **VNC (Virtual Network Computing)**—A remote display system that allows you to view a system's desktop environment—not only on the machine where it is running, but also from anywhere on the Internet and from a wide variety of machine architectures. Many programs do this—VNC just happens to be free and rather popular. Plus, it works on Windows, Linux, and UNIX (http://www.uk.research.att.com/vnc/).

- **Keystroke loggers**—Hundreds are available on the Internet, and they can be either hardware or software-based. Keystroke loggers record every keystroke pressed for a computer and can even e-mail you what they record.

- **Customized programs**—Add them to the Windows startup folder or configuration files (system.ini, win.ini, autoexec.bat, config.sys, and so on). For UNIX-based systems, you can employ entries in the /etc/rc.d directory.

There are cases when the attacker does not want to have a backdoor placed in the target system. Usually, this is in the case of corporate espionage, in which an attacker gains access to acquire a certain piece of information and leaves. In a situation involving corporate espionage, the attackers know what they want and has no interest in regaining access to the system at a later time. In these types of attacks, the attackers' main goal is to cover their tracks so no one will ever know what happened.

Where Are Attacks Coming From?

It is clear by now that the bad guys are out there on the Internet using all kinds of tools, from automated to those that target you specifically. Everyone knows that a public IP address is required to connect to the Internet. These addresses are allocated across the globe, so we should be able to find out where these attacks are going?

This is true, and the security company ISS (http://www.iss.net) has a Managed Security Service; of the 5052 security incidents it recorded between April 1, 2003 and June 20, 2003, they developed the graph shown in Figure 1-4 to shows where attacks originated by region.

Figure 1-4   Top Attack Regions from April 1, 2003 to June 20, 2003l

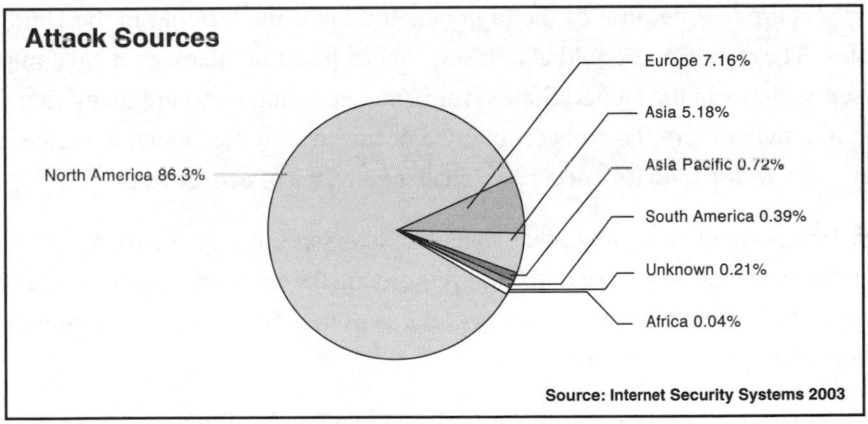

Another interesting aside from this report is that, because ISS was managing these security services for its customers, it knows each customer's business sector. This being said, Figure 1-5 shows the business sectors that these attacks targeted.

Figure 1-5   Attacked Business Sectors

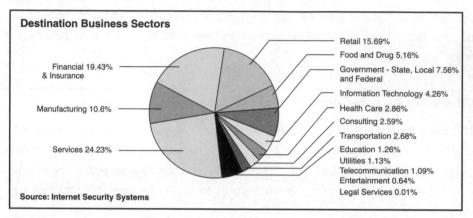

Destination Business Sectors

Retail 15.69%
Food and Drug 5.16%
Government - State, Local 7.56% and Federal
Information Technology 4.26%
Health Care 2.86%
Consulting 2.59%
Transportation 2.68%
Education 1.26%
Utilities 1.13%
Telecommunication 1.09%
Entertainment 0.64%
Legal Services 0.01%

Financial 19.43% & Insurance

Manufacturing 10.6%

Services 24.23%

Source: Internet Security Systems

I found this insight into business sectors that were targeted interesting. I guess everyone wonders how the insurance companies come up with rates and decisions!

Another interesting observation is that most attacks originate in the United States—in fact, it is a majority at over 82 percent, is it not? The truth could be that these numbers are true because of the high penetration of the Internet in the United States. These numbers could also be erroneous because attackers have compromised systems in the United States from another country and are using that system to attack others. There is probably a occurrence of the latter, but there is no way to know for sure. Isn't security a challenging area of networking?

This brings up an interesting point about liability—specifically, a term that is just now entering the vocabulary of the lawyers around the world: ***downstream liability***. In a nutshell, if your company does not take steps to protect itself and is used to attack others, it may be liable.

This situation can become a concern for anyone involved in network security, and it will not be long before a lawyer decides to bring this matter to court. When it comes to network security, not all the liability issues have been sorted out from a legal standpoint; although, they will be eventually—on that point, I trust lawyers!

Network Security Organizations

This section examines some of the exploits and vulnerabilities that are available to attackers. Prior to that though, it is important to look at where you can go to learn about vulnerabilities that are currently known.

At one time, each vendor or manufacturer was responsible for tracking all the vulnerabilities that affected its products. The result was that different companies would report that same vulnerability, thereby causing some confusion—or perhaps they would not acknowledge the vulnerability until it became public. The network security industry realized that this was not efficient, and it created CVE (common vulnerabilities and exposures). Do not misunderstand; CVE is not a database of vulnerabilities, but a dictionary. The CVE website, found at: http://www.cve.mitre.org/, defines its role as follows:

> **CVE** is a list of standardized names for vulnerabilities and other information security exposures. CVE aims to standardize the names for all publicly known vulnerabilities and security exposures. It is a dictionary, *not* a database. CVE's goal is to make it easier to share data across separate vulnerability databases and security tools. Although CVE might make it easier to search for information in other databases, CVE should not be considered as a vulnerability database on its own merit. It is a community-wide effort. CVE's content is a result of a collaborative effort of the CVE Editorial Board, which includes representatives from numerous security-related organizations like security tool vendors, academic institutions, and government, as well as other prominent security experts. The MITRE Corporation maintains CVE and moderates Editorial Board discussions.

CVE is beginning to gain more acceptance and use as it develops, and I look forward to seeing where it leads. Until then, several databases and checklists are considered essential resources for those who are interested or involved in network security. These organizations offer a variety of white papers, e-mail groups, forums, alerts, best practices, and educational opportunities to further increase your knowledge.

CERT Coordination Center

CERT (http://www.cert.org) defines itself as a center of Internet security expertise. It is located at the Software Engineering Institute, a federally funded research
and development center operated by Carnegie Mellon University. Its information
ranges from protecting your system against potential problems, to reacting to current problems to predicting future problems. CERT work involves handling computer security incidents and vulnerabilities, publishing security alerts, researching
long-term changes in networked systems, and developing information and training to help you improve security at your site.

SANS

SANS (http://www.sans.org/) defines itself as the trusted leader in information
security research, certification, and education. The SANS (SysAdmin, Audit, Network, Security) Institute was established in 1989 as a cooperative research and
education organization. The SANS Institute enables more than 156,000 security
professionals, auditors, system administrators, and network administrators to
share the lessons it is learning and find solutions to the challenges it faces. At the
heart of SANS are the many security practitioners in government agencies, corporations, and universities around the world who invest hundreds of hours each year
in research and teaching to help the entire information security community. Many
SANS resources, such as news digests, research summaries, security alerts, and
award-winning papers are free to all who ask. Income from printed publications
funds university-based research programs. Income from SANS educational programs fund special research projects and the SANS training program.

Center for Internet Security (CIS)

CIS (http://www.cisecurity.com) defines its mission as helping organizations
around the world effectively manage the risks related to information security. CIS
provides methods and tools to improve, measure, monitor, and compare the security status of your Internet-connected systems and appliances, and those of your
business partners. CIS is not tied to any proprietary product or service. It manages

a consensus process whereby members identify security threats of greatest concern and participate in the development of practical methods to reduce the threats. This consensus process is already in use and has proved viable in creating Internet security benchmarks that are available for widespread adoption.

SCORE

Score (http://www.sans.org/score/) defines itself as a cooperative effort between SANS/GIAC and the Center for Internet Security (CIS). SCORE is a community of security professionals from a wide range of organizations and backgrounds who work to develop consensus regarding minimum standards and best-practice information. It essentially acts as CIS's research engine. After consensus is reached and best practice recommendations are validated, CIS can formalize them as best practice and minimum standards benchmarks for general use by industry at large.

SCORE Objectives:

- Promote, develop, and publish security checklists.

- Build these checklists via consensus and through open discussion via SCORE mailing lists.

- Use existing references, recruit GIAC-certified professionals, and enlist subject matter experts where and whenever possible.

Internet Storm Center

Internet Storm Center (http://isc.sans.org/) defines itself as a center that gathers more than 3,000,000 intrusion detection log entries every day. It is rapidly expanding in a quest to do a better job of finding new storms faster, isolating the sites that are used for attacks, and providing authoritative data on the types of attacks that are being mounted against computers in various industries and regions around the globe. Internet Storm Center is a free service to the Internet community. The SANS institute supports the work with tuition paid by students attending SANS security education programs.

ICAT Metabase

ICAT (http://icat.nist.gov/icat.cfm) defines itself as a searchable index of information on computer vulnerabilities. It provides search capability at a fine granularity and links users to vulnerability and patch information.

Security Focus

With over 2.5 million unique users annually, Security Focus (http://www.security-focus.com/) is the largest community of security professionals available anywhere. Demographically, the Security Focus Online community consists of highly educated security professionals who hold technical or corporate management job titles within the security marketplace. The Security Focus Online venue is organized into seven focus areas, or channels: Home, The Basics, Microsoft, UNIX, IDS, Vulnerabilities, and Incidents; together these channels generate over seven million page views monthly. They are packed with compelling, late-breaking content featuring News, Columnists, InFocus articles, Vulnerabilities, Advisories, Events, Library, and much more. Security Focus Online is the security professional's morning "newspaper" worldwide.

Learning from the Network Security Organizations

These organizations did not exist five years ago, and the increase in threats across the Internet from attackers of all types has supported their birth and growth. You should explore each website because there is a wealth of information that takes you beyond what is presented here. The following section reviews some of the ways vulnerabilities and exploits are used in attacks.

One of the useful things that manufacturers are doing these days is setting methods for users and white hat hackers (good guys) to report security issues with their products. For example, Cisco has provided this information to you online:

http://www.cisco.com/en/US/tech/tk583/tk372/
technologies_security_advisory09186a00800b13d6.shtml#ContactPSIRT

Overview of Common Attacks and Exploits

This section reviews some of the more commonly used attacks and exploits that are available to attackers. It should by no means be considered complete because new attacks are being discovered at an alarming rate every day. For a more complete list or more information on the exploits listed here, refer to any of the organizations presented in the previous section:

- **Denial of Service (DoS)**—A denial of service attack attempts to force the target into a failure condition, thereby denying its services to others. There are several ways in which a failure condition can be induced, such as flooding the target with attempts to connect.

- **Distributed Denial of Service (DDoS)**—This type of attack uses a collection of unknowing accomplices to attack a target from multiple locations at once. See http://grc.com/dos/grcdos.htm for a good example of this type of attack.

- **SYN flood attack**—A SYN flood attack occurs when a network becomes so overwhelmed by SYN packets initiating incomplete connection requests that it can no longer process legitimate connection requests (thereby causing high CPU, memory, and NIC usage) and resulting in a DoS.

- **UDP flood attack**—Similar to the ICMP flood, UDP flooding occurs when UDP packets are sent with the purpose of slowing down the system to the point that it can no longer handle valid connections. Port 53–DNS flooding is the hallmark modus operandi of this kind of attack.

- **Port scan attack**—Port scan attacks occur when packets are sent with different port numbers with the purpose of scanning the available services, in hopes that one port will respond.

- **Ping of death**—The TCP/IP specification requires a specific packet size for datagram transmission. Many ping implementations allow the user to specify a larger packet size, if desired. A grossly oversized ICMP packet can trigger a range of adverse system reactions, such as DoS, crashing, freezing, and rebooting.

- **IP spoofing**—Spoofing attacks occur when an attacker attempts to bypass the firewall security by imitating a valid client IP address, e-mail address, or user ID. This becomes important when an attacker decides to exploit trust relationships that exist between computers. Usually, administrators set up trust relationships between multiple computers; one of the side benefits to this is a single login for all.

- **Land Attack**—Combining a SYN attack with IP spoofing, a land attack occurs when an attacker sends spoofed SYN packets that contain the victim's IP address as both the destination and source IP address. The receiving system responds by sending the SYN-ACK packet to itself, thereby creating an empty connection that lasts until the idle timeout value is reached. Flooding a system with such empty connections can overwhelm the system, resulting in a DoS condition on the target system.

- **Tear drop attack**—Tear drop attacks exploit the reassembly of fragmented IP packets. In the IP header, one of the options is offset. When the sum of the offset and size of one fragmented packet differ from that of the next fragmented packet, the packets overlap, and the server attempting to reassemble the packet can crash.

- **Ping scan**—Similar to a port scan attack, a ping scan attack occurs when an attacker sends ICMP echo requests (or pings) to different destination addresses in hopes that one will reply and, therefore, uncover a potential target's IP address.

- **Java/ActiveX/ZIP/EXE**—Malicious Java or ActiveX components can be hidden in web pages. When downloaded, these applets install a Trojan horse on your computer. Similarly, Trojan horses can be hidden in compressed files such as .zip, .gzip, and .tar, and executable (.exe) files. Enabling this feature blocks all embedded Java and ActiveX applets from web pages and strips attached .zip, .gzip, .tar, and .exe files from e-mail.

- **WinNuke attack**—WinNuke is a hacker application whose sole intent is to cause any computer on the Internet that is running Windows to crash. WinNuke sends out-of-band (OOB) data—usually to NetBIOS port 139— to a host with an established connection and introduces a NetBIOS fragment overlap that causes many machines to crash. This is yet another reason that NetBIOS should not be allowed into or out of a network.

- **Smurf**—The little blue folks are not coming back to make your day; rather, **ping** (ICMP) is being used to target devices via an intermediate device, thus hiding the attacks from the true source. You can read more about Smurf attacks at http://www.cert.org/advisories/CA-1998-01.html.

- **Brute Force**—In a brute force attack, an attacker tries to guess passwords through techniques such as repeatedly trying to log in to an account by using a dictionary of potential passwords.

- **Source Routing**—Source routing is an option in an IP packet's header that defines how packets are routed. When this option is on many firewalls, rules are bypassed, thereby allowing access to your network. For example, the IP header information can contain routing information that can specify a different source IP address than the header source. This causes the packets to be routed in a different direction. Following are several other ways to control the routing of ICMP packets:

  - **Record route**—An attacker sends packets where the IP option is 7 (Record Route). This option is used to record the route of a packet. A recorded route is composed of a series of Internet addresses that an outsider can analyze to learn details about your network's addressing scheme and topology.

  - **Loose source route**—An attacker sends packets where the IP option is 3 (Loose Source Routing). This option provides a means for the source of a packet to supply routing information for the gateways to use to forward the packet to the destination. This option is a loose source route because the gateway or host IP is allowed to use any route of any number of other intermediate gateways to reach the next address in the route.

  - **Strict source route**—An attacker sends packets where the IP option is 9 (Strict Source Routing). This option provides a means for a packet's source to supply routing information for the gateways to use to forward the packet to the destination. This option is a strict source route because

the gateway or host IP must send the datagram directly to the next address in the source route, and only through the directly connected network indicated in the next address to reach the next gateway or host specified in the route.

- **ICMP flood**—An ICMP flood occurs when ICMP pings overload a system with so many echo requests that the system expends all its resources responding until it can no longer process valid network traffic. Several different types of ICMP messages exist, each with their own purpose, and attackers can use them:

  - **ICMP Echo Reply**—(Code 0, Echo Reply) A response to a ping. Many firewalls allow ping responses so internal people can gain access to external resources. Therefore, they are an effective flooding technique.

  - **ICMP Host Unreachable**—Code 3, Destination Unreachable) An error message from a host or router indicating that a packet you sent did not reach its destination.

  - **ICMP Source Quench**—(Code 4, Source Quench) A response indicating congestion on the Internet. Someone might be trying to flood your network with these packets in an attempt to convince your machines to slow down data transmission.

  - **ICMP Redirect**—(Code 5, Redirect) A message advising to redirect traffic—for example, for network X directly to gateway G2 because this is a shorter path to the destination. Someone might be trying to redirect your default router. This could be from a hacker trying to execute a man-in-the-middle attack against you by causing you to route through his own machine.

  - **ICMP Echo Request**—(Code 8, Echo Request) These are ping request packets that are commonly used. They might indicate hostile intent of someone trying to scan your computer, but they might be part of the normal network functionality.

  - **ICMP Time Exceeded for a Datagram**—(Code 11, Time Exceeded in Transit) A message indicating that a packet never reached its target because something timed out.

- — **ICMP Parameter Problem on Datagram**—(Code 12, Parameter Problem on Datagram) A message advising that something unusual is going on; this probably indicates an attack.

- — **Large ICMP Packet**—An ICMP packet with a length greater than 1024 can cause trouble for some devices because ICMP packets are not normally this size.

- **Sniffing packets**—The use of a sniffer is a passive attack that allows a network Interface card to be placed into a special mode: promiscuous. Do not be fooled into thinking that there is no danger because it is a passive attack. In fact, for an attacker to get a sniffer on your LAN, serious security issues have already occurred. Now that attacker can see most of the packets on your LAN with a sniffer, there is a definite threat.

This is simply a short list of the thousands of vulnerabilities that are known today. Now imagine the effectiveness of a coordinated attack using some these vulnerabilities. It puts it in a different perspective, doesn't it?

Chapter Summary

This chapter examined the ways an attacker selects his targets, as those of opportunity or those of choice. Ultimately, you learned that everyone is a target, and the true differentiator comes when attackers either stumble across a target that is unprotected or in which there is perhaps a deeper and more malicious intent in the attacker's selection.

After attackers determine that you are a target, they employs six common steps, which form the components of the attack whose goal is the ultimate compromise of a system.

This chapter also discussed online places to learn more about network security. These places were the "good guys," and it is important to point them out because most locations on the Internet are the bad guys; be careful visiting these websites! Instead, read the last part of this chapter, where a few of the attacks and possible exploits were discussed. The following chapter discusses the next step in understanding network security—security policies, which are the first step in protection.

Chapter Review

Each chapter concludes with a "Chapter Review Section." In a question-and-answer format, the "Chapter Review Section" tests the basic ideas and concepts covered in each chapter. In tandem with the "Chapter Objectives" and "Chapter Summaries," the "Chapter Review Section" build upon and reinforce key ideas and concepts. "Chapter Review Section" are composed of a series of topical questions, and answers to the "Chapter Review Section" are included in Appendix A, "Answers to Chapter Review Questions," at the back of this book.

1. What is a target of opportunity?

2. What is a target of choice?

3. What is the purpose of footprinting?

4. Which of the following are ways by which an attacker can gain access?

    a. Operating system attacks

    b. Application attacks

    c. Misconfiguration attacks

    d. Script attacks

    e. All of the above

5. List four of the network security organizations.

6. Briefly explain why it is important for an attacker to cover his tracks.

7. Social engineering can be damaging without an overt attack ever happening. Explain why.

8. What kind of information might be found if an attacker dumpster dives at your place of work?

9. DNS information gained through WHOIS is used for what kind of reconnaissance?

10. What two free reconnaissance tools are available with most versions of the Windows operating system?

What You Will Learn

By the end of this chapter, you should know and be able to explain the following:

- ✔ What role does a security policy play in my network

- ✔ How do I create a security policy?

- ✔ How do I deal with any security policy violations?

Being able to answer these key questions will allow you to understand the overall characteristics and importance of a network security policy.

CHAPTER 2

Security Policies and Responses

Being defeated is often a temporary condition. Giving up is what makes it permanent. —Marlene vos Savant

Having security policies is the most essential first step to protecting and securing your network. Policies provide the basis for defining what is acceptable and appropriate behavior within your company and network. At the most fundamental level, policies form the "rule of law" against which everything else is judged.

Consider a security policy that is analogous to rules and laws found in your neighborhood. What would life be like? If you wanted to accomplish anything worthwhile, it would be unbearable. Viewed in this light, a security policy defines what is acceptable or not inside and outside your network. This is a fundamental definition of the role of security policy, yet there are many additional reasons that define a security policy's usefulness:

- Sets the expectations for procedures

- Defines appropriate behavior

- Communicates an operational and business consensus

- Provides a foundation for HR action if unacceptable behavior occurs

- Defines roles and responsibilities of each group in securing the company

- Assists in prosecuting legal action if unacceptable behavior occurs

- Provides definitions for concepts and ideas that are crucial in securing your network

- Allows for required tools to be defined by justifying funds for network security

Having a security policy allows and enables everyone within a company to clearly understand who is responsible for what and sets the policies and processes of each department within your organization. For example, customer service will understand their responsibilities in protecting sensitive customer information, human resources will understand what is expected of employees, and manufacturing and development will know how to protect the results of expensive research and development. Of course, the most important result of a security policy will be what a security policy means to an IT department. From the security policy, the IT staff knows what to configure on servers, the tools they need, rules for firewalls, virtual private network (VPN) settings, and so on—the list is endless.

You might wonder what some of the most commonly used security policies are and what areas of IT should consider using a policy? The SANS Security Policy Project (http://www.sans.org/resources/policies) provides a variety of security policies, some of the more common of which are described in Table 2-1.

Table 2-1   Common Security Policies

Policy Name	Description
Acceptable Encryption	Provides guidance that limits the use of encryption to those algorithms that have received substantial public review and have been proven to work effectively. Additionally, provides direction to ensure that applicable laws and regulations are followed.
Acceptable Use	Outlines who can use company-owned computer equipment and networks. It covers company computers located on company premises and in employees' homes.
Analog Line	Explains the analog and ISDN line acceptable use and approval policies and procedures. Separate rules apply to lines that are to be connected for the sole purpose of faxing and receiving and lines that are to be connected to computers.

Table 2-1   Common Security Policies (continued)

Policy Name	Description
Application Service Providers	Describes the company's requirements of Application Service Providers (ASPs). (ASPs combine hosted software, hardware and networking technologies to offer a service-based application.) It refers to and incorporates the separate ASP Standards Policy.
ASP standards	Defines the minimum-security criteria that an application service provider (ASP) must meet be considered for use.
Audit	Provides the authority for members of the Information Security Department team to conduct a security audit on any system owned by the company or installed on the company's premises.
Automatically Forwarded E-mail	Prevents the unauthorized or inadvertent disclosure of sensitive company information.
DB Credentials	States the requirements for securely storing and retrieving database usernames and passwords (that is, database credentials) for use by a program that accesses a database running on one of the company's networks.
Dial-in Access	Establishes rules that protect electronic information from being inadvertently compromised by authorized personnel using a dial-in connection.
Extranet	Describes the policy under which third-party organizations connect to the company's networks for the purpose of transacting business.
Information Sensitivity	Helps employees determine what information can be disclosed to non-employees, and the relative sensitivity of information that should not be disclosed without proper authorization.
Internal Lab Security	Establishes information security requirements for labs to ensure that confidential information and technologies are not compromised, and that production services and other interests are protected from lab activities.

continues

Table 2-1   Common Security Policies (continued)

Policy Name	Description
Anti-Virus	Establishes requirements that must be met by all computers connected to company's networks to ensure effective virus detection and prevention.
Password	Establishes a standard for creation of strong passwords, the protection of those passwords, and the frequency of change.
Remote Access	Defines standards for connecting to company's network from any host. These standards are designed to minimize the potential exposure from damages such as the loss of sensitive or company confidential data, intellectual property, damage to public image, damage to critical internal systems, and so on.
Risk Assessment	Empowers the Information Security Department to perform periodic information security risk assessments for the purpose of determining areas of vulnerability, and to initiate appropriate remediation.
Router and Switch Security	Describes a required minimal security configuration for all routers and switches connecting to a production network or used in a production capacity.
Server Security	Establishes standards for the base configuration of internal server equipment that is owned and/or operated on company premises or at web hosting locations.
Virtual Private Network	Provides guidelines for remote access IPSec or L2TP VPN connections to the company's corporate network.
Wireless Communication	Establishes standards for access of company's network via secured wireless communication mechanisms.

In addition to knowing what is expected, every person or department in a company is affected by a security policy. As you can see from the following list, each group within an organization is affected:

- **Generic user**—Because users access network resources, your policy impact them the most.

- **Management team**—This group is ultimately concerned with the protection of corporate resources and data while monitoring the financial impact.

- **Accountants, legal, and investors**—Understand that the company's responsibility to protect itself depends on such policies while recognizing the positive impact a security policy can have.

- **Security management team**—This group's role is defined in the policy to pinpoint what group is being tasked with security policy enforcement.

The following section discusses what could be viewed as the most important first question for designing a security policy: who and what to trust.

Defining Trust

Trust is a central theme in many aspects of security and must be foremost in your mind when discussing security policies. In a perfect world, there would be no issues with trust; you would trust everyone, and they would always do the right thing. Unfortunately, that is not realistic, nor does it take into account other factors such as bugs in network resources. Again, trusting the resources on your network would be great, but remember that buggy hardware and software is commonplace in networking.

A security policy can be written with the belief that no one in an organization is to be trusted; however, that would not likely work. It is a well-known fact that users circumvent policies that are too restrictive. Therefore, a balance between trust and securing the network must be struck. This balance is different for each organization, but the need for security does not change.

When considering the level of trust to write into a security policy, consider the following items and keep them in mind as your policy is being developed:

- Determine who receives access to each area of your network

- Determine what they can access and how

- Balance trust between people and resources

- Allow access based on the level of trust for users and resources

- Use resources to ensure trust is not violated

- Define the appropriate uses of your network and its resources

There are many other things to consider beyond this short list, including your company's politics and users' reactions. A security policy cannot possibly account for every consideration, but it is important to understand the reactions a security policy brings out in people.

According to the SANS Security Policy Project, security policies should emphasize what is allowed, not what is prohibited. Where appropriate, supply examples of permitted and prohibited behavior. This way, there is no doubt; if not specifically permitted by the security policy, the behavior in question is prohibited. The security policy should also describe the ways to achieve its goals. Table 2-2 lists the security policy sections and describes their content.

Table 2-2   Generic Description of a Security Policy's Contents

Section Name	Content Guide
1.0 Overview	Justifies the reason for the policy and identifies the risks that the policy addresses.
2.0 Purpose	Explains why the policy exists and the goal that it is written to accomplish.
3.0 Scope	Defines the personnel that the policy covers. This might range from a single group in a department to the entire company.
4.0 Policy	This is the policy itself. It is often broken down into several subsections. Examples are often used to illustrate points or facilitate the user's understanding.
5.0 Enforcement	Defines the penalty for failure to follow the policy. It is usually written as "everything up to and including…" so a series of sanctions can be applied. Dismissal is typically the most severe penalty, but in a few cases, criminal prosecution should be listed as an option.
6.0 Definitions	Any terms that might be unclear or ambiguous should be listed and defined here.
7.0 Revision History	Dates, changes, and reasons are listed here. This ties into enforcement in that the infraction should be measured against the rules in place at the time it occurred, not necessarily when it was discovered.

Your security policy defines the resources that your organization needs to protect and the measures you will take to protect them. In other words, it is, collectively, the codification of the decisions that went into your security stance. Policies must be published and distributed to all employees and other users of your system. Management should ensure that everyone reads, understands, and acknowledges their role in following them and in the penalties that violations can bring.

As stated previously, you can trust everyone or trust no one; neither option works effectively when trying to balance productivity and security. Users all have differing views as to a network's security needs, and they all have a certain level of inherent fear. Users fear that their jobs might be more difficult as a result of security, or that they might be punished if they make a mistake or forget to do something. Ultimately, people at any level do not like to feel restricted when they are trying to work. These kinds of attitudes are normal, emotional reactions, so they must be understood and managed appropriately for the security policy to provide balanced protection for your company. Building involvement in security policy development by including representatives from the areas listed in Table 2-3 is highly recommended.

Table 2-3   Members of the Policy Review Team (from the SANS Security Policy Project)

Representative From	Duties
Management	Someone who can enforce the policy. This is often a senior member of the HR staff.
Information Security Department	Someone who can provide technical insight and research.
User Areas	Someone who can view the policies the way a user might view them.
Legal Department	Possibly part time, but someone who can review policies with respect to applicable laws. For multinational firms, this review is exponentially more complicated.
Publications	Someone who can make suggestions on communicating the policies to the members of the organization and getting their buy in. Also, a good writer is always helpful.

The personal minefield can be avoided if you ask the involved groups for their input as part of the policy development process. This allows you to do a little social engineering for the good folks by allowing these groups to participate in the process; they will more readily accept increased security restrictions in this case.

The following section reviews some actual security policies that my company (Granite Systems) uses and helps define how we treat security.

Acceptable Use Policy

SANS (http://www.sans.org) provides a wide range of security policies that are freely available on its website. These policies are based on these publicly available policies. Visiting SANS will complement what you learn from and implement based on this chapter. Granite Systems (http://www.granitesystems.net) based their policies on those recommended by SANS and have graciously allowed the publication of its internal practices in this book.

In this policy, the company's IT Security Department is known simply as the *Corporate Security Team* for *Granite Systems*. *Granite Systems* and other Granite Systems-specific departments appear in *italics* throughout the policy; if you want to reuse this policy, you can replace these designations with your own.

Policy Overview

The *Corporate Security Team's* intentions for publishing an Acceptable Use Policy are not to impose restrictions that are contrary to *Granite Systems'* established culture of openness, trust, and integrity. *Corporate Security* is committed to protecting *Granite Systems'* employees, partners, and the company from illegal or damaging actions by individuals, either knowingly or unknowingly.

Internet/intranet/extranet-related systems, including but not limited to computer equipment, software, operating systems, storage media, network accounts providing electronic mail, WWW browsing, and FTP, are the property of *Granite Systems*. These systems are to be used for business purposes that serve the interests of the company, its clients, and its customers.

Effective security is a corporatewide team effort involving the participation and support of every *Granite Systems* employee, contractor, business partner, or any affiliates who deal with information and information systems. It is the responsibility of every computer user to know the guidelines contained within this security policy and to conduct their activities accordingly.

Purpose

The purpose of this security policy is to outline the acceptable use of computer equipment at *Granite Systems*. These rules are in place to protect the employee and *Granite Systems*. Inappropriate use exposes *Granite Systems* to risks, including but not limited to virus attacks, compromise of network systems and services, and legal issues.

Scope

This security policy applies to employees, contractors, consultants, temporaries, and other workers at Granite Systems, including all personnel affiliated with third parties. This policy applies to all equipment that is owned or leased by *Granite Systems,* to include personal equipment that might come in contact with the corporate IT infrastructure.

General Use and Ownership

1. While *Granite Systems' Corporate Security Team* desires to provide a reasonable level of privacy, users should be aware that the data they create on the corporate systems remains the property of *Granite Systems*. Because of the need to protect *Granite Systems'* network, management cannot guarantee the confidentiality of information stored on any network device belonging to *Granite Systems*.

2. Employees are responsible for exercising good judgment regarding the reasonableness of personal use. Individual departments are responsible for creating guidelines concerning personal use of Internet/intranet/extranet

systems. In the absence of such policies, employees should be guided by departmental policies on personal use and, if there is any uncertainty, employees should consult their supervisor or manager.

3. The *Corporate Security Team* recommends that any information that users consider sensitive or vulnerable be encrypted. For guidelines on information classification, see the *Corporate Security Team's* Information Sensitivity Policy. For guidelines on encrypting e-mail and documents, go to Security Team's Awareness Initiative.

note

In many cases, you will see a security policy that references other policies within an organization. This is considered reasonable and considered a best practice. This allows you to keep a policy specific to the topic at hand. Consider the preceding points, which reference encryption of data. Realistically, everyone within an organization must read and sign an acceptable use Security Policy; however, compare that to those who would be expected to encrypt data, a vastly different list and type of person. Thus, these policies are kept separate, thereby allowing or preventing confusion on the part of the user.

4. For security and network maintenance purposes, authorized individuals within *Granite Systems* may monitor equipment, systems, and network traffic at any time, per the *Corporate Security Team's* Audit Policy.

5. *Granite Systems* reserves the right to audit any and all networks and related systems on a periodic or ad hoc basis to ensure compliance with this policy.

note

Items 4 and 5 are extremely important because they allow your organization to notify all personnel that you can and will monitor and audit the network in all ways and on a regular, as-needed basis. It is crucial for these statements to be present because this allows employees to "know" that they will be watched in some fashion.

Security and Proprietary Information

1. The user interface for information contained on Internet/intranet/extranet-related systems should be classified as either confidential or not confidential, as defined by corporate confidentiality guidelines, the details of which can be found in the *Granite Systems* Human Resources policies. Examples of confidential information include, but are not limited to the following:

    — Company private or confidential

    — Corporate strategies or projections

    — Competitor-sensitive or competitive analyses

    — Trade secrets, patents, test results

    — Specifications, operating parameters

    — Customer lists and data

    — Research data

    Employees should take all necessary steps to prevent unauthorized access to this information. If an employee suspects that such information has been released outside the company, he should notify *Corporate Security* immediately.

2. Keep passwords secure and do not share accounts. Authorized users are responsible for the security of their passwords and accounts. System-level passwords should be changed quarterly; user-level passwords should be changed every six months.

3. All PCs, laptops, and workstations should be secured with a password-protected screensaver with the automatic activation feature set at 10 minutes or less, or by logging off (Ctrl-Alt-Delete for Win2K users) when the host will be unattended.

note

The items discussed in 2 and 3 presuppose that best practices are, in fact, being used. This means there is a dependency that servers require users to change passwords *and* that these passwords follow specific guidelines, as you will see later in the section, "Password Policy."

4. Use encryption of information in compliance with Corporate Security Acceptable Encryption Use policy.

5. Because information contained on portable computers is especially vulnerable, special care should be exercised. Protect laptops in accordance with the "Laptop Security Tips."

6. Postings by employees from an *Granite Systems* e-mail address to newsgroups should contain a disclaimer stating that the opinions expressed are strictly their own and not necessarily those of *Granite Systems*, unless posting is in the course of business duties.

7. All hosts used by the employee that are connected to the *Granite Systems* Internet/intranet/extranet, whether owned by the employee or *Granite Systems*, shall be continually executing approved virus-scanning software with a current virus database.

note

This portion of the policy reflects the strong trend of people checking e-mail from multiple PCs and different physical locations. Consider an employee who might check his free web mail service at work and download a file that contains a virus without realizing it. The goal here is to ensure that, when at work, an approved virus checker catches this virus. However, if an employee accesses the same e-mail from a home PC that she uses to connect to the corporate network, the vulnerability and ramifications should be closely considered.

8. Employees must use extreme caution when opening e-mail attachments received from unknown senders that might contain viruses, e-mail bombs, or Trojan horse code. When in doubt, employees are advised to manually scan the document and contact *Corporate Security* before opening them.

Unacceptable Use

The following activities are, in general, prohibited. Employees can be exempted from these restrictions during the course of their legitimate job responsibilities (For example, systems administration staff might have a need to disable the network access of a host if that host is disrupting production services.)

Under no circumstances is an employee of *Granite Systems* authorized to engage in any activity that is illegal under local, state, federal or international law while utilizing *Granite Systems*-owned resources.

The lists that follow are by no means exhaustive, but they attempt to provide a framework for activities that fall into the category of unacceptable use. If an employee has any questions regarding the appropriateness of an action, he should contact *Corporate Security* for clarification.

System and Network Activities

The following activities are strictly prohibited, with no exceptions:

1. Violations of the rights of any person or company protected by copyright, trade secret, patent, or other intellectual property or similar laws or regulations, including, but not limited to the installation or distribution of "pirated" or other software products that are not appropriately licensed for use by *Granite Systems*.

2. Unauthorized copying of copyrighted material including, but not limited to digitization and distribution of photographs from magazines, books, or other copyrighted sources, copyrighted music, and the installation of any copyrighted software for which *Granite Systems* or the end user does not have an active license is strictly prohibited.

3. Exporting software, technical information, encryption software, or technology in violation of international or regional export control laws is illegal.

The appropriate employee manager should be consulted prior to export of any material that is in question.

note

These first several instances are important for a security policy and an organization on many different levels. Consider probably the most vocal and legally active organizations on the Internet:

- Recording Industry Association of America (http://www.riaa.org)
- Report Cable Theft (http://www.cabletheft.com/)
- Business Software Alliance (http://www.bsa.org/)

These organizations monitor theft, pirating, copyright violations, and so on, and prosecute those who engage in these activities. Individuals and businesses have been the primary legal targets of those engaged in this activity; they have been successful and are set to tackle educational institutions and the pirating that goes on from their campuses.

4. Introduction of malicious programs into the network or server (for example, viruses, worms, Trojan horses, e-mail bombs, and so on).

5. Revealing your account password to others or allowing use of your account by others. This includes family and other household members when work is being done at home.

note

Note that no one in the company will ever ask for your password. In the event of a technical difficulty, they will reset the password. Never reveal your password to anyone and, if asked, report the request to corporate security immediately.

6. Using an *Granite Systems* computing asset to actively engage in procuring or transmitting material that is in violation of sexual harassment or hostile workplace laws in the user's local jurisdiction.

7. Making fraudulent offers of products, items, or services originating from any *Granite Systems* account.

8. Making statements about warranty, expressly or implied, unless it is a part of normal job duties.

9. Effecting security breaches or disruptions of network communication. Security breaches include, but are not limited to, accessing data of which the employee is not an intended recipient or logging in to a server or account that the employee is not expressly authorized to access, unless these duties are within the scope of regular duties. For purposes of this section, "disruption" includes, but is not limited to, network sniffing, pinged floods, packet spoofing, denial of service, and forged routing information for malicious purposes.

10. Port scanning or security scanning is expressly prohibited unless prior notification to *Corporate Security Team* is made.

11. Executing any form of network monitoring that will intercept data that is not intended for the employee's host, unless this activity is a part of the employee's normal job/duty.

12. Circumventing user authentication or security of any host, network, or account.

13. Interfering with or denying service to any user other than the employee's host (for example, denial of service attack).

14. Using any program/script/command, or sending messages of any kind with the intent to interfere with or disable a user's terminal session via any means, locally or via the Internet/intranet/extranet.

15. Providing information about or lists of *Granite Systems* employees to parties outside *Granite Systems*.

E-mail and Communications Activities

1. Sending unsolicited e-mail messages, including the sending of "junk mail" or other advertising material to individuals who did not specifically request such material (e-mail spam).

2. Any form of harassment via e-mail, telephone, or paging, whether through language, frequency, or size of messages.

3. Unauthorized use or forging of e-mail header information.

4. Solicitation of e-mail for any other e-mail address, other than that of the poster's account, with the intent to harass or to collect replies.

5. Creating or forwarding "chain letters," "Ponzi," or other "pyramid" schemes of any type.

6. Use of unsolicited e-mail originating from within *Granite Systems'* networks of other Internet/intranet/extranet service providers on behalf of, or to advertise, any service hosted by *Granite Systems* or connected via *Granite Systems'* network.

7. Posting the same or similar nonbusiness-related messages to large numbers of Usenet newsgroups (newsgroup spam).

Enforcement

Any employee found to have violated this policy might be subject to disciplinary action, up to and including termination of employment.

Conclusion

Every security policy should end with a few common elements to clear up any potential miscommunication and confusion on the part of the user now that he understands what is permitted and what is not:

1. **Enforcement**—The most important element is the enforcement and the ramifications to an employee if these policies are violated.

2. **Definitions**—Not every employee or user will understand some of the terminology used in a policy; therefore, it is a good idea to provide yet another level of clarification by defining industry-specific terms.

3. **Revisions**— Changes are always applied to policies such as these. The source of these changes alter with time; however, it might be a change in

management, new laws, or perhaps a clarification of older laws, new threats against your network's security, your company has decided it wants to become certified (for example, ISO), or perhaps your company has new technology that needs to be covered. All these factors might require a policy change, and it is wise to document the changes.

While these kinds of policies have a tendency to upset people who think they are *entitled* something from their employer, in fact they are not; they are there to contribute to the company's business goals. This fundamental truth allows the policy to protect the company, its employees, and everyone associated with it. Quoting from *Star Trek II: The Wrath of Khan*, "The needs of the many outweigh the needs of the few." Being one of a few power users in my organization, I do not look forward to approving policies; however, it is the right thing to do for the company.

Password Policy

SANS (http://www.sans.org) provides a wide range of security policies that are freely available on its website. These policies are based on these publicly available policies. You should visit SANS and use discussions in this chapter to spark your ideas. Granite Systems (http://www.granitesystems.net) based these policies on those recommended by SANS and allowed me to present them here.

In this policy, the company's IT Security Department is known simply as the *Corporate Security Team* for *Granite Systems*. *Granite Systems* and other Granite Systems-specific departments will appear in *italics* throughout the policy; if you want to reuse this policy, you can replace these designations with your own.

Overview

Passwords are an important aspect of computer security. They are the first line of protection for user accounts. A poorly chosen password might result in the compromise of *Granite Systems'* entire corporate network. As such, all *Granite Systems* employees (including contractors and vendors with access to *Granite*

Systems systems) are responsible for taking the appropriate steps for selecting and securing their passwords, as outlined in the following sections.

Purpose

The purpose of this policy is to establish a standard for the creation of strong passwords, the protection of those passwords, and to define how often you should change them.

caution

Passwords should be changed on a regular basis because user passwords are the first thing an attacker will try to crack. Most systems automatically prompt a user to change a password after a set amount of time has elapsed. In fact, many of the newer operating systems apply some intelligence to a user's password, thus forcing the user not to use words that can be guessed or found in a dictionary. If you are not using these features or are not sure whether they are a part of your systems, it is a good idea to research the matter and activate them.

Scope

The scope of this policy includes all personnel who have or are responsible for an account (or any form of access that supports or requires a password) on any system that resides at any *Granite Systems* facility, has access to the *Granite Systems* network, or stores any nonpublic *Granite Systems* information.

note

An account can be defined and expanded to included e-mail, keypad locks, FTP, shared drives, and so on. All passwords used to access these kind of resources should follow some sort of password policy, as discussed in other portions of this policy.

General Policy

All system-level passwords (for example, root, enable, NT admin, application administration accounts, and so on) must be changed on at least a quarterly basis.

- All production system-level passwords must be part of the *Corporate Security Team's* administered global password management database.

note

Not every organization has such a grandiose sounding "global password database" way of tracking passwords and, frankly, it is not necessary for most organizations. However, you must track passwords and how often they are changed in some manner. This allows you to ensure that your policy is being followed. Of course, ensure that you restrict access to whatever tool you put in place.

- All user-level passwords (for example, e-mail, web, desktop computer, and so on) must be changed at least every six months. The recommended change interval is every four months.

- User accounts that have system-level privileges granted through group memberships or programs such as administrator or root must have a unique password from all other accounts held by that user.

- Passwords must not be inserted into e-mail messages or other forms of electronic communication.

- Passwords must never be given out to anyone, regardless of their position in the company. Employees are instructed to contact *Corporate Security* if anyone asks for your password, *before* giving it out.

- Where SNMP is used, the community strings must be defined as something other than the standard defaults of "public," "private," and "system," and

must be different from the passwords used to login interactively. A keyed hash must be used where available (for example, SNMPv2).

note

This last part means changing the default passwords for the device in question. This is important, and it is amazing how many organizations have never changed the default passwords. When I run across a device for which I do not know the default password, I always consult this site:

http://www.cirt.net/cgi-bin/passwd.pl

At the time of this writing, there are over 162 vendors with a total of 1132 default passwords and an ever-growing list for wireless devices and their passwords (SSID).

All user-level and system-level passwords must conform to the guidelines described in the following section.

General Password Construction Guidelines

Passwords are used for various purposes at *Granite Systems*. Some of the more common uses include user-level accounts, web accounts, e-mail accounts, screen-saver
protection, voicemail password, and local router logins. Because few systems have support for one-time tokens (that is, dynamic passwords that are only used once), everyone should be aware of how to select strong passwords.

Poor, weak passwords have the following characteristics:

- The password contains less than eight characters.

- The password is a word found in a dictionary (English or foreign).

- The password is a common usage word such as the following:

  — Names of family, pets, friends, coworkers, fantasy characters, and so on

  — Computer terms and names, commands, sites, companies, hardware, software

— The words Granite Systems, energy, Granite Systems, or any derivation

— Birthdays and other personal information such as addresses and phone numbers

— Word or number patterns like aaabbb, qwerty, zyxwvuts, 123321, and so on

— Any of the previous words spelled backward

— Any of the previous words preceded or followed by a digit (for example, secret1, 1secret)

— Sports teams or famous players

note

Chapter 10, "Tools of the Trade," discusses word lists and dictionaries; however, while discussing passwords, it is also appropriate to mention word lists and dictionaries in this chapter. A word list is simply a list of words, such as words from the dictionary, sports teams, industry terms, slang words, names; or all these lists are available in many different languages on the Internet. A good online source is http://wordlist.sourceforge.net/.

Attackers use these word lists as the basis of an attack, hoping someone would use a derivation of a word found on one of these lists. Just to be sure, they also inject numbers. This capability of attackers is the basis for the preceding portion of this policy.

Strong passwords have the following characteristics:

■ Contain both upper- and lowercase characters (for example, a-z, A-Z)

■ Have digits and punctuation characters and letters (for example, 0-9, !@#$%^&*()_+|~-=\`{}[]:";'<>?,./)

■ Are at least eight alphanumeric characters in length

■ Are not words in any language, slang, dialect, jargon, and so on

■ Are not based on personal information, names of family, and so on

- Passwords should never be written down or stored online. Try to create passwords that you can remember easily. One way to do this is create a password based on a song title, affirmation, or other phrase. For example, the phrase might be: "This May Be One Way To Remember," and the password could be: "TmB1w2R!" or "Tmb1W>r~," or some other variation. NOTE: Do not use either of these examples as passwords.

Password Protection Standards

Do not use the same password for *Granite Systems* accounts as for other non-Granite Systems access (for example, personal ISP account, option trading, benefits, and so on). Where possible, do not use the same password for various *Granite Systems* access needs. For example, select one password for the engineering systems and a separate password for IT systems. Also, select a separate password to be used for an NT account and a UNIX account.

Do not share *Granite Systems* passwords with anyone, including administrative assistants or secretaries. All passwords are to be treated as sensitive, confidential *Granite Systems* information.

Following is a list of "don'ts":

- Do not reveal a password over the phone to ANYONE.

- Do not reveal a password in an e-mail message.

- Do not reveal a password to the boss.

- Do not talk about a password in front of others.

- Do not hint at the format of a password (for example, "my family name").

- Do not reveal a password on questionnaires or security forms.

- Do not share a password with family members.

- Do not reveal a password to coworkers while on vacation.

If someone demands a password, refer him to this document or have him call someone in the *Corporate Security Team*.

Do not use the "Remember Password" feature of applications (for example, Eudora, Outlook, Netscape Messenger).

Again, do not write passwords down and store them anywhere in your office. Do not store passwords in a file on *any* computer system (including Palm Pilots or similar devices) without encryption that has been approved by the *Corporate Security Team.*

Change passwords at least once every six months (except system-level passwords, which must be changed quarterly). The recommended change interval is every four months.

If an account or password is suspected to have been compromised, report the incident to the *Corporate Security Team* and change all passwords immediately.

The *Corporate Security Team* or its delegates can perform password cracking or guessing on a periodic or random basis. If a password is guessed or cracked during one of these scans, the user will be required to change it.

Enforcement

Any employee found to have violated this policy might be subject to disciplinary action, up to and including termination of employment.

Conclusion

Every security policy ends with a few common elements. These elements clear up all potential miscommunication and confusion on the part of the user, now that she understands what is permitted and what is not.

1. **Enforcement**—The most important element is the enforcement and the ramifications to an employee in the event that these policies are violated.

2. **Definitions**—Not every employee or user understands some of the terminology used in a policy; thus, it is always a good idea to provide yet another level of clarification by defining industry specific terms.

3. **Revisions**— Changes are always applied to policies such as these. The source of these changes alter with time, however; it might be a change in management, new laws, clarification of older laws, new threats against your network's security, your company has decided it wants to become certified (for example, ISO), or perhaps your company has new technology that needs to be covered. All these factors might require a policy change, and it is wise to be able to document the changes.

Users always try and get around the restrictions placed on them via a password policy—no one likes to remember the cryptic passwords required in such a policy. If a user does remember a password that meets these guidelines, do not worry— he will have to change it soon!

Unfortunately for users, they will have to remember and follow this policy. Note that password security is the first step in protecting your network; as such, beginning with the right expectations of your users helps to ensure that the overall security of your organization is preserved.

The next section examines a security policy that is targeted at virtual private networks (VPNs) and what to look for to ensure their security.

Virtual Private Network (VPN) Security Policy

Chapter 7, "IPSec Virtual Private Networks (VPNs)," covers VPNs in more detail; however, because this chapter covers security policies, the growth of VPNs that are in use today demands inclusion of a sample policy for VPNs here. This policy is prefaced by a brief definition of what a VPN is, but you should refer to Chapter 7 for the full scope of this technology.

VPNs are becoming popular and have matured considerably in the last several years. Many companies are using them as a means of securely connecting small remote offices or users of every description. The connections can be made secure through the use of IPSec (IP Security) and L2TP (Layer Two Tunneling Protocol) and with the increasing prevalence of high-speed Internet connections such as DSL or cable VPNs becoming very affordable. Therefore, it becomes important to have a security policy to regulate their use so that all traffic is properly secured.

SANS (http://www.sans.org) provides a wide range of security policies that are freely available on its website. These security policies are based on these publicly available policies. I strongly encourage you to visit SANS and use the discussions in this chapter to spark your ideas. *Granite Systems* (http://www.granitesystems.net) based these policies on those recommended by SANS and have allowed me to present them here.

In this policy, the company's IT Security Department is known simply as the *Corporate Security Team* for *Granite Systems*. *Granite Systems* and other Granite Systems-specific departments appear in *italics* throughout the policy; if you want to reuse this policy, you can replace these designations with your own.

Purpose

The purpose of this policy is to provide guidelines for Remote Access IPSec or L2TP virtual private network (VPN) connections to the *Granite Systems* corporate network.

note
VPNs based on IPSec are preferred over those using L2TP because they are generally considered more secure.

Scope

This policy applies to all *Granite Systems* employees, contractors, consultants, temporaries, and other workers, including all personnel affiliated with third parties that utilize VPNs to access the *Granite Systems* network. This policy applies to implementations of VPN that are directed through a VPN Concentrator or VPN-aware Firewall.

Policy

Approved *Granite Systems* employees and authorized third parties (customers, vendors, and so on) can utilize the benefits of VPNs, which are a "user managed" service. This means that the user is responsible for selecting an Internet service provider (ISP), coordinating installation, installing any required software, and paying associated fees.

note

Although some companies might provide (that is, pay for) broadband or dial-up Internet connections for some of its employees, this is usually on a case-by-case basis. In general, companies leave that responsibility up to its employees, and that is, therefore, expressed in the corporate security policy.

Additionally:

1. It is the responsibility of employees with VPN privileges to ensure that unauthorized users are not allowed access to *Granite Systems* internal networks.

2. VPN use is to be controlled using either a one-time password authentication such as a token device or a public/private key system with a strong pass phrase.

3. When actively connected to the corporate network, VPNs force all traffic to and from the PC over the VPN tunnel; all other traffic is dropped.

4. Dual (split) tunneling is NOT permitted; only one network connection is allowed.

5. *Split-tunneling* is a method of configuring a VPN and is either on or off. Essentially, if split-tunneling is on, users are allowed to simultaneously connect to the corporate network and the Internet. This presents a danger to the corporate network's security because if an attacker were to take control of the computer creating a VPN to the corporate network, the attacker could also gain access to the companies network via the VPN. It is therefore considered best practice to disable split-tunneling.

6. VPN Concentrators are set up and managed through *Granite Systems* network operational groups.

7. All computers connected to *Granite Systems* internal networks through VPN or any other technology must use the most up-to-date antivirus software that is the corporate standard and can be downloaded through the corporate intranet. This also includes personal computers.

8. VPN users are automatically disconnected from *Granite Systems'* network after thirty minutes of inactivity. The user must then log in again to reconnect to the network. Pings or other artificial network processes are not to be used to keep the connection active.

9. Users of computers that are not *Granite Systems*-owned equipment must configure the equipment to comply with *Granite Systems'* VPN and Network Security policies.

10. Only VPN Clients approved by the *Corporate Security Team* can be used.

11. By using VPN technology with personal equipment, users must understand that their machines are a de facto extension of *Granite Systems'* network and, as such, are subject to the same rules and regulations that apply to Granite Systems-owned equipment; that is, their machines must be configured to comply with all Corporate Security Policies.

Conclusion

Every security policy should end with a few common elements; these elements clear up all potential miscommunication and confusion on the part of the user now that he understands what is and is not permitted:

1. **Enforcement**—The most important element is the enforcement and the ramifications to an employee if these policies are violated.

2. **Definitions**—Not every employee or user understands some of the terminology used in a policy; thus, it is always a good idea to provide yet another level of clarification by defining industry-specific terms.

3. **Revisions**—Changes are always applied to policies such as these. The source of these changes alter with time, however; it might be a change in management, new laws, or perhaps a clarification of older laws, new threats against your network's security, your company has decided it wants to become certified (for example, ISO), or perhaps your company has new technology that needs to be covered. All these factors might require a policy change, and it is wise to document the changes.

VPN technology is ever-evolving, faster than most. As discussed, businesses are deploying VPNs in ever-increasing numbers; therefore, it is crucial that all organizations have policies governing their use. If there is a mistake with a VPN, the consequences can be costly from both a security and financial perspective.

The next section covers the security policy that is necessary when corporate business partners or other third parties need to connect to your organization's network—a very sensitive situation, indeed.

Extranet Connection Policy

This security policy deals with "how to handle" and "the requirements" necessary for those not affiliated with your organization to connect to and access resources on the network.

The "who's" and "why's" behind such a request vary greatly and, when considering them, you should review the section on trust in Chapter 1, "Here There Be Hackers!" before making a decision. Requests will come to you from the following parties:

- Contractors trying to do legitimate work with your company

- Business partners of all sorts

- Customers, usually large and requiring special handling

This security policy provides the necessary guidelines for answering such requests and the requirements to be placed on the requestor. It also allows for the members of the IT Staff to deal with pushy and insistent people, making this policy a virtual panacea.

SANS (www.sans.org) provides a wide range of security policies that are freely available on its website. These policies are based on these publicly available policies. You should visit SANS and use the discussions in this chapter to spark your ideas. Granite Systems (http://www.granitesystems.net) based these policies on those recommended by SANS and allowed the policies to be presented here.

In this policy, the company's IT Security Department is known simply as the *Corporate Security Team* for *Granite Systems*. *Granite Systems* and other Granite Systems-specific departments appear in *italics* throughout the policy; if you want to reuse this policy, you can replace these designations with your own.

Purpose

This document describes the policy under which third-party organizations or consultants connect to the *Granite Systems* network for the purpose of conducting business that is related to *Granite Systems*.

Scope

Regardless of whether a dedicated telecommunications circuit (such as frame relay or ISDN), broadband, or VPN technology is used for the connection, connections between third parties that require access to nonpublic *Granite Systems* resources fall under this policy. Connectivity to third parties such as Internet service providers (ISPs) that provide Internet access for Granite Systems or to the Public Switched Telephone Network (PSTN) do *not* fall under this policy.

note
Some clarification is warranted for that last part, where the policy seems to make an exception for the corporate Internet access and telephone usage through the PSTN. These are excepted because they are commodities purchased by your company; as such, if you requested that the phone company follow this policy prior to getting telephones, trust me, you would never get any results.

Security Review

All new extranet connectivity will go through a security review with the *Corporate Security Team*. The security review ensures that all access matches the business requirements in the best possible way, and that the principle of **least access** is followed.

Third-Party Connection Agreement

All new connection requests between third parties and *Granite Systems* require that the third party and *Granite Systems* representatives agree to and sign the *Third-Party Agreement*. This agreement must be signed by the *Vice President* of the *Sponsoring Organization* as well as a representative from the third party who is legally empowered to sign on behalf of the third party. The signed document is to be kept on file with the company's *Legal Department* and *Corporate Security Department*.

Business Case

All production extranet connections must be accompanied by a valid business justification, in writing, that is approved by the *Director of Corporate Security*. Included in this business case is the identification of the network resources that are requesting to be accessed.

Point of Contact

The *Granite Systems Sponsoring Organization* must designate a person to be the point of contact (POC) for the extranet connection. The POC acts on behalf of the *Sponsoring Organization* and is responsible for those portions of this policy and the *Third-Party Agreement* that pertain to it. In the event that the POC changes, the relevant extranet organization must be informed promptly.

Establishing Connectivity

Sponsoring Organizations within *Granite Systems* that want to establish connectivity to a third party are to file a new site request with the *Corporate Security* team. The sponsoring organization engages the *Corporate Security* Team to address security issues that are inherent in the project. The *Sponsoring Organization* must provide full and complete information as to the nature of the proposed access to the extranet group and *Security Team*, as requested.

All established connectivity must be based on the least-access principle, in accordance with the approved business requirements and the security review. In no case does *Granite Systems* rely upon the third party to protect *Granite Systems'* network or resources.

Modifying or Changing Connectivity and Access

All changes in access must be accompanied by a valid business justification and are subject to security review. Changes are to be implemented via corporate change management process. The *Sponsoring Organization* is responsible for notifying the *Corporate Security Team* when there is a material change in their originally provided information so that security and connectivity evolve accordingly.

Terminating Access

When access is no longer required, the *Sponsoring Organization* within *Granite Systems* must notify the extranet team responsible for that connectivity; this terminate the access. This might mean a modification of existing permissions up to terminating the circuit, as appropriate. The *Corporate Security Teams* must conduct an audit of their respective connections annually to ensure that all existing connections are still needed and that the access meets the needs of the connection. Connections that are deprecated and are no longer being used to conduct *Granite Systems* business are terminated immediately. Should a security incident or a finding that a circuit has been deprecated and is no longer being used to conduct *Granite Systems* business necessitate a modification of existing permissions or termination of connectivity, *Security Team* notifies the POC or the *Sponsoring Organization* of the change before taking any action.

Conclusion

Every security policy should end with a few common elements. These elements clear up all potential miscommunication and confusion on the part of the users now that they understands what is and is not permitted:

1. **Enforcement**—The most important element is the enforcement and the ramifications to an employee if these policies are violated.

2. **Definitions**—Not every employee or user understands some of the terminology used in a policy; thus, it is always a good idea to provide yet another level of clarification by defining industry-specific terms.

3. **Revisions**—Changes are always applied to policies such as these. The source of these changes alter with time, however; it might be a change in management, new laws, or perhaps a clarification of older laws, new threats against your network's security, your company has decided it wants to become certified (for example, ISO), or perhaps your company has new technology that needs to be covered. All these factors might require a policy change, and it is wise to document the changes.

It is always a touchy subject to grant such access to those outside your company. One of the things that happens is that employee A works with business partner Z, who needs to access some resource on your network; to complete the business, employee A promises partner Z access. Alternatively, it is someone in management that makes a promise.

These scenarios are common, and this policy helps ensure that, if such a requirement is needed, the proper due diligence is taken before making any promises given this established process.

Perhaps the fastest growing certification authority is the International Standards Organization (ISO). The following section briefly discusses how ISO has entered into the security arena. It is fitting to bring it to your attention because more and more companies are becoming ISO-certified to one degree or another.

ISO Certification and Security

Compliance with any internationally recognized standard is becoming more important. As a result, and because standards relevance is a common currency of instant legitimization, many companies are pursuing such a course. The ISO offers many standards, and all are valuable in their own right. For purposes of this discussion, the concern lies with standard ISO17799.

The ISO17799 standard is extremely comprehensive in its security coverage, and it contains a significant number of controls that are arranged into nine different areas:

- **Business continuity planning**—Details how to allow businesses to continue operating after a major failure or disaster.

- **System access control**—Outlines the control and access to information of all types within an organization and, more importantly, how to detect unauthorized activities.

- **System development and maintenance**—Covers the process of protecting assets and building security into all aspects of the organization's IT systems, software, and data.

- **Physical and environmental security**—Ensures that unauthorized access or damage is prevented, regardless of the intent.

- **Compliance**—Allows organizations to know (via auditing) that they are not violating any civil law, statutory, regulatory, or contractual obligations, and informs them of any security requirements.

- **Personnel security**—Discusses how to reduce the risk of human error, theft, and misuse, thereby allowing minimization of damage from security incidents and malfunctions, and learning from such incidents.

- **Security organization**—Outlines how to maintain and manage the security of information within an organization.

- **Computer and operations management**—Details how to minimize risk while increasing security to ensure the safeguarding of information to prevent loss, modification, or misuse.

- **Asset classification and control**—Describes how to maintain the appropriate protection of corporate assets and to ensure that information assets receive an appropriate level of protection.

The ISO certification is briefly discussed here, but the standard is perhaps one of the most comprehensive and will be growing in use. To learn more, visit the ISO website at http://www.iso.org.

When delivering the security policy to users, you must then determine the most effective manner in which to present them to help facilitate compliance and support from your users. This is often much easier said than done.

Many discussions on the concepts and goals of security policies always seem to gloss over the delivery of these policies. Yet it is crucial for everyone to understand and more importantly support these policies. To not reach for this goal and to make the effort dooms the policy to failure and backlash from users because they will resent the policy from the beginning.

Handling these types of situations is similar to handling interpersonal relationships. Beyond good interpersonal skills, consider the following additional suggestions:

- Ensure that all policies are presented during new employee orientation.

- Always allow a sample of the personnel affected by a security policy to review it and provide input comment before implementing.

- Provide a security policy refresher course.

In general, you should keep policies short, less than two pages. There is no need to complicate the situation. Occasionally, you might have to go over, but not usually. In closing, ensure that your policies are updated annually, if not sooner, to reflect the changes of the past year.

Sample Security Policies on the Internet

Of course, the policies presented here are simply one means of meeting an organization's needs; what works well for one organization might not be ideal for another. Thus, you should refer to the following additional resources on security policies:

- http://www.sans.org/rr/catindex.php?cat_id=50—This site contains articles and papers written by GIAC-certified professionals.

- http://www.ietf.org/rfc/rfc2196.txt?Number=2196—The Site Security Policies Procedure Handbook.

- http://www.securityfocus.com/data/library/
Why_Security_Policies_Fail.pdf—A white paper (PDF).

Some general websites with information security policies include the following:

- http://www.security.kirion.net/securitypolicy/

- http://www.network-and-it-security-policies.com/

- http://www.brown.edu/Research/Unix_Admin/cuisp/

- http://iatservices.missouri.edu/security/

- http://www.utoronto.ca/security/policies.html

- http://irm.cit.nih.gov/security/sec_policy.html

- http://w3.arizona.edu/~security/pandp.htm

- http://secinf.net/ipolicye.html

- http://ist-socrates.berkeley.edu:2002/pols.html

- http://www.ruskwig.com/security_policies.htm

- http://razor.bindview.com/publish/presentations/InfoCarePart2.html

- http://www.jisc.ac.uk/index.cfm?name=publications

Chapter Summary

This chapter discussed what many view as simply paperwork when, in reality, a security policy reflects your company's commitment to security. It included key concepts in writing a security policy, such as determining who and what to trust and who to involve in the writing and crafting of a security policy.

This chapter also presented a variety of sample security policies. These security policies reflect the current trends and major areas upon which companies can improve. Specifically, these areas include what is considered acceptable use of corporate IT resources, how to ensure that you have effective passwords, when and how to use VPNs, and what restrictions to use when connecting your network to a business partner's network.

Chapter 3, "Overview of Security Technologies," discusses the use of technologies that have evolved to support and enhance network security. Many of these technologies are used today without the reader understanding when or where they are operating. After reading this chapter, you should understand the benefits of these technologies, where they operate, and some of their associated risks.

Chapter Review

1. How important is it to involve other departments and employees in the crafting of security policies?

2. True or false: It is a well-known fact that users circumvent security policies that are too restrictive. Explain your answer.

3. What are three things that you should keep in mind when writing or reviewing a security policy?

4. Why is it important to include an enforcement section in every security policy?

5. An Acceptable Use Policy defines what kind of expectations for users?

6. When and under what circumstances should you reveal your password to someone?

7. Which of the following sample passwords would be considered effective when checked against the corporate password policy?

   a. wolfpack

   b. thomas67

   c. simonisnot4

   d. sJ8Dtt&efs

   e. Missing$4u

8. Define VPN and the role it can play within a company's network infrastructure.

9. VPNs support a technology called split tunneling: define this technology and explain whether it should be used in a network?

10. How frequently should security policies be updated or reviewed?

What You Will Learn

This chapter discusses the use of technologies that have evolved to support and enhance network security. Many of these technologies are used today without the user really understanding when or where they are operating. After reading this chapter, you will understand the benefits of these technologies, where they operate, and some of the risks associated with them. By the end of this chapter, you should know and be able to explain the following:

✔ How packet filtering can be employed to reduce simple threats to a network

✔ Precisely what is stateful packet inspection, and why we need firewalls to use this technology

✔ The role and placement of proxy technology

✔ Network Address Translation (NAT) and how it is being used to allow the Internet to continue to grow

✔ How Public Key Infrastructure (PKI) has the potential to protect the flow of information in a global manner

✔ Identify several authentication technologies and how they are used to secure network resources

Being able to answer these key questions and understand the concepts behind them will allow you to understand the overall characteristics and importance of the security technologies covered in this chapter. By the time you finish this book, you will have a solid appreciation for network security, its issues, how it works, and why it is important.

Overview of Security Technologies

A man travels the world over in search of what he needs and returns home to find it. — Author Unknown

So far, this book has painted in broad strokes the steps an attacker could possibly take to gain access to sensitive resources. The first step in protecting these resources is the global security policy created by combining the many aspects discussed in Chapter 2, "Security Policies and Responses." This chapter introduces some of the more broadly used security technologies. Each of these technologies contains a concept or specific role that increases the security of your network when designed and implemented in a layered design.

Security First Design Concepts

Network security can be a many-headed beast with regard to the potential attacks and threats against the network. The resources and opinions on this subject are incredible, and opinions vary greatly depending on whom you ask. For example, a simple Google search on "designing a secure network" returns almost half a million results. Looking in any bookstore also reveals almost as many!

The point is that experts in each area of network design have written so much on designing a secure network that to try to do the subject justice here is beyond the scope of this book. Current texts on network security offer a granular approach to the subject. This book illustrates good network security design principles to build

the strongest possible foundation for the reader. However, we cover some important design concepts of which you must be aware:

- *Layered security*—A network that implements layered security truly understands that a single point of defense is doomed to eventual failure. Thus, as Figure 3-1 demonstrates, implementing security consistently throughout a network at as many points as possible is considered good design. This concept of layering a network's security is the single-most important design concept in this chapter.

Figure 3-1   Layered Security Points

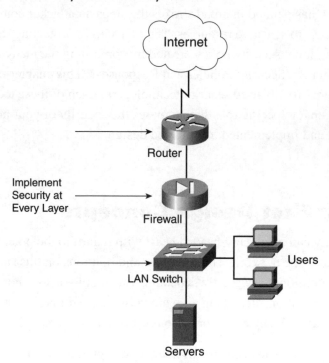

- **Controlling access**—The network is ultimately your responsibility and, as a result, you determine what is allowed into your network. One highly recommended practice is to make access decisions with the mindset of "block everything, and only allow what is needed to conduct business." This has also been referred to as the *Policy of Least Privilege (POLP)*. This is the default action of Cisco firewalls.

- **Role Specific security**—When deciding upon access and privilege (that is, trust), one of the most useful templates to use is based on a user's role within the organization. For example, a web developer would clearly need access to the organization's website, while an administrative assistant would not.

- **User awareness**—Stories abound about users writing down passwords, changing them five times in a row, and then using their original password again. It is not that users are intentionally bypassing security; they do not understand the purpose of the security. Thus, user awareness through training is essential to get users to understand the importance of security. One great idea for getting users to attend training and learn why it is important is to serve ice cream with all the trimmings. This method appeals to a base need, but it is also effective and fun; you will become a very popular person! It is crucial to have your user truly aware of security and supportive of security policies.

- **Monitoring**—Perhaps one of the most forgotten aspects of security is monitoring. Many organizations believe that it is enough simply to have security. They forget that monitoring their systems to ensure that they remain secure and are not subject to attack is also crucial. Chapter 9, "Intrusion Detection and Honeypots," discusses the methods that are used to monitor for attacks: Intrusion Detection Systems (IDS). A strongly recommended practice is to include provisions for IDS when designing a network's security solution.

- **Keep systems patched**—Patching/upgrading systems is a fundamental task that is often forgotten by system administrators with their busy schedules. Fortunately, many newer operating systems can remind you when new updates are available. For example, I use an Apple PowerBook G4 running OS X (a.k.a. Jaguar); within this operating system is a built-in functionality that automatically checks for updates, as shown in Figure 3-2.

The only downside in this example is that I do not yet have an Apple iPod, which would require this update. Regardless, you can understand the point: Always make the time to check for patches for your systems because hackers are always pushing to find and exploit. For Windows users, Microsoft has also included this automatic update functionality in newer versions of its operating systems.

Figure 3-2   MAC OS X Automatic Update Functionality

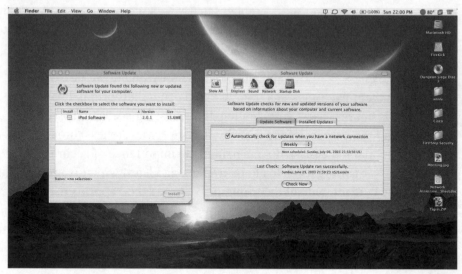

■ **Response team**—Security concerns will inevitably be brought to you in some form or another. Perhaps your systems have become the target of an attack or you have detected that the compromise and damage has already been done. This aspect of design deals with how an organization responds to an attack and deals with whatever situation it is experiencing. It is best to include and consider response teams and the process of responding in practice rather than when you are under pressure and the situation is extreme. So design it now; the benefits come later. Practice makes perfect, and dry runs can help point out a plan's flaws that do not seem evident at the time the plan is written.

These first-step security design considerations will allow you to understand how to begin securing any network. The next section begins to discuss the specifics of how security technologies are used and their roles in protecting a network.

Packet Filtering via Access Control Lists (ACLs)

As you probably already know, all information that flows across the Internet uses TCP/IP and, in turn, this information is sent in small pieces known as packets. In the early days of the Internet, filtering based on packets was common and, in many cases, routers in many networks still use packet filtering. Packet filters are often used as a first defense in combination with other firewall technologies. Today, their most common implementation is seen in the access control lists of routers at the perimeters of networks.

Packet filtering is one of the oldest and most common types of packet inspection technologies available. It begins by inspecting a packet's contents and applying rules to determine whether a packet should be dropped or allowed. Although many characteristics are possible within a TCP/IP packet's header (that is protocol, port, and so on), this discussion refers to filtering based on the source or destination IP address, as shown in Figure 3-3.

Figure 3-3   Packet Filtering at Layer 3 of the TCP/IP Model

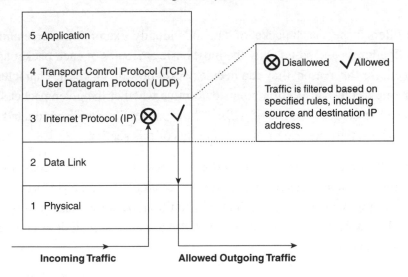

The method used to configure and deploy packet filters on Cisco routers is known as *access control lists (ACLs)*. The two main types of ACLs are standard ACLs, which filter based on IP address, and extended ACLs, which look further into a packet header, if so configured.

note

Standard ACLs are source address-based and extended ACLs are source-based and destination-based and have more capabilities, such as specifying port or protocol. The following ACL styles for IP are supported:

- **Standard IP ACLs**—Use source addresses for matching operations
- **Extended IP ACLs (control plane only)**—Use source and destination addresses for matching operations, and optional protocol type and port numbers for finer granularity of control
- **Named ACLs**—Use source addresses for matching operations

Refer to the following URL for more information about ACLs and Cisco devices (Cisco.com account required):

http://www.cisco.com/en/US/partner/products/sw/secursw/ps1018/products_tech_note09186a00800a5b9a.shtml#types

Packet filters inspect each packet of data individually, examining source and destination IP address and ports. Only the most basic attributes of each packet are examined; for this reason, they can decide packet flow quickly. The characteristics of each one of these inspection points determine whether the given packet should be allowed or denied. The use of ACLs is how packet filtering is conducted on Cisco devices; they are one of the focal points of this section.

Because every packet of every connection is checked against the access control rules, larger, complex packet-filtering rule bases could decrease performance of the device upon which they are applied. In addition, because packet filters can check only low-level attributes, they are not secure against malicious code hiding in the other layers.

The use of ACLs is one of the most confusing topics to many. As you will see in the following section, a good understanding of ACLs can be less confusing when superimposed on a good analogy that relates to real life.

Grocery List Analogy

This analogy is just one way to introduce and explain the concepts behind packet filtering via ACLs. You must consider certain key principles while considering this grocery list analogy. Table 3-1 begins the analogy by comparing packet filtering via ACLs with creating a grocery list.

Table 3-1 ACL Analogy Overview

ACL Characteristics	Grocery List Analogies
[ACLs are effective]	Following a list is efficient and saves money.
[Top-down processing]	The order of the items on the list is important.
[Place denies first]	There are items that are not on the list, so do not buy them.
[Always have a permit]	A list must always include things that are permitted.
[Implicit deny all]	You can only buy what is on the list.

In planning a turkey dinner, my wife and I discovered that we needed some things to finish cooking; we decided to make a list. This way, I would not forget what we needed when I went to the store. We knew that we had the following things, so they are not going on the grocery list:

- Turkey

- Stuffing

- Bread

- Cheese

In other words, I cannot buy these ingredients because my wife says that we do not need them. When I make a list of the things I am allowed to buy, my list is rather broad. I am happy with the list; it will do the job, so I am ready to head to the grocery store to get the following items:

- Milk

- Pie

- Potatoes

- Gravy

- **Buy nothing else**

This list is broad because there are many types of milk and *many* types of pies. Because we need these ingredients, I can buy them. This broad grocery list analogy can relate directly to a standard ACL when expressed as follows:

```
[standard acl] Regular Grocery List
[deny] Turkey
[deny] Stuffing
[deny] Bread
[deny] Cheese
[permit] Milk
[permit] Pie
[permit] Potatoes
[permit] Gravy
[implicit deny all else] **Buy nothing else**
```

Notice the last line; my wife imposes this restriction on me because I have a great deal of affection for chocolate ice cream and sale items. Now, she does not have to actually *say the words to me* because, after 16 years of marriage, I implicitly understand that I am not allowed to buy anything else.

I decide to show my list to my wife to make sure I did not miss anything. She reviews the list and decides I need more specific instructions because it is important to buy the right "kind" of groceries. She begins writing on my list:

```
[extended acl] Extended Grocery List (i.e. wife's version)
[deny] Turkey
[deny] Stuffing
[deny] Bread
[deny] Cheese
[permit] Milk - 2% White
[permit] Pie - Mrs. Smiths Pumpkin
[deny] Potatoes - Red as a guest is allergic to this type
[permit] Potatoes - any potatoes other than red is okay
[permit] Gravy - White Country
[implicit deny all] **Buy nothing else**
```

This type of list allows for a more granular level of filtering or, in my case, a more rewarding return home with the ingredients I was permitted to buy. Did you notice the difference between the two lists? The first list was rather broad and not specific at all, while the second list was extremely specific and told me not only exactly what not to buy, but more specifically what I was permitted to buy. Ultimately, the implicit understanding is that everything else is denied. You probably relate to the challenges of shopping when you are married and are also wondering how this relates to ACLs and packet filtering.

Packets have identifiable characteristics that access lists use to classify them and take an action—either permit or deny. Consider Example 3-1, which shows what a standard access list based on my analogy might look like.

Example 3-1   Analogy as a Standard Access List

```
access-list 10 deny any turkey
access-list 10 deny any stuffing
access-list 10 deny any bread
access-list 10 deny any cheese
access-list 10 permit any milk
access-list 10 permit any pie
access-list 10 permit any potatoes
access-list 10 permit any gravy
```

The standard access list in a Cisco device is primarily used to filter packets based on IP addresses. In addition, numbering them identifies a standard access list; specifically, they use 1–99 and 1300–1399 as identification numbers. If you were to take this example a technical level deeper and use IP addresses and subnets, it would look like Example 3-2 in a Cisco device's configuration.

Example 3-2   Standard Access List Filtering Packets

```
access-list 10 permit any 192.168.10.0
access-list 10 permit any 192.168.20.0
access-list 10 permit any 192.168.30.0
access-list 10 permit any 192.168.40.0
```

You are probably wondering what happened to the **deny** statements? With Cisco ACLs, there is that implicit **deny** everything else at the end, which you do not "see" in the configuration. Thus, you do not have to enter the **deny** statements. You could take the standard ACL and expand it to be even more specific by using an extended ACL; this is what my wife did when she gave me more specific instructions.

Because they are designed to identify packets, ACLs fulfill many roles in the world of networking. After a packet is identified, it can be acted upon in some manner. This action might include sending it after a more important packet, or perhaps filtering the packet. Figure 3-4 shows the placement of an ACL to filter packets.

Figure 3-4   Placement of Packet Filters

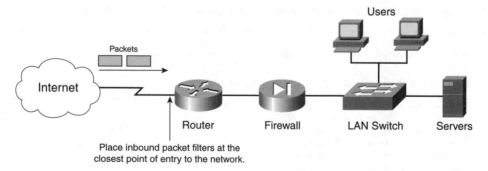

Limitations of Packet Filtering

It is time to talk about the drawbacks of using packet filtering. Certainly, you can stop many things with their use. Consider that you have a web server in a DMZ; all web/HTTP traffic must be able to reach this server. This server happens to be running Microsoft's IIS web server software, and an attacker decides to directly attack the web server using web/HTTP traffic. Because the attack targets vulnerabilities in IIS, the packets are allowed. So, although packet filtering is not good security (on its own), it most certainly is another technique that will increase the depth of your security.

note

You can find additional ACL information and techniques at the following Cisco.com URL (Cisco.com account required):

http://www.cisco.com/en/US/partner/products/sw/iosswrel/ps1835/
products_configuration_guide_chapter09186a00800ca7c0.html

The next section takes packet filtering a step further by discussing stateful packet inspection.

Stateful Packet Inspection (SPI)

This section discusses the more advanced technique of packet inspection: *Stateful Packet Inspection (SPI)*. To understand how SPI operates, you must briefly review the TCP/IP model.

note

Many people are confused about the relationship between the OSI reference model and the TCP/IP model—simply put, the use of OSI is as a reference for developers whereas, in education, *functionally* TCP/IP is used. Therefore, you must use the TCP/IP model when inspecting packets.

In Figure 3-5, you can see the five layers of the *TCP/IP model*. The stateful inspection component is concerned with how TCP (Layer 4—transport) makes connections. Tracking the state of the TCP connection is done via Layer 4 of the TCP/IP model.

Figure 3-5   TCP/IP Model

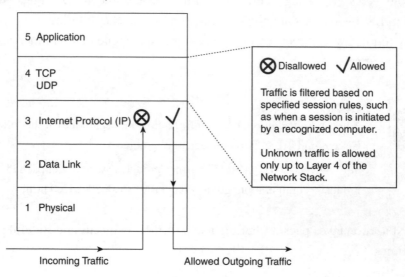

In most cases, SPI occurs in a firewall, which sits behind the router that connects your network to the Internet. If you have implemented packet filtering on the router as your first line of defense, the next line of defense will be SPI at the firewall, as shown in Figure 3-6.

Figure 3-6   Placement of Stateful Packet Inspection

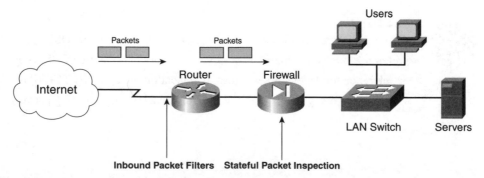

This placement and added security allows for the defense in depth to be layered at yet another level, with the goal of completely securing the network via multiple layers of protection.

SPI is usually implemented in a firewall so the TCP/IP connections can be inspected more closely. Thus, this technology is considered *connection aware* in that SPI monitors and understands that a connection between two computers usually consists of many packets that flow back and forth between the computers. Stateful inspection of packets occurs during the first packets that are used to create this connection. As the connection is *inspected*, an entry is created in a table. Then, as future packets are received, they are verified against entries in this table to see whether they belong to an existing and recorded connection. If the packets pass this verification phase, they are allowed to pass. At a very high level, that is how SPI occurs. The following section examines this process in more detail.

Detailed Packet Flow Using SPI

Because this book strives to always present best practices regarding network security and the associated technologies, this more detailed discussion is based on the assumption that the external router is in place and that it is configured to pre-screen connection attempts into the network by using packet filtering. Therefore, picking up the packet as it passes through the router and its packet filtering, the next step is the packet arriving at the firewall:

1. When a packet arrives at the firewall, a decision must be made to determine whether the packet should be allowed (forwarded) to the internal network.

2. The device performing the stateful packet inspection takes each arriving packet and inspects its headers to determine whether they match the set of rules that control what kind of packets are allowed.

3. When inspecting the packet's headers, the inspection includes the packet's source and destination addresses, its protocol type (TCP, UDP, ICMP, and so forth), its source and destination ports, flags set on the packet (SYN, ACK, FIN, RST, and so on), or other such basic header information. Incoming packets are inspected until enough information has been gathered from the packets received (using information such as TCP sequence numbers) to determine the connection's "state."

4. This inspection data is compared against the rule set that has determined what should be allowed and what should be denied. For example, all HTTP traffic *only* might be allowed to a web server, while other traffic should be denied trying to access the web server. This is a common rule wherein only a certain type of traffic should only be allowed to a certain server.

5. Depending on the connection status, this inspection information is then compared to a stateful table that would have entries for each TCP/IP connection the device has allowed. For example, most devices allow everyone from inside the network to access anything they want outside the network, and that connection would have formed an entry in the state table. Rather than allowing all packets that meet the rule set's requirements to pass, only those packets that are part of a valid, established connection are permitted.

6. Ultimately, packets are either permitted or denied depending on these inspection steps. Because these rules/tables are only consulted once, complex inspection rules do not greatly impact performance.

SPI rules are not as easy to create as packet-filtering rules because of the added level of complexity. However, they are certainly worth the money and effort because they add an additional level of security to your network. They are also fast and can handle large amounts of network traffic. If the metrics recorded for the connection do not match the entry in the connection database, the connection is dropped.

note
Usually, firewalls are the devices of choice for performing stateful packet inspection; however, routers can also be used in this role. However, this is not advised because mixing network devices' roles alters the functions they were designed to perform. Some might argue that you can successfully combine roles and devices; perhaps this might be appropriate in the distant future—for today and for the networks I am responsible for securing, I advise against it.

Limitations of Stateful Packet Inspection

Although SPI devices have improved scalability and benefits over packet filtering, they are not the ultimate point of protection for your network. Consider the following two major disadvantages of stateful packet inspection:

■ **No application level inspection**—SPI cannot look at a packet any higher than Layer 4 of the OSI reference model. In practice, this is how attacks are able to succeed against servers that are accessible in some manner and protected by firewalls performing stateful packet inspection.

■ **No connection state for every TCP/IP protocol**—Certain protocols within TCP/IP have no method of tracking the state of their connection between computers. Specifically, ICMP or UDP have no connection state; thus, in the layered model, these protocols should be subjected to packet filtering because they have no connection state to track.

This section discussed the capability of security devices, such as firewalls, to track the state and thereby the validity of a connection to determine whether it should be allowed into the protected area of your network. The next section focuses on the various means of further ensuring the validity of packets entering your network by using additional security to inspect them at Layer 5 (application) of the TCP/IP model.

Network Address Translation (NAT)

The Internet has grown larger than anyone ever imagined. Although its exact size is unknown, the current estimate is that there are about 100 million hosts and over 350 million users actively on the Internet. This is more than the entire population of the United States. In fact, the Internet is effectively doubling in size each year.

When IPv4 addressing first appeared, everyone thought there were plenty of addresses to cover any need. Theoretically, you could have 4,294,967,296 unique public addresses (2^{32}). The actual number of available public addresses is smaller (somewhere between 3.2 and 3.3 billion) because of the way that the addresses

have been separated by the Internet Engineering Task Force (IETF) into classes (A, B, C) and the need to set aside some of the addresses for multicasting, testing or other specific uses (Class D).

note

In addition to arranging groups of IPv4 addresses into classes, you might be wondering what happened to the millions of public IPv4 addresses that I said were no longer available. To ensure that every network in need of private IP addresses can have them, the Internet Engineering Task Force (IETF) has set aside a large range of addresses for internal network routing by means of Network Address Translation (NAT). Many of these addresses are referred to as *private IP addresses*; these addresses are not accessible on the public Internet, thus the word "private." Private addresses are to be used within any organization that needs them, and never on the Internet. The addresses used on the Internet are referred to as *public IP addresses*.

With the explosion of the Internet and the ever-increasing need for IP addresses in home networks and business networks, the number of available IPv4 addresses is simply insufficient. The obvious solution is to redesign the IP addressing scheme to allow for more possible addresses. This is being developed in a solution known as IPv6, but it will take many years to implement because it requires the modification of the Internet's entire infrastructure. As a result, the process of converting from IPv4 to IPv6 has been slow and will likely continue slowly as NAT further extends the life of IPv4.

NAT allows organizations to resolve the problem of IP address depletion when they have existing networks and need to access the Internet. Sites that do not yet possess NIC-registered IP addresses must acquire them from the Internet Assigned Numbers Authority (IANA) and American Registry for Internet Numbers (ARIN), who delight in causing bureaucratic delay. Many sites do not pass their unfriendly bureaucratic examination; therefore, NAT is the solution for most.

note

The Internet Assigned Numbers Authority (IANA) has reserved the following three blocks of the IP address space for private networks:

- 10.0.0.0–10.255.255.255 (10/8 prefix)
- 172.16.0.0–172.31.255.255 (172.16/12 prefix)
- 192.168.0.0–192.168.255.255 (192.168/16 prefix)

NAT allows companies to use *public IP addresses on the outside of the network* (that is, on those devices that connect directly to the public Internet). However, as discussed, there probably will not be enough public IP addresses for every network printer, PC, server, switch, router, wireless device, and so forth to be assigned a public IP address. These devices need an IP address to connect with TCP/IP, so we use *private IP addresses on the internal network.* The use of private IP addresses inside our network provides for all devices to now communicate using TCP/IP, which was the goal. However, you must activate NAT because the private IP addresses are not allowed out onto the Internet.

Network Address Translation (NAT) is deployed and implemented on a device (firewall, router, or computer) that sits between an internal network using private IP addresses and the Internet, which uses public IP addresses. The device performing the *Address Translation* from private to public is usually a firewall and, to a lesser extent, a router. The device performing NAT usually sits with one part connected to the internal network and another part connected to the Internet (or some external network). Figure 3-7 shows the placement of NAT as part of a layered defense.

Figure 3-7   Placement of NAT in a Network

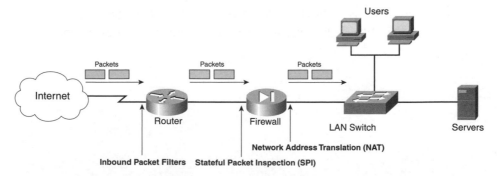

Discussion of how NAT also provides an additional level of security to your network is discussed later in the section, "Increasing Network Security." NAT has many forms and can work in several ways:

- *Static NAT*—Provides for mapping a private IP address to a public IP address on a one-to-one basis. This is particularly useful when a device needs to be accessible from outside the network. For example, if your web server has an internal IP address of (10.0.0.1) and it needs to be accessible from the Internet—it is your web server, after all! NAT must to be *statically* configured to allow users who go a public IP address to always be translated to 10.0.0.1. The use of static NAT is quite common for devices like web servers, which must always be accessible from the Internet.

- *Dynamic NAT*—Provides for mapping a private IP address to a public IP address from a group of registered IP addresses. In this type of NAT, there is a one-to-one relationship in the mapping from private to public. For example, if your PC was assigned an internal IP address of 10.0.0.2 and your co-worker was 10.0.0.3, each of you would be assigned a public IP address at the firewall via NAT as your traffic went to the Internet. Dynamic NAT is helpful, but it might not be the right solution in many cases. For example, what if your other co-worker wanted to access the Internet and the firewall was out of available public IP addresses? He would be denied. This could introduce a serious problem; therefore, NAT overloading was developed.

- *NAT Overloading*—A form of dynamic NAT that provides for the translation of multiple private IP addresses to a single public IP address by using different TCP ports. This is also known as Port Address Translation (PAT) or single address NAT. Its many names are not important, but how it functions is crucial. Because over 64,000 TCP ports are possible per single IP address, NAT allows for an effective means of providing Internet access to many users who have been assigned private IP addresses. This type of NAT is the most commonly used because it serves large numbers of users at once.

Increasing Network Security

Solving the IPv4 address depletion problem was the leading reason for the development of NAT. NAT also provides for yet another layer of security to protect your network. In general, using NAT makes it more difficult for an attacker to

- Map the target's network topology and determine connectivity

- Identify the number of systems running on a network

- Identify the type of machines and the operating systems they are running

- Implement denial of service (DOS) attacks such as SYN (synchronize/start) flooding, port scans, and packet injection

NAT's Limitations

It is clear that the introduction of NAT to the realm of networking and the Internet has solved or at least extended the IP address depletion problem. Many people have asked if networks will ever evolve to IPv6 now that NAT works so well. The question is not really if, but when will this conversion will take place. For example, the Asia/Pacific region of the world is leading the implementation of IPv6 with many networks already using it.

As connectivity and convergence increase, the need for additional IP addresses will grow and expand. We will therefore make the change to IPv6 eventually; NAT has simply delayed the inevitable. NAT is useful and has brought advantages; however, it does have some limitations:

- **Issues with UDP**—NAT tracks and controls connections based on state and, as discussed earlier in this chapter, UDP has no inherent mechanism to determine state. Thus, NAT has no way of knowing whether a packet is part of an ongoing conversation or an isolated transmission. NAT devices then need to guess at how long a conversation involving UDP should remain open after the last packet; this is known as the idle time. Cisco firewalls provide the functionality to set idle time on UDP sessions to limit such cases.

- **Sensitive protocols**—Some protocols hide, alter, or otherwise obscure aspects of the packets that NAT requires to properly perform the translation. For example, Kerberos, X-Windows, remote shell, and session initiation protocol (SIP) can have trouble operating through a NAT device. This trouble is caused by applications that have embedded IP addresses in the packets where this issue occurs. Cisco firewalls have nice fix-ups for different protocols, such as Skinny for telephony, that allow these applications to work when the fix-up is applied.

- **Interferes with encryption and authentication systems**—Many data encryption systems attempt to ensure the integrity of packets by ensuring that packets were not tampered with in transit. By its very design tampers, NAT with packets, thus causing encryption and authentication technologies to not work well with NAT (by default).

- **Complicated logging**—When devices are logging through a device, the correlation of the logs requires users to understand the translations being performed by NAT. Correlation of system logs with the NAT system can thus become highly complicated and tedious to understand which internal systems were actually involved.

- **One size fits all**—If your organization is using PAT, and one person in the company authenticates to a protected resource outside of your company, it's possible that the rest of your organization now has access to that resource as well. Remember that if you're using PAT, you're only using one IP address that has been multiplexed using port numbers. The protected resource that requires authentication sees all conversations from your company as coming from the same IP address.

The final point to reinforce is that NAT is useful in many regards, from allowing an entire company to access the Internet to providing an additional layer of security. If you go back to the network referenced in figures throughout this chapter, you can see that including NAT adds another layer of protection, as shown in Figure 3-7.

The following section of this chapter looks at how security can be further deepened through tools and technologies that look deeper into a TCP packet.

Proxies and Application Level Protection

Stateful packet inspection firewalls are enhanced versions of packet filtering. The devices used here provide additional enhancements by analyzing the packets at the application layer. Several types or technologies can be used to implement this protection, and they are known by many different names. Although each technology operates slightly differently, their goal is the same: to increase the security of your network.

Application level firewalls provide the most secure type of data connections because they can examine every layer in the TCP/IP model of the communication process. To achieve this level of protection, these firewalls—also known as *proxies*—actually mediate and control connections by intercepting and inspecting every connection. If the proxy determines that the connection is allowed, it opens a second connection to the server from itself on behalf of the original host, as shown in Figure 3-8.

Figure 3-8   Proxy Placement

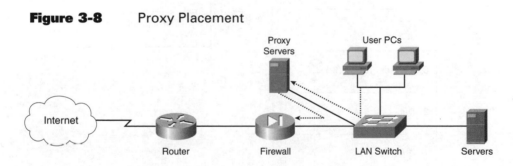

The data portion of each packet must be stripped off, examined, rebuilt, and sent again on the second connection. As shown in the list and in the following sections, different types of firewalls can be used to accomplish this:

- **Standard proxy firewalls**—A proxy firewall does not route packets; it simply forwards them, and it operates at the application layer of the TCP/IP model. Functionally, a proxy firewall receives packets from one interface, inspects the packets according to the defined rule set, and passes the packets out to the other interface if they are permitted. A connection is never made from the outside to the inside byPCs; as far as the PCs inside the firewall know, all of their information is coming from the proxy firewall.

■ **Dynamic proxy firewalls**—Originally developed from the concepts described for standard proxy firewalls, a dynamic proxy firewall was designed to take the benefits of standard proxies and add the benefits of packet filtering. A dynamic proxy firewall performs a complete inspection of the packet; when a connection is first made and, after it is approved, the faster and weaker packet filtering mechanism handles all additional packets. To summarize, connections are first inspected at the application layer, and then at the network layer.

Because these proxy firewalls have full visibility into the application layer of the TCP/IP model, they can look for more specific pieces of data than any other type of technology discussed thus far. For example, they can tell the difference between an e-mail and java data contained within a packet, as shown in Figure 3-9.

Figure 3-9   Proxy Packet Inspection

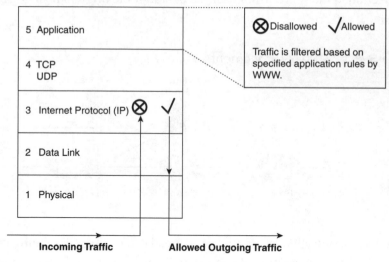

As the packet is inspected entering the proxy in Figure 3-9, all aspects of the TCP/IP header information is removed from the *actual data* and inspected with the data. The information gathered by this inspection would then be compared against the firewalls rules, and the packet would then either be denied or permitted based on this comparison. If the packet was deemed as something that should be permitted, the proxy firewall stores the connection information from the headers, rewrites the headers, and transmits the packet accordingly. If the packet were denied, it would be thrown in the bit bucket.

note

Have you never heard of the ***bit bucket***? It is a lighthearted way of saying trash or garbage can. When saying that a packet is thrown in the bit bucket, this really means that the router, firewall, or proxy has chosen to discard the packet; because all data is ultimately only bits (1s and 0s), we have proof that nerds have a sense of humor.

Limitations of Proxies

Hopefully by now, you have realized that everything has a limitation or associated drawback. Sales and marketing would love for you to believe that their new security gizmo is perfect for solving all of your problems. Reality is frequently not the rosy picture they would like us to believe, and proxy firewalls are no different. Following are some of the limitations of proxy firewalls:

- **Reduced performance**—This thorough examination and handling of packets means that proxy firewalls are very secure and generally slow. Reduced performance could result because of the inspection of essentially every part of every packet being subjected to this level of security.

- **Not always current**—As new protocols and applications are developed, proxy servers must be expanded to recognize what is acceptable or not. This expansion means that, to stay current, new proxies must be developed and tested; this takes time and results in a security device that might not always be current.

From a security standpoint, the most secure firewall is a standard proxy firewall that inspects all traffic on an application layer. However, that is not always the most practical solution in many of today's networks. Careful planning and understanding of the required network security and the traffic therein is important for developing a strong security solution. For example, a landscaping company has different security needs than a company that builds electronic components for the government.

Of the two types of firewalls discussed—stateful and proxy—it is crucial that you use at least one of them as part of your layered approach to network security. Add to them the presence of packet filtering on your edge router and a firewall device

that also uses NAT, and you will have developed the beginnings of a layered defense. The following section examines how content filters can also be used to protect your network and its users.

Content Filters

Content filtering is a subject so vast that its implications and possible solutions have spawned entire businesses that are dedicated to providing the right solution for you, regardless of whether you are a home user or a large business. Everyone seems to be faced with the need to filter some sort of content at every aspect of how they connect. Consider some of the challenges that have recently emerged into politics and the media:

- **Public libraries and pornography**—For some reason, there is a group of people who think people have the right to surf pornography on computers that tax dollars pay for. Making this issue worse is the fact that they are doing this in the middle of libraries— the same place where children go to read. Content filters could be used in libraries to disallow access to this type of content. Businesses are also using content filters to filter out user attempts at going to sites on the Internet.

  Unfortunately, the problem is not only about pornographic web sites—there are also those sites dedicated to drug use, criminal activity, terrorism, violence, threaten the safety of children, and hate-oriented material.

- **SPAM**—If you have e-mail, you have spam—of that there can be no doubt. All types of businesses are fighting back against spam, and it has always been a fight to detect and stop spam. Every time a solution is discovered, spammers get more creative and do something different. For example, many people spell out their e-mail addresses out now—*tom dot thomas at netcerts dot com*—in hopes of fooling the programs that search for e-mail addresses. It might for a little while, but it will not last long. In the arena of spam prevention, content filters can identify those annoying ads for low mortgage rates. They are so silly; who would want to get a mortgage with a company that had to spam to get your business?

- **Viruses and trojan horses**—Many of the ways viruses are spread follow the growth patterns of the Internet. Virtually everyone who connects to the Internet has e-mail—thus sending a malicious attachment in an e-mail has become commonplace. Content filters would examine the content of such attachments and filter them before any damage was done.

- **Malicious web pages**—Attackers can now code into web pages ways to learn more about you when you visit those pages, and they can do this in many ways. Content filters would be able to examine the actual HTML code that makes the website and filter it as needed.

- **Increased organization success**—You might be wondering how content filtering can increase a corporation's overall success? Companies and government agencies can face significant risk because of their employees' behavior. Consider the implications to any organization if an employee were to access offensive or illegal material via that organization's network? For example, employees visiting websites with offensive content can create a hostile work environment, negatively affect morale/productivity, and might lead to potentially costly legal fees with the resulting negative bad press. Do you recall the concept of downstream liability discussed in Chapter 1, "Here There Be Hackers!"? If an employee were to access child pornography, the organization could be held liable, have assets seized (network), and suffer additional negative publicity.

Internet access has become critical to businesses, and the rewards to many organizations can be high. However, issues arise where employees have unmanaged access to the Internet, as just discussed. None of the technologies discussed thus far address the potential security risks just listed. You might be correctly thinking that not all of these risks are applicable to your organization, and that might be true. The goal of this chapter is to discuss the technology surrounding content filtering, which could clearly be applied to many different problems, depending on your need. Benefits of content filtering include the following:

- Reduce or eliminate legal liability by not letting your organization's resources be used in a compromising manner or through the inadvertent disclosure of confidential information.

- Optimize employee productivity; who wants to pay someone while they are surfing the Internet for pleasure?

- Improve reporting on employee Internet usage. This is critical because you might feel protected or safe. There is no way to know for sure unless you are also watching what is happening on your network.

- Enforce company Internet access policies that would be documented in the Acceptable Use Security Policy, as discussed in Chapter 2, "Security Policies and Responses":

  — Disallow the accessing illegal or offensive material

  — Prevent the downloading of unauthorized software

There are a variety of ways to filter the content of packets as they flow through your network. Entire companies and tons of products provide any type of filtering service for you from span to content. To do them justice by explaining them all is beyond the scope of this chapter. There are some common fundamental similarities, regardless of the product selected.

note

Your organization's Acceptable Use Policy should inform the employee of what is expected from him as a user of corporate resources, and the content monitoring/filtering monitors and reports on compliance.

The key to content filtering solutions is the ability to monitor and filter content from the Internet, chat rooms, instant messaging, e-mail, e-mail attachments, Word, PowerPoint, and from web browsers. There are several ways to filter traffic, and they can be classified into two main categories:

- **Client-based filtering**—This filtering solution involves loading software onto individual PCs that check content and filter it according to a defined set of rules. In the case of home users, this is the most common type of solution and usually comes in the form of a subscription to a server that contains updates.

■ **Server-based filtering**—In this filtering solution, individual client PCs do not require specialized software to be loaded because everything is being loaded and controlled by a server that the client PC's in turn access. This type of filtering is commonly used for e-mail spam and virus detection; all e-mail comes into a central server, which is the most logical place to filter it.

For content filtering, a device such as a proxy server or Cisco content engine forces all web traffic through it so the user requests to view web pages. Users can be inspected to determine if the request should be permitted or denied. Content filtering is accomplished using a library or database of terminology, words, and phrases as the set of rules defining what is not allowed.

In many cases, requests are regarded as the replies; for example, some attempts to access a website might be able to be classified via the database/library when the client makes a request (such as http://www.showmeporno.com), while other requests might require the filtering device to analyze the content of the web page before making a filtering decision.

These same examples of browsing the Internet using content filtering is extremely similar to how spam and virus filtering is accomplished. Ultimately, a database contains ways of identifying what should be filtered and what should not. As traffic enters the network, it is verified against this database. For example, many products and tools can be used at the server level to identify and stop spam. Nothing is ever 100 percent accurate, so many e-mail clients also have some sort of built-in way of allowing users to further identify spam e-mail.

Limitations of Content Filtering

Content filtering can play a large role in protecting your network and ensuring the proper use of network resources. However, it does have some disadvantages that, if you are aware of them, will allow for the filtering to operate better:

■ An estimated three to five million websites are introduced to the Internet as new or renamed every single week. This makes the tracking of good/bad sites extremely difficult to do and requires dedicated service to ensure that your filters are always up to date.

- Content is always changing; in addition to new websites, new ways to spam, new viruses, and other threats make it difficult to keep on top of the changes.

- Nothing is perfect, so you can expect to see false positives to a certain degree. Therefore, retaining some sort of control of the system is important, and blind reliance on outside classifications is probably not a good idea—for example, www.msexchange.com being seen by content/URL filter as "m sexchange" rather than "ms exchange."

Content filtering is probably in use in your network in some form or another. The extent of its implementation varies widely depending on the size and sensitivity of your business. The following section looks at a manner of completely securing your network: PKI.

Public Key Infrastructure (PKI)

Have you ever bought anything online or otherwise engaged in some sort of electronic commerce on the Internet? Most likely, you saw the little lock in the corner of your browser window that told you that this was a secure transaction. With what you have learned so far in this book, do you honestly believe that?

The little key or lock in your browser means that you are on a website (server) that is using a *Secure Socket Layer (SSL)* certificate, so you can rest assured that they are who they say they are. Go ahead—buy and enter your credit card number!

note
The little lock means that an SSL connection has been engaged. Anyone can cause a secure connection to take place, so be careful even when you see a little lock.

Have you ever noticed that, while you are conducting e-commerce, the http:/.... changes to https://...? The presence of the "s" means that you are using HTTP over SSL to communicate back and forth.

Ultimately, what is actually occurring is that your web browser is taking in the SSL certificate, contacting whoever certified it to ensure its validity, and then proceeding to communicate in a secure mode with the server so you can complete your transaction in complete security. Do you still believe that this is a good system?

Did I mention that this SSL certificate session is 40 bits in length? Certain aspects of the certificate that reside on the server are 1024 bits. Compare this 40-bit length to an IP address, which is 32 bits in length or 3DES encryption at 128 bits. You should never feel 100 percent secure when conducting e-commerce at this stage in the Internet's evolution because the security is not there yet. As the use of e-commerce continues to rise, the level of fraud is increasing even more. This trend is taking a toll on the growth and confidence in e-commerce and online transactions of all kinds. Of course, none of this is ever talked about in polite sales and marketing circles. Not to fret—an advance in securing e-commerce is coming in the form of PKI.

Public Key Infrastructure (PKI) is an evolving technology that will eventually become an IETF standard. The goal of PKI is to provide a foundation for a system that will support a variety of security services, such as data integrity, data confidentiality, and non-repudiation. PKI will provide this through a combination of hardware, software, procedures, and policies so users can communicate and exchange information securely, regardless of location.

This system involves the verification and authentication of each side of a transaction over a network. Consider for a moment the impact that online credit-card fraud has on people and businesses. At this time, everyone is losing when fraud occurs—the people because they had their credit card or identity stolen, and the businesses because they are trying to provide a service while remaining profitable.

PKI provides for authentication through the use of advanced digital certificates and certification authorities to verify and authenticate the validity of each side of a transaction. This transaction could be something as sensitive as an online Internet purchase, or as straightforward as exchanging sensitive information via e-mail. PKI is going to be the next step in the evolution of secure communication and e-commerce.

Additional PKI resources can be found online at the following locations:

http://www.pki-page.org/

http://www.pkiforum.org/

PKI's Limitations

PKI is not yet a standard because the IETF has yet to ratify any RFC relating to PKI at press time. In researching PKI, I began to think this was a great next step—even more so when my wife's identity was stolen, coupled with the lack of concern by our law-enforcement agencies. The ease with which people dismissed the crime was amazing, not to mention the fact that businesses felt it was just a risk whose loss they had to absorb. Certainly then, PKI would be a good step; however, there are some serious challenges in its future:

- E-commerce is working and flourishing on the Internet, regardless of the occasional risks involved.

- Scary laws in states like Utah and Washington are on the books, saying that if someone were to crack your key or use it illegally, you are still responsible for the debt they created. Having seen the bills created by the thief of my wife's identity, this is extremely worrisome to me if I am ever forced to use PKI!

- Security is today, and it is likely to continue to be under PKI the responsibility of the certificate holder. Thus, you must trust that they have taken all the necessary precautions without exposing new vulnerabilities. PKI is coming; however, there are still some questions in my mind about it.

- PKI does not support a single login infrastructure, so users will have to log in and authenticate multiple times to access different resources; this is a recipe for disaster. Users will find ways to "simplify" (that is, defeat) the security PKI provides, and mistakes will happen.

So, is a technology like PKI good or bad? That is difficult to say because PKI is not really mature enough to be called a standard. However, it does provide for increased security that could help in many areas. The verdict on PKI is still up in the air and is subject to the whims of the PKI vendors and how they listen and evolve their products.

The following section looks at some methods that are currently available for authenticating access to the network.

AAA Technologies

Today, we live in a world where almost everything must be protected from misuse and nothing is free. It does not matter if you are a system administrator, manager, student, or a network engineer. If you access services via a network, you always need three things:

- Authentication

- Authorization

- Accounting

These components are collectively known as *AAA* (pronounced triple A). As discussed in the following sections, each of these components plays an important role.

Authentication

Authentication ensures that the network's user is who she claims to be. This is important because you do not want that person accessing the network if she is not supposed to. Usually a shared secret or a trusted third-party software application provides authentication.

Authentication allows the network administrators to identify who can connect to a network device or Internet by including the user's username and password. Normally, when a user connects to a router remotely via Telnet, the user must supply only a password to gain access to the router. This is functional but not secure because, if the router is connected to the Internet, an attacker could try and try to

connect, and you might never know that this was occurring. All the attacker would have to do is guess a single password to access your router. How hard could that be when he has all the time in the world?

When someone logs into one of your network devices and makes a change, how do you know who the person is and what he has done? With AAA authentication, whenever a user logs on, the user must enter a username and password pair (which network administrator has assigned). The following code snippet shows an example of a remote user accessing a Cisco router with AAA configured to request a username:

```
User Access Verification

Username: tom_thomas

Password: xxxxxxxx

MyCiscoRouter>
```

As shown in the preceding example, the user must enter a valid username and password to gain access to the router. Typically, a database that contains the valid usernames reside locally on the router or on a remote security server.

Authorization

Related to authentication is authorization, which comes into play once authentication is complete. After the user is authenticated, there must be a way to ensure that the user is authorized to do the things he is requesting. For example, if you are a normal user, you do not have the permissions to access all the files in a file system. Using ACLs or policies provides authorization.

Authorization allows administrators to control the level of access users have after they successfully gain access to the router. Cisco IOS Software allows certain access levels (called *privilege levels*) that control which IOS commands the user can issue. For example, a user with a 0 privilege level cannot issue any IOS commands. A user with a privilege level of 15 can perform all valid IOS commands. The local or remote security server can grant access levels.

You can display your privileged level on a Cisco router with the **show privilege** command, as shown in the following command line.

```
MyCiscoRouter#show privilege

Current privilege level is 15

MyCiscoRouter#
```

Authorization can also dictate the types of protocol activity in which the user can engage, such as allowing a user to invoke only FTP, Telnet, or HTTP traffic. Keep in mind that the higher the privilege, the more capabilities a user has with the IOS command set.

Accounting

Accounting occurs after the authentication and authorization steps have been completed. Accounting allows administrators to collect information about users and the actions that they take when connected to network devices. The information gathered through accounting can provide forensic evidence of tampering or hacking because you have a roadmap of the user's times/dates and activities. Specifically, administrators can track which user logged into which router, which IOS commands a user issued, and how many bytes were transferred during a user's session. For example, accounting enables administrators to monitor the routers that have had their configurations changed. A router or a remote security server can collect accounting information.

note
If you still use dialup to access the Internet, you are using AAA when you authenticate and receive authorization into your service provider's network. Accounting is the process in which the network service provider collects network usage information for billing relating to how long you were connected, capacity planning, and other purposes. This is important for the service provider—there is no such thing as a free lunch.

After AAA is configured, you can use external security servers to run external security protocols—such as RADIUS or TACACS—that will stop unauthorized access to your network. Both RADIUS and TACACS can be implemented on Cisco network devices and will be reviewed in the upcoming sections.

note

You must use AAA if you intend to use RADIUS or TACACS security server protocols. As AAA collects the information, it sends it to the security servers to determine each of the characteristics associated with AAA.

Remote Authentication Dial-In User Service (RADIUS)

RADIUS is a client-server based system that secures a Cisco network against intruders. RADIUS is a protocol implemented in Cisco IOS Software that sends authentication requests to a RADIUS server. A RADIUS server is a device that has the RADIUS daemon or application installed. RADIUS must be used with AAA to enable the authentication, authorization, and accounting of remote users. When a RADUIS server authenticates a user, the following events occur:

1. The remote user is prompted for a username and password.

2. The username and password is encrypted and sent across the data network.

3. The RADIUS server accepts or rejects a username and password pair. In some instances, a user might be asked to enter more information (this is called a challenge response). For example, if a user's password has expired, a RADUIS server prompts the user for a new password.

note

Traffic between the Network Access Server (NAS) and RADIUS is *not* encrypted—as opposed to TACACS, which does encrypt authentication message traffic.

note

A RADIUS server is usually software that runs on various platforms, including Microsoft NT servers or a UNIX host. RADIUS can authenticate router users, authenticate vendors, and even validate IP routes.

The following steps are required to enable RADIUS on a Cisco router:

Step 1   Use the **aaa new-model** command. AAA must be used with RADIUS.

Step 2   Specify the RADIUS server with the **radius-server host** command, as shown in Example 3-3.

Step 3   Specify the password used between the router and the RADIUS server.

note

Of course, you must also ensure that you have entered users and passwords into the radius server before activating RADIUS.

Example 3-3 displays the required configuration for a Cisco router to authenticate users from the RADIUS server with the host address 10.99.34.50.

Example 3-3   RADIUS Configuration

```
radius-server host 10.99.34.50
radius-server key <password>
```

Let's move on to TACACS, which is an alternative protocol to RADIUS that also works with AAA.

Terminal Access Controller Access Control System (TACACS)

Cisco IOS supports three versions of TACACS: TACACS, extended TACACS, and TACACS+. All three methods authenticate users and deny access to users who do not have a valid username and password.

The first version of TACACS provides simple password verification and authentication. Accounting is limited in that only requests and denials are listed. Next, extended TACACS replaced the first version of TACACS. TACACS+, also referred to as TACACS plus, provides detailed accounting and must be used with AAA (in other words, the **aaa new-model** command must be enabled). TACACS+ supercedes the earlier releases of TACACS. In general, *TACACS* provides a centralized security system that validates users from any remote location. Typically, TACACS runs on a Windows Server or UNIX operating system. When a TACACS server authenticates a user, the following events occur:

1. The remote user is prompted for a username and password.

2. The username and password is sent across the data network and is authenticated.

3. The TACACS server accepts or rejects the username and password pair. The user might be asked to enter additional information (called a challenge response).

For example, a challenge response might appear when an error occurs during authentication. TACACS+ requires AAA, but TACACS and extended TACACS do not use AAA.

The configuration tasks required to enable TACACS+ on a Cisco router are as follows:

Step 1   Use the **aaa new-model** command. AAA must be used with TACACS+.

Step 2   Specify the TACACS+ server with the **tacacs-server host** command.

Step 3   Specify the authentication key used between the router and the TACACS+ server.

Step 4   Because TACACS+ must be used in conjunction with AAA, you must specify TACACS+ authentication, authorization, and accounting.

Example 3-4 displays the required configuration for a Cisco router to authenticate users from the TACACS+ server with the host address 10.99.34.50.

Example 3-4 TACACS Configuration

```
aaa new-model

aaa authentication enable default tacacs+

! Sets router to use the tacacs server to authenticate enable
! password

aaa authorization exec tacacs+

! Sets tacacs+ plus to authorize exec commands on local router

aaa accounting exec start-stop tacacs+

! Accounting information is gathered for exec commands

tacacs-server host 10.99.34.50

tacacs-server key <password>
```

Example 3-4 is a basic TACACS + configuration; you can set other configuration options to enable complex AAA commands.

caution
If you enable AAA on a router, you could get locked out if you are not careful. If you fat finger any commands and exit out of your configuration, you might not be able to re-enter.

TACACS+ Versus RADIUS

Comparing the two server protocols, RADIUS and TACACS+, shows that both require AAA to be enabled on a Cisco router (unless you use the older versions of TACACS+, namely TACACS and extended TACACS). RADIUS and TACACS+ both require a username and password pair to obtain access. The difference between the two protocols is in the protocol itself and the fact that TACACS+ is a centralized validation service, while RADIUS is based on client/server technologies.

Chapter Summary

This chapter began with discussion of the importance of a layered network security design. This layering of security provides a deeper level of protection for your network. You want to avoid what I call the orange syndrome, where there is only a single layer of protection before you get to the "good stuff." You do not want attackers to defeat a single layer and get to the good stuff in your network.

This chapter looked at many technologies that you could use to provide a layered approach to security:

- Packet filtering via ACLs

- Stateful packet inspection

- Network Address Translation

- Proxies and application level protection

- Content filters

- Public key infrastructure

- AAA technologies

Separately, each of these technologies is just a single layer of protection, but combined, they provide you with several layers of protection and keep the good stuff safe.

Chapter Review Questions

The following questions assist in reinforcing the concepts that we covered in this chapter.

1. What are the six security design concepts you should consider when looking at the security technologies for securing your network?

2. What rule is always implicitly present at the end of every packet filter?

3. When a device is performing stateful packet inspection, what characteristics in a packet's header are inspected, and why are they important?

4. What are some limitations of stateful packet inspection?

5. Define the differences between public and private IP addresses.

6. Compare and contrast the three different versions of NAT and identify which of them is the most commonly used.

7. What are the two types of proxy firewalls?

8. Why is content filtering so important to networking?

9. What is the potential value of PKI to securing a network and e-commerce?

10. AAA provides security for what aspect of a network?

11. Search the Internet and find three potential vendors that can offer an effective RADIUS solution. Describe what features about each are beneficial.

What You Will Learn

By the end of this chapter, you should know and be able to explain the following:

✔ The difference between DES and 3DES, including their limitations

✔ The function and role of MD5 plays in securing connections

✔ The differences between PPTP and L2TP

✔ The breadth and scope of SSH and how it is more secure than Telnet

Being able to answer these key questions will allow you to understand the overall characteristics and importance of network security. By the time you finish this book, you will have a solid appreciation for network security, its issues, how it works, and why it is important.

CHAPTER 4

Security Protocols

The wisest mind has something yet to learn. — Author Unknown

Some of you might be wondering why this chapter is called "Security Protocols" since, in the IT realm, the term protocol is usually reserved for routing protocols of some sort. The best routing protocol is Open Shortest Path First (OSPF), and you should learn more about it when you can. At this time, however, the discussion focuses on security. According to Newton's *Telecom Dictionary*, a protocol is defined as, "a set of rules governing the format of messages that are exchanged between computers and people."

In the realm of security, a *security protocol* is defined as a secure procedure for regulating data transmission between computers. This chapter concerns the methods of encrypting data securely for transmission over a network. Later chapters cover the means of transporting data securely.

This chapter will allow you to develop an understanding of how data can be secured. In many ways, being able to protect data through encryption is yet another layer of a network's security.

Consider the fact that each day, information is being disclosed to people whom you do not wish to have it; more often than not, this is sensitive information. In many cases, this is not intentional, nor is it related to criminal activity or attackers in any way. Do you find this difficult to believe? Think about the following points:

- Sensitive data is placed on servers connected to your LAN for other people to access.

- Sensitive data is copied to floppy disks, CDs, and DVDs, or printed and handed to the recipient.

- Sensitive data is e-mailed across the network, or perhaps the Internet.

- Sensitive data is transmitted in some other manner.

- Sensitive data is placed on a web server.

Certainly, these common examples of "business as usual" and "how we do business" are easily recognizable scenarios to everyone. We have all done this at some time or another. The danger here is that the sensitive data is being sent *in the clear*; this means that anyone can read the data if they intercept it intentionally or accidentally, or even unintentionally (have you ever sent an e-mail to the wrong person?). You might ask yourself what possible kind of data could be used in a negative manner. Consider the following types of data:

- **Personal data**—Have you ever entered your address, phone number, date of birth, and so on into a web page or an e-mail?

- **Financial data**—Do you use Quicken or other money-management software on your computer? Is that computer ever connected to a network? What about checking bank account information online, tracking stocks you own, or entering credit-card data online?

- **Customer data**—Does your company enter customer information into a database or take orders online?

- **Medical data**—When was the last time you walked into a hospital or doctor's office and did not see a computer? Last time I was there, the doctor had a Palm Pilot with all my data loaded onto it. What would happen if he lost it or it was stolen?

These are the most commonly known types of data, but what about movies, music, new product plans, future projections, source code, and so on?

Most of the time, there is no danger of any sort; however, this is not always the case. When there is a mistake, it can be extremely serious. The point here is that everyone and every company has data that is important and that they would not want shared. This chapter discusses ways to protect this data.

note
When discussing encryption, the password is often referred to as the key; keep in mind that these two terms can be and are used interchangeably.

DES Encryption

In 1972, the National Institute of Standards and Technology (NIST), known at the time as the National Bureau of Standards, decided that a strong cryptographic algorithm was needed to protect nonclassified information. Historically, this was right around the time that the Internet as we know it today was beginning to expand into colleges and universities across the country and around the world. This was one of the driving factors behind the NIST decision to have a way for people to protect their data.

In typical government fashion, a public proposal was developed that outlined the specifications for this new cryptographic algorithm. The algorithm was required to be cheap, easily distributable, flexible for inclusion into many applications, and very secure.

In 1974, IBM submitted the Lucifer algorithm, which appeared to meet most of the design requirements NIST outlined in its proposal. Lucifer appeared to be a good solution and included the specification to be 128 bits in length. NIST did not have the technical knowledge to completely evaluate Lucifer, so it enlisted the help of the National Security Agency (NSA).

In the mid-1970s, the NSA was distrusted because of its secretive activities. The Cold War was occurring at this time, and the NSA was fulfilling its role in the nation's security. The NSA advised NIST that the 128-bit key had to be shrunk to 56 bits, thus significantly weakening the protection offered by the *Data Encryption Standard (DES)*.

 note

The NSA was also accused of changing the algorithm to plant a "back door" in it that would allow agents to decrypt any information without having to know the encryption key. These fears proved unjustified, and no such back door has ever been found.

NIST adopted the modified Lucifer algorithm as a federal standard on November 23, 1976, and changed its name to the Data Encryption Standard (DES). The algorithm

specification was published in January 1977, and with official backing by the government, it became a widely employed algorithm in a short amount of time.

In the late 1970s and early 1980s, when the best desktop computers were from Atari and Commodore, the security offered by DES was ideal. However, as computers became faster, the added element of people "looking" at DES, shortcuts were found; it was quickly realized that the 56-bit key was not large enough to be used as the basis for security.

In 1997, NIST discontinued its endorsement of DES and began to work on a replacement cryptographic algorithm known as the Advanced Encryption Standard (AES). Everyone loves a challenge, and the company RSA Security began sponsoring a series of DES challenges to see who could crack DES in the shortest amount of time. In the beginning, DES was cracked in days; however, more recently coming in at 22 hours, 15 minutes, the DES Challenge III was solved by the Electronic Frontier Foundation's "Deep Crack" in a combined effort with distributed.net. The foundation used a specially developed computer called the DES Cracker and a worldwide network of nearly 100,000 PCs, with which it was able to test over 245 billion keys per second. You can visit the RSA DES Challenge web page here:

http://www.rsasecurity.com/rsalabs/challenges/des3/index.html

This illustrates that any organization with moderate resources can break through DES with some effort these days. Despite the growing concerns about its vulnerability, financial services and other industries worldwide still widely use DES to protect sensitive online applications.

Encryption Strength

DES is 56 bits, meaning that the key to decrypt DES will be 56 bits in length. Basic mathematics tells us that, if there are 56 bits, they are made up of 8 bytes of 7 bits per byte ($8 * 7 = 56$). If you are thinking that each byte has 8 bits, you are correct. You can, therefore, have 128 values to choose from for each character from the normal ASCII character set. ASCII, however, has 256 characters; this is double the capacity of DES, and that means that there are two possible keys for DES (that is, there are always two ASCII characters that are interchangeable). In addition, the last bit on a DES key is ignored.

The strength of any *encryption* algorithm lies in the fact that it would take a long time to guess the used key. You can see the possible number of combinations through some simple math:

128^8= 128 * 128 * 128 * 128 * 128 * 128 * 128 * 128 =
72,057,594,037,927,936 (72 thousand plus billion) possible combinations

Each bit can have two states: off or on (0 or 1). There are normally 8 bits in a byte; because 8 bytes exist here, this makes 64 bits in total. Also, DES uses only 7 bits in the byte because one is ignored, as mentioned previously. This makes 56 bits in total. Converting the preceding byte calculations into bits would result in the following:

$256^8 = 2^{64}$

$128^8 = 2^{56}$ which is how the strength of DES being 56-bit encryption is expressed

Let's put this math into a real-world example. Consider that you know a piece of data has been encrypted using DES and you are trying to crack the key. Your computer has the ability to try 1 million different keys every minute. If you had to try all 72 thousand billion possible keys, it would take your computer 137,096 years to try every possible key. This seems pretty impressive, doesn't it? This certainly was the argument that led NIST and the NSA to support DES in the 1970s. However, computers have advanced quite a bit since then. The DES Crack Challenge employed technology that was trying 254 billion different keys per second.

Limitations of DES

Chapter 2, "Security Policies and Responses," discussed having a password policy that includes special characters and numbers to increase the effectiveness of the

passwords (keys) in use. Assume for a moment that people or companies are either not listening to the policy or think it is irrelevant. What effect might this have on the ability to crack a DES encrypted password (key)?

Assume that someone encrypts some important data using a key that contains normal characters—say, any letter between A and Z. Perhaps it is his mother's name, favorite sports team, or hometown? Using only normal letters makes a password/key hundreds of thousands of times easier to crack.

The entire alphabet consists of 26 characters; because there are two possible combinations (mathematically) for each, there are really only 13 in binary. Looking at this using numbers, it can be expressed as follows:

> If we have the entire alphabet, we have 26 characters; that reduces the number of possible combinations from thousands of billions down to 208 billion (208,827,064,576).

As explained previously, this number is reduced further because DES is not using all the bits in a byte to a very manageable 815 million (815,730,721). The end result is a password that can be cracked very quickly if you use only letters. You can see how quickly the key could be cracked if your computer could try a million different keys per minute—in less than 14 hours, your password could be cracked. In practice, however, most people who are using just letters of the alphabet are using them in the form of a word; those can be cracked in minutes.

Triple DES Encryption

DES was a fantastic answer to a problem in the 1970s; what the developers did not expect or anticipate was how much the world would change in less than 30 years. They did not understand that they were on the leading edge of the IT revolution. Ultimately, however, technology has made the protection level of DES such that it left businesses needing another solution.

The DES algorithm became obsolete. To fill the gap, Triple DES (written as **3DES**) was developed from the original DES algorithm. The development of 3DES happened quickly because it was based on the existing DES algorithm.

Looking at the names of the two different algorithms, you might be inclined to believe that 3DES makes your encryption three times more difficult to break. 3DES actually makes your encryption five billion, trillion, trillion times harder to break—that is, $5 * 10^{33}$.

The 3DES algorithm uses three separate keys when running its encryption algorithm and associated computations. Through the use of three separate keys, the key length has effectively been increased from 8 to 24 characters, thereby resulting in 168 bits-worth of encryption strength. Mathematically, this means that the number of possible key combinations can be expressed as

$$2^{168} = 3.7 * 10^{50} \text{ (370 trillion trillion trillion trillion) different combinations}$$

Earlier in this chapter, I mentioned what would happen if you could crack keys at the rate of 1 million per minute. I have no idea how long it would take using 3DES, but I will be long gone from this earth by the time you finish. This is why 3DES is considered so strong. You can read more about cracking 3DES in financial ATM applications in the article, *Extracting a 3DES Key from an IBM 4758*, which you can find online at http://public.planetmirror.com/pub/descrack/.

Encryption Strength

3DES is an extension of DES that takes three keys and encrypts the data, as shown in Figure 4-1.

Figure 4-1   Triple DES Encryption Steps

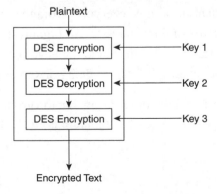

The overall procedure to encrypt data is the same in 3DES and DES; however, in 3DES, the encryption process is repeated three times. The plain text data, such as an MS-Word document, is encrypted with the first key. The result is then encrypted with the second key, and that result is then encrypted with the third key—hence the name 3DES.

Limitations of 3DES

The resulting actions of having to encrypt every piece of plain text data three times means that 3DES runs slower than normal DES. If used properly with three different keys, 3DES is several magnitudes stronger than DES.

You want to avoid having the same key for each of the three encryption steps. If any of the keys are the same, the end result is that you are using a slower version of DES. As discussed in this section, 3DES is a much stronger method of encryption than DES and is used today in many places.

Message Digest 5 Algorithm

With the development of the Internet and the evolution of the world to become oriented in data and connectivity, we have also learned that *"there be hackers"* out there. This means that you must be concerned with issues such as security, authenticity, and integrity of data.

These issues are important for almost everyone, from the military/government to healthcare/personal records to financial data. All organizations require secret or private data to be kept from those who should not have access to it. Security in the form of authenticity and integrity of data is being driven as follows:

- **Authenticity** is responsible for ensuring that the group or person sending the data is who he says he is. A digital signature is an example of the importance of authenticity.

- **Integrity** is responsible for ensuring that the data is not altered during transmission and that exactly what was sent was received. Have you ever downloaded a software application or operating system patch? It is important that the downloaded file has not lost any of its integrity; this is the importance of integrity.

Message Digest 5 (MD5) is one of the best available methods of ensuring that these security needs are met. A message-digest algorithm is designed to accept data and generate fixed length output; this output is called a *hash* value, fingerprint, or a message digest and is the key to the security that MD5 provides.

note

The term "hash" apparently comes by way of analogy with its standard meaning in the physical world: to "chop and mix." When teaching, I often run across technologies that hash. I find that the best way to explain a hash and make it memorable to students is through an analogy. A hash is basically a grinder that takes something recognizable—like beef or pork—hashes it, and the result is something based on the original, but is unique. In this case, it is hamburger or sausage, of course! Try and put that back together.

Developed in 1994 by Rivest, MD5 is a one-way hash algorithm that takes any length of data and produces a 128-bit nonreversible fingerprint known as a hash. (RFC 1321 officially describes MD5.) This output hash/fingerprint cannot be reverse engineered to determine the data that was used to produce it. Functionally, this means that it is impossible to derive the original file contents from the MD5; this is why they call it one-way.

note

A one-way hash is the result of an algorithm that turns data of any type into a string of digits, thus creating a *digital signature*. These digital signatures are then used to verify the authenticity and integrity of data. *Like a written signature, the purpose of a digital signature is to guarantee that the individual sending the message really is who she claims to be.*

It is important to note that MD5 does not actually encrypt or alter any data. Rather, it creates a hash from which the data's authenticity and integrity can be determined. Because MD5 does not encrypt data, it is not restricted by any exportation rules. You can freely use and distribute this MD5 anywhere in the world.

note

Authentication is the process of identifying an individual or device based on the correct username and password combination. Authentication does not determine what an individual is allowed to access, but merely that they are who they claim to be. Authorization defines what an individual is allowed to access—assuming that he has been authenticated, of course!

The following section looks at MD5 in action and where you might have unknowingly encountered MD5. The actual mathematics of how MD5 creates these hashes is beyond the scope of this book. Readers wanting to learn more about MD5 are encouraged to read RFC 1321, "The MD5 Message-Digest Algorithm" (http://www.isi.edu/in-notes/rfc1321.txt).

MD5 Hash in Action

If you own a computer, you have most likely experienced MD5 without even knowing it. MD5 plays a large role in networking, and it can help you in a variety of ways:

- When downloading files from the Internet, you can use MD5 to ensure that the downloaded file has been unaltered after being made available on a server. The MD5 hash is calculated after a file is downloaded.

- Ensure that the integrity of system files is maintained—various tools, such as tripwire (covered later), use MD5 to monitor and consistently verify that operating system files have not been altered. This protects crucial systems and alerts administrators if something has changed because the hashes no longer match.

When using a one-way hash operation like MD5, you can compare a calculated message digest against the received message digest to verify that the message has not been tampered with. This comparison is called a *hash check*.

MD5 checksums are widely used in software development to provide assurance that a downloaded file or patch is unaltered. By verifying a published MD5 checksum and comparing MD5 checksum on record with the software provider with a downloaded file's checksum, a user can be sure that the file is the same as that offered by the developers if a match occurs.

This comparison procedure protects everyone by providing a measure of protection when downloading software and by ensuring that there are no trojan horses or computer viruses. As previously discussed, this is the definition of a digital signature. Digital signatures are especially important for electronic commerce and are a key component of most authentication schemes. To be effective, digital signatures must be unbreakable, which is an idealistic goal. As a viable compromise, the signature must be able to be independently verifiable, difficult to break, and have a design that allows its strength to increase and evolve. As demonstrated in the discussion of DES, the growth of technology can overtake security if you do not take the proper precautions or follow up on updated security needs.

Point-to-Point Tunneling Protocol (PPTP)

This section discusses the Point-to-Point Tunneling Protocol (PPTP), which was developed by Ascend Communications, Microsoft Corporation, 3Com/Primary Access, ECI Telematics, and U.S. Robotics.

PPTP operates at Layer 2 of the OSI reference model and is based on the Point-to-Point Protocol (PPP) standard for dialup networking that allows any user with a PPP client to use an ISP to connect to the Internet. PPTP builds on the functionality of PPP, which is used for traditional dialup networking, by allowing users to connect securely via a VPN (covered in Chapter 6, "Router Security") to secure networks such as that of their employers or business partners.

note

One of the most difficult aspects about writing a book is always remaining focused on the technology at hand without getting distracted by other technologies. When researching various aspects of PPTP, I ran across a competing technology that I must share:

Pigeon Packet Transfer Protocol (PPTP) is a new revolutionary wireless packet transfer technology. Instead of physical cable media, network packets are attached to the backs of pigeons and transferred between locations by air. Visit http://www.ne2.com.

Point-to-Point Tunneling Protocol (PPTP) is a protocol (or a set of communication rules) that allows corporations to extend their own corporate network through private "tunnels" over the public Internet. Effectively, a corporation uses a wide-area network (WAN) as a single large local-area network (LAN). A company no longer needs to lease its own lines for wide-area communication, but can securely use the public networks. This kind of interconnection is known as a virtual private network (VPN).

PPTP Functionality

PPTP packages data within PPP packets and then encapsulates the PPP packets within IP packets (datagrams) for transmission through an Internet-based VPN tunnel. PPTP supports data encryption and compression of these packets. PPTP also uses a form of *Generic Routing Encapsulation (GRE)* to move data to and from its final destination.

PPTP-based Internet remote access VPNs are by far the most common form of PPTP VPN. However, PPTP VPNs are not the most common VPNs in use. IPSec is by far the more secure and popular. Cisco IOS Software does allow the use of PPTP VPNs; however, you should definitely consider the shortcomings, which are explained in the section, "Limitations of PPTP." When PPTP tunnels are established with a two-step creation process:

1. The user wanting to connect using a PPTP client connects to his ISP using PPP dialup networking (in most cases, traditional modem or ISDN)—or perhaps the user is permanently connected via cable modem, for example.

2. The PPTP client is launched, and it creates a control connection via TCP (port 1723) between the client and the server, thereby establishing the tunnel.

After the PPTP tunnel is established, two types of rather obvious packets of information flow through this tunnel: *control messages*, which manage the PPTP tunnel, and *data packets*.

PPTP relies on the inherent functionality of PPP to maintain the connection, encapsulate packets, and authenticate users. PPTP uses the ***Challenge Handshake Authentication Protocol (CHAP)*** or the ***Password Authentication Protocol (PAP)***.

PPTP directly handles maintaining the VPN tunnel and transmits data through the tunnel. PPTP also supports some additional security features for VPN data beyond what PPP provides.

PPTP remains a popular choice for VPNs, thanks to Microsoft. PPTP clients are freely available in all popular versions of Microsoft Windows. Windows servers and certain Cisco devices can function as PPTP-based VPN servers to terminate PPTP client connections.

Limitations of PPTP

As just discussed, the extensive use of Microsoft products is driving PPTP in many ways. Although other PPTP providers are available because many organizations have Windows servers, it is natural to want to use what you have. There are some limitations and drawbacks to using PPTP that revolve around its use in general.

The PPTP standard does not define how authentication and data encryption tasks are to be handled. This means that two different vendors might produce a PPTP-capable device or client, and yet they might not be able to work together, which introduces compatibility issues within an organization using different PPTP implementations. For example, if Vendor A implements PAP and Vendor B implements CHAP, they will not interoperate.

Concerns also persist around the security involved in the use of PPTP connections when compared with other available solutions—specifically, surrounding the implementation of Microsoft's PPTP solution, which is the leader by far.

A company called Counterpane Internet Security is a managed security services provider founded by Bruce Schneier, who is also the current CTO. Mr. Schneier is also an author who helped developed several encryption technologies—specifically, Blowfish and Twofish. These folks have written some excellent and detailed papers on a variety of security-related subjects. Specifically, Bruce Schneier of Counterpane and Mudge of L0pht Heavy Industries conducted detailed analysis on Microsoft's implementation of PPTP. In their own words, they summarize their findings:

> *"The Point-to-Point Tunneling Protocol (PPTP) was designed to solve the problem of creating and maintaining a VPN over a public TCP/IP network using the common Point-to-Point Protocol (PPP). Although the protocol leaves room for every type of encryption and authentication imaginable, most commercial products use the Microsoft Windows NT version of the protocol. This is the implementation that we cryptanalyze in this paper.*
>
> *We have found Microsoft's authentication protocol to be weak and easily susceptible to a dictionary attack; most passwords can be recovered within hours. We have found the encryption (both 40-bit and 128-bit) to be equally*

weak, and have discovered a series of bad design decisions that make other attacks against this encryption possible. We can open connections through a firewall by abusing the PPTP negotiations, and can mount several serious denial-of-service attacks on anyone who uses Microsoft PPTP."

If you would like to read the entire paper or refer others to it, you can find it at

http://www.counterpane.com/pptp-paper.html

This additional paper from Counterpane Internet Security covers its findings and analysis of Microsoft's implementation of CHAP—including both of the versions, MS-CHAP and MS-CHAPv2, respectively:

http://www.counterpane.com/pptpv2-paper.html

For a little humor regarding the findings, refer to the FAQs:

http://www.counterpane.com/pptp-faq.html

If you have taken the time to read through some of these papers on the Counterpane website, you are probably wondering how you can implement a VPN securely if PPTP is not advised. The primary alternative to PPTP is an IPSec-based VPNs. IPSec is an open standard that has been developed under the direction of the Internet Engineering Task Force (IETF) in its normal public process and is not owned by any one company. This is an important distinction because the manner in which Microsoft has implemented PPTP has made it proprietary to them. The following section examines the Layer 2 Tunneling Protocol (L2TP), which is also an extension of PPP, we will discuss IPSec in the VPN chapter.

Layer 2 Tunneling Protocol (L2TP)

Layer Two Tunneling Protocol (L2TP) is an extension of the Point-to-Point Tunneling Protocol (PPTP) that is documented in RFC 2661 and is used to enable the operation of a virtual private network (VPN) over the Internet. RFC 3193 defines using L2TP over a secure IPSec transport. In this approach, L2TP packets are

exchanged over User Datagram Protocol (UDP) port 1701. IPSec Encapsulating Security Payload (ESP) protects UDP payload to ensure secure communication. Cisco and Microsoft agreed to merge their respective L2TP, thereby adopting the best features of two other tunneling protocols: PPTP from Microsoft and *Layer 2 Forwarding (L2F)* from Cisco Systems.

The two main components that make up L2TP are the L2TP Access Concentrator (LAC), which is the device that physically terminates a call, and the L2TP Network Server (LNS), which is the device that terminates and possibly authenticates the PPP stream.

In this regard, L2TP is similar to PPTP in its use of PPP and in both function and design. In this blending of two of the largest IT related companies, some areas definitely benefited—specifically, the area of securing sensitive data.

L2TP Versus PPTP

L2TP and PPTP have a variety of features and benefits in common that reflect their original design and function within networking. These similarities are as follows:

- Both provide a logical transport mechanism for sending PPP payloads.

- Both provide tunneling and encapsulation so that PPP payloads based on any protocol can be sent across an IP network.

- Both rely on the PPP connection process to perform user authentication and protocol configuration.

Although L2TP and PPTP share some similarities, they are different in the following ways:

- With PPTP, data encryption begins after the PPP connection process (and therefore PPP authentication) is completed. With L2TP/IPSec, data encryption begins before the PPP connection process.

- L2TP/IPSec connections use either DES or 3DES.

- PPTP requires only user-level authentication, and L2TP requires the same user-level authentication, as well as computer-level authentication through a computer certificate.

The following section discusses some of L2TP's important benefits and how it can be used more securely than its predecessor, PPTP.

Benefits of L2TP

ISPs have been able to build VPN solutions using L2TP (because of its Internet standard status) as the method in which customers gain the benefits of VPNs within a carrier's network. Some of the more specific benefits of L2TP include the following:

- Because it is standards-based, interoperability of L2TP capable devices between vendors is greatly increased.

- L2TP VPNs have become *products for service providers.*

- In Cisco-powered networks, end point-to-end point quality of service (QoS) can be provided through the use of QoS technologies such as DiffServ to categorize and handle traffic accordingly.

- IPSec is responsible for encryption, which is also standard-based (that is, defined in an RFC). IPSec provides per-packet data origin authentication (proof that the authorized user sent the data), data integrity (proof that the data was not modified in transit), replay protection (prevention from resending a stream of captured packets), and data confidentiality (prevention from interpreting captured packets without the encryption key). By contrast, PPTP provides only per-packet data confidentiality.

- Support for multiprotocol environments because, by design, L2TP can transport any routed protocols, including IP, IPX, and AppleTalk. L2TP also supports any WAN transmission technology, including Frame Relay, ATM, X.25, or SONET. It also supports LAN media such as Ethernet, Fast Ethernet, Token Ring, and FDDI.

In many ways, L2TP is the best of both vendors (Cisco and Microsoft); personally, I think Microsoft was the big winner because its tinkering with PPTP left a lot to be desired. The following section examines how L2TP functions.

L2TP Operation

As discussed previously, L2TP allows for the support of legacy protocols and over the tunnel through the use of GRE. This permits an architecture to be created that allows L2TP tunnels to connect rather easily over the public Internet or dialup.

> **note**
> Traditional dialup networking services support only registered IP addresses, thereby limiting the types of applications that are implemented over VPNs.

Figure 4-2 shows the most common architecture that is used when an L2TP network is implemented. In this figure, note that the equipment shown is what an ISP or carrier would use when implementing a complete LT2P solution with all the aspects and benefits that we have described. It is commonplace for companies to use a subset of this design.

Figure 4-2 L2TP Network Architecture

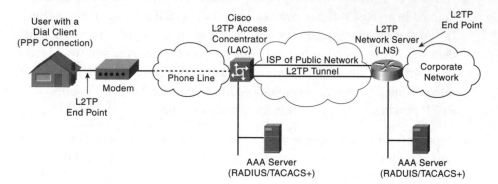

L2TP will use the Internet and its network connections to make it possible for its endpoints to be in different geographic locations. In Figure 4-2, the users PC creates a dialup connection (Layer 2) to the *L2TP Access Concentrator (LAC)*, which then authenticates them using the AAA Server and forwards the connection, which is encrypted, to the L2TP Network Server.

L2TP's greatest security strength is its use of IPSec, which provides connections with confidentiality, per packet authentication, and anti-replay protection for control and data packets. In contrast, the Microsoft Point-to-Point Encryption (MPPE) used by PPTP encrypts only data and does not prevent forgery or replay, like IPSec does.

The following list describes the actual call-sequence steps as home users dial into their ISP to create an L2TP connection to their corporate office:

1. The remote user uses the analog telephone system or broadband to initiate a PPP connection from her home to an ISP.

2. The ISP network LAC accepts the connection at its Point of Presence (POP), and the PPP link is established.

3. After the end user and LNS negotiate LCP, the LAC partially authenticates the end user with CHAP or PAP. The username, domain name, or DNIS is used to determine whether the user is a VPDN client. This is how ISPs can offer these services because each company and user is unique. The AAA Server connected to the LAC defines each user.

4. If the user is not a VPN client (using L2TP), authentication continues, and the client accesses the Internet as a normal user. If the user is a VPN client, her connection names a specific endpoint (the *L2TP network server [LNS]*) where the user's VPN terminates. The user's information is sent to the AAA server, which is connected to the LNS, for further authentication.

5. The tunnel end points—the LAC and the LNS—authenticate each other before any data is transmitted from the user into the tunnel.

6. After the VPN tunnel (using L2TP) is created, an L2TP session is created for the end user to the corporate network.

The end result is that the exchange process appears to be between the dialup client and the remote LNS exclusively, as if no intermediary device (that is, the LAC) is involved. Figure 4-3 offers a visual representation of the L2TP incoming call sequence with its own corresponding sequence numbers. Note that the sequence numbers in Figure 4-3 are not related to the sequence numbers described previously.

Figure 4-3   L2TP Creation Steps

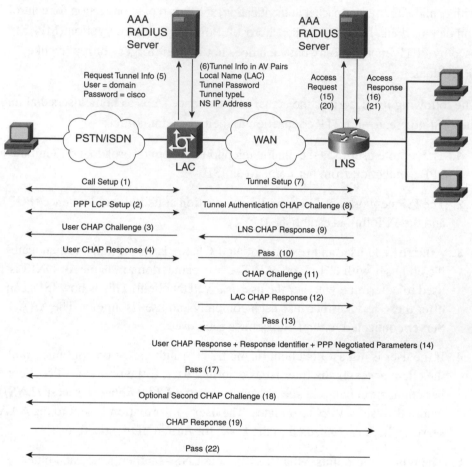

The following section examines one of my favorite protocols and tools for IT professionals today: Secure Shell (SSH). It is also a good security solution; no good book could be written without mentioning it, so I have to include it!.

Secure Shell (SSH)

Secure Shell, or SSH as it is more commonly known, is used to log in to a remote computer system, much in the same way that Telnet has been used in the past for the same purpose. The big difference between Telnet and SSH, however, is that SSH provides significantly enhanced security for your connection. SSH is a program that provides an encrypted communications path between two hosts over an untrusted, potentially insecure network such as the Internet. Therefore, it prevents users' passwords and other sensitive data from being transmitted across the network in clear-text form. SSH solves the most important security problem on the Internet: hackers stealing or cracking passwords.

Used since 1995, SSH1 was designed to replace the nonsecure UNIX rcommands (rlogin, rsh, and rcp). These protocols provided UNIX users with a variety of useful tools; however, they were fraught with security concerns. The IETF released SSH2 in 1997 and improved the security and functionality of SSH1. At this time, SSH1 is slowly being phased out in favor of SSH2.

note

You might be wondering what the difference is between SSH1 and SSH2 and whether they are compatible. In a nutshell, they are not compatible, and SSH2 is a complete rewrite of SSH1 resulting in a completely different protocol implementation. SSH2 encrypts packets more securely and references only host keys because it exchanges a hash.

The most common usage of SSH is for creating a secure command shell (remote login) like the more common protocol, Telnet. However, SSH takes the basic functionality and vulnerabilities of Telnet and solves them in a manner that has made SSH the de facto connection standard.

SSH extends Telnet capabilities both in features and functionality. Today, SSH is available on virtually all computer platforms: Macintosh, Microsoft Windows, UNIX, Linux, and so on.

Typical SSH applications include remote access (login) to computer resources over the Internet or via some other untrusted network where you want to perform one of the three core SSH capabilities:

- Secure command shell

- Secure file transfer

- Secure Port forwarding

Although remote login is the primary use of SSH, the protocol can be used as a general purpose cryptographic tunnel that is capable of copying files, encrypting e-mail connections, and triggering remote execution of programs.

SSH Versus Telnet

Telnet is terribly insecure for so many reasons, except that it has no protection, encryption, or any way to protect your password or any activity you are conducting via Telnet. A simple Google search reveals the following as proof positive:

```
Excerpt from Google.com

Searched the web for telnet vulnerabilities .
Results 1-30 of about 53,400 .    Search took 0.32 seconds.
```

Perhaps you need another example relating to network security to make the point about Telnet's insecurities a bit stronger. Look at Figure 4-4; here, I used a freely available tool, ettercap, that I installed on my Apple Powerbook and intercepted a Telnet session from another PC to a Cisco router.

Let me help you understand what is happening in this figure. Upon starting etter-cap, I activated its ARP Spoofing feature and inserted my laptop (using ettercap) into the communication session between the PC (192.168.254.70) and the Cisco router (192.168.254.99), as shown in the top box of the figure.

Figure 4-4   ettercap Reveals Telnet use of Plain text

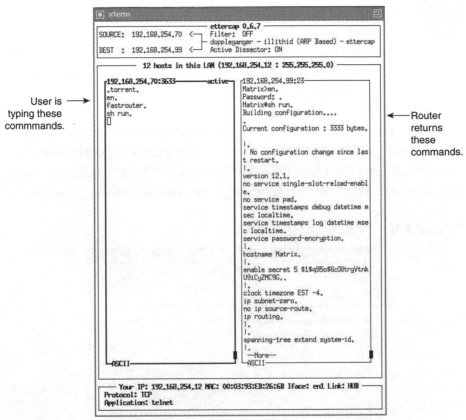

After seeing and selecting the Telnet session that was running between them, ettercap began capturing the ASCII characters being transmitted in both directions. The left column includes characters being transmitted from the PC and the right column shows the router's characters. Thus, you can see that I logged in, input the password, entered enable mode, input my password, and executed a **sh run** command. The router prompts for passwords and its configuration is also shown as well (right window).

note

ettercap is a multipurpose sniffer/interceptor/logger for switched LAN. It supports active and passive dissection of many protocols (even ciphered ones) and includes many features for network and host analysis. If you are interested in learning more about ettercap, it can be found here:

http://ettercap.sourceforge.net

Of course, no proof to this level would be complete without showing you what SSH sends and how our little ettercap tool "sees" it. In Figure 4-5, I connected to a Cisco Firewall using SSH1 with DES (the only version of SSH that Cisco currently supports, unfortunately); as you can see, my actions and passwords are not visible.

Figure 4-5   SSH Encrypts All Data

SSH is clearly better than Telnet because it has encryption; however, the benefits of SSH do not stop there. SSH offers additional features and benefits as follows:

- Denies IP Spoofing of packets, thereby ensuring you know that host that is sending the packets.

- Encrypts packets to prevent the interception of clear text passwords and other data by intermediate hosts.

- IP source routing by preventing a host from pretending that an IP packet comes from another, trusted host.

- Prevents the manipulation of data by people in control of other devices along the route of your packets.

A much simpler way of looking at this is that SSH does *trust* any device other than the one with which it is trying to establish a secure connection. On the other hand, Telnet trusts anyone and pretty much anything; if I had wanted to, I could have taken over the Telnet connection shown in ettercap, erased the routers' configuration and that is truly disturbing.

SSH Operation

To review, SSH is used to connect two different hosts using an encrypted communication session. In its simplest mode of operation, SSH uses TCP to connect to a host, and authenticates using a username and password; authentication is successful, and SSH begins encrypting data.

Depending on the version of SSH, a variety of different *encryption methods* can be available for use, as shown in Table 4-1.

Table 4-1   SSH Encryption Methods

Encryption Method	SSH1	SSH2
DES	Yes	No
3DES	Yes	Yes
IDEA	Yes	No
BLOWFISH	Yes	Yes
TWOFISH	No	Yes
ARCFOUR	No	Yes
CAST-128-CBC	No	Yes

Connecting keys are used during the authentication phase of SSH. Depending on the version of SSH used, either an RSA or DSA key is used with a pair created, one public and one private. Depending on the version of SSH, a variety of different *authentication* methods can be available for use, as shown in Table 4-2.

Table 4-2   SSH Authentication Ciphers

Authentication Cipher	SSH1	SSH2
RSA	Yes	No
DSA	No	Yes

The private key is stored encrypted while the public key is stored on the users'
machine if they authenticates properly. This allows SSH software clients to connect
automatically because the key is stored for use any time the user starts a connection.

Tunneling and Port Forwarding

SSH brings an interesting feature to the realm of security: the concept of forwarding certain traffic (identified by port number) via SSH in a tunnel. The two most
common protocols to take advantage of this feature are FTP and X Windows. This
forwarding feature provides SSH with the ability to utilize these other protocols
for conducting operations on the host terminating the SSH connection. Perhaps
the other end is a web server, and you want to upload new files over the Internet or
you want desktop type access to the device using X Windows.

note

The best SSH client I have found and recommend is SecureCRT, from
VanDyke Software (http://www.vandyke.com). This GUI tool provides
for some excellent built-in benefits, such as automatic logging, customizable scripts, and adjustable buffers.

Figure 4-6 shows easy configuration of port forwarding. Notice also that X Windows
can be easily forwarded because it is so commonly used in conjunction with SSH.

Figure 4-6   SecureCRT Allows SSH Tunneling

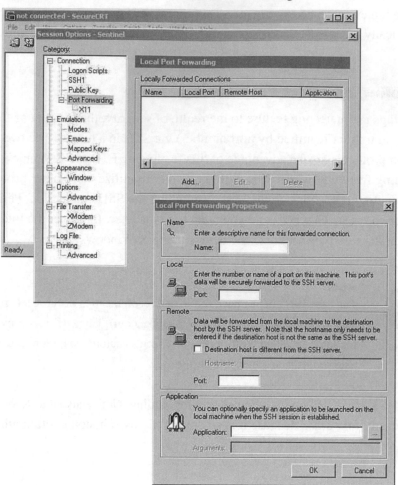

Limitations of SSH

SSH version 1 (SSH1) had several bugs and problems, so choose SSH version 2 (SSH2) if you have a choice. Choosing version 2 eliminates most of the limitations.

SSH does not help you protect any of your internal systems (PCs, servers, and so on); therefore, after an attacker gains access to one of those systems, he has access to SSH and it, too, can be subverted for his use.

The ability to tunnel through an SSH connection might make you think that it would be a good alternative to a VPN, but that is not the case. A better solution would be tunneling via SSH through a VPN connection—now that is a secure connection!

This section of the chapter covered SSH rather broadly and gave you enough information to understand what is happening. If you would like to learn more about SSH, I recommend the following book:

> Barrett, Daniel J. and Richard Silverman. *SSH, The Secure Shell: The Definitive Guide*. Cambridge, MA: O'Reilly & Associates; 2001.

In summary, SSH is a popular and powerful tool for encrypting TCP sessions over a network. It is most commonly used for remote login, but also has other uses for increasing your network's security.

Chapter Summary

This chapter discussed the importance and functionality of the DES and 3DES encryption technologies. You saw the math that is involved in each encryption technology in order to demonstrate the difficulty of cracking them—unless simple passwords are used, such as passwords with all letters.

There are several ways to tunnel and protect traffic within a network, and this chapter covered two methods: PPTP and L2TP. It discussed each of the benefits and recommended L2TP because it combines the best aspects of Microsoft and Cisco technologies. This chapter concluded with a discussion of SSH and the value it brings to your network.

Chapter Review Questions

The following questions will reinforce the concepts that were covered in this chapter.

1. How long, in bits, is the DES key?

2. In 3DES, the same key is used to encrypt at each of the three stages: true or false?

3. Define a hash in your own words.

4. What is used to create a digital signature?

5. Define authentication and provide an example.

6. Define authorization and provide an example.

7. A hash check occurs at what point in the operation of MD5?

8. Of the security protocols covered in this chapter, which of them use generic routing encapsulation (GRE)?

9. Describe several security benefits of L2TP.

10. What are the three core SSH capabilities?

What You Will Learn

By the end of this chapter, you should know and be able to explain the following:

- ✔ Who needs a firewall and why firewalls are used to protect network resources

- ✔ How a firewall is a technological expression of your organization's written security policy

- ✔ When a DMZ is appropriate and the security benefits you gain by deploying a firewall with a DMZ

Being able to answer these key questions will allow you to understand the overall characteristics and importance of network security. By the time you finish this book, you will have a solid appreciation a firewall's roll, its issues, how it works, and why it is important.

CHAPTER 5

Firewalls

Courage is resistance to fear, mastery of fear—not absence of fear.

— Mark Twain

The Internet is an exciting and wonderful place to browse and explore. It has been likened to the Wild West, The Great Frontier, and other grandiose achievements of mankind. In reality, the World Wide Web is merely a collection of routers and servers that make up the largest wide-area network (WAN) in recorded history. This collection of networking gear provides mail servers, websites, and other information storage and retrieval systems and is all connected to the Internet and accessible to every person who is also connected. It has even been said that the Internet contains the collective institutional knowledge of mankind.

Wow! What awesome potential! The entire collective knowledge of mankind is stored on magnetic media just waiting for people to download and learn. Entire books have been written on the Internet's potential and its impact on our lives. We are concerned with this network's security, so we must ask what kinds of safeguards are in place to protect such an unbelievable amount of information.

Is there some organization that polices the Internet much in the same way the State Police cruise the highways? How about a federal agency that snoops around and double checks every possible device connected to the Internet? The answer to these questions is no; there is no unifying organization that is responsible for protecting the Internet. The job of securing and maintaining the doorways to the Internet halls of knowledge is left up to the person or persons responsible for publishing the information in the first place. Each website is fronted by a corporate Internet connection or Internet service provider (ISP), whose job it is to make sure

that hackers (the bad guys) do not make a mess of the carefully stored and catalogued information of the website in question. And just how does one protect a website, mail server, FTP server, or other information sources accessible from the web? The answer is one word: Firewall. The sole purpose of these dedicated hardware devices is to provide security for your network.

A *firewall* is a security device that sits on the edge of your Internet connection and functions as an Internet Border Security Officer. It constantly looks at all the traffic entering and exiting your connection, waiting for traffic it can block or reject in response to an established rule. The firewall is law and protection in a lawless global web. It is ever vigilant in its mission to protect the internal network resources connected to it.

The Internet has made so much information available to individual users as, over the years, access to this information has evolved from an advantage to an essential component for both individuals and businesses. However, making your information available on the Internet can expose critical or confidential data to attack from everywhere and anywhere in the world— the Internet is literally a worldwide network. This means that, when I connect to the Internet in Raleigh, North Carolina, I can be subject to attacks from Europe, Asia, and so on. Firewalls can protect both individual computers and corporate networks from hostile intrusion from the Internet, but you must understand your firewall to use it correctly.

This 24-hour/365-day-a-year "electronic Robocop" has a very important job: to keep the bad guys out and let the good guys get to the resources they need to do their jobs. Sounds pretty simple, right? On paper it sounds like a walk in the park, but in reality, configuring a firewall "properly" is far from easy.

In some cases, a badly configured or feature-inadequate firewall can be worse than no firewall at all. This is difficult to believe, isn't it? Nonetheless, it is true. This chapter dissects a firewall's duties to understand what makes it operate and how it does its job.

Firewall Frequently Asked Questions

Before looking at the overall operation of a firewall, the following sections examine and answer some of the fundamental questions surrounding them.

Who Needs a Firewall?

This is perhaps the most frequently asked security question. If you plan on connecting to the Internet, you need a firewall. It does not matter if you connect from home or your company is connecting—**you need a firewall, period**! The increased penetration of broadband Internet services to the home and their always-on Internet connections make home security even more important.

Why Do I Need a Firewall?

You read about security threats in the papers or hear about them on the evening news almost every day: viruses, worms, denial-of-service (DoS) attacks, hacking, and new vulnerabilities to your computer. For example, SoBig, Blaster, LovSan, SQL Slammer, Code Red, NIMDA, and MyDoom have all appeared on the evening news. Unless you have not read a newspaper or watched the news in the last year, you surely have heard at least one of these names.

It is no secret: hackers are out there, and they are out to get us. Often, we do not know who they are, but we do know where they are and where we do not want them to be (in our network). Like pirates of old roamed the seas, hackers roam the wide expanses of the Internet. You do not want them to enter your network and roam among the computers that connect to it.

You know that you must protect your network from these attackers, and one of the most efficient methods of protecting your network is to install a firewall. By default, any good firewall prevents network traffic from passing between the Internet and your internal network. This does not mean that the firewall will stop all traffic—that defeats the purpose of being on the Internet. It does mean that the firewall is configured to allow only web browsing (HTTP/port 80) to access it

from the Internet. Along the way, the firewall provides Stateful Packet Inspection (SPI) rules to every incoming packet (as discussed previously in Chapter 2, "Security Policies and Responses.")

The alternative to having a firewall is allowing every connection into your network—nor would there be any sort of packet inspection to determine whether an attack is hidden within one of the incoming packets. Not having a firewall is ill advised and will make your organization wide open to everyone on the Internet.

Do I Have Anything Worth Protecting?

I often hear people say: *"I understand that if I had something worth protecting, I would definitely need a firewall. However, I do not have anything an attacker would want, so why should I worry about a firewall?"*

Networks and their resources are important to the way our society conducts business and operates. In practical terms, this means that there is value to your network and having it operate effectively. This increased role of networks means that you definitely have something worth protecting to some degree, as documented in the following list:

- **Downstream liability**—This sounds like a confused fishing show title, but it is perhaps the next big step in the legal evolution of the Internet. Downstream liability involves allegations that an attacker has taken control of a target computer (yours) and used it to attack a third party. Assume that it is your company's computer that has been compromised by a hacker. Your company's failure to protect its own systems has resulted in the damaging of a third party; the attacker used your computer as a weapon against the third party. Your company is therefore negligent because it has failed in its duty to protect against reasonable risks—specifically, no firewall was in place. The prudent person's obligation here is to use reasonable care. A more detailed definition can be found in Prosser, Wade, and Schwartz's *Cases and Materials on Torts*: "…requiring the actor to conform to a certain standard of conduct, for the protection of others against unreasonable risks." Who says Hollywood liberalism doesn't contribute to society?

- **Lost data**—You have probably heard the stories of companies that lost all their business data in the September 11th attacks, and many of them did not recover. What if your company experienced the same loss because you did not have a firewall and an attacker deleted your data because they could? What would happen to your business? Would it cost money to re-create everything? Would you suffer lost sales?

- **Compromise confidential data**—Every organization has data it considers confidential and, if lost, might cause financial problems, legal difficulties, or extreme embarrassment. These things might be caused by the loss of customer information such as credit card numbers, secret plans for the new weight loss formula, or secret plans that end up in the hands of a competitor. The list goes on, and when you have been hacked, you must assume the worst. Perhaps, this is why most cybercrimes go unreported.

- **Network downtime**—Have you ever gone to an ATM machine or a grocery store to get cash and paid with your cash card in the swipe card readers? The networks allowing these devices to operate usually work fine; however, if they were not protected, an attacker might cause them to go down. The loss of revenue from these networks can quickly grow if they are unavailable. Downtime is the bane of any network, and a cost is always associated with these types of events.

Ultimately, everyone has something worth protecting, and failure to do so is ill advised; it is just a matter of time before something happens. The next question is, *"What does a firewall do to protect my network?"*

What Does a Firewall Do?

A firewall examines traffic as it enters one of its interfaces and applies *rules* to the traffic—in essence, permitting or denying the traffic based on these rules. As shown in Figure 5-1, a firewall filters both inbound and outbound traffic.

Figure 5-1   Firewall in Operation

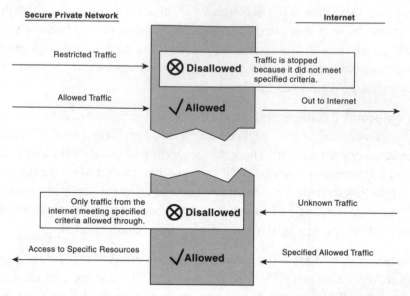

Firewalls, like access control lists (ACLs), can filter traffic based on source/destination IP addresses, protocol, and the *state* of a connection. In other words, normally you might not allow FTP into your network (via the firewall), but if a user inside your network begins an FTP session, it is allowed because the session was *established* from inside the network. By default, firewalls trust all connections to the Internet (outside) from the trusted internal network (inside).

A firewall can also log connection attempts with certain rules that might also issue an alarm if they occur. Finally, firewalls allow you to perform Network Address Translation (NAT) from internal private IP addresses to public IP addresses. The section, "Firewall Operational Overview," discusses the roles of a firewall; however, here we tie the firewalls back to Chapter 2's security policies discussions by examining how a firewall enforces your security policy.

Firewalls Are "The Security Policy"

What kind of traffic is allowed into or out of your network? How do you secure your network against attacks? What is your security policy? What happens to the people who do not follow the security policy? Who is responsible for writing and updating the security policy?

All these questions are valid, and they all deserve answers. Having a network that connects to the Internet via a firewall is only the first step to security; because this book is about first steps, this would be a perfect place to start. You should now know that the security policies form the basis of how these rules are put into production.

Do you remember the old saying, "No job is ever finished until the paperwork is done?" Well, no security solution is even remotely close to complete until you establish a written narrative of the rules and regulations that govern your organization's security posture. This written version of your security rules and regulations is known as a security policy. Now, this "policy" document is very different in nature and scope than a security plan," so be sure that you understand what makes a policy unique from every other security document an organization maintains. And just what is it that makes a security policy different from a security plan? Drum-roll please....

PUNISHMENT! That is correct, a security policy includes what is permissible and what will happen to you if you do not live by the law of the land. If you do not follow the rules, you can be

- Fired or dismissed

- Demoted

- Demoted and fined

- Fired, dismissed, and demoted

- Demoted, dissed, and dismissed

- All of the above

All kidding aside, the security policy document spells out in clear language exactly what the law is, who enforces it, and what happens to you if you break it. It is all about the consequences of user actions.

Having said that, how can a firewall be the security policy? Simple—a firewall does what it does by following the "rules" configured by a network engineer or Information Security Officer (ISO). These rules should align perfectly with a written narrative version found in the security policy document you have on your shelf, next to the box of 5-inch Floppy Disks at the back of the server room or sitting useless in some manager's office. Grab that old dusty binder and check it out. You should see that the security policy document contains information and a listing of the network rules, as covered in Chapter 2. The interesting thing is that all the rules in the policy document should also be configured on the firewall.

note

Wait a minute! We have a hand in the front row. Yes…you with the confused look on your face. Your question is, "Why is the binder that contains the security policy so dusty and located in such an obscure place?" As strange as that might sound, go ahead and sit down. I will tell you the answer to that question is that most organizations either do not have a security policy, or the one they have is so old that it was written during a previous presidential administration.

The configuration rules entered on a firewall should align perfectly with the rules outlined in an organization's security policy. If you were to examine the firewall's configuration file, you might see something like Example 5-1, which is a portion of a Cisco PIX Firewall Configuration.

Example 5-1   Sample PIX Firewall Rules

```
conduit permit tcp host 216.186.xx.xxx eq smtp any
conduit permit tcp host 216.186.xx.xxx eq www any
conduit permit tcp host 216.186.xx.xxx eq pop3 any
conduit permit tcp host 216.186.xx.xxx eq ftp any
```

The **conduit permit** statements in Example 5-1 are most likely in keeping with some security policy statement that dictates what services are allowed, by name, to enter the protected network and the destinations to which those services are allowed to travel. These statements are your network's security plan, and the security policy defines them.

note

Today, conduits are slowly being replaced with access control lists in an effort to standardize the Cisco product line. Access lists were covered in Chapter 4, "Security Protocols." For completeness, conduits are shown here.

In an effort to expand on the Firewall-Policy analogy, examine some additional security policy bullet points and how a firewall aligns with them:

■ A security policy outlines what action will be taken in response to circumstances that arise.

■ A security policy document is constantly evolving and changing to meet new security needs.

■ A security policy dictates both acceptable and unacceptable usage parameters.

If you perform a point-by-point comparison of a security policy with a firewall configuration, you see that firewalls act in conjunction with a written security policy document, as shown in Table 5-1.

Table 5-1   Comparing Security Policies and Firewall Configurations

	Security Policy	Firewall Configuration
Ability to respond to circumstances	Yes	Yes
Constantly Evolving	Yes	Yes
Dictates Behavior	Yes	Yes

The intention of this section is not to convince you that a firewall is a replacement for a security policy document, but to get you thinking about security as an all-encompassing philosophy of plans, policies, and security devices. You must put a great deal of thought into a complete solution—not simply rely on a single aspect to protect your network. When you are ready to plan your firewall's configuration and develop the rules permitting or denying traffic, you should use your security policy as the starting point. Firewalls are the physical and logical manifestations of your security policy.

Firewall Operational Overview

Every long journey begins with the first step. Before delving too deep into other areas of security appliance behavior, it is essential to understand how a firewall performs its magic.

Most firewalls (*most, not all*) rely on **Stateful Packet Inspection (SPI)** to keep track of all outbound packets and the responses these packets might generate. Keeping track of the hosts on the protected network that are generating outbound packets keeps rogue or unsolicited WAN packets from entering an external interface.

In other words, a firewall that uses SPI, as discussed in Chapter 3, "Overview of Security Technologies," watches all traffic that originates from an inside host, tracks the conversation from that host to the desired destination, and ensures that the inbound response to that request makes it back to the host that started the whole thing in the first place.

note
A firewall that is not stateful in design and configuration is rather incomplete and should not be used to protect your network. This chapter focuses on firewalls that track the state of a connection. As a reference point, all Cisco PIX Firewalls are considered stateful.

The dual purpose of packet inspection and filtering of packets is one of the most fundamental responsibilities of a firewall. The following list includes the most common rules and features of firewalls:

- **Block *incoming* network traffic based on source or destination**—Blocking unwanted incoming traffic is the most common feature of a firewall and is the main reason for a firewall: stopping unwanted traffic from entering your network. This unwanted traffic is usually from attackers, thus the need to keep it out.

- **Block *outgoing* network traffic based on source or destination**—Many firewalls can also screen network traffic from your internal network to the Internet. For example, you might want to prevent employees from accessing inappropriate websites.

- **Block network traffic based on content**—More advanced firewalls can screen network traffic for unacceptable content. For example, a firewall that is integrated with a virus scanner can prevent files that contain viruses from entering your network. Other firewalls integrate with e-mail services to screen out unacceptable e-mail.

- **Make internal resources available**—Although the primary purpose of a firewall is to prevent unwanted network traffic from passing through it, you can also configure many firewalls to allow selective access to internal resources, such as a public web server, while still preventing other access from the Internet to your internal network. In many cases, this can be accomplished by using a DMZ, which is where the public web server would be located (DMZs are discussed later in the section, "Essentials First: Life in the DMZ.")

- **Allow connections to internal network**—A common method for employees to connect to a network is using virtual private networks (VPNs). VPNs allow secure connections from the Internet to a corporate network. For example, telecommuters and traveling salespeople can use a VPN to connect to the corporate network. VPNs can also connect branch offices to each other. Some firewalls include VPN functionality and make it easy to establish such connections.

■ **Report on network traffic and firewall activities**—When screening network traffic to and from the Internet, it is also important to know what your firewall is doing, who tried to break into your network, and who tried to access inappropriate material on the Internet. Most firewalls include a reporting mechanism of some kind or another. A good firewall can also log activity to a syslog or other type of archival storage receptacle. Perusing firewall logs after an attack has occurred is one of a number of forensic tools you have at your disposal.

Firewalls in Action

Are you thoroughly confused at this point? Look at the Figure 5-2 for a bit more clarity of this process. Please refer to the list, which explains the steps shown in the figure a bit more in-depth.

Figure 5-2   Firewall in Operation

④ Firewall checks connection state table for a match; If a match exists, the connection is allowed.

① Outbound Request to View www.avoidwork.com

③ Inbound Reply to View Website

Firewall

Router

Internet (www)

Host A

Inside   Outside

Web Server www.avoidwork.com

② Firewall records outbound request and connection data then forwards request out to the router (i.e. Internet).

Before looking at the list of steps illustrated in Figure 5-2, it is important to point out that many firewalls just have two physical interfaces in them, and 99 percent of them are based on Ethernet. These interfaces are called inside (protected) and outside (unprotected) and are deployed in relation to *your network*. Thus, in practice, the outside interface connects to the Internet, and the inside interface connects to your internal network:

1. Host A, an Apple PowerBook G4, opens a web browser and wants to view a web page from the www.avoidwork.com web server.

   Host A sends the request outbound through the firewall.

2. The firewall sees the request originated with Host A and is destined for www.avoidwork.com.

   a. The firewall notes the outbound request and expects that the reply will come only from the www.avoidwork.com web server.

   b. A session marker is placed in the firewall's session state table that will track the communication process from start to finish.

   c. Connection metrics are also placed in the marker that is being maintained by the firewall for this conversation.

3. The reply to Host A's web page request is sent back from the www.avoidwork.com web server to Host A via the firewall.

4. The firewall checks its session state table to see if the metrics being maintained for this session match the outbound connection. If all the stored connection details match exactly, the firewall allows the inbound traffic.

Consider one last issue regarding stateful firewalls in general. If a firewall maintains connection state context regarding inbound and outbound connections, the possibility of a hacker "spoofing" or "forging" a packet with the intention of penetrating your network becomes difficult. When attackers try to send packets to get through a firewall, incorrect or missing connection state information means that the session is terminated and most likely logged for later review.

note

Many firewalls examine the source IP addresses of packets to determine if they are legitimate. An attacker would conduct an IP Spoofing attack to try to gain entry by "spoofing" the source IP address of the packets sent to the firewall. If the firewall thought that the packets originated from a trusted host because they had the correct source IP address, the firewall might let the packets through unless other criteria failed to be met. This reinforces the principle that technology alone does not solve all security problems. In addition, you need the involvement of your company's management and, you guessed it, a security policy. Cisco firewalls use adaptive security algorithm (ASA) as a method of dynamically appending a number to the translated session to make it even more difficult for a hacker to hijack a translated session.

See http://www.cisco.com/en/US/partner/products/sw/secursw/ps2120/products_configuration_guide_chapter09186a008017278b.html#29996. (This requires a Cisco.com account.)

Implementing a Firewall

The choice of available firewalls is almost mind-boggling these days; they come in every shape, size, and parameter. When I am designing a firewall solution for a customer, the first thing I want to know is what will the firewall's responsibilities be?

The type of firewall you install depends on your exact requirements for protection and management, as well as the size of your network or what is to be protected by the firewall. Firewalls usually fall into one of the following categories:

- **Personal firewall**—A personal firewall is usually a piece of software that is installed on a single PC to protect only that PC. These types of firewalls are usually deployed on home PCs with broadband connections or remote employees. Of course, any time someone wants to deploy a firewall, it is a good idea. Some of the more well known personal firewalls can be found at these websites:

  http://www.zonelabs.com

  http://www.tinysoftware.com

  http://www.firewallguide.com

Operating system manufacturers such as Apple and Microsoft have responded to this need by integrating personal firewalls within them. Apple's OS X (Panther) comes with an IP Firewall, and Windows XP has a similar firewall.

- **All-in-one firewall**—These kinds of firewalls are widely used by broadband (cable or DSL) subscribers who have the benefit of a single device that offers the following features and functionality: router, Ethernet switch, wireless access point, and a firewall. If this type of firewall appeals to you, please make sure that you take care to determine the firewall's abilities, and be skeptical of the security you can gain from these devices regardless of who makes them.

note

Cable modems provide an "always on," very fast Internet connection over cable television wiring. In addition to connecting your television to this cable, you also connect a cable modem to the wiring, and you suddenly have a high-speed Internet connection. DSL provides the same benefits and uses telephone lines instead of cable.

- **Small-to-medium office firewalls**—These firewalls, such as the Cisco PIX 501 or 506, are designed to provide security and protection for small offices.

- **Enterprise firewalls**—These firewalls, such as the Cisco PIX 515, are designed for larger organizations with thousands of users. As a result, they have additional features and capacity, such as more memory and extra interfaces.

Cisco firewalls all run the same version of operating system that have the same reporting and management capabilities regardless of model. Larger models are needed when there are demands for larger numbers of connections and capacity.

Normally, a firewall is installed where your internal network connects to the Internet. Although larger organizations also place firewalls between different parts of their internal network that require different levels of security, most firewalls

screen traffic passing between an internal network and the Internet. For example, if a large organization allows business partners to connect directly to its network, you typically find a firewall controlling what is allowed into their network from their partners. This placement of an internal firewall is definitely considered best practice.

No matter what type of firewall you choose, you must define the filters that will support your security policy.

Determine the Inbound Access Policy

As network traffic passes through a firewall, the traffic is subject to the rules defined within the firewall. Because 99 percent of all networks use private IP addresses on the inside of their networks, you can expect almost every firewall to be using Network Address Translation (NAT)—as discussed in Chapter 3.

note

Packets coming in from the Internet in response to requests from local PCs (users) are addressed to the firewall's outside interface. The firewall is likely using NAT and tracking the state of each inside user request. The firewall is dynamically allocating port numbers on the outside interface using NAT. Thus, allowing multiple users to use a public IP address so their requests can be routed on the Internet is the essence of NAT. The use of a single IP address and port numbers to translate addresses is known as port address translation (PAT). These port changes are also made rapidly, making it difficult for an attacker to make assumptions about which port numbers to use.

If all your LAN traffic were destined to the Internet, the inbound access policy would be straightforward in its design. The firewall permits only inbound traffic in response to requests from hosts on the internal LAN. The firewall tracks all outbound requests in its state table, as previously discussed.

However, there will come a time when specific requests from the outside must be allowed and controlled through the firewall. Notice that I did *not* say that this was a good idea or that you should do it.

note

The realities of the real world will make companies want to have their own e-mail or web servers without spending money on a new firewall that has a DMZ interface, which is where you place these servers whenever possible. The section, "Essentials First: Life in the DMZ," discusses the purpose and role of a DMZ interface.

Allowing direct access from the Internet (outside) through your firewall is perilous, but common practice. The key to security in these types of implementations is to strictly define the traffic types you will allow and the port number. For example, permitting IP to any location inside your network is inappropriate. For example, you should permit Internet HTTP (port 80) traffic to your web server (IP address: 10.10.10.10). This allows only HTTP port 80 traffic to the web server from the Internet, which is much smarter. Do you think you should do anything else?

Of course you should, if you are now a believer in a layered security model to protect your network. Because many vulnerabilities and attacks use HTTP and port 80, the firewall cannot detect many of them because you have permitted that traffic through—see how this is a catch 22? A strongly recommended practice is to add layers of security in the form of a personal firewall, Intrusion Detection System (IDS), and virus software. Also, before you implement these configurations, make sure that your security policy outlines the best practices and what steps are needed to maintain security. If you do not have a security policy, this is a great catalyst to make the decision to start one!

Determine Outbound Access Policy

All firewalls screen traffic that is coming into a firewall, but a well-implemented and designed firewall also screens outgoing user traffic.

Recall the earlier discussion of proxy servers and how they can be used to control and monitor traffic that leaves your network. They are a good example of a device that defines an outbound access policy.

Additionally, recall the earlier discussion about placing a firewall between your network and connections to business partners. This type of firewall usage and placement is also where you would apply and control traffic bound from your network to theirs.

You might also want to use your main firewall to control what IP addresses are allowed to exit; specifically, you should allow only IP addresses that are found on your internal network out, thus preventing spoofing of IP addresses.

Perhaps, there are also certain places on the Internet where you do not want users to go. Alternatively, you might want to specify the locations they are allowed to go to because every other destination will be denied by default.

The next section looks at the next aspect of firewall and network security the Demilitarized Zone (DMZ).

Essentials First: Life in the DMZ

The *Demilitarized Zone (DMZ)* is a term used in the military to define a buffer area between two enemies. Perhaps the most commonly acknowledged DMZ in the world has been the DMZ between North and South Korea, which separates them because they have not yet signed a permanent peace treaty since the Korean War. Perhaps this is an interesting piece of military and political trivia that you did not know, but how does it relate to securing your network and firewalls?

Connecting web, mail, and FTP servers to the Internet can be dangerous and, in some cases, simply not advised. If your company has a self-hosted public website complete with e-mail servers, you might consider using a two-interface (Inside and Outside) firewall and have the firewall create translation rules that direct the inbound traffic to the correct servers on your private network. While that might seem like a pretty safe thing to do, it could be disastrous if a talented hacker sets his sights on you. Well, some really smart people got together a long time ago and said, "Hey—let's put a third interface in the firewall and call it a DMZ." Adding the third interface to a standard firewall made things both easier and quite a bit safer when deploying Internet accessible servers and services (www, e-mail, and so on).

Sending traffic from the Internet inbound directly to your private network is a *bad* idea. It is so bad that it is amazing that some organizations even consider it. If you were going to sell computers out of your house, you would not want people coming all the way inside your house to buy one, would you? Of course not; you would want to set up a little shop in the garage or the front porch, thus preventing people that you do not know from wondering all over your house and tampering with your comic book collection or going into your fridge and making a sandwich.

A DMZ is an interface that sits between a trusted network segment (your company's network) and an untrusted network segment (the Internet), providing physical isolation between the two networks that is enforced by a series of connectivity rules within the firewall. The physical isolation aspect of a DMZ is important because it allows only Internet access to the servers that are isolated on the DMZ and not directly into your internal network, as shown in Figure 5-3.

Figure 5-3   DMZ Placement and Function

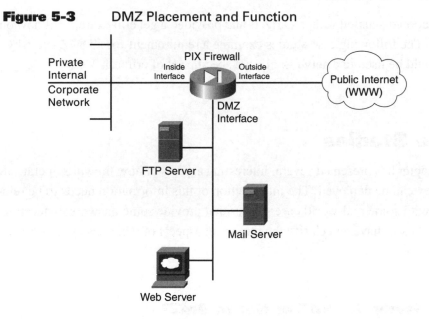

In Figure 5-3, the segment connected to the DMZ interface houses the mail, web, and FTP servers. Rules applied to the DMZ interface prevent traffic from the Internet from going beyond the segment attached to it.

The biggest benefit to a DMZ is in isolating all unknown Internet requests to the servers on the DMZ and no longer allowing them into your internal network. However, there are some additional benefits to deploying a firewall with a DMZ that will help you better understand what is happening in your network and thereby increase security:

- Auditing of DMZ traffic

- Locating an Intrusion Detection System (IDS) on the DMZ

- Limiting routing updates between three interfaces

- Locating DNS on the DMZ

This section discussed what a DMZ is and provided a general example of how one is used. The following case studies examine a requirement for a DMZ and why one should be used in a network given a specific set of criteria.

Case Studies

This chapter has presented several interesting aspects of how firewalls operate and how they can be deployed. The introduction of this information needs to be reinforced with some real-world case studies that provide some answers to questions you might still have and clarify the important aspects of what has already been covered.

Case Study: To DMZ or Not to DMZ?

The Carpathian Corporation has decided that it no longer wants to pay its ISP to host its web and mail servers. The IT department has decided that it will use two older servers to provide these services to its clients and company staff. The IT staff is planning on hosting these servers at its corporate office and are unclear whether it should purchase a firewall that has a DMZ interface.

If the Carpathian Corporation wants to continue with its proposed plan for "self hosting," it needs to consider the security-related issues that are relevant to the solution being suggested. It is taking the right steps by asking what security ramifications should be addresses. The Carpathian IT staff needs to take a good look at the risk factors involved with providing for its own Internet services (www and mail) and where the pitfalls might be:

- **Question/Security Issue #1**—Will Internet traffic be allowed to travel to servers on the private network, or is there another solution?

  Answer— The web and mail servers will be attached to the DMZ segment. They will not be dual homed or have conflicts of security in its implementation.

- **Security Issue #2**—How will the IT staff ensure that inbound network traffic will stay confined to the segment containing the web and mail servers?

  Answer—The DMZ interface rule set will not allow external traffic to reach the private network, by nature of configured connectivity rules. This will keep the inbound Internet traffic confined to the DMZ segment only.

- **Security Issue #3**—What measures will be taken to hide the private network from the inbound network traffic?

  Answer—The DMZ interface will not have routes to allow this to occur.

The Carpathian IT Staff is into the "What is a DMZ and why do we need one?" frame of mind. The answers should be obvious at this point: use a firewall with a third or DMZ interface. The previous section gave us the basic mechanics of the DMZ interface and a typical deployment scenario.

Case Study: Firewall Deployment with Mail Server Inside the Protected (Internal)

This chapter has described the business needs of deploying a mail server on your internal network and the ramifications of allowing this to happen with regards to the security of your network. Ultimately, however, deploying a mail server internally is still common practice and deserves a look at a basic implementation of this solution.

note

By default, Cisco Systems lists a variety of configuration settings when viewing the configuration files of its devices. In the following case study, several configuration files are shown for clarity purposes. To illustrate the case study, comments are made surrounding key configuration entries; however, we do not discuss every command because that is beyond the scope of this book. Additional information can be found at Cisco.com.

This scenario presents a small to medium-sized corporate network, as shown in Figure 5-4. As the configuration in Example 5-2 shows, there is only a mail server inside, but it could also be a web server or DNS.

Figure 5-4   Firewall Deployment with Mail Server Inside

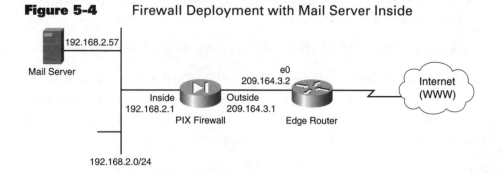

Example 5-2   PIX Firewall Inside Mail Server Configuration

```
nameif ethernet0 outside security0
 nameif ethernet1 inside security100

!--- These commands name and set the security level for each PIX interface.
Through these commands, the firewall will know which interface is considered
untrusted (outside) and trusted (inside).

 enable password 8Ry2YjIyt7RRXU24 encrypted
 passwd 2KFQnbNIdI.2KYOU encrypted
 hostname SECURE-FIREWALL
 domain-name noplace.com
 fixup protocol ftp 21
 fixup protocol http 80
 fixup protocol h323 1720
 fixup protocol rsh 514
 fixup protocol smtp 25
 fixup protocol sqlnet 1521
 no names

 access-list smtp permit tcp any host 209.164.3.5 eq smtp

!--- Create an access list permitting SMTP (email) traffic from anywhere to the
host at 209.164.3.5 (the mail server's public IP address). This list is named
smtp. Add additional lines to this access list as required if there is a web or
DNS Server. This is the first step in creating a rule that permits traffic into
your network if it is destined for a specific IP address.

Note: There is only one access list allowed per interface per direction (for
example, inbound on the outside interface). Because of limitation, any
additional lines needing to be placed in the access list must be specified here.
If the server in question is not SMTP, replace the occurrences of SMTP with www,
DNS, POP3, or whatever else might be required. The access-list command was
introduced in PIX Software Release 5.0; it is used here instead of a conduit
statement.

 pager lines 24
 logging on
 logging timestamp
 no logging standby
 logging console debugging
 logging monitor debugging
 logging buffered debugging
 logging trap debugging
 no logging history
 logging facility 23
 logging queue 512

 interface ethernet0 auto
 interface ethernet1 auto

!--- Set each Ethernet interface to auto-detect its media type.

 mtu outside 1500
```

continues

Example 5-2   PIX Firewall Inside Mail Server Configuration (continued)

```
mtu inside 1500
ip address inside 192.168.2.1 255.255.255.0
ip address outside 209.164.3.1 255.255.255.0

!--- Define the IP address for each interface.

no failover
arp timeout 14400

global (outside) 1 209.164.3.129
nat (inside) 1 192.168.2.0 255.255.255.0

!--- Specify that any traffic originating inside from the 192.168.2.x network
will be NAT'd (via PAT) to IP address 209.164.3.129 if such traffic passes
through the outside interface destined to the Internet.

static (inside,outside) 209.164.3.5 192.168.2.57 netmask
255.255.255.255

!--- The preceding command defines a static translation between the legal public
IP address 209.164.3.5 on the outside interface and the private RFC1918 IP
Address of 192.168.2.57 on the inside. These are the addresses to be used by
the server located inside the firewall. On older PIX IOS's, a conduit and static
command pair is required for inbound traffic; the conduit command opened the
doorway and the static command defined the path. You would generally never see
one without the other.

access-group smtp in interface outside

!--- Applies the access list named smtp inbound on the outside interface. With
this command, the access list named smtp that you previously created is applied
to the interface and the presence of the static statement, coupled with the
access list, will not allow your design to function. Because the access list
(smtp) is applied inbound, the PIX will now check all incoming packets against
this list, dropping all packets not explicitly permitted.

route outside 0.0.0.0 0.0.0.0 209.164.3.2 1

!--- Set the default route to be via the outside interface and the nxt hop is
209.164.3.2. The PIX assumes that this address is that of a router.

timeout xlate 1:30:00 conn 1:00:00 half-closed 0:10:00 udp 0
timeout rpc 0:10:00 h323 0:05:00
timeout uauth 0:00:00 absolute
aaa-server TACACS+ protocol tacacs+
aaa-server RADIUS protocol radius
no snmp-server location
no snmp-server contact
snmp-server community public
no snmp-server enable traps
floodguard enable
terminal width 200
Cryptochecksum:d66eb04bc477f21ffbd5baa21ce0f85a
: end
```

Case Study: Firewall Deployment with Mail Server in DMZ

This chapter has taken care to describe the business needs of deploying a mail server on your internal network and discussed the ramifications of allowing this to happen with regard to the security of your network. Ultimately, however, deploying a mail server internally is still common practice and deserves consideration of a basic implementation of this solution.

note

By default, Cisco Systems lists a variety of configuration settings when viewing their devices' configuration files. In the following case study, several configuration files are shown for clarity purposes. To illustrate the case study, comments are made surrounding key configuration entries; however, not every command is discussed because that is beyond the scope of this book. Additional information can be found at Cisco.com.

This scenario presents a small to medium-sized corporate network, as shown in Figure 5-5. As the configuration in Example 5-3 shows, only a mail server exists on the DMZ; however, it could also be a web server or DNS.

Figure 5-5   Firewall Deployment with Mail Server in DMZ

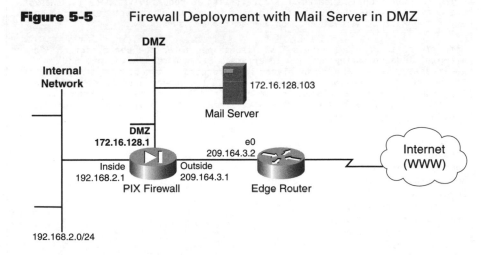

Example 5-3   PIX Firewall DMZ Mail Server Configuration

```
nameif ethernet0 outside security0
nameif ethernet1 inside security100
nameif ethernet2 dmz security50
```

!--- These commands name and set the security level for each PIX interface.
Through these commands, the firewall knows which interface is considered
untrusted (outside), trusted (inside)and DMZ. Notice the numeric values in this
configuration example. Here we have the least secure interface outside assigned
a security value of 0, as it should be. The inside interface is considered
secure, so it has a value of 100, with the DMZ being somewhere in between at 50.

```
enable password 8Ry2YjIyt7RRXU24 encrypted
passwd 2KFQnbNIdI.2KYOU encrypted
hostname SECURE-FIREWALL
domain-name noplace.com
fixup protocol ftp 21
fixup protocol http 80
fixup protocol h323 ras 1718-1719
fixup protocol h323 h225 1720
fixup protocol ils 389
fixup protocol rsh 514
fixup protocol rtsp 554
fixup protocol smtp 25
fixup protocol sqlnet 1521
fixup protocol sip 5060
fixup protocol skinny 2000
no names
```

```
access-list smtp permit tcp any host 209.164.3.5 eq smtp
```

!--- Create an access list permitting SMTP (e-mail) traffic from anywhere to
the host at 209.164.3.5 (the mail servers public IP address). This list is named
smtp. Add additional lines to this access list as required if there is a web or
DNS Server. This is the first step in creating a rule that permits traffic into
our network if it is destined for a specific IP Address.

Note: There is only one access list allowed per interface per direction (for
example, inbound on the outside interface). Because of limitation, any
additional lines needing to be placed in the access list must be specified here.
If the server in question is not SMTP, replace the occurrences of SMTP with www,
DNS, POP3, or whatever else might be required. The access-list command was
introduced in PIX Software Release 5.0; it is used here instead of a conduit
statement.

```
pager lines 24
logging on
logging timestamp
no logging standby
logging console debugging
logging monitor debugging
logging buffered debugging
logging trap debugging
no logging history
logging facility 23
```

Example 5-3 PIX Firewall DMZ Mail Server Configuration (continued)

```
logging queue 512

interface ethernet0 auto
interface ethernet1 auto
interface ethernet2 auto

!--- Set each Ethernet interface to auto-detect its media type.

mtu outside 1500
mtu inside 1500
mtu dmz 1500
ip address inside 192.168.2.1 255.255.255.252
ip address outside 209.164.3.1 255.255.255.252
ip address dmz 172.16.128.1 255.255.255.0

!--- Define the IP address for each interface.

no failover
arp timeout 14400

global (outside) 1 209.164.3.129
nat (inside) 1 192.168.1.0 255.255.255.0

!--- Specify that any traffic originating inside from the 192.168.2.x network
will be NAT'd (via PAT) to IP address 209.164.3.129 if such traffic passes
through the outside interface destined to the Internet.

static (dmz,outside) 209.164.3.5 172.16.128.103 netmask 255.255.255.255

!--- The preceding command defines a static translation between the legal public
IP address 209.164.3.5 on the outside interface and the private RFC1918 IP
Address of 172.16.128.103 on the inside. These addresses are to be used by the
server located on the firewall's DMZ interface.

static (inside,dmz) 192.168.1.0 192.168.1.0 netmask 255.255.255.0

!--- This static essentially prevents the translation of the internal corporate
subnet of 192.168.1.x when that subnet sends packets to the DMZ, perhaps to
check e-mail. Literally speaking, it creates a translation from 192.168.1.x to
192.168.1.x.

access-group smtp in interface outside

!--- Applies the access list named smtp inbound on the outside interface. With
this command, the access list named smtp you previously created is applied to
the interface, and the presence of the static statement coupled with the access
list will not allow our design to function. Because the access list (smtp) is
applied inbound, the PIX now check all incoming packets against this list,
dropping all packets that are not explicitly permitted.

route outside 0.0.0.0 0.0.0.0 209.164.3.2 1
```

continues

Example 5-3   PIX Firewall DMZ Mail Server Configuration (continued)

```
!--- Set the default route to be via the outside interface, and the next hop is
209.164.3.2. The PIX assumes that this address is that of a router.

!
timeout xlate 3:00:00
timeout conn 1:00:00 half-closed 0:10:00 udp 0:02:00 rpc 0:10:00 h323 0:05:00 si
p 0:30:00 sip_media 0:02:00
timeout uauth 0:05:00 absolute
aaa-server TACACS+ protocol tacacs+
aaa-server RADIUS protocol radius
aaa-server LOCAL protocol local
no snmp-server location
no snmp-server contact
snmp-server community public
no snmp-server enable traps
floodguard enable
terminal width 80
Cryptochecksum:d66eb04bc477f21ffbd5baa21ce0f85a
: end
```

Firewall Limitations

A firewall is a crucial component of securing your network and is designed to address the issues of data integrity or traffic authentication (via stateful packet inspection) and confidentiality of your internal network (via NAT). Your network gains these benefits from a firewall by receiving all transmitted traffic through the firewall. The importance of including a firewall in your security strategy is apparent; however, firewalls do have the following limitations:

- A firewall cannot prevent users or attackers with modems from dialing into or out of the internal network, thus bypassing the firewall and its protection completely.

- Firewalls cannot enforce your password policy or prevent misuse of passwords. Your password policy is crucial in this area because it outlines acceptable conduct and sets the ramifications of noncompliance.

- Firewalls are ineffective against nontechnical security risks such as social engineering, as discussed in Chapter 1, "Here There Be Hackers!"

- Firewalls are a bottleneck of traffic because they concentrate traffic and security in a single spot, resulting in a potential single point of failure.

note
The FBI's arrest of the phone masters cracker ring in 1999 brought several
of these security issues to light. These hackers were accused of breaking
into credit-reporting databases belonging to Equifax Inc. and TRW Inc. as
well as the databases of Nexis/Lexis and Dun & Bradstreet. They also
broke into AT&T Corporation, British Telecommunications Incorporated,
GTE Corporation, MCI WorldCom, Southwestern Bell, and Sprint
Corporation. In doing so, these hackers did not use any high-tech attack
methods. The phone masters used a combination of social engineering and
dumpster diving, both used by attackers that have very little technical
skill, as discussed in Chapter 1.

Chapter Summary

This chapter covered the world of firewalls and their role in securing a network.
Not everyone believes in the value of these devices, and our discussions in this
regard allowed us to answer these naysayers and show them the folly of their
ways. We provided further proof of the importance of firewalls by expanding on
their pure technical aspects, while expressing the fundamental truth that firewalls
are the manifestation of a company's security policy.

Operationally, this chapter covered how firewalls function, where and when to
implement them, and how to design the access policies that are necessary to
define access into your network. Furthermore, the chapter introduced the DMZ
interface as an evolution in firewalls and how they provide special locations for
various Internet servers. The chapter concluded with several brief case studies
demonstrating firewalls in action, followed by some of their limitations.

Chapter Review Questions

The following questions assist in reinforcing the concepts covered in this chapter.

1. Who needs a firewall?

2. Why do I need a firewall?

3. Do I need a firewall?

4. How is a firewall an extension of a security policy?

5. What is the name of the table in a firewall that tracks connections?

6. What fundamental does a DMZ fulfill?

7. What are four benefits of a DMZ?

8. Can firewalls enforce password policies or prevent misuse of passwords by users?

What You Will Learn

By the end of this chapter, you should know and be able to explain the following:

- ✔ The major components of Content-Broad Access Control (CBAC)

- ✔ The value of using the IOS-based intrusion detection functionality and the Cisco Firewall Feature Set (FFS)

- ✔ The breadth and scope of techniques used to secure your router

Being able to answer these key questions will allow you to understand the overall characteristics and importance of network security. By the time you finish this book, you will have a solid appreciation for network security, its issues, how it works, and why it is important.

CHAPTER 6

Router Security

Be the change you wish to see in the world. —Mahatma Gandhi

Everyone is getting online as rapidly as possible in whatever way they can; if you are reading this book, you are probably the person your family calls to "fix" the Internet. Perhaps the best T-shirt I never bought was the *"No, I will not fix your computer" from ThinkGeek.com*, as shown in Figure 6-1.

Figure 6-1   No, I Will Not Fix Your Computer

The point is that most people do not understand that the Internet operates because of routers. They think that individuals have more control and security than they do because their PC connects to the Internet. Of course, this is not the case—there

are no guarantees on the Internet, which is a wild and fast place. Everyone tries to do a good job, but unexpected events occur.

As people seek to leverage the unparalleled possibilities of Internet communications, they need secure solutions that

- Protect internal networks from intrusion

- Provide secure Internet and remote access connections

- Enable network commerce through the World Wide Web

Today, the Internet is the focus of powerful new technologies that dramatically enhance communications with remote customers, suppliers, partners, and employees. Users must be confident that network transactions—especially over public networks—are secured.

Cisco IOS Software runs on over 80 percent of Internet backbone routers and an equally high percentage of corporate network routers that connect to the Internet. Cisco IOS Software provides complete network services and enables networked applications. Cisco IOS security services offer many options for building custom security solutions for Internet, intranet, and remote access networks to provide end-to-end network security.

A critical part of an overall security solution is a network firewall, which monitors traffic crossing network perimeters and imposes restrictions according to security policy. As discussed in Chapter 5, "Firewalls," firewalls are not routers, and they are used to connect the Internet to your corporate network. Routers used to connect to the Internet are known as *edge routers*; they form the outermost perimeter of your network.

Perimeter routers are found at any network boundary, such as between private networks, intranets, extranets, or the Internet. Firewalls most commonly separate internal (private) and external (public) networks.

The Cisco IOS Firewall Feature Set, available as a Cisco IOS Software option, provides an advanced security solution that protects networks from security violations. This integrated router security solution provides one element in a system of security solutions available from Cisco Systems.

This chapter discusses the use of routers, the purpose of a firewall IOS, and what it is. Where within your network will you be applying this type of protection? This chapter explains the use and placement of this type of security technology and its advantages and disadvantages.

A firewall is a security device that sits on the edge of your Internet connection and functions as an Internet Border Security Officer by constantly looking at all the traffic entering and exiting your connection, looking and waiting for traffic to block or reject in response to an established rule. The firewall plays the role of law and protection in a lawless global web, ever vigilant in its mission to protect the internal network resources that connect to it.

In contrast, the edge router provides connectivity to the Internet for businesses, and most people view it as a necessary device that provides them with connectivity. Having a router, however, means that it will handle (route) every single packet that wants to enter or leave the network. It is the role of the firewall to determine what is permitted or denied. However, if you have a router as the first layer into your network, shouldn't you use that router as part of your layered security strategy?

Of course, you should. You have paid for the router, spent time configuring it, and blindly trusting that it is inherently secure is a mistake. Even if your company spent tens of thousands of dollars on other security solutions, the router handling everything might not have had its configuration hardened to protect it and your network. The router is essentially in the default out of the box (OOB) condition. Consider that an attacker gained control of your router. Because that router literally *sees* every single IP packet, what might the attacker learn? What might he then be able to do? The router is a smart network device that holds a key position and handles crucial information. Network security is often thought of in terms of servers, firewalls, VPNs, and how to protect IT resources. This chapter covers how to protect the router and then expand its capabilities to further protect your network with an additional layer of security through the use of the Cisco Firewall Feature Set IOS.

By securing the router and thus increasing your network's security, you can accomplish the following:

- Prevent routers from unintentionally *leaking information* about your network to attackers

- Prevent the disabling of your routers (and thus your network) by attackers or accidental misconfiguration

- Prevent the use of your routers as platforms to launch an internal attack or to be used to attack others

- Reduce the load on the firewall and internal network as bad packets and thus stop associated attacks at the edge of your network

- Quickly activate an additional layer of security to further protect your network

These accomplishments revolve around the security and functionality of the router and your network. As such, they are concerned with the big picture; however, the firewall feature set available for routers has additional security benefits.

Not everyone wants to spend the money, time, effort, or expertise needed to correctly configure the firewall functionality on a router. The reality is that many companies allow the firewall to be the stateful packet inspection device. However, *everyone* should use a router as a layer in the defense of his network. The discussion and debate should center not on "if" but "how" the router should be configured. Here are three ways to configure your edge router:

- **Router with basic configuration**—Get the router, put a basic configuration in it, connect it to your LAN and the Internet, and you are finished. There is nothing fancy here, and absolutely no security or value to your network!

- **Router as a choke point**—As discussed in Chapter 3, " Overview of Security Technologies," all routers come with the capability to filter traffic based on access control lists (ACLs). Access lists can be developed to filter traffic based on type and destination at the router turning it into a choke; if the traffic is not permitted, it is denied! This is the minimum that should be accomplished!

■ **Router as a packet inspector**—To have the router perform more advanced filtering, this type of router is deployed with the firewall feature set on it. This router is the best of the three, and it is also the most difficult to achieve. Anything in life that is worth having is never free—you must work for it!

This chapter does not cover what a router secures or protects with a basic configuration because it does nothing to help increase your network's security. Rather, this chapter focuses on how a router functions as a choke point through the use of static access lists and as a screening device through more advanced access lists.

Edge Router as a Choke Point

A *choke point* came to the world of networking courtesy of the Internet's military heritage. A choke point refers to a single point in which everything will try and either enter or leave your network. In this application of the term choke point, it is a router. The edge router is the single point from which the entire Internet gains access to your network. The router then is also a single point of failure, but that is an entirely separate discussion.

Edge routers that operate as choke points increase your network's security by restricting the flow of data between your network and the Internet (or another network).

A successful network security implementation is based on understanding what happening in the network. This knowledge forms the basis of what should be used to filter network activity so inappropriate activity can be identified. Network activity should be restricted to permit acceptable service only. Chokes provide a great way of implementing a coarse level of control, and monitoring that can be fine-tuned using intelligent filters, such as proxy and stateful firewalls.

The value of edge routers being configured as choke points is that they can prevent access to specific devices and applications in a performance-friendly way. This increase in security is typically provided through the use of standard and extended access control lists that can address traffic concerns at Layers 2, 3, and 4

of the OSI reference model. The fact that their performance does not *normally* suffer results from the fact the router must read the contents of the IP packet anyway to make a decision on where to forward the packet. It does not take much more work to toss out the packet or permit it into the network.

The use of ACLs gives network engineers a high degree of control and filtering capabilities over packets traversing the router. Figure 6-2 demonstrates a common example of the rules and placement of a choke router. On a side note, can you figure out what network device is missing from this figure?

Figure 6-2   Edge Router as a Choke Point

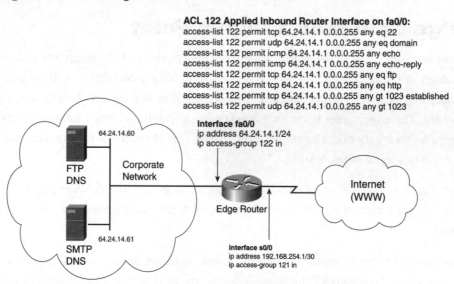

ACL 122 Applied Inbound Router Interface on fa0/0:
access-list 122 permit tcp 64.24.14.1 0.0.0.255 any eq 22
access-list 122 permit udp 64.24.14.1 0.0.0.255 any eq domain
access-list 122 permit icmp 64.24.14.1 0.0.0.255 any echo
access-list 122 permit icmp 64.24.14.1 0.0.0.255 any echo-reply
access-list 122 permit tcp 64.24.14.1 0.0.0.255 any eq ftp
access-list 122 permit tcp 64.24.14.1 0.0.0.255 any eq http
access-list 122 permit tcp 64.24.14.1 0.0.0.255 any gt 1023 established
access-list 122 permit udp 64.24.14.1 0.0.0.255 any gt 1023

Interface fa0/0
ip address 64.24.14.1/24
ip access-group 122 in

FTP DNS   64.24.14.60   Corporate Network

SMTP DNS   64.24.14.61

Edge Router   Internet (WWW)

Interface s0/0
ip address 192.168.254.1/30
ip access-group 121 in

ACL 121 Applied Inbound on Router Interface s0/0:
access-list 121 permit tcp any any eq 22
access-list 121 permit udp any any gt 1023
access-list 121 permit icmp any any gt 1023
access-list 121 permit icmp any any echo-reply
access-list 121 permit icmp any any unreachable
access-list 121 permit icmp any any administratively-prohibited
access-list 121 permit icmp any any time-exceeded
access-list 121 permit icmp any any packet-too-big
access-list 121 permit tcp any 64.24.14.60 eq ftp
access-list 121 permit tcp any 64.24.14. 61 eq smtp
access-list 121 permit tcp any 64.24.14.61 eq domain
access-list 121 permit udp 64.24.14.61 eq domain

This edge router that is acting as a choke point into the corporate network permits only the following traffic into the corporate LAN:

- Inbound mail delivery to the e-mail (SMTP) server at IP address 64.24.14.61

- FTP file transfers to the FTP server at IP address 64.24.14.60

- DNS (zone transfers via UDP and name lookup requests via TCP) to the DNS server at IP address 64.24.14.61

- TCP and UDP traffic above port 1023 to allow outbound connections from the private network to function

- Only specific types of ICMP

- All other traffic is denied access to the edge router

As a user on the corporate LAN, the edge router permits only you to establish connections out to the Internet as follows:

- SSH [port 22]

- DNS [port 53]

- FTP [ports 20 and 21]

- HTTP [port 80]

The use of a choke point router to limit access (both in and out) for known services (below port number 1023) leaves the network largely exposed. Because the majority of today's applications utilize ports above 1023 and not all IP stack and application implementations follow the 49152 through 65535 dynamic/private port guidelines, filtering above 1023 can affect the operation of applications that you want to function and, therefore, cannot deny this port range.

Did you discern what was missing in this figure? If you guessed a firewall performing stateful packet inspection (SPI) and network address translation (NAT), you were correct and are making progress toward becoming a security guru!

Limitations of Choke Routers

Choke routers are useful and can protect your network as previously demonstrated; however, they are only part of the solution and are likely to stop only a *script kiddie.* An experienced attacker or one who has already read this book understands that the network is not completely protected. Some of the limitations of choke routers are as follows:

- Choke routers running regular IOS cannot look at the higher layers of the OSI reference model (Layers 5–7). However, use of enhanced IOS facilitates the use of Network Based Application Recognition (NBAR), which allows a router to detect and block many of the more common worms. You can find a useful article regarding this point at: http://certcities.com/editorial/columns/story.asp?EditorialsID=76.

- Choke routers do not adequately address protocol and application security concerns; you would have no idea if your connections were being spoofed.

- Choke routers do not have the ability to perform SPI without potentially serious upgrades.

While choke routers do not address the preceding concerns, they are quite valuable for implementing broad network and service access policies (that is, what users on the Internet can access).

caution

Creating static ACLs require some thought and a lot of testing. A poorly written ACL can have adverse effects on the network in terms of performance and service availability. A strongly recommended practice is to write the ACL out on paper first to ensure that you have it designed to accomplish your filtering goals. Also, do not ask for help on your ACLs until you have repeated the mantra—there is an implicit deny all at the end of every ACL that the Cisco IOS does not display. The Cisco TAC will thank me for including that requirement because everyone forgets it—myself included, at times!

Edge Router as a Packet Inspector

By now, you should readily agree that using your edge router as a part of your layered security strategy will bring benefits to your network. Using the edge router as a choke point is certainly useful; however, there are some limitations to its use that might be important to you. Perhaps your company is involved in government contracts, so you must have the highest possible level of security. Or perhaps you are working for the government. Regardless, the next level up in security is the use of Cisco Firewall Feature Set (FFS) on the edge router.

At the heart of Cisco's Firewall Feature Set IOS is ***Context-Based Access Control (CBAC)***. CBAC is a stateful packet inspection engine that extends the router's filtering capability to the application layer (Layer 7) of the OSI reference model. It accomplishes this by using CBAC-based access lists. (Get used to access lists because they never go away; they only get reconstituted for another new cool technology.)

As the heart of the Firewall Feature Set tracks TCP, ICMP (as of Cisco IOS Software Release 12.2.15T), and UDP-based application packet, CBAC flows between hosts on either side of the firewall (router), thus performing SPI, which qualifies the use of the *firewall features* in its title; *however,* this type of IOS is no replacement for a dedicated stateful firewall.

note

Routers that perform "firewall-like" operations are sometimes referred to as "routerwalls." Remember, the key term here is "firewall-like," which means that it can sort of function as a firewall but should not be used to replace a bonafide, dedicated firewall appliance.

CBAC is a hybrid of security architectures rather than a single pure implementation, such as a dedicated firewall. This hybrid architecture gives the FFS IOS the flexibility to function as both a router and firewall, making it ideally suited for use

in providing increased security on the edge of your network. The edge of your network is truly the best place for this type of security technology.

note

The Cisco Firewall Feature Set IOS is supported on almost every Cisco router platform. The caveat is that additional memory is typically required to deploy and use this version of IOS. In many cases, your router will need two things to run the Firewall Feature Set IOS: additional memory and appropriate IOS software license. For some reason, Cisco memory has not been reduced in price like PC memory; therefore, you will be incurring additional cost. However, I strongly recommend that you look for bundled deals that contain the router, memory, and IOS that you need.

Benefits of the Firewall Feature Set

Although the goal of this book is not to provide a lot of marketing hype, this technology begs an exception because it is the Cadillac of IOS.

The Firewall Feature Set IOS is particularly useful for businesses that are interested in a cost-effective way of extending perimeter security across all network boundaries, specifically branch-office, intranet, and extranet perimeters. In addition, it is appropriate for small and medium-sized businesses that need a cost-effective router that includes an integrated firewall with intrusion-detection capabilities. Some benefits of the Cisco IOS Firewall Feature Set are

- **Dynamic filtering**—CBAC allows return path filtering for TCP, UDP, and ICMP that creates dynamic *stateful* entries based on the bidirectional communication sessions in the filtering of access lists when a conversation is first established. CBAC allows the creation of these, provided there are permit statements in extended access lists that are unique. This eliminates the need to leave any statically open ports; in other words, CBAC will open ports dynamically only when traffic matches an ACL. The ports that are opened dynamically are limited in lifespan (the duration of the conversation) and only to specific hosts, thus limiting the opportunity for external attacks. Some of the filtering capabilities include the following:

— **Standard and Extended Access Control Lists (ACLs)**—Apply controls over access to specific network segments, and define which traffic passes through a network segment or the router, thus protecting your network.

— **Lock and Key–Dynamic ACLs**—Grant temporary access through firewalls upon user identification (username/password).

— **Per User Authentication and Authorization**—Provides the ability to control user access by IP address and interface as determined by the security policy. This is known as *authentication proxy*.

■ **TCP sequence numbers tracking**—CBAC monitors the outbound communication session sequence numbers and the inbound communication session that TCP uses to track the state of the communication stream. This sequence number tracking provides protection against man-in-the middle and other session hijacking attacks because incorrect sequence numbers get packets discarded. As discussed in previous chapters, this is the essence of SPI.

■ **Tracking of communication session states**—CBAC tracks half-open, open, and closed TCP sessions to provide defense against TCP-SYN DOS attacks. Session number and transmission per minute rates are tracked using high and low, administrator-defined thresholds.

■ **UDP and ICMP connection tracking**—These two protocols are difficult to monitor because they do not have the characteristics that are necessary to be tracked statefully, like TCP. This does not alleviate the need to do so; therefore, CBAC tracks them through the use of dynamic filtering and timers that approximate conversation status. At press time, this technique is perhaps one of the most advanced means of validating the transmission of these protocols.

■ **Session logging**—As a security device, a firewall must protect first and foremost. However, trailing ever so slightly behind protection is the ability to log and provide an audit trail. Important functionality to include in session logs includes details about transactions—communication termination, time

stamps, source host, destination host, ports, and total number of bytes transmitted. This information is useful, depending on the culture of your company and has a variety of uses. CBAC provides support for per-application auditing in real time. Reporting is provided through the standard IOS logging mechanism with support for local and remote reporting to a syslog server.

- **Application specific monitoring**—CBAC examines packet flows for many application-specific protocol violations, along with single-path TCP, UDP, and ICMP flows. If CBAC detects a violation, the conversation is blocked and the relevant channels are closed. Application packet inspection is available for the following protocols, which have been the targets of many vulnerabilities:

  — *CU-SeeMe (Port 7648)*—Peer-to-peer videoconferencing.

  — *FTP (Port 21)*—Client-server File Transfer Protocol.

  — *H.323 (Port 1720)*—Packet-based multimedia communication protocol (VoIP) that inspects Q931 and H.245 control messages to open additional UDP channels for video and audio data; this also includes SIP (Port 5060) Session Initiation Protocol.

  — *ICMP Inspection*—Throughout this book, you have seen the uses of ICMP to troubleshoot network issues and by attackers to discover your network topology and exploit your network. The firewall feature set employs packet inspection to trust only the ICMP messages generated from within the internal network.

  — *MCGP (Port 2427)*—Media Control Gateway Protocol (VoIP).

  — *MSRPC (Port 135)*—Microsoft Remote Procedure Call Protocol (provides system-to-system process communication).

  — *Net show (Port 1755)*—Microsoft's streaming media platform.

  — *R-EXEC (Port 512)*—Berkeley remote command protocol (UNIX).

  — *R-SHELL (Port 514)*—Berkeley remote shell protocol (UNIX).

   — *RTSP (Port 544)*—Real-Time Streaming Protocol (multimedia and VoIP).

   — *SMTP (Port 25)*—Simple Mail Transfer Protocol for detecting invalid SMTP commands; eliminates requirement for external mail relay in "demilitarized zones."

   — *SQLnet (Port 1521)*—Client-server middleware for client-to-database and database-to-database communication. Inspects redirect messages from Oracle listener processes; opens port for clients to connect to servers.

   — *Stream Works (Port 1558)*—Streaming media platform (now owned by Real Networks).

   — *SUNrpc (Port 111)*—Sun Microsystems' remote procedure call protocol (NFS).

   — *Real Audio (Port 7070)*—Real Networks' streaming media platform.

   — *Telnet (Port 23)*—Virtual terminal protocol.

   — *TFTP (Port 69)*—Trivial File Transfer Protocol.

   — *VDOlive (Port 7000)*—Streaming media protocol.

- **Java applet blocking**—At the edge router, you can set the level of protection in place against Java applets. The router can be configured to filter or completely deny access to Java applets that are not embedded in an archive or compressed file—you decide.

- **Virtual private networks (VPNs)**—Provide secure data transfer over the Internet; reduce implementation and management costs for remote branch offices and mobile users/employees; enhance quality of service and reliability; standards-based for interoperability. VPNs are becoming extremely popular with the increasing prevalence of high-speed broadband Internet access at reasonable costs. Chapter 7, "IPSec Virtual Private Networks (VPNs)," covers VPNs in greater detail.

A robust and layered security policy entails more than setting up a firewall. Cisco FFS IOS Software is an ideal method for implementing increased security at the edge of your network, thus allowing easier enforcement of security policies and increased network security. The FFS also offers a means of providing forensic analysis of connections in the event of a security breach or suspected breach.

Content-Based Packet Inspection

As discussed in Chapter 5, many dedicated firewalls have security defined on a per-physical interface level. This is the concept of an interface that connects to outside your network to the Internet—for example, versus an interface that connects to the inside of your network. An interface connected to the public Internet clearly has a higher security requirement than an internal interface. This belief is similar across every type of firewall. Remember, it is important to know who to trust and who not to trust.

The Cisco IOS Firewall Feature Set, however, operates on a router, and the mass of gray matter in San Jose had a divinely inspired moment that allowed them to take the mission of a router (route packets) and that of a firewall without the dependency of trust. A firewall innately understands trust through its use of inside and outside interfaces. A router running FFS must be manually configured to understand trust. For example, you might decide to not allow inbound (defined as "from the outside in") Telnet, so you should set up an ACL to block TCP Telnet port 21, or also not allow SNMP traffic into a network from the Internet.

This means that the FFS does not function entirely like a true firewall, but you have probably already figured that out.

The FFS allows for the inspection of a packet's contents, which is extremely effective when securing your network. Consider that if you allow port 80 (HTTP) in, security is intact as long as it is going to your web server, right? *Wrong! You have a false sense of security.* Attackers know that if you have a website, you must allow HTTP traffic to reach it; therefore, they send HTTP packets with the contents of packets containing malicious code designed to attack the web server. Yikes! Is that a newsflash for you? Do not despair—CBAC is there!

Using the IOS IDS, CBAC, allows for the inspection of packet contents based on a simple concept: *inspection precedes access*. After the inspection, the packet can be filtered accordingly, as shown in Figure 6-3.

Figure 6-3   CBAC Security Controls

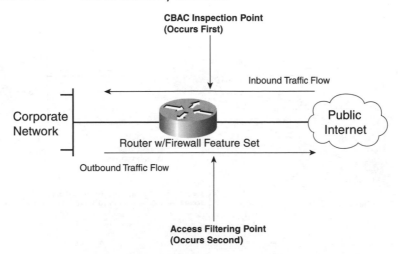

Of course, you can have multiple points of inspection in the form of ACLs. The only requirement of the FFS and CBAC is that the filtering must occur *after* the inspection. Having the FFS determine access based on conversation direction maintains the capability for the router to continue to function primarily as a router.

From a design standpoint, you must do some careful thought and traffic analysis before implementing CBAC, particularly in environments requiring the use of an "explicit permit" access model. Now, take a look at the security process followed by a router equipped with the FFS IOS. This list is also reflected in Figure 6-4.

Figure 6-4 Cisco's Firewall Feature Set IOS in Action!

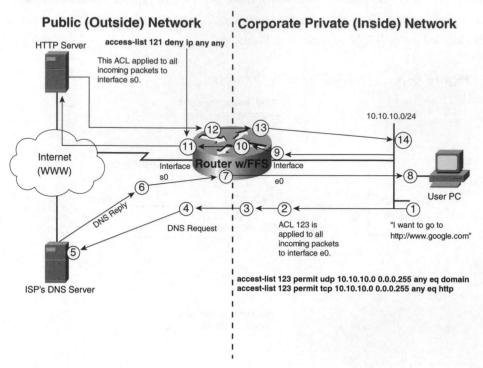

1. A user is on the *inside* of a corporate network; from his PC he types **http://www.google.com** in his web browser and presses **Enter**.

   Before the connection with the Google website can be established, the user's PC issues a DNS domain name lookup to translate the URL to an IP address.

2. The DNS lookup packet arrives at the router's inside Ethernet interface. The DNS packet (a UDP datagram) is evaluated against access list 123, which looks at all incoming packets to the inside router's Ethernet interface.

   If the DNS packet is permitted by access list 123, it is forwarded; if not, the router discards the packet automatically (implicit deny all).

3. After the DNS lookup packet is permitted by access list 123, it is inspected by CBAC, which inspects the packet and records the state information in its state table, specifically:

Source IP Address and Port Number

Destination IP Address, Port Number and Protocol

4. CBAC takes the state data it gathered and dynamically creates a temporary permit statement to access list 121 (applied on *serial* interface to all packets that want to enter the router). The new access list **permit** statement permits only the return traffic from the destination host (DNS Server in this example) to the user's PC when it has the same protocol and port numbers. The rule is prepended (put in front of) the static statements that are already in access list 121. Remember that UDP is not connection-oriented, so this poses some challenges in tracking a connection, unlike TCP, which has a connection set up.

5. The DNS lookup packet (UDP port 53) is forwarded out of the router's serial interface, processed by the DNS server, and a reply is sent back to the user's PC. The dynamic UDP DNS entry remains in access list 121 for five seconds. If the router does not receive a reply within that five-second period, the temporary access list statement for this connection is cancelled.

6. When the DNS reply packet arrives inbound to the router's serial interface, it is evaluated against the inbound access list 121 and is permitted because it belongs to an established session that was tracked and will be permitted by CBAC.

7. When permitted to enter the routers serial interface, the CBAC inspects the DNS reply AC and forwards it to the user's PC. Because the session is UDP-based, the state entry remains for the default timer and is then removed, along with the dynamic ACL entry.

note
In terms of a router running the FFS processing packets, the initial session packet is process-switched. Any additional packets belonging to the same session are fast-switched.

8. The DNS reply arrives at the user's PC now that it knows the IP address of the Google web server. Now that the PC knows the website's IP address, the initial HTTP session is initiated. Because HTTP (WWW) uses TCP, the first packet sent is a SYN (synchronization) to begin the synchronization using the TCP 3-way handshake.

9. The HTTP packet arrives at the router's inside Ethernet interface. It is evaluated against the outbound access list 123 and is permitted because it is a HTTP port 80 packet.

10. When the HTTP packet is permitted by access list 123, it is inspected by CBAC, which inspects the packet and records the state information in its state table, specifically:

    Source IP Address and Port Number

    Destination IP Address, Port Number and Protocol

11. The packet is forwarded on to the destination web server. Based on the state table information, a temporary return traffic permit access list entry is prepended to access list 121. Because HTTP uses TCP, this temporary entry remains for up to 30 seconds for a SYN-ACK (synchronization-acknowledgment) response from the destination web server. If no reply is received within the time limit, the dynamic entry is retracted and the state table entry purged.

12. When the reply packet arrives at the router's serial interface, it is evaluated against the inbound access list 121 and accepted because the temporary permit entry has been added by CBAC.

13. After being permitted to enter the router's serial interface, CBAC inspects the packet for protocol-specific violations. If the header or data field information contain a known violation, CBAC discards the packet and closes the session. If the packet is error-free, it is forwarded onto the origin host.

14. In the case of HTTP and other multisession protocols, in which several communication sessions are created to complete a task, CBAC continues to update the state table and serial interface access list accordingly.

All the CBAC-created temporary access list entries are removed when each communication session is completed, depending on the type of protocol being used:

- ICMP and UDP sessions are removed based on configurable inactivity timers.

- TCP sessions are removed five seconds after the exchange of FIN packets. In the event of an RST packet, the session is terminated and corresponding ACL entries are removed immediately.

- By default CBAC:

  — Starts deleting half-open sessions when its counters reach 500.

  — Stops deleting half-open sessions when its counters see the number drop to 400.

- A huge number of "half-open" sessions being seen in a large chunk could mean that a DoS attack has begun in the form of a port scan or some other type of scan that uses incomplete, "half-open" sessions to gather information.

Intrusion Detection with Cisco IOS

The Cisco IOS Firewall IDS acts as an in-line *intrusion detection* sensor, watching packets and communication sessions as they flow through the router and scanning each packet to see whether it matches any of the IDS signatures.

Cisco developed its Cisco IOS Software-based intrusion detection capabilities in the Cisco IOS Firewall Feature Set with flexibility in mind so individual attack signatures could be disabled in case of false positives. Also, while it is preferable to enable both the firewall and intrusion detection features of the FFS CBAC security engine to support a network security policy, each of these features can be enabled independently and on different router interfaces.

The Cisco IOS Firewall Feature Set includes intrusion detection technology in addition to basic firewall functionality. The Cisco FFS IOS acts as a *limited* in-line intrusion detection sensor, watching packets and sessions as they flow through the router (this is the inline aspect of its operation—scanning each packet to determine whether the contents match any of the IDS signatures it knows about). When the router detects suspicious activity—in other words, when it believes that a packet contains an attack signature—it responds accordingly before network security can be compromised and logs the suspicious activity by using *syslog* and by communicating directly with a server running the Cisco Secure IDS Software.

note

System Message Logging (syslog) provides a means for the system and its running processes to report various types of system state information. There are three classes of system state data: error, informational, and debug. Cisco IOS Software provides an extensive system message and error reporting facility. In fact, IOS uses over 500 service identifiers known as "facilities" to categorize system state data for error and event message reporting. System logging data is an important resource in diagnosing problems in general and, when issued by the firewall feature set, it allows for the reporting of events.

The Firewall Feature Set has limited intrusion detection capabilities because the attack signatures that allow it to identify various attacks are *coded* into the IOS and cannot change unless a new version of IOS is created with new signatures. The router would then require having the newer IOS uploaded to it. This contrasts with a dedicated IDS device that can have new signatures loaded rather easily. In practice, this means that the engineers responsible for your network's security must ensure that the attack signatures are always as current as possible. The network administrator can configure the IDS-enabled router to choose the appropriate response to various threats. When packets in a session match a signature, the IDS system can be configured to take the following actions:

- Send an alarm to a syslog server or a Cisco Secure IDS Director (centralized management interface)

- Drop the offending packet

- Reset the TCP connection

Security best practice procedures recommend that you use the drop and rest actions together. In practice, this would mean that when the FFS IDS receives a packet that matches on its IDS attack signatures, the packet is dropped, thereby preventing it from reaching the targeted device in your network. Because attacks come in the form of multiple packets, simply dropping only one packet is not enough to protect your network. The FFS IDS will proactively send a *reset* to the device that sent the offending packet, thereby causing the connection to drop. This combination response is effective because the specific packet and the communication session are dropped.

When to Use the FFS IDS

Cisco IOS Firewall IDS capabilities are ideal for providing additional visibility at intranet, extranet, and branch-office Internet perimeters. Networks of all sizes and complexity will enjoy a more robust protection against attacks on the network and can automatically respond to threats from internal or external hosts.

The Cisco IOS Firewall with intrusion detection is intended to satisfy the security goals of all customers and is particularly appropriate for the following scenarios:

- Enterprise customers who are interested in a cost-effective method of extending their perimeter security across all network boundaries—specifically branch-office, intranet, and extranet network perimeters.

- Small and medium-sized businesses that are looking for a cost-effective router that has an integrated firewall with intrusion-detection capabilities.

- Service provider customers that want to set up managed services, providing their customers with firewalling and intrusion detection, all housed within the necessary function of a router.

FFS IDS Operational Overview

By now, it should be apparent that understanding packets is fairly important in networking. This is a realization that comes slowly for some people; however, after you accept this truth, networking should become much easier to understand. Everything is a packet, and all network devices are designed to do something with a packet. Sometimes, this is forwarding the packet to its destination, inspecting it, or even altering it in some way to accomplish a goal. This understanding is something that many hackers have figured out, and they use this knowledge to serve the dark side. That is melodramatic, but truthful because it is no fun rebuilding a server at 3:00 a.m. because it has been compromised, or dealing with a rampant virus that brings a network to its knees. This book is not designed to make you an expert at packets, but it introduces you to many of the fundamental truths of network security that provide a solid understanding of how the real world functions. If you need to learn more, you can build on this beginning. That being said, you do not have to live at the packet level; simply knowing that it is there and that it functions is the basis for everything *networking*.

note

Perhaps the person I respect the most who educates people about living at the packet level is Laura Chappell. Visit her and her many online resources at http://www.packet-level.com/.

Cisco developed its Cisco IOS Software-based intrusion detection capabilities in the Cisco IOS Firewall with flexibility in mind so individual attack signatures could be disabled in case of false positives. Also, although it is preferable to enable the CBAC security engine's firewall and intrusion detection features to support a network security policy, each of these features can be enabled independently and on different router interfaces.

The Cisco IOS IDS acts as an in-line intrusion detection sensor, watching packets as they traverse the router's interfaces and acting upon them in a definable fashion.

The Cisco IOS Firewall's Intrusion Detection System (Cisco IOS IDS) identifies the most common attacks using signatures to detect patterns of misuse in network traffic (*attack signatures*). The Cisco IOS Firewall Feature Set's intrusion detection signatures were chosen from a broad cross-section of intrusion detection signatures. The signatures represent severe breaches of security, the most common network attacks, and information gathering scans.

In Cisco IOS IDS, signatures are categorized into four types:

- **Info atomic signature**—Atomic signatures can detect patterns as simple as an attempt to access a specific port on a specific host, such as a port scan.

- **Info compound signature**—Compound signatures can detect complex patterns, such as a sequence of operations distributed across multiple hosts over an arbitrary period of time. In general, both kinds of informational signatures detect attackers' information-gathering activities.

- **Attack atomic signature**—Detect patterns where an attacker is attempting to access a single host device.

- **Attack compound signature**—A signature that detects complex attack activities that are spread across multiple hosts over an arbitrary period of time.

The intrusion detection signatures included in the Cisco IOS Firewall were chosen from a broad cross-section of intrusion detection signatures that represent the most common network attacks and information gathering scans that are not commonly found in an operational network.

tip
The following URL lists attack signatures in numerical order by their signature number in the Cisco Secure IDS Network Security Database. After each signature's name is an indication of the type of signature (information or attack, atomic or compound):

http://www.cisco.com/en/US/products/sw/iosswrel/ps1835/
products_configuration_guide_chapter09186a00800ca7c6.html

The following describes the packet auditing process with Cisco IOS IDS:

1. You create an audit rule, which specifies the attack signatures that should be applied to packet traffic and the actions to be taken when a match is found. An audit rule can be as flexible and specific as needed to meet the goals of your security policy. An example rule follows in which you suspect or want to prevent the spamming of e-mail messages, so the IDS is configured to audit all SMTP traffic and ensure that there are no more than 100 recipients:

```
ip audit smtp spam 100
```

2. You apply the audit rule to an interface on the router, specifying a traffic direction (*in* or *out*). The following example applies the audit rule to look at all inbound SMTP traffic to the router:

```
ip audit smtp in
```

3. If the audit rule is applied to the *in* direction of the interface, packets passing through the interface are audited before the inbound ACL has a chance to discard them. This allows an administrator to be alerted if an attack or information-gathering activity is underway, even if the router would normally reject the activity. It is considered best practice to apply IDS audit rules inbound because they are inspected.

4. If the audit rule is applied to the *out* direction on the interface, packets are audited after they enter the router through another interface. In this case, the inbound ACL of the other interface might discard packets before they are audited. This could result in the loss of IDS alarms, even though the attack or information-gathering activity was thwarted.

5. Packets going through the interface that match the audit rule are audited by a series of modules, starting with IP; then either ICMP, TCP, or UDP (as appropriate); and finally, the application level.

6. If a signature match is found in a module, the following user-configured actions occur:

   — If the action is **alarm**, the module completes its audit, sends an alarm, and passes the packet to the next module.

   — If the action is **drop**, the packet is dropped from the module, discarded, and not sent to the next module.

   — If the action is **reset**, the packets are forwarded to the next module, and packets with the reset flag set are sent to both participants of the session, if the session is TCP.

If there are multiple signature matches in a module, only the first match fires an action. Additional matches in other modules fire additional alarms, but only one per module. IDS can reset only a TCP-based connection because this protocol has a SYN ACK and the all-powerful RST, which the IDS can send back to the attacker's TCP-based session and shut down that application. UDP is not connection-oriented, so this is not something that can be reset—thus the need for ACLs on a blocking device such as a router or PIX Firewall.

FFS Limitations

CBAC enhances the effectiveness of IOS routers as security devices. Used in conjunction with other available security enhancements, IOS routers can be used for more than packet forwarding, thus increasing their ROI and allowing administrators to cost-effectively implement more secure networks. Of course, there is no perfect security device. That being said, there are some operational issues and limitations to CBAC of which administrators should be aware:

- Intrusion detection's performance impact depends on the configuration of the signatures, the level of traffic on the router, the router platform, and other individual features enabled on the router such as encryption, routing, and so on. Enabling or disabling individual signatures does not alter performance significantly; however, signatures that are configured to use ACLs have a significant performance impact because the more you ask the router to inspect a packet, the greater its effect on router performance.

- For auditing atomic signatures, there is no traffic-dependent memory requirement. For auditing compound signatures, CBAC allocates memory to maintain the state of each session for each connection since by definition compound signatures are going to multiple machines. Memory is also allocated for the configuration database and for internal caching.

- CBAC inspection is not performed on packets with the source or destination address of the firewall interfaces. This impacts the router's operation two different ways:

  — vty (that is, Telnet) sessions between administrators and the firewall are not inspected.

  — Management, authorization, and accounting (TACACS/RADIUS) traffic is not inspected because it too is destined to the router's interface.

- Encrypted packet payloads, such as those used in VPNs, are not inspected unless the router is the encrypted link endpoint.

In general, having the more advanced functions available does increase the security of your router and network. However, these functions do not address the best practices in making the router a secure device when you are not employing them. The following section discusses this aspect of securing a router because, given the cost and effort needed to maintain the FFS, you are likely only going to deploy it at the edge of your network; therefore, protecting the inside devices is covered next.

Secure IOS Template

So far, this chapter has covered the different ways of securing your router and using it as a supplement to a dedicated firewall. This section explores how to harden your router and some of the best practices available for making the router a more secure device on your network. For the sake of brevity, you will not see coverage of every single ACL and command that is possible to secure your router. There are a couple reasons for this choice:

- The physical constraints of this book do not allow it, so content must be prioritized. Some of the items that are left out are specific to certain businesses in networking (ISPs, for example); most networks easily use the remaining items.

- Certain parts of the recommendations such as TACACS and RADIUS are covered in previous chapters, so there is no need to cover them again here.

This section is not meant to teach you how to secure your router with brief explanations so that you can decide which commands are appropriate for your network. You can apply these commands and suggestions today!

The complete Secure IOS Template can be found online at the INRGI website:

http://www.inrgi.net/security/secure_ios_template.htm

This website has all the latest commands and suggestions because security is an ever-changing world!

tip

The Cisco SDM Security device manager is a mature, sound GUI tool that is now a shipping standard with the security/VPN routers. This GUI offers a robust setup and configuration of VPN and CBAC; it also does a router analysis and locks down the router, but it offers suggestions to the user about how to do it:

http://www.cisco.com/en/US/products/sw/secursw/ps5318/index.html

The configuration commands in Example 6-1 are in **bold** text so they stand out from the supporting comments, which are highlighted for readability. The secure template assumes the topology in Figure 6-5.

Figure 6-5   Figure 6-5Secure Template Topology

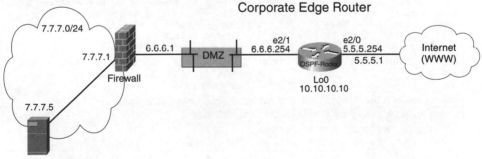

Example 6-1 Secure IOS Template

```
!
```
The Nagle congestion control algorithm is something that many companies turn on
to improve the performance of their Telnet session to and from the router. When
using a standard Telnet, which is based on TCP. TCP is implemented via TCP to
send keystrokes between machines; TCP tends to send one packet for each keystroke
typed. On larger networks, many small packets use up bandwidth and contribute
to congestion. John Nagle's algorithm (RFC 896) helps alleviate the small-packet
problem in TCP. In general, it works this way: The first character typed after
connection establishment is sent in a single packet, but TCP holds any additional
characters typed until the receiver acknowledges the previous packet. Then the
second, larger packet is sent and additional typed characters are saved until
the acknowledgment comes back. The effect is to accumulate characters into
larger chunks and pace them out to the network at a rate matching the round-trip
time of the given connection. Keepalives ensure that no TCP connections via the
router get hung.

```
!
service nagle
!
```
Enabling TCP keepalives on incoming connections ensures that any sessions left
hanging by remote system crashes or disconnections will not block or use up the
available router vty (Telnet) ports.

```
!
service tcp-keepalives-in
service tcp-keepalives-out
!
```
By default, log messages are not time stamped or marked in anyway that would
allow you to know when they occurred. You should activate time stampings in all
debug messages and log entries down to the millisecond to ensure that you can
determine the relevance of each message and ensure that your router's clock is
set properly—otherwise it will not be very effective! The following setting
will produce entries that are similar to the following:

```
Sep  4 23:58:11.437: %LINK-3-UPDOWN: Interface FastEthernet0/10, changed state
to up
```

The command line options in the timestamps command are as follows:
- debug: all debug information is time stamped
- log: all log info is time stamped
- datetime: the date and time is include in the syslog message
- localtime: the local time of the router is used in the log message
show-time zone: the time zone defined on the router is included (useful if the
network crosses multiple time zones and we suggest standardizing on single time
zone if this is the case)
- msec: time accuracy to milliseconds – useful if NTP is configured.

```
!
service timestamps debug datetime msec show-timezone localtime
service timestamps log datetime msec show-timezone localtime
!
```

Example 6-1   Secure IOS Template (continued)

By default, a syslog message contains the IP Address of the interface it uses
to leave the router. You can require all syslog messages to contain the same IP
Address, regardless of the interface they use. Many large enterprise networks
or ISPs use the loopback IP Address to more clearly identify the routers in their
network. This keeps their syslogs consistant and allows them to enhance the
security of their syslog server. You can also set this interface destination to
be any active interface on the router if you do not have a loopback interface
configured.

!

`logging source-interface loopback0`

!

The 'service password-encryption' command provides minimal security for user,
line, ppp, radius and assorted other passwords and keys that must be stored in
the IOS configuration file. The command causes passwords in the config file to
be encrypted with a reversible encryption that keeps people from finding your
passwords by glancing at your configurations. Note that this encryption does not
provide real protection; we recommend considering the use of the enable secret
password or TACACS/RADIUS controlled logins.

!

`service password-encryption`

!

By default, Cisco has enabled routers to now act as DHCP clients by default;
this is really not a necessary service to have running, so shut it off. Also,
given the issues with TCP and UDP small servers, make sure they are off! For
example, one of the small servers is "Chargen," which is a character generator
service that is used to generate a stream of characters for diagnostic purposes.
Then there is the "echo" service that merely echos back every character that is
sent to it. Pointing the "chargen" service at the "echo" service creates a loop
that causes an enormous amount of traffic to be generated and will eventually
overwhelm the router's CPU and RAM resources; thus, we have the makings of a
very serious denial of service attack (DoS). The easiest way to prevent this
kind of attack from happening is to disable these services on the router. The
commands to do so are "no tcp-small-servers"—disables echo, chargen, discard
and daytime; "no udp-small-servers"—disables echo, chargen and discard.

!

`no service udp-small-servers`
`no service tcp-small-servers`
`no service dhcp`
!

Not all services are bad; in fact, this new entry to the service category is
quite useful. Essentially, by enabling it, your syslog entries are numbered to
ensure that they are not tampered with to hide hacking from you! Cisco helps us
with our servers—aren't they nice?

!

`service sequence-numbers`

!

`hostname OSPF-Rocks`

!

Logging is a must in almost every case, so turn it on! Plus, with all the logging
we are doing in this configuration, it might be a good idea to rate limit the
log messages sent per second to not overwhelm your server because the entries
can climb rapidly when you are logging ACLs!

!

continues

Example 6-1   Secure IOS Template (continued)

```
logging 7.7.7.5
logging buffered 16384 debugging
logging rate-limit ?
!
```

When a message is sent to the console port of the router, this results in CPU interrupt occurring in order for the log message to be delivered to the console port and, considering the level of logging that is going on, disable console logging until needed. Console logging is very effective when troubleshooting; you are physically attached to the router, so keep this command ready.

```
!
no logging console
!
```

Almost all passwords and other authentication strings in Cisco IOS configuration files are encrypted using the weak, reversible scheme used for user passwords. To determine which scheme has been used to encrypt a specific password, check the digit preceding the encrypted string in the configuration file. If that digit is a 7, the password has been encrypted using the weak algorithm. If the digit is a 5, the password has been hashed using the stronger MD5 algorithm. Even though *enable secret* is used for the enable password, do not forget *service password-encryption* so that the remaining passwords are stored in the configuration with type 7 encryption rather than in plain text. Of course, the most secure password type is enable secret, so use it with some CAPITAL letters and some Num83r2; it makes brute force attacks harder. The encryption algorithm type 7 used in *enable password* and *service password-encryption* is reversible. The enable secret command provides better security by storing the enable secret password using a non-reversible cryptographic function. The added layer of security encryption it provides is useful in environments where the password crosses the network or is stored on a TFTP server.

```
!
enable secret <PASSWORD>
no enable password
!
```

Use TACACS+ for AAA login authentication. Ensure that the local account is case-sensitive, thus making brute-force attacks less effective.

```
!
aaa new-model
aaa authentication login default group tacacs+ local-case
aaa authentication enable default group tacacs+ enable
aaa authorization commands 15 default group tacacs+ local
aaa accounting exec default stop-only group tacacs+
aaa accounting commands 15 default stop-only group tacacs+
aaa accounting network default stop-only group tacacs+
tacacs-server host 7.7.7.5
tacacs-server key OSPF-r0ck2
!
```

In the event that TACACS+ fails, use case-sensitive local authentication or, if TACACS+/RADIUS is not available in your network, local AAA. The use of local authentication keeps attackers guessing, and the router more secure; remember, security is all about layers of defense.

```
!
username <USERNAME> password <PASSWORD>
!
```

Example 6-1 Secure IOS Template (continued)

```
Do I really need to explain why you should not use the built-in web server?
Sometimes Cisco takes the web too far—it is a router, Jim!
!
no ip http server
!
Allows us to use the low subnets and go classless, which are areas that have not
typically been used.
!
ip subnet-zero
ip classless
!
Why these services are still on by default and in IOS is anyone's guess; however,
for your sanity and the security of your network, turn them off. As Cisco's IOS
has evolved, some of these services have become turned off by default; however,
it is always considered best practice to ensure that they are turned off.
!
no service pad
no ip source-route
no service finger
no ip bootp server
no ip domain-lookup
!
TCP intercept helps prevent SYN-flooding attacks by intercepting and validating
TCP connection requests. In intercept mode, the TCP intercept software
intercepts TCP synchronization (SYN) packets from clients to servers that match
an extended access list. The router responds, and they are allowed to communicate
if it is a valid connection.
!
ip tcp intercept list 120
!
IOS watches and manages a TCP connection for 24 hours after no activity. Why?
Who knows? Regardless, it should be changed.
!
ip tcp intercept connection-timeout 60
!
Keep half-open sockets open only 10 seconds instead of the default 30 seconds.
all the while waiting for a response.
!
ip tcp intercept watch-timeout 10
!
These commands determine when TCP intercept should deactivate or activate; in
this case, 1500 and 6000, respectively—the defaults are not very realistic at
900 and 1100.
!
ip tcp intercept one-minute low 1500
ip tcp intercept one-minute high 6000
!
```

continues

Example 6-1   Secure IOS Template (continued)

Cisco Systems has added a *core dump* facility to its IOS. This core dump facility operates like many other similar systems. When a router crashes, a copy of the core memory is kept. Before the memory is erased on reboot, the Cisco router can be set up to copy the core dump out to a server. An account (FTP, TFTP, or RCP) and sufficient disk space (equal to the amount of memory on the router per dump) must be set up and allocated. Catch core dumps in case of a router crash; this is very important with a "security router" because a denial-of-service (DOS) attack might have been successful and crashed your router, so it is good to know what happened. We have configured our Network Management server inside our firewall to accept FTP connections from the router. Make sure that you give the core dump files a unique name, as shown in the following lines. It is recommended that access to the "Cisco core dump" account be made as secure as possible. For example, do not send core dumps to the same FTP server as the one used to provide generic anonymous or user FTP accounts.

```
!
ip ftp username <FTP SERVER USERNAME>
ip ftp password <PASSWORD>
exception core-file <UNIQUE FILE NAME>
exception protocol ftp
exception dump 7.7.7.5
!
```

TFTP is the most common tool for uploading and downloading IOS upgrades or configurations. The TFTP server's security is critical. That means using security tools that only allow a TFPT connection to be successful based on the source IP address. Cisco's IOS allows TFTP to be configured to use a specific IP interfaces address. This allows a fixed ACL on the TFTP server based on a fixed address on the router. This fixed IP Address is commonly the loopback interface if it is configured as these interfaces are frequently used in managing a router. However, if you are using loopback interfaces in your network, the interface closest to the TFTP server should be used; the command is shown below. FTP is also included because it was previously configured in this template.

```
!
ip tftp source-interface <SOURCE INTERFACE>
ip ftp source-interface <SOURCE INTERFACE>
!
```

CEF is an advanced, Layer 3 switching technology inside a router. It defines the fastest method by which a Cisco router forwards packets from ingress to egress interfaces. The ip cef command enables CEF globally, not all router support CEF so check your docs.

```
!
ip cef
!
```

Set the time zone properly. It is best to standardize on one time zone for all routers and servers, thus making problem tracking easier.

```
!
clock timezone GMT 0
!
```

Example 6-1   Secure IOS Template (continued)

NTP is *the* most overlooked feature on many networks. The Network Time Protocol
(NTP) is a protocol designed to time-synchronize a network of machines. It
provides a precise time base for networked workstation, servers, and other
devices on the network. NTP runs over UDP, which in turn runs over IP. An NTP
network usually gets its time from an authoritative time source, such as a radio
clock or an atomic clock attached to a timeserver. NTP then distributes this
time across the network. NTP is extremely efficient; no more than one packet per
minute is necessary to synchronize two machines to within a millisecond of one
another. Many system administrators configure time synchronization for servers
but do not continue that first step to include network devices. If you wish to
compare the syslog information from devices all over your network, you must
synchronize the time on all of them. Comparing logs from various network devices
is essential for many types of troubleshooting, fault analysis, and security
incident tracking. Without precise time synchronization between all the various
logging, management, AAA and security functions, this sort of comparison would
be impossible. When activating NTP, synchronize the router's clock with a local
(trusted and authenticated) NTP server. The SECRETKEY must be the same on both
the router and the NTP server. Note that NTP is slow to get synchronized properly
in the beginning; it is a Cisco thing, so be patient!

```
!
ntp authentication-key 6767 md5 <SECRETKEY>
ntp authenticate
ntp update-calendar
ntp server 7.7.7.5
!
```

Configure the loopback0 interface as the source of our log messages. This is
often used for routing protocols also because a logical interface does not go
down; thus, it is very reliable. Assign an IP address that uniquely identifies
this router. One trick is to allocate a netblock for use as the router loopback
netblock.

```
!
int loopback0
 ip address 10.10.10.10 255.255.255.255
 no ip redirects
 no ip unreachables
 no ip proxy-arp
 !
```

Configure and thus activate the null0 interface as a place to send naughty
packets. This becomes the "roach motel" for packets—they can route in, but they
cannot route out.

```
!
interface null0
 no ip unreachables
 !
interface Ethernet2/0
 description Unprotected interface, facing towards Internet
 ip address 5.5.5.254 255.255.255.0
 !
```

continues

Example 6-1   Secure IOS Template (continued)

Do we run CEF verify? Yes, if the data path is symmetric, but no if the data
path is asymmetric. Use the ip verify unicast reverse-path interface command on
the input interface on the router at the upstream end of the connection. This
feature examines each packet received as input on that interface. If the source
IP address does not have a route in the CEF tables that points back to the same
interface on which the packet arrived, the router drops the packet.
!
```
 ip verify unicast reverse-path
```
!
Apply our template ACL, more on what this ACL is covering later in the
configuration, but applying it is crucial to its success.
!
```
 ip access-group 2010 in
```
!
Rate limiting traffic to protect the router and by default your infrastructure
is extremely important. The values might be tweaked to meet your needs but, in
general, we recommend the following. Allow UDP to use no more than 2 Mb/s of the
pipe; caution, however, if you are running video on demand as it uses UDP
packets.
!
```
 rate-limit input access-group 150 2010000 250000 250000 conform-action transmit
exceed-action drop
```
!
Allow ICMP to use no more than 200 Kb/s of the pipe.
!
```
 rate-limit input access-group 160 500000 62500 62500 conform-action transmit
exceed-action drop
```
!
Allow multicast to use no more than 5 Mb/s of the pipe.
!
```
 rate-limit input access-group 170 5000000 375000 375000 conform-action transmit
exceed-action drop
```
!
Disables the sending of ICMP redirect messages to learn routes; let the hackers
wonder!
!
```
 no ip redirects
```
!
Disables the sending of ICMP protocol unreachable and host unreachable messages
and, once again there is no reason to allow ICMP to educate hackers about your
network.
!
```
 no ip unreachables
```
!
Dropping IP directed broadcasts makes routers less susceptible to a denial-of-
service attack. The configuration command "no ip directed-broadcast" means that
the translation of directed broadcast to physical broadcasts is disabled. If
enabled, a broadcast to a particular network could be directed at a router
interface, producing effects that might be undesirable and potentially harmful.
An example of the ill effects of directed broadcasts being enabled is the so-
called SMURF attack.

Example 6-1   Secure IOS Template (continued)

```
!
 no ip directed-broadcast
!
```

Cisco IOS Software examines IP header options on every packet. It supports the
IP header options Strict Source Route, Loose Source Route, Record Route, and
time stamp, which are defined in RFC 791. If the software finds a packet with
one of these options enabled, it performs the appropriate action. If it finds a
packet with an invalid option, it sends an ICMP Parameter Problem message to the
source of the packet and discards the packet. The IP protocol provides a
provision that allows the source IP host to specify a route through the IP
network. This provision is known as source routing, which is specified as an
option in the IP header. If source routing is specified, Cisco IOS forwards the
packet according to the specified source route in the IP header. This feature
is employed when you want to force a packet to take a certain route through the
network. The default is to perform source routing. As a general rule of thumb,
if you are not using IP source routing, turn it off. IP source routing is a well-
known security vulnerability used in attacks against a system or to bypass
firewalls.

```
!
 no ip source-route
!
```

The configuration "no ip proxy-arp" means that the router does not respond to
ARP requests for other hosts on the network connected to this interface if it
knows the MAC address of those hosts. Again, this is to prevent undesirable
effects on the connected network and potential security problems. In other
words, do not have the router pretend to be something its not.

```
!
 no ip proxy-arp
!
```

Disables the sending of ICMP mask reply messages. The default for Cisco routers
is not to do this, but it never hurts to input the command anyway just to be sure.

```
!
 no ip mask-reply
!
```

Enables IP accounting with the ability to identify IP traffic that fails IP
access lists, thereby allowing your router to log all naughty business. Be sure
to check it.

```
!
 ip accounting access-violations
!
```

If you allow multicast in your network or participate in the MBONE, the following
multicast filtering steps help to ensure a secure multicast environment. These
must be applied per interface.

```
!
 ip multicast boundary 30
!
```

Keep flow data for analysis. If possible, export it to a cflowd server.

```
!
 ip route-cache flow
!
interface Ethernet2/1
 description Protected interface, facing towards DMZ
```

continues

Example 6-1 Secure IOS Template (continued)

```
 ip address 6.6.6.254 255.255.255.0
!
```

Do we run CEF verify? Yes ,if the data path is symmetric. No, if the data path is asymmetric. See above interface description for more information on this command.

```
!
 ip verify unicast reverse-path
!
```

If we are using Reverse Path Forwarding, comment out the ACL below.

```
!
 ip access-group 115 in
!
```

The following commands have been described previously; for additional information, refer to earlier in the configuration file.

```
!
 no ip redirects
 no ip unreachables
 no ip directed-broadcast
 no ip proxy-arp
 ip accounting access-violations
 ip multicast boundary 30
 no ip mask-reply
 ip route-cache flow
!
```

Source routing allows the path to be specified in a packet. This could allow the packet to bypass firewalls, and so on. Disable this feature!

```
!
 no ip source-route
!
```

This is a default route to the Internet (could be a routing protocol instead).

```
!
ip route 0.0.0.0 0.0.0.0 5.5.5.1
!
```

Route to network on the other side of the firewall.

```
!
ip route 7.7.7.0 255.255.255.0 6.6.6.1
!
```

The following static routes will black hole networks that are not supposed to be routable on the public Internet. Be *very* careful about enabling these when running TCP Intercept. The TCP Intercept command directs the router to act as a TCP socket proxy. When the router receives the SYN packet, the router (instead of the destination) initially responds with the SYN¦ACK. This is where the interaction between TCP Intercept and black hole routes causes a problem. If you create black hole routes for all bogon ranges and point them to the null device, and if someone launches a SYN flood from a bogon range, the router sends the SYN¦ACK to the null device. The router is not (yet) intelligent enough to realize that it has done this, and the TCP Intercept queue begins to build quickly. By default, the timeouts are not aggressive enough to work through this problem.

```
!
```

Example 6-1   Secure IOS Template (continued)

```
<<<Output Omitted for Brevity go to: http://www.inrgi.net/security/
secure_ios_template.htm >>>
!
```
Export our NetFlow data to our NetFlow server, 7.7.7.5. NetFlow provides some statistics that can be useful when tracing back to the true source of a spoofed attack. We also use the source as the loopback interface, which is a best practice.
```
!
ip flow-export source loopback0
ip flow-export destination 7.7.7.5 2055
ip flow-export version 5 origin-as
!
```
Log anything interesting to the syslog server. Capture all of the logging output sent from the loopback interface; this makes ID of this router in the various places recording data easy and uniform to identify.
```
!
logging trap debugging
logging source-interface loopback0
logging 7.7.7.5
!
<<<Output Omitted for Brevity go to: http://www.inrgi.net/security/
secure_ios_template.htm >>>
!
```
Do not share Cisco Discovery Protocol (CDP) information from your secure router because CDP contains crucial bits of information about your network topology, device configuration, network devices that are in use, IP addresses, and so on. This command disabled CDP globally. If you require CDP on an interface, use cdp run and disable cdp (not cdp enable) on the Internet-facing interface. In other words, use CDP *only* on interfaces where it is needed—*never globally*. Note that Cisco ships all devices with CDP enabled by default starting with IOS 11.1CA.
```
!
no cdp run!
```
SNMP is *very* important for network management, particularly in conjunction with MRTG to track usage statistics. To keep SNMP access even more secure, treat the COMMUNITY string as a password; keep it difficult to guess by using a combination of CAPS, lowercase, and numbers. Ultimately a SNMP community string *is* the password for SNMP Services so the string should follow your corporate password policy. This is important because the community string is *not encrypted*. Then, further protect access by including an access control list (ACL) that determines what network/hosts can access SNMP, *only* if they have the proper community string. Now that is a real layered security approach!

If SNMP is going to be used in read/write mode, think very carefully about the configuration and why there is a requirement to do this because configuration errors in this scenario could leave the router very vulnerable. I have developed and seen tools that, through the use of SNMP Read/Write, can automatically reset password and alter configurations. If possible, put an ACL at the edge of your network to prevent potential attackers from probing your network via SNMP. There are many publicly and commercially available tools that will scan *any* network on the Internet via SNMP. This could map out your entire network and/or discover a device that has had SNMP left open. When performing security audits and vulnerability assessments, I have done an SNMP Walk on devices and learned a great deal about a person's network.

continues

Example 6-1 Secure IOS Template (continued)

```
!
snmp-server community <COMMUNITY> RO 20
snmp-server location Raleigh, NC (in the country)
snmp-server contact INGRI: Tom Thomas [tothomas@netcerts.com]
snmp-server host 192.168.254.70 <COMMUNITY>
!
```

In the configuration, this ACL would appear at a different location; however, for completeness, I have moved it here for easy reference. Access list 20 permits SNMP access to this device if the requests come from the server (IP Address: 7.7.7.5) and by default if access is not permitted and is then denied when using Cisco ACLs. Notice that I entered the normally invisible *deny any* command because I have added the *log* keyword at the end. The inclusion of this keyword has the router log denied all SNMP query attempts to our syslog server.

```
!
access-list 20 remark ACL TO CONTROL SNMP ACCESS
access-list 20 permit 7.7.7.5
access-list 20 deny any log
!
```

Introduce yourself with an appropriately stern banner that reflects the level of security and monitoring applied to your network. It is also important to set everyone's expectations accessing the router and what happens if attacks are made against it. Although we are just showing the Message of the Day (MOTD) Banner, you should apply the same banner to the console port, aux port, AAA Login, and whenever a user accesses EXEC mode.

```
!
banner motd %
```

Warning!!! This system is solely for the use of authorized users and only for official purposes. Users must have express written permission to access this system. You have no expectation of privacy in its use and to ensure that the system is functioning properly, individuals using this system are subject to having their activities monitored and recorded at all times. Use of this system evidences an express consent to such monitoring and agreement that if such monitoring reveals evidence of possible abuse or criminal activity the results of such monitoring will be supplied to the appropriate officials to be prosecuted to the fullest extent of both civil and criminal law.

Unauthorized Access to this system is a violation of Federal Electronic Communications Privacy Act of 1986, and may result in fines of $250,000 and/or imprisonment (Title 18, USC). All IP traffic is logged and violators will be prosecuted.

```
%
!
```

Another type of banner available is the "exec" banner, which is displayed at the time a user has successfully authenticated and logged in when they enter exec mode on the router. Exec mode is analogous to super user (UNIX) or administrator (windows).

```
!
banner exec ^
```

Please note that this device is part of a production network and all configuration changes need to be approved in advance. All changes should be recorded and the configuration backed up.

```
^
```

Example 6-1   Secure IOS Template (continued)

```
!
```

Apply a password to the console port of a router. Requiring a password on the physical console port provides another layer of security by requiring anyone plugging into the device to supply a password. Including the transport input disables reverse Telnet and protects the physical ports against access.

The connection timeout value for Console and AUX ports on a router is 10 minutes. This timeout is controlled by the exec-timeout command, as shown in the configuration below. vty (Telnet) sessions do not have an associated timeout value. Leaving the vty timeout unchanged is generally regarded as bad practice because it will hog the few available ports on the router and could cause maintenance access problems in the time of emergencies. Notice that setting the idle timeout to 0 means that the session is left connected indefinitely.

```
!
line con 0
 exec-timeout 15 0
 transport input none
line aux 0
 exec-timeout 15 0
 transport input none
!
```

Apply an access control list (ACL) to the vty (Telnet) ports that define which systems by source IP Address can attempt to access this router via Telnet. Most IOS versions only support five vty ports; this means that when you look in the configuration and see "line vtty 0 4," there can be a maximum of five Telnet connections if you count 0 as a line (0, 1, 2, 3, 4). In the following example, we are configuring a group of vty lines (0-3) to all have the same operating parameters.

```
!
line vty 0 3
 access-class 100 in
 exec-timeout 15 0
 transport input telnet ssh
!
```

The definition of this access list is important to understand and would normally appear much earlier in the configuration; however, for ease of understanding, I have moved it to the relevant section. access control list 100 will deny everyone access to the router and permit connection attempts from the Network Management server (7.7.7.5) or the firewall (6.6.6.1); only if SSH (port 22) or Telnet (port 23) is used, we log every successful access and this allows us to monitor who is connecting, when, and how. Of course, we also log any denied access attempts to learn the same information. This also serves to create an audit trail of all access to the router through the use of a extended ACLs to log some additional data.

```
!
access-list 100 remark DEFINE TELNET ACCESS TO THE ROUTER
access-list 100 permit tcp host 7.7.7.5 host 0.0.0.0 range 22 23 log-input
access-list 100 permit tcp host 6.6.6.1 host 0.0.0.0 range 22 23 log-input
access-list 100 deny ip any any log-input
!
```

continues

Example 6-1 Secure IOS Template (continued)

```
Whenever possible, enable SSH connectivity because SSH is much more secure than
Telnet. Obviously, you must have an IOS image that supports SSH, and do not
forget to generate the key with crypto key generate RSA command.
!
Leave one vty safe (line #4) for emergency access, just in case. The host 7.7.7.8
is a secure host in the NOC. If all the vtys are occupied, this leaves one VTY
available and logging is also happening.
!
line vty 4
 access-class 105 in
 exec-timeout 15 0
 transport input telnet ssh
! NOTE: You can also use AAA during the login process as well.
!
access-list 105 remark VTY Access ACL
access-list 105 permit tcp host 7.7.7.8 host 0.0.0.0 range 22 23 log-input
access-list 105 deny ip any log-input
!
```

Chapter Summary

This chapter discussed ways and places in which a router can be used with a deeper purpose than it might have been implemented with. To this end, the chapter examined how a router can be used to prescreen your network as a *choke point* of entry. The next level was to have the router act as a more advanced packet inspection tool through the use of the Cisco IOS Firewall Feature Set and coupled with the Intrusion Detection feature. Both of these advanced technologies are not a replacement for dedicated devices of the same kind; however, they do offer a higher level of security in your network by adding additional layers of inspection and protection.

Next, the chapter focused on some of the more fundamental methods you can use immediately to secure the router itself. This information was presented in a real router configuration file, thus giving you a point of reference when comparing your router configurations with the suggestions provided here. The following chapter examines the steps you can take to use VPNs to increase network security.

Additional resources on security can be found online at

Increasing Security on IP Networks—An old, but essential document on some of the essentials to security and IP based networks: http://www.cisco.com/univercd/cc/td/doc/cisintwk/ics/cs003.htm

The Cisco INTERNET SECURITY ADVISORIES—An online list at the Cisco website of all its security advisories, including tutorials and details about how to protect yourself from some of the worst vulnerabilities on the Internet today (Cisco.com account required) at http://www.cisco.com/warp/customer/707/advisory.html.

Chapter Review Questions

1. Because every company that connects to the Internet has a router, should you deploy security on those routers?

2. What is the value of edge routers being used as choke points, and how effective can they be in increasing your network's security?

3. What technology is at the heart of the Cisco Firewall Feature Set IOS?

4. How does the firewall feature set employ dynamic filtering of packets using ACLs?

5. Can the Cisco IOS IDS have multiple points of packet inspection?

6. Temporary access control lists have timers associated with them. Define how they function based on protocol (ICMP, UDP, and TCP)?

7. What is the difference between atomic and compound signatures?

8. What happens when an attacker uses chargen and echo together? How would you stop this from occurring in a Cisco router?

What You Will Learn

By the end of this chapter, you should know and be able to explain the following:

- ✔ The difference between the different types of VPNs

- ✔ The benefits and goals of VPN technology and how should it be deployed

- ✔ Where the encryption modes are and the functions they play in VPNs

- ✔ The protocols being used during the operation of an IPSec VPN

Being able to answer these key questions will allow you to understand the overall characteristics and importance of network security. By the time you finish this book, you will have a solid appreciation for network security, its issues, how it works, and why it is important.

CHAPTER 7

IPSec Virtual Private Networks (VPNs)

Change is life giving, it helps us grow into someone greater than we already are.—Successories

As connectivity grows and personal mobility increases, the need for networks to adapt and provide services also continues to increase. Users do not understand the security concerns for the remote services that they demand for productively, regardless of location. Users that are traveling to other countries, in airports, customer sites, and so on are demanding the ability to connect to corporate resources to fulfill their jobs. With the increased levels of connectivity from T1s and wireless in airports, to Wi-Fi hot spots, and customers with high-speed connections, those people who are responsible for maintaining networks are faced with some difficult decisions. How should they provide the required IT services to users, regardless of their location, in a secure and reasonable manner?

Technology has evolved and the leading solution for these demands is Internet Protocol Security Protocol (IPSec) encrypted *virtual private networks (VPNs)*. Occasionally, a technology's name accurately reflects its function, and this is the case with VPNs.

note

The National Institute of Standards and Technology (NIST) has created AES, which is a new Federal Information Processing Standard (FIPS) publication that describes an encryption method. AES is a privacy transform for IPSec and Internet Key Exchange (IKE) and has been developed to replace the Data Encryption Standard (DES). AES is designed to be more secure than DES:

http://www.cisco.com/en/US/products/sw/iosswrel/ps1839/
products_feature_guide09186a0080110bb6.html

NIST was awaiting final acceptance of AES; in late 2003, the U.S. Department of Defense finally approved AES for use. You will probably see more AES in use with this announcement.

This chapter discusses the use of VPNs, how they function, the encryption provided by IPSec, and how these technologies can ensure that your network's security is maintained while increasing available services to your customers. Everyone has customers to whom they provide some degree of service, regardless of the field. However, in the case of VPNs, *customers* can be defined as anyone with the business need to connect securely to the corporate network to access resources. Customers can be mobile users (sales, system engineers), power users going online all the time, executives conducting your company's affairs, or business partners picking up or dropping off important information. *Resources* are defined here as any device that is not directly accessible from the Internet; these resources might include e-mail servers, file servers, Citrix servers, or network devices.

Arguably the hottest topic in data security today, virtual private networks (VPNs) are full of promise for businesses seeking to lower cost, increase flexibility and scalability, and ensure the security of their communications.

note

In May 2002, the technology industry research firm Gartner Dataquest reported that "the expansion of proven IP VPN implementations are expected to drive the worldwide IP VPN equipment market to $4.7 billion by 2006," up from just under $3 billion in 2002 and just over $2 billion in 2001. Growth of this magnitude—45.7 percent from 2001 to 2002— speaks to some of the strengths of VPNs in today's marketplace.

But what exactly does a VPN do, and how can it impact your business drivers—
lowering cost, mitigating risk, and increasing revenue? The popularity of VPN
technology is directly related to its potential to bring about significant return on
investment (ROI). For businesses paying the often staggering costs of private connections via leased lines or Frame Relay, the costs savings associated with deploying VPNs to replace these costly connections is significant. To understand the
value of a VPN to your business, you might want to consider the technologies that
VPNs most often replace:

- Site-to-site VPNs can take the place of expensive wide-area network (WAN)
  telco circuits by replacing private line services with VPNs that use the Internet instead.

- Remote access VPNs can eliminate or dramatically reduce long-distance
  dialup charges for connecting a remote sales force or small offices.

If your organization is making significant recurring investments in either WAN
telco circuits or long-distance remote access dialup charges, a VPN can provide
an alternative approach with a big payoff in cost savings and flexibility.

Before entering into a technical overview of the components and possibilities
involved in deploying a VPN, it is important to firmly understand the gist of the
VPN concept. Analogies work well because they introduce people with vastly different levels of knowledge and experience to a complex subject.

Analogy: VPNs Connect IsLANds Securely

Your network (LAN) is an island of sanity, order, and user services in an unpre-
dictable ocean known as the Internet. You know thousands of other islands exist
within this ocean; when you want to travel from island to island, you would hop
on a ferry and check out that website you had your eye on.

Now, you are on this ferry (TCP/IP) traveling over the ocean (Internet) to reach
something on an island (LAN) that is going to provide you with some sort of service (website). This makes perfect sense, right? Now, how many other people do

you see on that ferry—perhaps a few, or perhaps many thousands? The potential problem is that you have no security or privacy traveling from island to island; other people can see everything you see. Now, if you were reading the latest news on http://www.foxnews.com, who cares if you do not have privacy? However, if you were going to your company's island to check on something, this lack of privacy can have serious ramifications.

Because you are traveling on the worldwide ocean that is the Internet, you have no control over the wires, fiber, routers, or switches that make up the Internet. Nor do you get any guarantees of any sort. In other words, you might be able to reach some website or other server, but there are no guarantees. Remember, connecting to the Internet is a privilege and not a right! Having no control of the Internet means that you are susceptible to security issues, and this becomes especially true if you want to connect two private networks using a public resource such as the Internet.

note

When conducting a network assessment of a customer's network, I observed that the company had no firewalls at any of its four sites, which were all connected to the Internet. This is a serious concern, but what struck me as a real issue is that this customer had configured Microsoft servers at each of the locations to trust one another over the public Internet! All a hacker would have had to do was hijack that trust, and the network would be totally compromised; in fact, it had occurred several times. I had to shake my head in disbelief—do not let this happen to you! Use VPNs!

As the person in charge of connecting your island to another, you are directed to connect your island with a new one that was just purchased. Your island decides to build a bridge to this other island so there is an easier, more secure, and direct way for people to travel between the two. It is expensive to build and maintain this bridge, even though the island you are connecting with is close. But the need for a reliable, secure path is so great that you do it anyway.

This situation is a lot like having a private wide-area network (WAN). The bridges (private lines) are separate from the ocean (Internet), yet they can connect the islands (LANs). Many companies have chosen this route because the need for security and reliability drives the connection from their remote offices to their main office.

Your island would like to connect to a second island that is much farther away, but you decide that the cost to build a bridge are simply to high to justify. You quickly learned that, if the offices are far apart, the cost could be prohibitively high, just like trying to build a bridge that spans a great distance. However, the need is still there.

note

Many businesses have a tendency to allow IT to drive the evolution of their business, and while this is appropriate for some, most businesses must reverse this thinking. The needs of the business should drive the evolution of a company's IT infrastructure. To me, this is a fundamental truth because businesses are not in business to build a big IT department or network! Nerds, take note. The 90s are over, and reality has unfortunately returned in the form of the proven business model.

Are you wondering when VPNs are going to fit into this analogy? You have established that you need increased security, and the first option was to build a bridge; however, that is too expensive. You could give everyone who needs the ability to travel between islands privately and securely a submarine. A submarine is a perfect analogy for a VPN because, like a submarine, VPNs have the following amazing properties:

- They can be very fast.

- They are easy to take with you.

- They can hide you from others.

- Additional cost is minimal after they are first deployed.

- They protect you when you are traveling.

- VPN-aware PDAs are the latest entry into the VPN market.

- The Cisco VoIP SoftPhone application also works well over a VPN, turning your PC into a secure telephone.

It might not be easy to take a submarine with you; however, I am sure you understand this analogy. There are several different ways to implement VPNs, and the following sections examine the three types of VPNs. Another good analogy would be the concept of the Stargate portals. You must get the symbols right on both sides (the SA for VPN), and you must have a Stargate on the other side that is "on" for the hyperspace tunnel to form (the VPN tunnel)....

VPN Overview

A virtual private network (VPN) is an encrypted network connection that uses a secure tunnel between endpoints via the Internet or other network, such as a WAN. In a VPN, dialup connections to remote users and leased-line or Frame Relay connections to remote sites are replaced by local connections to an Internet service provider (ISP) or other service provider's point of presence (POP). The increasing prevalence of Internet broadband connections to small remote offices and homes makes the use of cheaper access to the Internet attractive. As discussed, after the initial investment in VPNs, the cost to add more sites or users is minimal.

VPNs allow each remote user of your network to communicate in a secure and reliable manner using the Internet as the medium to connect to your private LAN. A VPN can grow to accommodate more users and different locations much easier than a leased line. In fact, scalability is a major advantage that VPNs have over typical leased lines. Unlike leased lines, where the cost increases in proportion to the distances involved, the geographic locations of each office matter little in the creation of a VPN.

caution

It is possible to have unencrypted VPNs that rely on some other type of encryption or routing for security—for example, MPLS VPNs. Only under very specific circumstances are these VPNs the appropriate solution for a network. Best practice dictates that you always encrypt your traffic over a VPN; failure to do so could be disastrous, and the responsibility will rest squarely on your shoulders.

A VPN allows a private intranet to be securely extended through IPSec encryption across the Internet or other network service, facilitating secure e-commerce and extranet connections with mobile employees, business partners, suppliers and customers. There are three main types of VPNs:

■ *Remote Access VPNs*—Allows individual dialup users to securely connect to a central site across the Internet or other public network service. This type of VPN is a user-to-LAN connection that allows employees who need to connect to the corporate LAN from the field. Their systems use special VPN client software that enables a secure link between themselves and the corporate LAN. Typically, a corporation that wants to set up a large remote access VPN provides some form of Internet dialup account to their users using an ISP. The telecommuters can then dial a toll-free number to reach the Internet and use their VPN client software to access the corporate network. A good example of a company that needs a remote access VPN would be a large firm with hundreds of salespeople in the field. Remote access VPNs are sometimes referred to as soft (as in software-based) VPNs, virtual private dialup networks (VPDN), or dial VPNs. Users pay a low "fixed cost" to a local ISP using a local call and therefore they incur no long-distance fees and do *not* have to establish a long-distance call directly to the corporate office. The user can then use the local ISP connection to establish a VPN tunnel over the Internet. CFOs prefer small, fixed costs to increasing long-distance costs.

■ *Site-to-site VPNs*—Used to extend a company's existing LAN to other buildings and sites through the use of dedicated equipment, so that remote employees at these locations can utilize the same network services. These types of VPNs are considered actively connected at all times. Site-to-site VPNs are sometimes referred to as hard (as in hardware-based) VPNs, intranet, or LAN-to-LAN VPNs.

- *Extranet VPNs*—Allows secure connections with business partners, suppliers, and customers for the purpose of e-commerce. Extranet VPNs are an extension of intranet VPNs with the addition of firewalls to protect the internal network. A good example would be companies that work closely with suppliers and partners to achieve common goals such as supply and demand relationships—for example, when one company has a demand for supplies and the supplier fulfills the demand based upon the company's needs. Working across an extranet, these two companies can share information more quickly.

All these VPNs aim to provide the reliability, performance, quality of service, and security of traditional WAN environments using lower cost and more flexible ISP or other service-provider connections. Figure 7-1 illustrates the three types of VPNs.

Figure 7-1   Types of VPNs

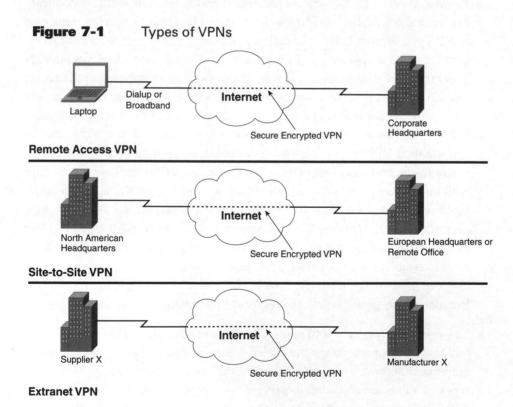

In Figure 7-1, all the VPNs are utilizing the Internet. VPN technology can also be used within your network to provide an additional layer of security to control access to sensitive information, systems, or resources. For example, VPN technology can be used to limit access to financial systems to certain users or to ensure that sensitive or confidential information is sent in a secure way. In this scenario, VPNs can encrypt and further secure traffic to sensitive systems. The following section discusses the placement of VPNs and the specific associated benefits.

VPN Benefits and Goals

A well-designed VPN can greatly benefit any company. Some of the benefits of implementing a VPN in your network include the following:

- Before the advent of VPN technologies, employees in remote locations would have to dial long-distance telephone numbers to reach their company's network. You want to reduce telecom costs as dedicated and long-distance dialup connections are replaced with local connections to the Internet through which users use a VPN client. Depending on the number of employees in the field, this alone can be a huge cost savings. For many smaller companies with limited financial breathing room, VPN solution providers can be a practical solution.

- You want to increase the productivity of your users by enabling them to securely access network resources regardless of their geographic location.

- You want to reduce the operational costs associated with dedicated WAN connections by replacing them with direct Internet connections such as business class broadband, through which remote sites will connect via a site-to-site VPN.

- You want to simplify your network's topology by adding VPNs strategically throughout your network.

- Your bandwidth needs are modest as sites need connectivity into your network. By using VPNs, you will gain a faster return on investment (ROI) than a traditional WAN solution.

- You want greater flexibility in deploying mobile computing, telecommuting, and branch office networking, easier e-commerce and extranet connections with business partners, suppliers and customers' external Internet access, and internal intranet and extranet access can be provided using a single secure connection.

- You want to reduce office costs by having users work from home three days a week. Home users typically have higher production and less stress.

Before implementing a VPN, you should spend a considerable amount of time contemplating what you want to accomplish with your VPN. During this exercise, before choosing a solution provider or hardware and software, you should consider which features are most important. Security, which is mentioned later, is one of the most important features of your VPN.

VPN Implementation Strategies

VPN implementation strategies are extremely varied because every vendor these days has a "VPN solution" for you! Some of the solutions are what they claim to be, and others have raised concerns among the security community, as discussed in Chapter 6, "Router Security." Because there is no widely accepted standard for implementing a VPN, many companies have developed turnkey solutions on their own. This section looks at some of the different potential components that are available from Cisco, and how single function devices such as firewalls can be used to fulfill a VPN role:

- **Firewalls**—If you did not have a firewall in place before reading Chapter 5, "Firewalls," you probably do now. Firewalls are crucial to the security of your network. Today, all Cisco firewalls support the combining of VPNs with stateful packet inspection (SPI). Solutions range from standards-based site-to-site VPNs leveraging the Internet Key Exchange (IKE) and IP security (IPSec) VPN standards. Cisco PIX firewalls encrypt data using 56-bit Data Encryption Standard (DES), 168-bit Triple DES (3DES), or up to 256-bit Advanced Encryption Standard (AES) encryption. An amazing piece of technology, the Cisco PIX Firewall combines dynamic Network Address Translation, proxy server packet filtration, firewall and VPN termination capabilities into a single piece of hardware. Instead of using Cisco IOS Software, this device has a highly streamlined OS that trades the capability to handle a variety of protocols for extreme robustness and performance by focusing on IP.

■ **VPN-capable routers**—Cisco routers can be upgraded to have the ability to use VPNs. These upgrades come in some form of the following, depending on the router model in question: IOS, memory, or dedicated VPN hardware. You can gain some unique features with the provision of scalability, routing, security, and quality of service (QoS). Based on Cisco IOS Software, there is a router suitable for every situation, from small office/home office (SOHO) access through central-site VPN aggregation, to large-scale enterprise needs.

■ **VPN Concentrator**—Incorporating the most advanced encryption and authentication techniques available, Cisco VPN Concentrators are built specifically for creating remote access user VPNs, which provide high availability, high performance, and scalability, and include components called scalable encryption processing (SEP) modules, which enable network engineers to easily increase capacity and throughput. VPN Concentrators are built to handle the requirements of VPNs and are available in models suitable for everything from small businesses with up to 100 remote-access users, to large organizations with up to 10,000 simultaneous remote users.

■ **Client Software**—Simple to deploy and operate, the Cisco VPN Client establishes secure, end-to-end encrypted tunnels to the VPN devices listed here. This thin design, IPSec-compliant software can be preconfigured for mass deployments, and the initial logons require little user intervention. The client software is available for the following operating systems: Windows 95, 98, Me, NT 4.0, 2000, XP, Linux (Intel), Solaris (UltraSparc-32bit), and MAC OS X 10.x.

Depending on the type of VPN (remote access or site-to-site), you must use specific hardware components to build your VPN. However, you should also consider the following:

■ **Manageability**—Manageability of a VPN concerns the amount of effort needed to successfully maintain the established network connectivity. Specifically, *PC Magazine* rates manageability by the "ease-of-use factors for

remote and local management options, including whether the device provides a browser-based interface or command line access" (*PC Magazine*, 2002).

- **Reliability**—Obviously, if the VPN software or hardware is unavailable when you need it, you are losing productivity and probably money. When choosing a solution, you should request "up-time" statistics for comparison.

- **Scalability**—As a company's business grows, oftentimes, so does its IT requirements. To grow your VPN infrastructure quickly and cost-effectively, it is important to choose a solution that has scalability in mind. The last thing an IT manager wants to do is start from scratch and replace his VPN infrastructure because of a bottleneck in its growth potential.

When selecting the right device to provide VPN services to your network, you must be aware of the limitations. For example, a router's IOS can terminate VPNs, but that is a manual process to configure and it requires a deeper understanding than if you were to use a PIX Firewall with its VPN Configuration Wizard available in the GUI. There is also the Cisco VPN Concentrator, which offsets the PIX or IOS as the powerful GUI that eases the management of many different VPN policies. The Cisco VPN Concentrator offers intuitive instructions on setting up these different policies and groups, thus allowing many different users into a network with different enforcement groups associated to that group. I typically bring up the concentrator when the customer has limited staffing and needs many different VPN policy needs. The IOS with PIX is a little more difficult to set up and manage for this particular need. Do not forget scalability, either.

Split Tunneling

Many VPN users are already behind firewalls, and they need to access resources only through a VPN. Traditional VPNs do not allow users to also access network resources on their local segment while they are connected to their corporate VPN at the same time. This becomes an issue when, for example, these users must access a system via a VPN *and* print to a local network printer. To correct this potential problem, a feature has been introduced known as *split tunneling*.

Split tunneling occurs when a remote VPN user or site is allowed to access a public network (the Internet) at the same time that he accesses the private VPN, without placing the public network traffic inside the tunnel first. This is not always the best feature to enable, however, because it could allow an attacker to compromise a computer that is connected to two networks. Figure 7-2 illustrates an overview of how split tunneling works.

Figure 7-2   Split Tunneling Overview

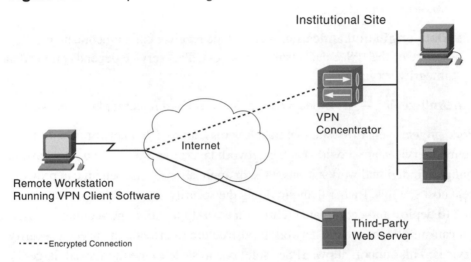

Overview of IPSec VPNs

IPSec has become the de facto standard for creating VPNs in the networking industry. Several vendors have implemented it and, because the Internet Engineering Task Force (IETF) has defined IPSec is defined in an RFC, interoperability between vendors makes IPSec the best option for building VPNs. IPSec offers a standard means of establishing authentication and encryption services between peers. For purposes of this discussion, IPSec peers are devices that form each end of a VPN tunnel. IPSec acts at the network layer of the OSI reference model, protecting and authenticating IP packets between participating IPSec devices

("peers"), such as Cisco routers or firewalls. IPSec provides the following network security services:

- **Data confidentiality**—The IPSec sender can encrypt packets before transmitting them across a network. If a hacker cannot read the data, it is of no use to him.

- **Data integrity**—The IPSec receiving endpoint authenticates all packets sent by the IPSec sender to ensure that the data has not been altered during transmission.

- **Data origin authentication**—The IPSec receiver can authenticate the source of the IPSec packets that were sent. This service depends on the data integrity service.

- **Anti-replay**—The IPSec receiver can detect and reject replayed packets.

IPSec protects sensitive data that travels across unprotected networks, and IPSec security services are provided at the network layer; therefore, you do not have to configure individual workstations, PCs, or applications. This benefit can provide a great cost savings. Rather than providing the security services that you do not need to deploy and coordinate security on a per-application, per-computer basis, you can simply change the network infrastructure to provide the needed security services. This support allows IPSec solutions to scale to medium-sized, large-sized, and growing networks, where a secure connection between many devices is required.

IPSec provides enhanced security features, such as better encryption algorithms and more comprehensive authentication. Corporate networks connected to the Internet can enable flexible and secure VPN access with IPSec. With IPSec technology, customers can now build VPNs over the Internet with the security of encryption protection against wire tapping, eavesdropping, or other attacks that intrude on private communications.

note
Only IPSec-compliant systems can take advantage of this protocol. Also, all devices must use a common key, and each network's firewalls must have similar security policies set up.

IPSec provides authentication and encryption services to protect unauthorized viewing or modification of data within your network or as it is transferred over an unprotected network, such as the public Internet. IPSec can encrypt data between various devices, such as

- Router to router
- Firewall to router
- Firewall to firewall
- User to router
- User to firewall
- User to VPN concentrator
- User to server

IPSec is a framework of open standards defined by the IETF. IPSec provides security for transmission of sensitive information over unprotected networks, such as the Internet. Figure 7-3 shows the three most common types of VPNs.

Figure 7-3   VPN Connectivity Overview

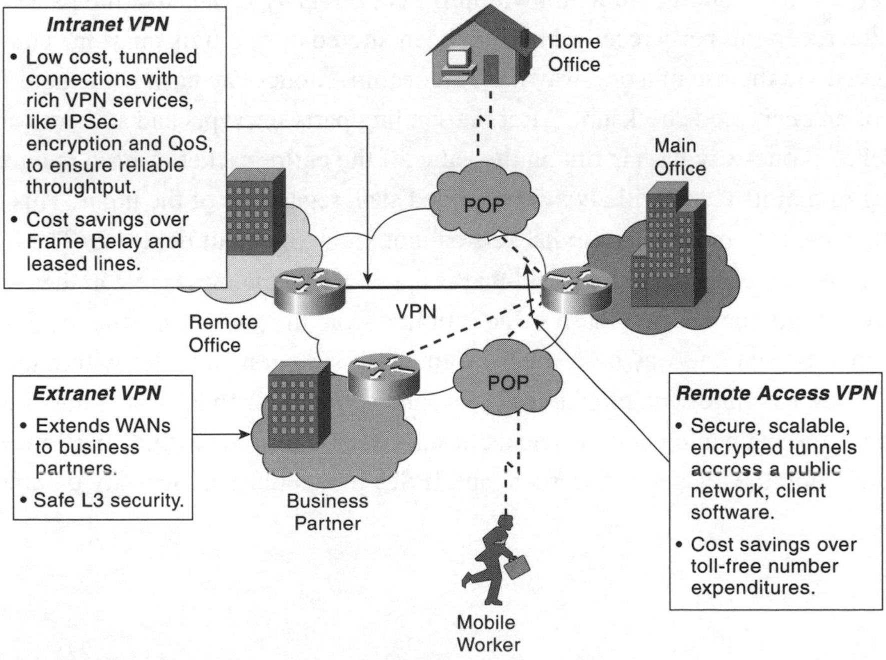

Intranet VPN
- Low cost, tunneled connections with rich VPN services, like IPSec encryption and QoS, to ensure reliable throughtput.
- Cost savings over Frame Relay and leased lines.

Extranet VPN
- Extends WANs to business partners.
- Safe L3 security.

Remote Access VPN
- Secure, scalable, encrypted tunnels accross a public network, client software.
- Cost savings over toll-free number expenditures.

Home Office

Main Office

POP

POP

VPN

Remote Office

Business Partner

Mobile Worker

Authentication and Data Integrity

To establish trust, *authentication* verifies the identity of the two VPN endpoints and the users sending traffic through the VPN. An endpoint could be a VPN client, VPN Concentrator, firewall, or router. Authentication is a process of IPSec that occurs after data encryption and before decryption on the receiving end. It is a necessary function within IPSec to ensure that both the sending and receiving parties are who they claim to be. With IPSec, each peer must be manually configured with a preshared key (usually agreed upon out of band) and a static list of valid peers, thereby creating a possibly large table within the router, which would take up memory resources.

note

Users can also be authenticated via digital certificates, or you can also require a machine to have a digital certificate to even begin the connection process; then, the user certificate can be processed to finalize the connection. Although it is beyond the scope of this book, further discussion on certificates can be found at http://www.netsol.com.

Data integrity is another function within IPSec. *Integrity* means that the packet that the receiving party received has not been altered during transmission. This is achieved via the use of a one-way hash algorithm. A one-way hash is the equivalent of an encrypted checksum. After the sending party encrypts and authenticates a packet, a one-way hash is run on the value of the entire packet. A hash is interesting in that its result will always be a fixed size, regardless of the input. This is another security mechanism so hackers cannot know the input field size. The one-way hash creates an encrypted field that is appended to the message. On the receiving end, the one-way hash value is pulled from the packet, and the receiving end runs its own one-way hash. Because the hash is run on variables within the packet such as time sent, number of bytes, and so on, both ends' hash value must be the same—meaning that the packet has not been tampered with. If the values are different, the packet is discarded, and IPSec renegotiates its security parameters.

Tunneling Data

Tunneling is what VPNs rely on to create a private network over the Internet. Basically, this is the process of taking an entire packet of data and encapsulating it within another packet before sending it over a network. The network must understand the outer packet's protocol to enter and exit the network. Tunneling requires three different protocols to work:

- **Passenger protocol**—The original data packet, usually IP, which is to be encrypted into the VPN. If you so desire, other protocols such as IPX or NetBEUI could be included.

- **Encapsulating protocol**—The protocol (GRE, IPSec, L2F, PPTP, L2TP) that is wrapped around the original data (that is, encapsulated). IPSec is the de facto standard that is used as the encapsulating protocol at this stage, and it allows for the entire passenger packet to be encrypted and protected. IPSec must be supported at both tunnel interfaces for proper operation.

- **Carrier protocol**—The protocol the network uses and over which the information travels. The original packet (passenger protocol) is encapsulated inside the encapsulating protocol, which is then put inside the carrier protocol's header (usually IP) for transmission over the public network.

 note
The encapsulating protocol also often carries out the encryption of the data. As you can see, protocols such as IPX and NetBEUI, which are not normally transferred across the Internet, can safely and securely be transmitted. Or, you could put a packet that uses a private (non-routable) IP address inside a packet that uses a globally unique IP address to extend a private network over the Internet. There techniques can make these protocols work through the use of GRE and IPSec.

Tunneling works well with VPNs because you can use protocols that are not supported on the Internet inside an IP packet, and it can still be sent safely. At the beginning of a VPN tunneled transmission, a data packet from the source LAN is wrapped or encapsulated with new header information that allows intermediary

networks to recognize and deliver it. After this is done and the transmission is complete, the tunneling protocol "header" is stripped off, and the original packet is transferred to the destination LAN for delivery.

Although tunneling allows data to be carried over third-party networks, tunneling alone does not ensure privacy. To secure a tunneled transmission against any interception and tampering, all traffic over the VPN is encrypted. In addition, VPNs typically include additional features, such as firewalls at the perimeters.

In site-to-site VPNs, the encapsulating protocol is usually IPSec or generic routing encapsulation (GRE). GRE includes information about what type of packet you are encapsulating and about the connection between the client and server. The difference depends on the level of security needed for the connection, with IPSec being more secure and GRE having greater functionality. IPSec can tunnel and encrypt IP packets, whereas GRE can tunnel IP and non-IP packets. When you need to send non-IP packets (such as IPX) over the tunnel, IPSec and GRE should be used together.

Encryption Modes

IPSec has two encryption modes: tunnel and transport. Each mode differs in its application and in the amount of overhead added to the passenger packet. These different modes of operation are summarized briefly in that tunnel encrypts the packet header and the payload of each packet, while transport encrypts only the payload.

Tunnel Mode

This is the normal way in which IPSec is implemented between two PIX Firewalls (or other security gateways) that are connected over an untrusted network, such as the public Internet. All discussions involving IPSec will be on the tunnel mode. Tunnel mode encapsulates and protects an entire IP packet. Because it encapsulates or hides the packets to be successfully forwarded, the encrypting routers themselves own the IP addresses that are used in these new headers. Tunnel mode can be employed with either or both ESP and AH. Using tunnel mode results in additional packet expansion of approximately 20 bytes associated IP header, a new IP header must be added for the packet with the new IP header, as shown in Figure 7-4.

Figure 7-4   Tunnel Mode

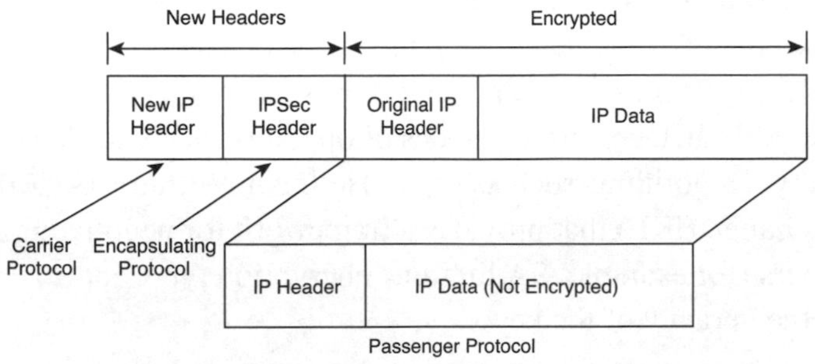

Transport Mode

This method of implementing IPSec is typically done with L2TP to allow the authentication of remote Windows 2000 VPN clients. Chapter 5 already covered this concept, so this chapter focuses on IPSec and tunnel mode. In tunnel mode, IPSec encrypts the entire packet and writes a new IP header into the packet, which masks the original source and destination information. Tunnel mode is inherently more secure than transport mode (because of the fact that the entire original packet is encrypted, not just the payload as in transport mode), as shown in Figure 7-5.

Figure 7-5   Transport Mode

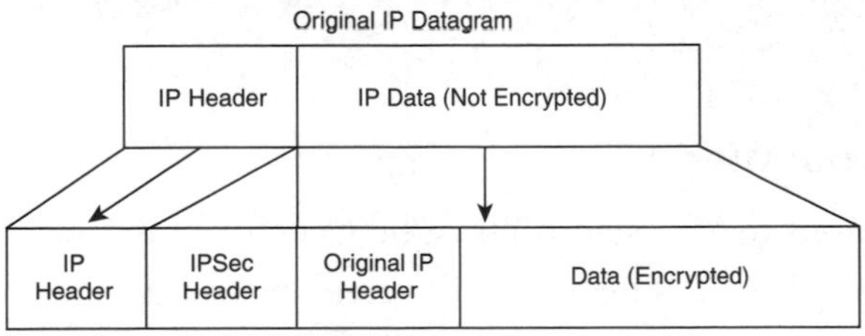

IPSec Protocols

IPSec uses three complementary protocols that, when used together, form a cohesive and secure standards-based framework that is ideally suited for VPNs. Following are the three protocols described in the IPSec standards:

- *Internet Security Association Key Management Protocol (ISAKMP)*— Describes the phase of negotiating the IPSec connection to establish the VPN; *Oakley* defines the method to establish an authenticated key exchange. This method can take various modes of operation and can also derive keying material via algorithms such as Diffie-Hellman. Within ISAKMP is Internet Key Exchange (IKE) that provides a framework for negotiating security parameters (for example, SA lifetime, encryption type, and so on) and establishing the veracity of the keys.

- *Encapsulated Security Protocol (ESP)*—Provides data confidentiality and protection with optional authentication and replay-detection services. ESP completely encapsulates user data. ESP can be used either by itself or in conjunction with AH. ESP runs using the TCP protocol on ports 50 and 51 and is documented in RFC 2406.

- *Authentication Header (AH)*—Provides authentication and anti-replay services (optional). AH provides services to limited portions of the IP header and extended header, but does not provide for data encryption by applying a one-way hash to create a message digest of the packet. AH is embedded in the data to be protected (a full IP datagram, for example). AH can be used either by itself or with Encryption Service Payload (ESP). (Refer to RFC 2402.) This protocol has largely been superseded by ESP and is considered deprecated.

Security Associations

Security associations (SAs) establish trust between two devices in a peer-to-peer relationship and enable VPN endpoints to agree on a set of transmission rules by negotiating policies with a *potential* peer. Consider a security association like a contract that negotiates and then sets various parameters with regard to the connection parameters.

A security association is identified through an IP address, a security protocol identifier, and a unique security parameter index (SPI) value. The SPI value is a 32-bit number embedded in packet headers. The two types of security associations are

- *Internet Key Exchange (IKE)* — Provides negotiation, peer authentication, key management, and key exchange. As a bidirectional protocol, IKE provides a secure communication channel between two devices that negotiates an encryption algorithm, a hash algorithm, an authentication method, and any relevant group information. It uses key exchange based on Diffie-Hellman algorithms, and network administrators can closely tie IKE with policy management systems. To prevent a man-in-the-middle attack — when an attacker sniffs packets from the network, modifies them, and inserts them back into the network — a Diffie-Hellman enhancement called Station-to-Station (STS) protocol allows two devices in the Diffie-Hellman exchange to authenticate each other using digital signatures and public-key certificates.

- *IPSec Security Association (IPSec SA)* — IPSec SA is unidirectional and thus requires that separate IPSec SAs is established in each direction. IPSec SA is a two-phase, three-modes procedure. In Phase 1, two modes can be used: *main mode* and *aggressive mode*. In Phase 2, the only available mode is called *quick mode*. The end user has no control over which mode is chosen; rather, the selection is automatic and depends on the configuration parameters set up by both peers.

Both IKE and IPSec use SAs, although SAs are independent of one another. IPSec SAs are unidirectional and are unique in each security protocol. The security associations define which protocols and algorithms should be applied to sensitive packets and specify the keying material to be used by the two peers. SAs are unidirectional and are established separately for different security protocols (AH and/or ESP). IPSec SAs can be established in two ways:

- **Manual SAs with preshared keys** — The use of manual IPSec SAs requires a prior agreement between administrators of the PIX Firewall and the IPSec peer. There is no negotiation of SAs, so the configuration information in both systems should be the same for IPSec to process traffic successfully. Manual is easy to configure; however, it is difficult to change preshared keys

because the tunnel fails when you do, and the trouble is that preshared keys are usually never changed.

■ **IKE-established SAs**—When IKE is used to establish IPSec SAs, the peers can negotiate the settings they will use for the new security associations. This means that you can specify lists (such as lists of acceptable transforms) within the *crypto map* entry.

Internet Key Exchange (IKE)

This section describes the Internet Key Exchange (IKE) protocol and how it works with IPSec to make VPNs more scalable. IKE is a hybrid protocol that uses part of Oakley and part of another protocol suite called Secure Key Exchange Mechanism (SKEME) inside the Internet Security Association and Key Management Protocol (ISAKMP) framework. You can see in Figure 7-6 that IKE is a true hybrid protocol.

Figure 7-6   IKE Composition

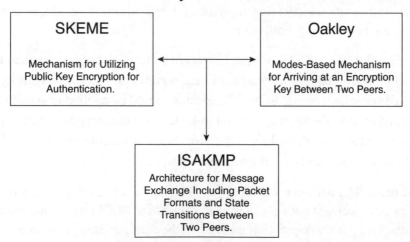

IKE establishes a shared security policy and is authenticated keys for services (such as IPSec) that require keys. Before any IPSec traffic can be passed, each router/firewall/host must be able to verify its peer's identity. This can be done by manually entering preshared keys into both hosts, by a Certification Authority (CA) service, or secure DNS (DNSSec). IKE is the protocol formerly known as ISAKMP/Oakley, and it is defined in RFC 2409.

note
A potential point of confusion is that the acronyms "ISAKMP" and "IKE" are both used in Cisco IOS Software to refer to the same thing. These two items are somewhat different, as shown in the next definition.

IKE is a protocol that IPSec uses for completion of Phase 1. IKE negotiates and assigns security associations (SAs) for each IPSec peer, which provides a secure channel for the negotiation of the IPSec SAs in Phase 2. IKE provides the following benefits:

- Eliminates the need to manually specify all the IPSec security parameters at both peers

- Allows you to specify a lifetime for the IPSec SAs

- Allows encryption keys to change during IPSec sessions

- Allows IPSec to provide anti-replay services

- Enables CA support for a manageable, scalable IPSec implementation

- Allows dynamic authentication of peers

IKE negotiations must be protected, so each IKE negotiation begins by the peer agreeing on a common (shared) IKE policy. This policy states the security parameters that will be used to protect subsequent IKE negotiations. After the two peers agree on a policy, a security association established at each peer identifies the policy's security parameters, and these SAs apply to all subsequent IKE traffic during the negotiation.

ISAKMP Overview

Internet Security Association and Key Management Protocol (ISAKMP) is a framework that defines the mechanics of implementing a key exchange protocol and negotiation of a security policy. ISAKMP is used for secure exchanges of both SA parameters and private keys between peers in an IPSec environment, as well as key creation and management.

ISAKMP provides for several methods of key management and provides secure transit of IPSec parameters between peers. It accomplishes this by using similar algorithms used by IPSec for the actual encryption of the data payload. Like IPSec, ISAKMP is not a protocol, but simply an interface to manage various ways of dynamic key exchange. ISAKMP defines various methods—such as digital signatures, certificates, and one-way hash algorithms—to ensure that negotiation of SAs between peers is handled securely.

Currently, the only supported protocol in ISAKMP is the Internet Key Exchange (IKE) protocol. When IKE is actively employed in the encryption process, many features become available to the IPSec communication process. Using public-key cryptography, IKE negotiates security parameters and key exchanges before the IPSec processing ever begins.

IPSec Operational Overview

IPSec's main task is to allow the exchange of private information over an insecure connection by negotiating the connection and providing the keys in a secure manner. IPSec uses encryption to protect information from interception or eavesdropping. However, to use encryption efficiently, both parties should share a secret key (password) that is used for both encrypting and decrypting the information as it enters and exits the VPN tunnel. IPSec uses IKE to establish the secure link so the

VPN forms and data connects. At a very high level, the sequence of events for an IPSec transaction is as follows:

1. One of the IPSec peers receives or generates interesting traffic on an interface that has been configured to initiate an IPSec tunnel for this *interesting* traffic.

2. Main mode or aggressive mode negotiation using IKE results in the creation of an IKE security association (SA) between two IPSec peers.

3. Quick mode negotiation using IKE results in the creation of two IPSec SAs between two IPSec peers.

4. Data starts passing over an encrypted tunnel using the ESP or AH encapsulation techniques.

These four seemingly simple steps require some additional examination. IPSec operates in two major phases to allow the confidential exchange of a shared secret key, as described in the sections that follow.

IKE Phase 1

IKE Phase 1 handles the negotiation of security parameters required to establish a secure channel between two IPSec peers. Phase 1 is generally implemented through the IKE protocol and is primarily concerned with establishing the protection suite for IKE messages. The sequence of events of IKE Phase 1 is as follows:

1. Phase 1 is the creation of the ISAKMP SA, where peers negotiate and agree upon parameters for IPSec SAs to follow. After Phase 1 is complete and a secure channel is established between peers, IKE moves into Phase 2.

2. If the remote IPSec peer cannot do IKE, you can use manual configuration with preshared keys to complete Phase 1.

Figure 7-7 shows the negotiation of the Phase 1 parameters through the use of SA.

Figure 7-7   IKE Phase 1 Operation

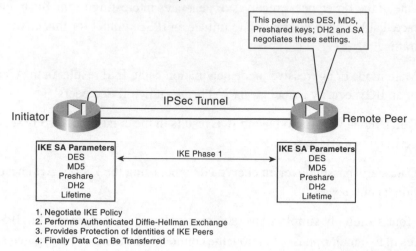

IKE's Phase I operation has two modes of operation: aggressive and main mode. Aggressive mode eliminates several steps in the authentication of IKE, reducing it to just three steps, whereas main mode uses the full four steps to authenticate. Although it's faster, aggressive mode is considered less secure than main mode, for obvious reasons. Cisco devices use main mode by default, but they will respond for peers using aggressive mode.

IKE Phase 2

IKE Phase 2 advances the security of the connection by using the secure tunnel established in IKE Phase 1 to exchange the additional security parameters required to actually transmit user data (see Figure 7-8).

In Phase 2, IKE negotiates SAs on behalf of IPSec, according to parameters configured in IPSec. The ISAKMP SA created in Phase 1 protects these exchanges.

Figure 7-8   IKE Phase 2 Operation

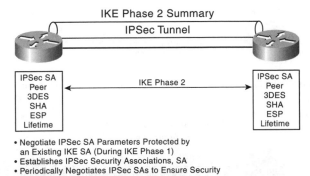

- Negotiate IPSec SA Parameters Protected by
  an Existing IKE SA (During IKE Phase 1)
- Establishes IPSec Security Associations, SA
- Periodically Negotiates IPSec SAs to Ensure Security
- Optionally Performs an Additional Diffie-Hellman
  Exchange If PFS Enabled

The secure tunnels used in both phases of IPSec are based on security associations (SAs) used at each IPSec endpoint. SAs describe the security parameters, such as the type of authentication and encryption that both end points agree to use.

Diffie-Hellman Algorithm

The *Diffie-Hellman algorithm* was the first public-key algorithm, and is still considered one of the best. IKE uses public-key cryptography to negotiate security parameters and protect key exchanges. Specifically, the Diffie-Hellman algorithm is used in the IKE negotiations to allow the two peers to agree on a shared secret by generating the key for use. This is why you will see that the Diffie-Hellman algorithm is used several times throughout the process.

In general, here is how the algorithm works: Each peer contains a private key. The Diffie-Hellman algorithm takes that private key and generates a public key. The public key is a product of the private key, but is such that the private key cannot be deduced by knowing the public key. The peers then exchange public keys, as shown in Figure 7-9.

Figure 7-9   Diffie-Hellman Key Exchange

Peer A

Peer B

R1 Private Key and
Public Key

R1 Private Key and
Public Key

1
1. Public keys are exchanged
in clear text.

2. Random Integer
generated.

2
2. Random Integer
generated.

+ Prime Number "A"

3
3. Each router uses the random
integer to generate a private key.

+ Prime Number "B"

4
4. R1 and R2 then combine with
the known prime number A and B
to generate a public key.

Shared Secret

note

Symmetric key algorithms use the same key for both encryption and decryption. Symmetric key algorithms offer significant advantages over public-key algorithms. The main advantage is speed because only one key is randomly generated, as opposed to two in public-key cryptography. The only problem with asymmetric key algorithms is the security involved in sharing the private key between peers over an unprotected link.

If peer A wants to pass encrypted traffic to peer B, peer A encrypts the traffic going to peer B with peer B's public key.

Peer B then uses its own private key to decrypt the message because its public key is derived from its private key. This ensures that only peer B can decrypt the message because only peer B knows its own private key.

This method allows for a secure communications channel to be established (ISAKMP SA) so that subsequent IPSec SAs can securely exchange key information in privacy without having to use a public-key algorithm to exchange their own keys every time encrypted traffic is passed. Figure 7-10 shows the various steps in ISAKMP Phase 1 and 2 negotiations.

Figure 7-10   VPN Connection Establishment

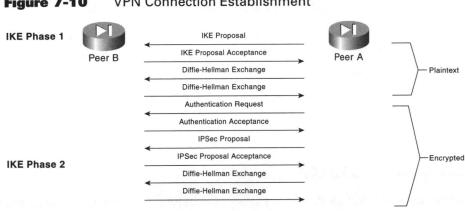

Figure 7-10 illustrates that traffic is already encrypted before the end of IKE Phase 1. This provides for a secure exchange of the IPSec proposals and keys performed on behalf of IPSec in IKE Phase 2.

In addition to providing a secure mechanism for key exchange and managing IPSec SAs, ISAKMP also provides several other important functions. ISAKMP can be configured to set IPSec SA Lifetimes, which allows for more control over how often keys are exchanged. It also allows for keys to change during communication without removing and recreating the IPSec SAs. With standalone IPSec, if keys are to change during communication, existing SAs are "torn-down" and rebuilt with the new keys. Because ISAKMP negotiates SAs for IPSec and protects them with its own SA, keys can be changed on-the-fly without recreating SA negotiations. This provides a substantial advantage over IPSec alone. ISAKMP also allows for dynamic authentication of peers and data integrity checks via the use of one-way hash algorithms.

Router Configuration as VPN Peer

I wanted to include one of the ways to configure a router with the ability to be part of a site-to-site VPN. I felt this particular configuration was important based on the fact that Cisco routers make up 80 percent of the routers in operation today. Therefore, it seemed that many networks could have their security greatly increased by using the router to terminate VPNs.

Configuring ISAKMP

IKE exists only to establish SAs for IPSec, but before it can do this, it must negotiate an SA (an ISAKMP SA) relationship with the peer. Because IKE negotiates its own policy, it is possible to configure multiple policy statements with different configuration statements, and then let the two hosts come to an agreement. ISAKMP negotiates the following:

- **Encryption algorithm**—Used to protect user data transmitted between two IPSec peers (DES or 3DES).

- **Hashing algorithm:** *MD5* **or SHA**—This selection specifies the hash algorithm used to ensure data integrity. The default is SHA-1. MD5 has a smaller digest and is considered slightly faster than SHA-1.

- **Authentication**—*RSA* signatures, RSA encrypted nonces (random numbers), or preshared keys. This selection specifies the method of authentication that is used to establish the identity of each IPSec peer. Preshared keys do not scale well with a growing network, but they are easier to set up in a small network.

- **Lifetime of the SA (in seconds)**—The default is 86,400 seconds or 24 hours. As a general rule, a shorter lifetime (up to a point) provides more secure IKE negotiations. However, with longer lifetimes, future IPSec security associations can be set up more quickly. However, as with many of the characteristics used in the VPN creation, the VPN tunnel activates and functions if the values do not match.

There is an implicit trade-off between security and performance when you choose a specific value for each parameter. The level of security provided by the default values is adequate for most organization's security requirements. If you are inter-operating with a peer that supports only one of the values for a parameter, your choice is limited to the other peer's supported value.

When the IKE negotiation begins, the peer that initiates the negotiation sends all its policies to the remote peer, which tries to find a match. The remote peer checks its policies in order of priority (highest priority first) until a match is found.

A match is made when both policies from the two peers contain the same encryption, hash, authentication, and Diffie-Hellman parameter values, and when the remote peer's policy specifies a lifetime less than or equal to the lifetime in the policy being compared. If the lifetimes are not identical, the shorter lifetime (from the remote peer's policy) is used.

If no acceptable match is found, IKE refuses negotiation and IPSec is not established. If a match is found, IKE completes negotiation, and IPSec security associations are created. Currently, there are two methods of configuring ISAKMP:

- Use preshared keys, which have the advantage of being simple to configure.

- Use a centralized *Certificate Authority (CA)*, which is a third-party entity that is responsible for issuing and revoking certificates. Each device that has its own certificate and public key of the CA can authenticate every other device within a given CA's domain. This solution has the advantage of being scalable throughout a large enterprise network.

 note
IKE negotiation is done on UDP port 500. IPSec uses IP protocols 50 and 51. Make sure that these are permitted on any access lists you have between the peers.

The following section discusses the use of preshared keys, which is by far the most common method of configuring ISAKMP.

Preshared Keys

If you use the IKE authentication method of preshared keys, you are setting the keys, or in other words, sharing them with the other peer with whom you plan on creating a VPN by manually configuring these keys on the device and its peer(s). You can specify the same key to share with multiple peers, but it is more secure to specify different keys to share between different pairs of peers. To configure a pre-shared key on the PIX Firewall, perform the following steps. Although configuring IKE is simple and you do not use a CA, it does not scale well. To configure IKE, you must

Step 1   Configure ISAKMP policy options.

Step 2   Configure ISAKMP key.

Configuring the ISAKMP Protection Suite

The following command creates the ISAKMP policy object. It is possible to have multiple policies, but there is only one in this example:

```
INRGI(config)#crypto isakmp policy 1
INRGI(config-isakmp)#
```

With the following **group** command, you can declare what size modulus to use for Diffie-Hellman calculation:

```
INRGI(config-isakmp)#group 2
```

Group 1 is 768 bits long, and group 2 is 1024 bits long. Why would you use one over the other? First of all, not all vendors support group 2. Secondly, group 2 is also significantly more CPU-intensive than group one; therefore, you would not want to use group 2 on low-end routers like the Cisco 2500 series or less. On the other hand, group 2 is more secure than group 1.

Because security is of primary concern, group 2 is used here (make sure the peer is also configured to use group 2). The default is group 1. If you select the default properties, the group 1 lines do not show up when you show the configuration command.

MD5 is the hashing algorithm as configured in the following command. Although implementing SHA and MD5 are both mandatory, not all peers can be configured to negotiate one or the other:

```
INRGI(config-isakmp)#hash md5
```

The following command shows the security association's lifetime—in this case, 500 seconds. If you do not set a lifetime, it defaults to 86,400 seconds, or one day. When the lifetime timer fires, the SA is renegotiated as a security measure:

```
INRGI(config-isakmp)#lifetime 500
```

The **authentication pre-share** command tells IKE what key to use:

```
INRGI(config-isakmp)#authentication pre-share
```

Two options for the **authentication** command besides the **pre-share** are

- **rsa-encr**—Configures RSA-encrypted nonces
- **rsa-sig**—Configures RSA signature

The **rsa-encr** and the **rsa-sig** options are addressed in the section, "Using a CA." For now, remember that **rsa-sig** is the default.

Configuring the ISAKMP Key

The following commands tell IKE what key to use. Remember that the peer, 192.168.10.38 in this case, must have the same key "Slurpee-Machine" in its configuration. I use this particular key because I am configuring a VPN to my good friend Cary's office and he is addicted to these cold delights:

```
INRGI(config-isakmp)#exit

INRGI(config)#crypto isakmp key Slurpee-Machine address 192.168.10.38
```

At this point, you are finished with IKE configuration. For the record, the following lines are the peer's IKE configuration:

```
crypto isakmp policy 1
 hash md5
 group 2
 authentication pre-share
crypto isakmp key Slurpee-Machine address 192.168.10.66
```

Configuring IPSec

Whether you use preshared keys or configure a CA, you still have to setup IPSec after you set up IKE. Regardless of which IKE method you use, the IPSec configuration steps are the same. To configure IPSec, you need to

Step 1 Create the extended ACL.

Step 2 Create the IPSec transforms.

Step 3 Create the crypto map.

Step 4 Apply the crypto map to an interface.

Step 1: Create the Extended ACL

The following command is a simple ACL that allows the routers to talk to one another (a Telnet from one router to the next, for example):

```
INRGI(config)# access-list 101 permit ip host 192.168.10.38
                host 192.168.10.66
```

A more realistic ACL looks like the following command:

```
INRGI(config)# access-list 101 permit ip 192.168.3.0 0.0.0.255
                10.3.2.0 0.0.0.255
```

This command is an ordinary extended ACL, where 192.168.3.0 is a subnet behind the router in question and 10.3.2.0 is a subnet somewhere behind the peer router. Remember that permit means encrypt, and deny means do not encrypt.

Step 2: Create the IPSec Transforms

A transform describes a security protocol (AH or ESP) with its corresponding algorithms. For example, ESP with the DES cipher algorithm and HMAC-SHA for authentication. A transform set represents a certain combination of security protocols and algorithms. During the IPSec security association negotiation, the peers agree to use a particular transform set for protecting a particular data flow. You can specify multiple transform sets, and then specify one or more of these transform sets in a crypto map entry. The transform set defined in the crypto map entry is used in the IPSec security association negotiation to protect the data flows specified by that crypto map entry's access list. During IPSec security association negotiations with IKE, the peers search for a transform set that is the same at both peers. When such a transform set is found, it is selected and applied to the pro-tected traffic as part of both peers' IPSec security associations. With manually established security associations, there is no negotiation with the peer, so both sides must specify the same transform set.

Create three transform sets, as done in the following command lines:

```
INRGI(config)# crypto ipsec transform-set PapaBear esp-rfc1829
INRGI(cfg-crypto-trans)# exit
INRGI(config)# crypto ipsec transform-set MamaBear ah-md5-hmac esp-des
INRGI(cfg-crypto-trans)# exit
NRGI(config)# crypto ipsec transform-set BabyBear ah-rfc1828
INRGI(cfg-crypto-trans)# exit
INRGI(config)#
```

The first set uses only ESP, the second set uses AH combined with ESP, and the last set uses only AH. During IPSec SA negotiation, all three are offered to the peer, which chooses one. Also, use the default tunnel mode for all three transform sets. Transport mode can be used only when the crypto endpoints are also the

communication's endpoints. The mode transport command under the transform-set configuration can specify the transport mode. Tunnel mode is used primarily for the VPN scenario.

Also note that esp-rfc1829 and ah-rfc1828 are based on the original RFCs for this technology and are obsolete transforms that are included for backwards compatibility. Not all vendors support these transforms, but other vendors support only these transforms. Finally, notice that the transform sets in the commands are not necessarily the most practical. For example, both "PapaBear" and "BabyBear" have substandard transform-sets. You should use esp-rfc1829 and ah-rfc1828 together in the same transform-set.

Step 3: Create the Crypto Map

Crypto maps specify IPSec policy. Crypto map entries created for IPSec pull together the various security settings that set up IPSec security associations, including the following:

- Which traffic should be protected by IPSec (per a crypto access list)

- Where IPSec-protected traffic should be sent (who the peer is)

- The local address to be used for the IPSec traffic

- What IPSec security should be applied to this traffic (selecting from a list of one or more transform sets)

- Whether security associations are manually established or established via IKE

- Other parameters that might be necessary to define an IPSec SA

For IPSec to succeed between two peers, both peers' crypto map entries must contain compatible configuration statements. When two peers try to establish a security association, they should each have at least one crypto map entry that is compatible with one of the other peer's crypto map entries.

Using the **ipsec-isakmp** tag tells the router that this crypto map is an IPSec crypto map. Although only one peer is declared in this crypto map, a given crypto map can have multiple peers. The session key lifetime can be expressed in either kilo-bytes (after x-amount of traffic, change the key) or seconds, as shown in the fol-lowing commands. The goal here is to make a potential attacker's efforts more difficult:

```
INRGI(config)# crypto map armadillo 10 ipsec-isakmp
INRGI(config-crypto-map)# set peer 192.168.10.38
INRGI(config-crypto-map)# set session-key lifetime seconds 4000
INRGI(config-crypto-map)# set transform-set MamaBear PapaBear BabyBear
INRGI(config-crypto-map)# match address 101
```

The **set transform-set** command is where you associate the transforms with the crypto map. In addition, the order in which you declare the transforms is signifi-cant. You most prefer "MamaBear" in this configuration, and then the rest in descending order of preference to "BabyBear."

The crypto map access list bound to the outgoing interface selects the IPSec pack-ets that are destined to an IPSec tunnel. IPSec packets that arrive from an IPSec tunnel are authenticated/deciphered by IPSec and are subject to the proxy identity match of the tunnel.

note
What happens if a packet does not meet the requirements for encryption? Simply put, that packet is then discarded into the bit bucket.

The **match address 101** command simply means to use access list 101 to deter-mine what traffic is relevant. You can have multiple crypto maps with the same name ("armadillo," in the following example) and different sequence numbers ("10," in the following example). The combination of multiple crypto maps and different sequence numbers allows you to mix and match classic crypto and IPSec. You can also modify your PFS configuration here. PFS group1 is the default in the example given here. You could change the PFS to group2 or turn it off all together, which you should not do.

Step 4: Apply the Crypto Map to an Interface

The following commands apply the crypto map to the interface. Remember to apply the crypto map to the egress interface, not the ingress one. If you have multiple crypto maps that you want to apply to this interface, you must tack the name onto the list in the **crypto map** command:

```
INRGI(config)# int e0
INRGI(config-if)# crypto map armadillo
```

Remember that crypto maps and their access lists are direction-based (either inbound or outbound,) and that traffic not matching the access list is still transmitted without being encrypted.

Firewall VPN Configuration for Client Access

Cisco PIX Firewalls can be configured to terminate client VPNs, thus allowing users to access corporate resources securely.

Used with IKE, dynamic crypto maps can ease IPSec configuration and are recommended for use in networks where the peers are not always predetermined. You use dynamic crypto maps for VPN clients (such as mobile users) and routers that obtain dynamically assigned IP addresses.

Dynamic crypto maps can only be used for negotiating SAs with remote peers that initiate the connection. They cannot be used for initiating connections to a remote peer. With a dynamic crypto map entry, if outbound traffic matches a **permit** statement in an access list and the corresponding security association is not yet established, the PIX Firewall drops the traffic.

A dynamic crypto map entry is essentially a crypto map entry that does not have all the parameters configured. The dynamic crypto map acts as a policy template where the missing parameters are later dynamically configured (as the result of an IPSec negotiation) to match a peer's requirements. This allows peers to exchange

IPSec traffic with the PIX Firewall, even if the PIX Firewall does not have a crypto map entry specifically configured to meet all the peer's requirements. Dynamic crypto maps are found for use by VPN Clients on PCs.

If the PIX Firewall accepts the peer's request at the point that it installs the new IPSec security associations, it also installs a temporary crypto map entry. This entry is filled in with the results of the negotiation. At this point, the PIX Firewall performs normal processing, using this temporary crypto map entry as a normal entry, and even requests new security associations if the current ones are expiring (based on the policy specified in the temporary crypto map entry). When the flow expires (that is, all the corresponding security associations expire), the temporary crypto map entry is removed.

Like regular static crypto map entries, dynamic crypto map entries are grouped into sets. A set is a group of dynamic crypto map entries all with the same *dynamic-map-name*, but each with a different *dynamic-seq-num*. If this is configured, the data flow identity proposed by the IPSec peer should fall within a permit statement for this crypto access list. If this is not configured, the PIX Firewall accepts any data flow identity proposed by the peer.

You can add one or more dynamic crypto map sets into a crypto map set via crypto map entries that reference the dynamic crypto map sets. You should set the crypto map entries that reference dynamic maps to be the lowest priority entries in a crypto map set (that is, use the highest sequence numbers).

note
Use care when using the **any** keyword in **permit** entries in dynamic crypto maps. If it is possible for the traffic covered by such a permit entry to include multicast or broadcast traffic, the access list should include deny entries for the appropriate address range. Access lists should also include deny entries for network and subnet broadcast traffic, and for any other traffic that should not be IPSec protected.

The procedure for using a crypto dynamic map entry is the same as the basic configuration described in the "Basic IPSec Configuration" section, except instead of creating a static crypto map entry, you create a crypto dynamic map entry. You can also combine static and dynamic map entries within a single crypto map set. Create a crypto dynamic map entry by performing the following steps:

Step 1   Assign an access list to a dynamic crypto map entry:

```
crypto dynamic-map dynamic-map-name dynamic-seq-num match address
  access-list-name
```

This determines which traffic should be protected and not protected.

For example:

```
crypto dynamic-map dyn1 10 match address 101
```

In this example, access list 101 is assigned to dynamic crypto map "dyn1." The map's sequence number is 10.

Step 2   Specify which transform sets are allowed for this dynamic crypto map entry. List multiple transform sets in order of priority (highest priority first):

```
crypto dynamic-map dynamic-map-name dynamic-seq-num set transform-set
  transform-set-name1 , [ transform-set-name2 , transform-set-name9 ]
```

For example:

```
crypto dynamic-map dyn 10 set transform-set myset1 myset2
```

In this example, when traffic matches access list 101, the security association can use either "myset1" (first priority) or "myset2" (second priority), depending on which transform set matches the peer's transform sets.

Step 3   Specify security association lifetime for the crypto dynamic map entry if you want the security associations for this entry to be negotiated using different IPSec security association lifetimes other than the global lifetimes:

```
crypto dynamic-map dynamic-map-name dynamic-seq-num set security-
  association lifetime {seconds seconds | kilobytes kilobytes }
```

For example:

```
crypto dynamic-map dyn1 10 set security-association lifetime 2700
```

This example shortens the timed lifetime for dynamic crypto map "dyn1 10" to 2700 seconds (45 minutes). The time volume lifetime does not change.

Step 4   Specify that IPSec should ask for PFS when requesting new security associations for this dynamic crypto map entry, or demand PFS in requests received from the peer:

```
crypto dynamic-map  dynamic-map-name dynamic-seq-num  set pfs  [group1
 | group2 ]
```

For example:

```
crypto dynamic-map dyn1 10 set pfs group1
```

Step 5   Add the dynamic crypto map set into a static crypto map set. Be sure to set the crypto map entries referencing dynamic maps to be the lowest priority entries (highest sequence numbers) in a crypto map set:

```
crypto map map-name seq-num  ipsec-isakmp dynamic  dynamic-map-name
```

For example:

```
crypto map mymap 200 ipsec-isakmp dynamic dyn1
```

Chapter Summary

This chapter discussed what a VPN is and the many benefits that it brings to networks everywhere. The most popular benefit of implementing VPNs is the cost reduction and overall financial savings. The reduction of bandwidth costs has made VPNs one of the best solutions available.

This chapter focused on the best available VPNs: IPSec-based VPNs. To understand how they protect your data, the chapter examined all those different levels,

phases, and types of processes that are involved in getting your data packets encrypted into your IPSec-based VPNs. This was a truly amazing task because the subject matter gets complicated quickly.

Chapter Review Questions

1. Is it possible to have unencrypted VPNs?

2. What are the three types of VPNs?

3. Select three VPN features and benefits and explain how your organization can directly benefit from each.

4. VPN Concentrators are designed for many users—explain how many and when they should be used.

5. Does the VPN Client Software for PCs support Apple's powerful new operating system, MAX OS X?

6. When does split tunneling occur?

7. In relation to a data stream, what role does authentication play in securing it?

8. When tunneling data in IPSec, what are the three protocols that play a role in process?

9. In site-to-site VPNs, what are the two different encapsulating protocols and what are the differences between the two?

10. Name three of the benefits of IKE.

What You Will Learn

By the end of this chapter, you should know and be able to explain the following:

- ✔ The essentials of wireless LANs, including their benefits and risks

- ✔ The major threats to a wireless network

- ✔ The breadth and scope of possible attacks and exploits that are available to attackers

Being able to answer these key questions will allow you to understand the overall characteristics and importance of network security. By the time you finish this book, you will have a solid appreciation for network security, its issues, how it works, and why it is important.

CHAPTER 8

Wireless Security

In the end, we will remember not the words of our enemies, but the silence of our friends. —Martin Luther King Jr. (1929-1968)

When was the last time you went on vacation to get away from it all? Perhaps to some remote beach or maybe a getaway to the country? Imagine that you walk out the patio door of your hotel room (an ocean view, of course) and admire the beauty of the sun setting on the ocean. The air is cool, so you decide to sit on the porch in your favorite lounge chair; the sea-gulls are playing, the waves are breaking in a rhythmic beat, and *beep-beep-beep*—your pager begins to go off!

Who could possibly be paging you while you are trying to relax and unplug? What emergency could be so grave that it would require you to be interrupted on this fantasy vacation?

According to the message on the display, there seems to be a problem with the company firewall/VPN/Exchange server/<insert emergency here>. It looks pretty serious, so you conclude that you need to log into your office network and take a look.

It is a good thing that you chose a hotel with high-speed Internet access, and that you brought your wireless access point. The access point is plugged into the high-speed LAN port via wireless so you can still enjoy the beautiful view. You cannot really avoid turning on the laptop that you were not planning to turn on while you were on vacation; you are needed for an emergency.

So, here you are on the patio booting up your laptop. You see the "blinky-blinky" of the wireless NIC's status lights. All systems are go!

You fire up Telnet and proceed to log in to the router/firewall and start snooping around to see what the problem could be. This should not take too long, you say to yourself. There is still plenty of time to enjoy the rest of the evening and perhaps have a nice dinner. An hour goes by and you have solved the problem. You are quite taken with yourself for being ingenious enough to diagnose and resolve the situation within a few tick-tocks.

Screeeech...stop the movie for a second. Unknowingly, the "vacationing uber tech" just caused his company to lose millions of dollars. How, you might ask, did this guy in the movie cause millions of dollars to be lost just by logging in to his company's router/firewall to fix a problem?

It was not the act of telnetting to the router/firewall that caused the problem; it was the fact that he used a wireless connection. You see, the company that uber tech worked for (yes, past tense cause he no longer works for them as a result) is a multinational corporation that was about to announce the creation of a new widget that was capable of converting discarded pizza boxes into SDRAM memory chips; a competitor of this revolutionary company not only wanted to stop this announcement—but they also wanted a copy of the plans for this widget so they could bring it to market first.

It seems that a hacker employed by the competitor was paid to follow vacationing uber tech and, at a convenient moment, break into his hotel room and download the contents of his laptop to a portable storage device, in hopes that the hacker could find some proprietary information about the widget. Upon seeing uber tech boot up his laptop, complete with wireless NIC, the hacker realized that he had struck gold and decided to do some long distance sniffing and hacking, courtesy of uber tech's unsecured wireless connection. Long-distance sniffing and hacking—sounds like a script from "Mission Impossible," doesn't it? Too far fetched to really happen? The truth is that this type of scenario occurs on a daily basis. Bad guys with wireless-enabled laptops steal information right out of the air with little effort. They use tools that are readily available on the Internet and can cause many problems for companies that do not take the time to understand the threats an unsecured wireless connection poses to their corporate network.

This chapter covers several topics related to wireless networking security and helps you identify, understand, and prevent the types of intrusions to which wireless connections are vulnerable from the outside. This chapter focuses on the commercial wireless products that are available and not the home version from Cisco subsidiaries such as Linksys. It is important to understand the differences; in this article describing the Cisco Linksys acquisition, there is a clear, related message:

> Take, for example, Cisco's Aironet wireless products. The Aironet products are the result of Cisco's significant investment in industry-leading WLAN and networking technology. Cisco Aironet solutions offer premium value in security, range, management, performance, features, and total cost of ownership as part of a complete, complex network. Linksys' products, on the other-hand, are developed using off-the-shelf silicon and software and focus on ease-of-use, price, and features that are important to consumers. As you can see by this example, the products are geared towards a different market with different needs.

> http://newsroom.cisco.com/dlls/hd_032003.html

Essentials First: Wireless LANs

This chapter discusses the use of Wireless LANs (WLANs), which are roaring into use almost every time you turn around—from airports, restaurants, and coffee shops, to people's homes. The growth of personal computers in the 1980s led to the creation of LANs and the Internet in the 1990s; this allowed for connections, regardless of geographic location. WLANs are proving to be the next technology growth area for the 2000s. Businesses are, of course, recognizing the benefits of WLANs and deploying them in ever-increasing numbers. Just as businesses were forced to provide security to PCs and the Internet, so too must businesses understand that, despite the productivity and mobility gains they provide, WLANs have associated security risks that must be addressed.

WLANs offer a quick and effective extension of a wired LAN. By simply installing access points to the wired network, personal computers and laptops equipped with wireless LAN cards can connect with the wired network at broadband speeds (or greater) from up to 300 yards away from the wireless access point. This means that computers are no longer tied to the infrastructure of wires—rather liberating, isn't it?

The majority of WLAN deployments have used a wireless transmission standard known as 802.11b. The IEEE 802.11b standard operates at the radio frequency of 2.4 Ghz—a frequency that is unregulated by governments. The 802.11b standard offers connectivity speeds of up to 11 Mbps, which provides enough speed to handle large e-mail attachments and run bandwidth-intensive applications like video conferencing. While the *802.11b* standard now dominates the wireless LAN market, other variations of the 802.11 standard are being developed, or have already been approved, to handle increased speeds. *802.11g* is the latest standard variation, which offers wireless speeds of up to 56 Mbps.

The various wireless standards are targeted to different industry segments as outlined in Tables 8-1 and 8-2.

Table 8-1   802.11a/WLAN Standard Characteristics

Standard	IEEE 802.11a, WLAN
Frequency wavelength	5 GHz
Data bandwidth	54 Mbps, 48 Mbps, 36 Mbps, 24 Mbps, 12 Mbps, 6 Mbps
Security measures	WEP, OFDM
Optimum operating range	150 ft. indoors, 300 ft. outdoors
Best suited for a specific purpose or device type	Roaming laptops in home or business; computers when wiring is inconvenient

802.11a never took off; however, the recently ratified 802.11g holds some interesting options to include increased speed and security as Table 8-2 documents.

Table 8-2   802.11g/Wi-Fi Standard Characteristics

Standard	IEEE 802.11g, Wi-Fi
Frequency wavelength	2.4 GHz
Data bandwidth	54 Mbps, 48 Mbps, 36 Mbps, 24 Mbps, 12 Mbps, 6 Mbps
Security measures	WEP, OFDM, AES (in Broadcom 54 g) and possibly WPA/Wi-Fi protected access
Optimum operating range	1000 ft. under ideal conditions; expect more like 150 ft. indoors and 300 ft. outdoors under normal conditions
Best suited for a specific purpose or device type	Roaming laptops in home or business; computers when wiring is inconvenient

Note that when 802.11b clients are granted access to an 802.11g wireless access point, security inevitably must be set (lowered) to allow 802.11b clients on; thanks to WEP and its problems, the entire network is reduced to a lowest common denominator.

What Is Wi-Fi?

The term *Wi-Fi (Wireless Fidelity)* is often used in discussions of 802.11 networks. Wi-Fi is most certainly the popular marketing word used today when talking about wireless (that is, Wi-Fi hot spots). The term Wi-Fi is fast becoming the common way to describe 802.11 wireless networks; it certainly is much quicker and easier to say, so we let marketing take the credit for making it the mainstream term.

Wi-Fi also refers to certification by the Wi-Fi Alliance, an international nonprofit association of 802.11 product vendors. 802.11 products that receive Wi-Fi certifi-

cation have been tested and found to be interoperable with other certified products. This means that you can use your Wi-Fi certified product with 802.11 Wi-Fi certified networks, whether they are Apple Computers or Windows-based networks. Although 802.11 products that do not have Wi-Fi certification might work fine with certified devices, the Wi-Fi Certified logo is your assurance of interoperability. You can learn more about the Wi-Fi alliance online at: http://www.weca.net/.

Benefits of Wireless LANs

I had not flown much on airplanes recently, but an important family event—my brother's wedding—allowed me the opportunity to fly. Not living near a major airport meant that I had to connect to reach my destination, so I experienced four different airports, each of which offered wireless connectivity to travelers, making layovers in airports a more productive time. Businesses all across the world are using this wireless capability and can easily be enabled for a relatively small financial investment. The benefits of deploying wireless LANs can be summarized as the following:

- **Attractive price**—Deploying a wireless LAN can be cheaper than a wired LAN because you do not have the need for wires; simply hook up an access point, and it can provide service to multiple computers.

- **Mobility**—Boost user productivity with the convenience of allowing them to wirelessly connect to the network from any point within range of an access point.

- **Rapid and flexible deployment**—Quickly extend a wired network with the ease of attaching an access point to a high-speed network connection.

- **Application agnostic**—As an extension of the wired network, WLANs work with all existing applications. As discussed previously, the standard protocol is TCP/IP, which is supported over all forms of wireless.

- **Performance**—WLANs offer a high-speed connection that, while equal to Ethernet, is quickly passing it in speed.

The benefits of WLANs are being recognized by individuals and businesses alike; recently the Gartner Group predicted that by 2005, 50 percent of the Fortune 1000 companies will have extensively deployed wireless networks, and that by 2010, the majority of Fortune 2000 companies will depend on wireless technology to meet their business and networking needs.

Wireless Equals Radio Frequency

The first technical concept you need to grasp when discussing what constitutes a threat to a wireless network is that 802.11 networks use radio frequencies to transmit the data back and forth between endpoints, just like the cordless phones or radios you have at home. The key difference is the frequency at which the signals are transmitted.

Radio waves can travel long distances, depending on the frequency being used. Some frequencies can transmit 300–400 feet, requiring little power to do so. Most older technology cordless phones and wireless NICs use the 900-MHz frequency as a carrier wave, which can travel quite a bit farther than most people realize. It is not uncommon for a 900-MHz cordless phone to give a user at least one or two city blocks of use before the handset loses its connection to the base unit. One or two city blocks translates roughly to 400–500 feet.

If your telephone handset can transmit out as far as 500 feet, it means that your wireless connection is capable of similar distances. If you have a Wireless access point (WAP) installed in your office or home, you can bet that people walking by outside are well within its operational envelope. The same holds true if you have a WAP installed in your small office, home office (SOHO) network. If an average WAP is installed in your living room and you live in an apartment complex, you might already be providing Internet service to most of the complex and not even realize it.

Wireless Networking

The term *wireless networking* refers to radio technology that enables two or more computers to communicate using standard network protocols such as IP, but without cables. Wireless networking hardware requires the use of underlying technology that deals with radio frequencies and data transmission. The most widely used standard is 802.11, which produced by the Institute of Electrical and Electronic Engineers (IEEE). This is a standard defining all aspects of Radio Frequency Wireless networking.

802.11b specifies that radios talk on the unlicensed 2.4GHz band at 11-Mbps transmission rate on one of 15 specific channels (in the United States, use is limited to only the first 11 of those 15 channels because of government regulations). Wireless network cards automatically search through these channels to find WLANs, so there is no need to configure client stations to specific channels. When the NIC finds the correct channel, it begins talking to the access point. As long as all the security settings on the client and AP match, communications across the AP can begin, and the user can participate as part of the network.

note

802.11g is a new high-speed wireless standard that allows users to transmit data at rates of up to 54 Mbps—nearly five times faster than 802.11b technology. Because it operates in the 2.4GHz frequency band, 802.11g is completely compatible with 802.11b and available for use worldwide. Apple currently has support for 802.11g in all its devices, with Cisco to follow shortly.

Modes of Operation

Two types of wireless networks are possible, and they differ on how wireless devices communicate to each other. WLANs operate either in ad-hoc or infrastructure. Ad-hoc networks have multiple wireless clients talking to each other as wireless peers to share data among themselves without the aid of a wireless access point. An infrastructure WLAN consists of several clients talking to a central device called an access point (AP), which is usually connected to a wired network like a corporate or home LAN:

■ *Infrastructure* — This mode of operation requires the use of a Basic Service Set (BSS); in other words, a wireless access point. The access point is required to allow for wireless computers to connect not only to each other but also to a wired network, as shown in Figure 8-1. Most corporate WLANs operate in Infrastructure mode because they require access to the wired LAN to use services such as printers and file servers.

Figure 8-1   Infrastructure Wireless Networking

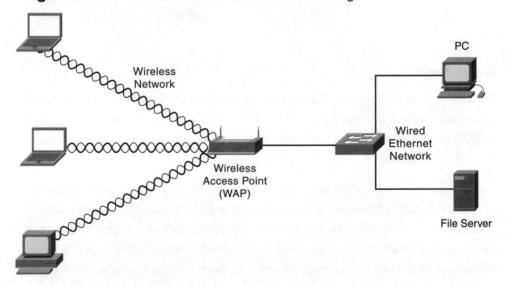

■ *Ad-Hoc* — Ad-hoc is also known as peer-to-peer wireless networking, as shown in Figure 8-2, where there are a number of wireless computers that need to transmit files to each other. This mode of operation is known as Independent Basic Service Set (IBSS). You can think of ad-hoc as being able to happen without the use of an access point. Each computer can communicate directly with all the other wireless enabled computers. They can share files and printers this way but are *unable to access wired LAN resources* unless one of the computers acts as a bridge to the wired LAN using special software. (This is called bridging.)

Figure 8-2   Ad-Hoc Wireless Networking

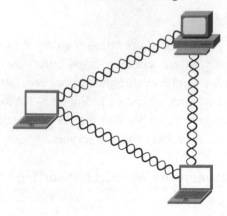

Coverage

Entirely too many wireless access points are available these days to cover them all, so this section focuses on the general coverage levels available. Your mileage might vary, so always check with your manufacturer and do a little WarWalking to see what is happening.

Every wireless access point has a finite range within which a wireless connection can be maintained between the client computer and the access point. The actual distance varies depending on the environment; manufacturers typically state both indoor and outdoor ranges to give a reasonable indication of reliable performance. Also, note that when operating at the edge of the range limits, the performance might drop because of deterioration of the quality of the wireless signal. Typical ranges are as follows:

- Typical indoor ranges are 150–300 feet but can be shorter if the building construction interferes with radio transmissions. Longer ranges are possible, but performance degrades with distance.

- Outdoor ranges are quoted up to 1000 feet, but again, this depends on the location and the environment.

In most cases, separate access points are interconnected via a wired LAN by providing wireless connectivity in specific areas such as offices or classrooms. Depending on the sophistication of the access point, the range can be modified by adjusting the power level on the AP. This might or might not be an option on some of the lower-end consumer level APs; however, on the Cisco Aironet 350, 1100, and 1200 series, this is possible. The ranges are 5 mw to 100 mw, which can be a useful method of controlling how far your signal reaches outside your company walls.

If a single area is too large to be covered by a single access point, multiple access points or wireless bridges can be used. If you choose to go this route, make sure that the access points you want to use have this feature because some do not.

Bandwidth Availability

Bandwidth on an 802.11b network is limited to 11 Mbps per access point. To dispel a lot of confusion, 11 Mbps refers to the *total possible bandwidth* per access point. Many people are used to the wired world, where switches are everywhere and each device gets the full 100 Mbps to the desktop. This is not the case with wireless; the 11 Mbps is divided among all users on that access point. If ten people access the same AP, communication to the wired world will be limited to the equivalent of approximately 1 Mbps per user.

So, you can solve the problem by simply adding another access point? I have not used the "it depends rule" since Chapter 4, "Security Protocols," so its use is way overdue and I am invoking it now. It depends; the 802.11b standard does not contain any specifications for load balancing across multiple access points. Devices that strictly adhere to the standard have no solution to the problem of finding your network becoming overpopulated.

The only way to manage this issue is to add another AP in the same area with a different network name and radio channel, effectively having more than one separate network with a maximum of three in use at the same area. Again, this is if you are using devices that adhere in this regard to the 802.11 standard. In reality, many manufacturers recognized that they would be severely limited in the number of

APs they could sell to businesses, so they developed proprietary load balancing solutions. Additional discussions of these solutions are beyond the scope of this book and should be referred to your vendor of choice.

WarGames Wirelessly

Like many of the beneficial technologies discussed in this book, wireless networks are also susceptible to a variety of threats; however, wireless is still a growing technology, and today you have the opportunity to protect and secure your network. This section takes a high-level look at some of those threats and why you should secure your network.

You might be familiar with the 1983 movie, *WarGames*, where a young man (played by Matthew Broderick) finds a back door into a military computer and unknowingly starts the countdown to World War III. The movie's young hacker executes this mayhem all over a modem, which coined the phrase *WarDialing*.

Fast-forward almost twenty years when London-based author, Ben Hammersley was writing and he wanted a cup of coffee or even a bit to eat from the café across the street. Ben installed a WAP that gave him the wireless access he wanted; he was a giving man, however, and decided to let his neighbors know that they could have free wireless Internet access. Disappointingly, no one took him up on his generosity. Enter Ben's friend, Matt Jones, who posted a set of runes on a website (http://www.blackbeltjones.com) with the intention of creating a set of international symbols that would let people know that a wireless connection is available. Ben took a piece of chalk and drew these runes on the curb in front of the café and became the first WarChalker. (See Figure 8-3.)

Shortly after Matt posted these symbols on the Internet (a.k.a. Black Belt Jones), word spread fast and these two individuals started an Internet phenomenon resulting in new words with such ominous names as WarChalking, WarSpying, WarSpamming, and WarDriving—all ultimately a part of the evolution of wireless access. To clarify, none of these new terms enhance the security of your network. They are simply terms that attackers use to describe their activities. The following sections review each of these threats.

Figure 8-3   WarChalking Symbols

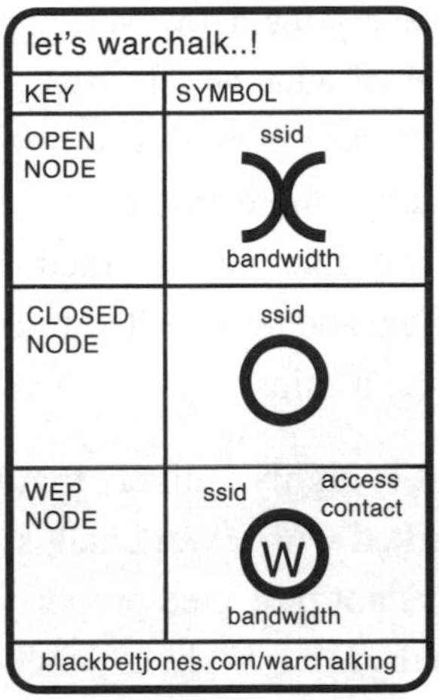

let's warchalk..!	
KEY	**SYMBOL**
OPEN NODE	ssid $)($ bandwidth
CLOSED NODE	ssid O
WEP NODE	ssid access contact W bandwidth
blackbeltjones.com/warchalking	

WarChalking

If you have ever seen a pirate movie in which a fancifully drawn treasure map displayed a large red X depicting where the ill-gotten gains were buried, you have some basic idea what role symbology has played in man's pursuit of riches. Much in the same way that the X marked the spot filled with gold, jewels, and silver, so did a series of runes depict areas of danger: which house a policeman might live in, or which houses were considered sympathetic to hobos during the great depression. For example, a rune in the shape of the pound sign "#" told fellow hobos that a crime had recently been committed and to avoid the area, or a casually drawn triangle might indicate that there were too many hobos working this area, so pickings were slim.

It was these "hobo hieroglyphics" from the Great Depression that inspired Ben and Matt to add a new dimension known as *WarChalking*. WarChalking is a practice that originated with the intention of telling fellow wireless warriors where they could get a free wireless connection on a corporate or private wireless network. The symbols utilized by these "WarChalkers" generally indicate whether the wireless access point is considered "open" or "closed," depicted either by two half-circles back to back or a single regular circle, respectively, and what sort of security is protecting this access point.

WarChalking in its original form turned out to be a momentary cult-like movement that was fascinating for everyone. However, in practice it has changed significantly to reflect the realities of what people are trying to accomplish. Very few people walk around drawing marks on buildings; however, people are "chalking" maps using GPSs to show exactly where wireless access can be gained. Searching the Internet reveals quite a few online maps marked for use (http://www.netstumbler.com/nation.php). One of the added benefits of putting the maps online is that they are not washed away when it rains.

From a security perspective, it is highly unlikely that you will ever *see* the side of your building or sidewalk marked with a WarChalk symbol; however, it is likely that if your wireless network is not protected properly, it will appear chalked on someone's map for anyone to use. You might be wondering how attackers are finding these access points. Consider the last time that you saw anyone walking around with a laptop and a GPS. It does happen, but it might not be obvious because WarWalkers typically use backpacks to conceal their activities. In addition to the limitations posed by equipment battery life, all this walking can become tiring. Enter the next wireless threat—WarDriving—where converters can power a laptop for as long as the car is running.

note

WapChalking—A variant of WarChalking set up by the Wireless Access Point Sharing Community, an informal group with a code of conduct that forbids the use of wireless access points without permission. The group uses the WarChalking marks as an invitation to wireless users to join their community. In WapChalking terms, the two half-moon open node mark means that a wireless access device is currently indicating factory default settings and is thus easily detected.

WarDriving

WarDriving makes finding open wireless networks simple and dramatically increases the search area exponentially. The act of WarDriving is simple: you simply drive around looking for wireless networks. Part of the appeal is that you can now use GPS systems connected to your laptop, which is then powered by your car. This makes the act of WarDriving accurate and potentially rewarding for those looking for your wireless network because they can cover a much larger area with a vehicle.

caution
Before delving too deeply into this subject, it is important to remember that WarDriving or "LAN jacking" an unwary subject's WAP is possibly illegal, depending on the part of the country in which you live. The reason you would consider even building an antenna in the first place is to remain as far away from the WLANs that you are sniffing in the first place. To get the latest information on legalities and updates on this front, consult your local computer club or perform an Internet search on "war driving and legalities."

It is disturbing that almost anyone can find your wireless network so easily, isn't it? Vendors turn everything on by default, regardless of network security concerns; this makes it easy for WarDrivers. By default, wireless access points broadcast a *beacon frame* that identifies (broadcasts the SSID) the wireless network they are a part of, every 10 milliseconds.

The average antennae on a wireless PCI card NIC is not sensitive enough to do a good job of zeroing in on low to medium-powered WAP signals, so many WarDrivers have resorted to using a USB wireless NIC outfitted with a homemade "directional Yagi" design antennae hardwired into the USB NIC, as shown in Figure 8-4 (http://3nw.com/pda/wireless/wi_fi_pringles_can_yagi_antenna.htm). Various designs yield better or worse results depending on the signal type of the wireless traffic you are trying to snoop. The wireless network is identified by a 32-bit character known as a *Service Set Identifier (SSID)*. For a WarDriver, the easiest networks to find are those that are broadcasting this SSID. Perhaps I do not have any special applications but only a laptop with Windows XP. From a security perspective, Windows XP is wireless-aware and perhaps too friendly because it easily picks up any SSID broadcasts and automatically tries to join any available wireless network. With such a friendly operating system, who needs all the special tools?

Figure 8-4   Pringles Can as a Yagi Antenna

By default, the SSID is included in the header of the wireless packets broadcast every 10 milliseconds from a WAP. The SSID differentiates one WLAN from another, so all access points and all devices attempting to connect to a specific WLAN must use the same SSID. A device is not permitted to join the wireless network unless it can provide the unique SSID. Because an SSID can be sniffed from a packet in plain text, it does not supply any security to the network, even though it does function as a wireless network password. It is strongly recommended that WAPs have the broadcasting of their SSID disabled.

The presence of an SSID in a wireless network means that those engaging in the search should have more powerful wireless antennas that allow them to pick up and detect wireless signals. For example, if you want to "LAN jack" 802.11b/2.4-Ghz wireless network connections, you would most likely opt for a "helix" or "helical" design, which is basically tubular in design with a series of copper wire wrappings around a central core. This custom-made antennae style can be difficult to build because of its exacting standards and rather pricey parts list. On the other hand, a "wave guide" style can be made from rather inexpensive components such as a Pringles can (as shown in Figure 8-4), coffee can, or juice can.

The basic premise of building these specialty "signal stealers" is to mount them on the roof or hood of your car, connect the antennae to your wireless NIC, and drive around town looking for unsecured access points. Again, WarDriving for the purposes of stealing Internet access and snooping around a private network is illegal and earns you a visit from men in blue suits with no sense of humor. WarDriving was invented by a man named Peter Shipley, who had the vision to take WarChalking to the next level:

> Most recently I invented Wardriving, while I am not the first person to go out and search for open wireless LANS (a few before me ventured around with in a with a laptop, pencil & paper manually scribbling notes). I was first to automate it all with dedicated software and a GPS. When I started this project the usage of WEP was around 15%, after going public with my findings, a year later WEP usage is now 33%. Thus it is good to know people are getting the message. Some maps I generated from these exercises can be found at *http:// www.dis.org/wl/maps/*.

Depending on your frame of reference (and why you are reading this book), you might be wondering whether WarDriving is a crime. Of course, those doing the WarDriving do not view it as such; however, those of you who own the wireless networks might have a slightly different perception. While doing research, I stumbled across a quote—supposedly from the FBI—that states their position as follows:

> Identifying the presence of a wireless network may not be a criminal violation, however, there may be criminal violations if the network is actually accessed including theft of services, interception of communications, misuse of computing resources, up to and including violations of the Federal Computer Fraud and Abuse Statute, Theft of Trade Secrets, and other federal violations.

Therefore, if you are deploying a wireless network, you are likely to have someone try and find it, so your security depends on that individual's understanding that it is his responsibility to ensure that he does not violate any local, state, or federal laws that might pertain to his area. To slightly rephrase: you have gone through all the trouble of purchasing equipment, learning the process, loading the tools, and setting everything up. *Your* wireless network is not secured, and law enforcement expects the WarDriver not to do anything illegal. Are you prepared to leave your network vulnerable to those who do not support this law-abiding scenario? If you are, go back to Chapter 1, "Here There Be Hackers!" and start reading again!

The FBI quote seems to be an accurate representation of law enforcement agency positions on WarDriving; contests are held to see who can find the most wireless networks. Individuals involved in the wireless industry and dedicated to a certain bias in this debate, clearly maintain these websites, but check them out:

> http://www.worldwidewardrive.org/

> http://www.wardriving.com/

You will find links to various WarChalked maps that show the GPS locations and, in many cases, much more about open wireless networks worldwide. In doing my research for this chapter, I stumbled across a few people who have taken WarDriving to the next level, literally, in the form of WarFlying.

WarFlying

I have heard only of two cases of *WarFlying*, but it is such an interesting endeavor that I just had to include it. WarFlying (a.k.a. WarStorming) is simply searching for wireless networks while flying in an airplane. However, because not many people have access to a small plane and the tools necessary to pull off WarFlying, the occurrences of WarFlying will be less than WarDriving. Because of the limited range of wireless LANs, the plane must fly below 1500 meters. WarFlying was first recorded in Perth, Australia.

WarFlying has some clear limitations because you do not have the ability (at least today) to triangulate on the access point, which could be several miles from where it was detected. Regardless, however, it is interesting, and I suggest checking out the three-part article on how Silicon Valley was WarFlown. I am not sure if that statement is grammatically correct; however, you get the point. Check out the rest of the story at http://www.arstechnica.com/wankerdesk/3q02/warflying-1.html.

WarSpamming

Everyone has received spam or junk mail; it is a plague on the Internet and, frankly, in my mailbox at home. I believe in free speech; however, that freedom does not give you the right to be heard. Fortunately, law makers and politicians around the world are beginning to notice our feelings on this matter and developing laws to penalize spammers. These laws might or might not be effective—time will tell. However, is it is becoming more difficult for spammers to source their spam from countries that are beginning to develop these laws. There are also organizations that list IP addresses of places where spam has originated from, so what is a spammer to do? Many are now sourcing their spam from other countries; this presents all sorts of logistical problems and additional costs to our spammers. As a spammer, what if I could drive downtown or hire someone to find an open wireless network, join that network, and send my spam?

Remember the concept of downstream liability discussed in Chapter 3, "Overview of Security Technologies?" It would be simple to find an open wireless network and join it to send spam. The attacker (spammer) could be sitting in a café across the street, and you might never know. Now fast-forward a bit; the spam is sent to thousands of people who report that they received it, and yet another wrinkle–the spam was pornographic in nature. Yes, it can be even worse than that (remember, we are not talking about people who have morals—they are driven by other goals and needs). A quick check reveals your network's IP address, which is then blacklisted and reported to your ISP— and do not forget about the new antispamming laws. The result is that all outgoing e-mail from your company is blacklisted. How embarrassing when *your* customers get the bounce message saying that your company is spamming, the ISP shuts off your Internet connection, and law enforcement comes knocking. Also, if you have one of those Internet connections where you are billed by usage, expect a *big* bill this month.

The truth of the matter in ***WarSpamming*** is that your network did, in fact, spam others and, while it might have been as a result of an attacker, you are now liable because your wireless network was not secured properly. Who do you think is responsible for that and are they looking for a new job? Expect to see WarSpamming increase as it becomes more difficult for spammers to operate. Those who want to do questionable things will always find a way; some will stop as it becomes too difficult, and others will not.

WarSpying

A nice follow-up to WarSpamming is WarSpying, which is a relatively new phenomenon coming to a wireless video network near you. The most popular method of WarSpying is using those wireless X10 cameras. X10 is the camera featured in pop-up ads all over the Internet and they invariably have some gorgeous woman in them. X10 is also a means by which to automate your home, as in a smart house; however, that topic is beyond the scope of this book.

WarSpying was first documented in the magazine 2600, an interesting read if you can find the few nuggets of technical worth from the rants *it prints*. Regardless, it outlined how to make a wireless device that can pick up wireless surveillance systems transmissions. Since then, many people have explored and documented the topic online, and there are now reports of people tapping into all sorts of cameras that are transmitting over a wireless network. You can learn more about WarSpying at http://rhizome.org/RSG/RSG-X10-1/.

Notice I have completely avoided all discussions of the other nefarious uses into which this could develop. The key is *awareness* and an understanding of how to protect your network.

Many places that sell kits to start someone WarDriving—plans, maps, and so on are also readily available. A simple Internet search shows the results:

> http://www.kenneke.com/index.html
>
> http://www.hotspotlist.com/
>
> http://www.wi-fiplanet.com/

This section was rather revealing about how wireless networks are found and, to a lesser degree, what some of the threats are. In addition, a variety of more specific threats are possible. Plus, after an attacker joins a wireless network, you have a host of other problems. The following sections examine these topics in more detail.

Wireless Threats

Wireless threats come in all shapes and sizes, from someone attaching to your WAP (Wireless access point) without authorization, to grabbing packets out of the air and decoding them via a packet sniffer. Many wireless users have no idea what kinds of danger they face merely by attaching a WAP to their wired network. This section discusses the most common threats faced by adding a wireless component to your network.

The airborne nature of WLAN transmission opens your network to intruders and attacks that can come from any direction. WLAN traffic travels over radio waves that the walls of a building cannot completely constrain. Although employees might enjoy working on their laptops from a grassy spot outside the building, intruders and would-be hackers can potentially access the network from the parking lot or across the street using the Pringles can antenna, as shown in Figure 8-2.

Sniffing to Eavesdrop

Because wireless communication is broadcast over radio waves, eavesdroppers who merely listen to the wireless transmissions can easily pick up unencrypted messages. Unlike wire-based LANs, the wireless LAN user is not restricted to the physical area of a company or to a single access point—the exception being those annoying areas that are not covered by the access, and it's always the office with a user who wants attention. The range of a wireless LAN can extend far outside the physical boundaries of the office or building, thereby permitting unauthorized users access from a public location like a parking lot or adjacent office suite. An attacker targeting an unprotected WAP needs only to be in the vicinity of the target and no longer requires specialized skills to break into a network. Anytime I do a network assessment for a customer in a shared office building, I almost always find one of two things:

- A neighboring business that has an open wireless network

- A neighboring user that has joined my customer's wireless network

If you want to examine the traffic going out over an Ethernet connection (wired or wireless), the best tool that comes to mind is the ubiquitous ***packet sniffer*** application. Packet sniffers allow the capture of all the packets going out over a single or multiple Ethernet connections for later inspection. These sniffer applications grab the packet, analyze it, and reveal the data payload contained within. The theft of an authorized user's identity poses one the greatest threats, and Figure 8-5 shows a freeware packet sniffer known as *Ethereal*, which is used on an Apple PowerBook G4 Laptop over a wireless Ethernet network to capture a mail application transmitting a username and password. (Names and passwords have been changed to protect the innocent, of course.)

Figure 8-5   **Wireless Sniffer Packet Capture**

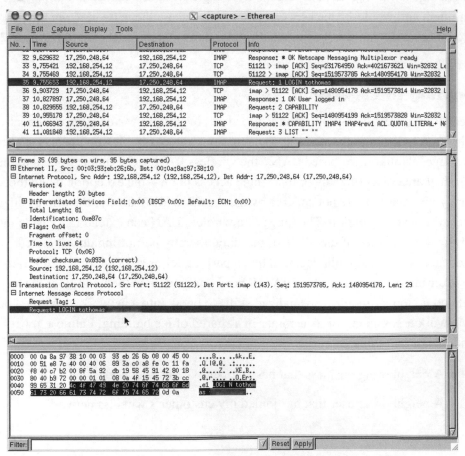

The intent here is to show you how packet sniffers can be used against known behavior. In this case, when users start their computers, one of the first things they do is check e-mail. Most e-mail servers do not require any sort of encryption and, because the wireless network is not transmitting anything encrypted, the data is sent in clear text. An attacker with a packet sniffer could now *steal the user identity* and log in to the mail server as the unaware user anytime.

If you have read through packet captures before and are familiar with the information they contain, you should have immediately recoiled in horror at the knowledge that wireless networks are sniffers readily available and several are free. If this is the first time you have seen a packet capture, you might be in for a shock as you find out the wealth of information contained in a packet's data payload. Imagine if you were a domain administrator logging in to the domain and checking your online bank account or other information that could be critically damaging if someone hijacked it.

Denial of Service Attacks

Potential attackers who cannot gain access to your Wireless LAN can nonetheless pose security threats by jamming or flooding your wireless network with static noise that causes wireless signals to collide and produce CRC errors. These denial of service (DoS) attacks effectively shut down or severely slow down the wireless network in a similar way that DoS attacks affect wired networks. This vulnerability is apparent, and being on a wired network does not reduce your vulnerability to viruses, attacks, or in any other way increase security; in fact, it will quite likely get worse.

note

Restaurants, hotels, business centers, apartment complexes, and individuals often provide wireless access with little or no protection. In these situations, it is possible to access other computers connected to a wireless LAN, thereby creating the potential for unauthorized information disclosure, resource hijacking, and the introduction of backdoors to those systems. When users take corporate laptops home and use them on wireless networks, the vulnerabilities to your network increase. I have been on network assessments reviewing wireless usage and found that many a CEO, CFO, or CTO has the IT staff set up a wireless device at home for them with the same characteristics they have at work (SSID, and so on). This makes it easy for them to work at home with no trouble; however, the corporate network is extremely vulnerable because an attacker can go after a corporate employee's home network and compromise his machine. When the employee goes to work, so does the attacker— now he is inside your corporate network. Common sense is needed her—and a commitment by everyone in the management team to secure the network. This means not mixing corporate and home security.

Perhaps a bit more common is when other wireless devices unintentionally cause a denial of service to your wireless data network—for example, that new cordless phone running on 2.4 Ghz, or placement of access points near devices that generate interference and affect their operation, such as microwaves. Not all reduction in wireless connectivity is related to attackers, so remember that wireless networks are based on radio signals, and many things (walls, weather, and wickedness) can affect them.

Rogue/Unauthorized Access Points

WAPs can be easily deployed by anyone with access to a network connection, anywhere within a corporation or business. In fact, most wireless deployments are in the home so people with laptops can use them in any room in the house. The ease with which wireless technologies can be deployed should be a concern to all network administrators.

Because a simple WLAN can easily be installed by attaching a WAP (often for less than $100) to a wired network and a $50 WLAN card to a laptop, employees are deploying unauthorized WLANs while IT departments are slow to adopt the new technology. Unauthorized WAPS are known more commonly as *Rogue APs*.

An executive of a large technology conglomerate was recently quoted as saying something like, "the hardest network to secure against wireless threats was one that had no wireless access at all" (or something very similar). What this executive meant was that, just because a company did not buy and install any wireless gear on their network did not mean that there wasn't any.

The concept behind wireless technology is to give people the freedom to roam around and still be connected to their network resources. The lure of this freedom is just too tempting to some folks in corporate America, so they go out and buy wireless gear on their own and hook it up to the office network. Now, you begin to see the problem.

note

In August 2001, Gartner Group reported that "at least 20 percent of enterprises already have rogue WLANs attached to their corporate networks" from authorized network users. Thus, risk-adverse organizations that consciously decide to delay WLAN deployment because of the security risks need to monitor their airspace to ensure that rogue WLANs do not inadvertently open a door for intruders. Stepping into the roll of the extremely paranoid, an attacker could be part of the cleaning crew in the evening and place a rogue access point into your network very easily.

If you can imagine how difficult it is to prevent people from bringing software from home and installing it on their work machines, it is ten times more difficult to prevent power users from "self adopting" wireless gear into the office LAN.

You might ask, "What is the harm in doing this?" The harm is that by installing an unauthorized access point, you have now extended an invitation to every hacker within a 500-foot radius to prowl your company's network, files, Internet access, printers, and any other devices currently connected to the private network.

Your network administrators take great pains to protect the corporate network from attackers and other "evildoers," and now there is a completely unprotected conduit into the company's holiest of holies: your internal corporate network.

A well-documented company has several security policies in place that govern every type of behavior when a user connects to the network. Rogue access points subvert these policies and open the doors to all varieties of bad things happening to the network.

To be perfectly fair to the employees who might commit this ultimate sin, it is important that the following information be made abundantly clear:

- Only authorized IT staff is to connect networking equipment.

- All devices that connect to the network, especially wireless access points, must conform to established security policies.

- Any devices that have been installed by anyone other than approved IT staff will become either the property of the company or will be rendered inert (that is, smashed into a million pieces).

- Hackers install rogue access points on a company network with the intention of stealing secrets and damaging data; this means no holiday bonuses because this kind of damage can cause a company to go out of business.

Finding rogue access points has become a little easier than in the past through the use of freely available software; the section entitled, "NetStumbler" delves into this. This same piece of software that made life easier for hackers has now become the favored tool of network security specialists for dealing with unauthorized wireless access points.

Attackers' Rogue AP Deployment Guidelines

I was going to call these "the rules for attackers to deploy rogue access points," but applying rules to those with criminal intent seemed an oxymoron. Attackers have developed some best practices that they have shared in their community and, by now, all honest network engineers are going to make WarDriving a frequent occurrence to protect your network. Following is a brief list of what you can do to prevent attackers from "casing the joint":

- Know what you are trying to gain before placing the access point.

- Plan for the use of the access point; this means place so that if you have your laptop out and "working," you do not look suspicious.

- Place the access point as discretely as possible while maximizing your ability to connect to it.

- Disable SSID Broadcasting, thus requiring the target's IT staff to have a wireless sniffer to detect it.

- Disable all network management features of the access point, such as SNMP, HTTP, Telnet.

- If possible, protect the access point's MAC address from appearing in ARP tables.

The obvious disclaimer here is that these actions are not something you should ever do without—and I *really* stress this—*written permission.* Many companies view even the accidental connection to their wireless network as an attack, so it is likely that you are going to be viewed as guilty until you prove your innocence.

It is also important to note that devices designed to jam radio signals have been around since before wireless ever became a standard. Because wireless is a radio frequency, it can be easily jammed.

Incorrectly Configured Access Points

Incorrectly configured access points are an avoidable but significant hole in WLAN security. Many access points are initially configured to openly broadcast SSIDs to authorized users. Many honest network administrators have incorrectly used SSIDs as passwords to verify authorized users. However, because the SSID is being broadcasted, this a large configuration error that allows intruders to easily steal an SSID and have the AP assume they are allowed to connect.

SSIDs act as crude passwords and are often used to recognize authorized wireless devices; thus, SSIDs should follow your corporate password policy and be treated as passwords. If you do not have a password policy, refer to Chapter 2, "Security Policies and Responses," and ensure the SSID cannot identify your company or business.

Network Abuses

Authorized users can also threaten the integrity of the network with abuses that drain connection speeds, consume bandwidth, and hinder a WLAN's overall performance. A few users who clog the network by trading MP3 files can affect the productivity of everyone on the wireless network. This ultimately leads to users who are trying to be productive complaining that the network is slow or that they keep losing connection. Based on experience, these types of issues are extremely difficult to identify and narrow down, especially if businesses decided to save money by using APs designed for home use rather than those designed for corporate use. Home-use APs do not come with the tools needed to help you.

Careless and deceitful actions by both loyal and disgruntled employees also present security risks and performance issues to wireless networks with unauthorized access points, improper security measures, and network abuses. Again, this recognizes the fact that the majority of security breeches and incidents come from inside, trusted individuals.

Wireless Security

You might be wondering why someone would want to use a wireless connection with all the insecurities that seem to go along with it. All is not lost, thanks to something known as Wired Equivalent Protocol, or is it Wireless Encryption Protocol—or it might even be Wired Equivalent Privacy. There seems to be some debate over exactly what WEP stands for among "industry experts." Regardless of how you spell or say it, WEP is an encryption algorithm that can be invoked to encrypt the transmissions between the wireless user and his Wireless access point (WAP).

From its inception, the 802.11b standard was not meant to contain a comprehensive set of enterprise level security tools. Still, the standard includes some basic security measures that can be employed to help make a network more secure. With each security feature, the potential exists for making the network either more secure or more open to attack.

Working on the layered defense concept, the following sections look first at how a wireless device connects to an access point and how you can apply security at the first possible point.

Service Set Identifier (SSID)

By default, the access point broadcasts the SSID every few seconds in beacon frames. Although, this makes it easy for authorized users to find the correct network, it also makes it easy for unauthorized users to find the network name. This feature is what allows most wireless network detection software to find networks without having the SSID upfront.

SSID settings on your network should be considered the first level of security and should be treated as such. In its standards-adherent state, SSID might not offer any protection against who gains access to your network, but configuring your SSID to something not easily guessable can make it more difficult for intruders to know what exactly they are seeing.

If you have your SSID configured to be any of the defaults cited in Table 8-1, you should change the SSID immediately.

Table 8-1   Default Wireless SSIDs

Manufacturer	Default SSID
3Com	101, comcomcom
Addtron	WLAN
Cisco	Tsunami, WaveLAN Network
Compaq	Compaq

continues

Table 8-1 Default Wireless SSIDs (continued)

Manufacturer	Default SSID
Dlink	WLAN
Intel	101, 195, xlan, intel
Linksys	Linksys, wireless
Lucent/Cabletron	RoamAbout
NetGear	Wireless
SMC	WLAN
Symbol	101
Teletronics	any
Zcomax	any, mello, Test
Zyxel	Wireless
Others	Wireless

A complete listing of manufacturers' SSIDs and even other networking equipment default passwords can be found at http://www.cirt.net/. As you can see, the SSIDs are readily available on the Internet, so it is a good idea to turn off SSID broadcasting as your first step.

Device and Access Point Association

Before any other communications take place between a wireless client and a wireless access point, the two must first begin a dialogue. This process is known as *associating*. When 802.11b was designed, the IEEE added a feature to allow wireless networks to require authentication immediately after a client device associates with the access point, but before the access point transmission occurs. The goal of this requirement was to add another layer of security. This authentication can be set to either *shared key authentication* or *open key authentication*.

You need to use open key authentication because shared key is flawed; although that is counter-intuitive, this recommendation is based on the understanding that other encryption will be used.

Wired Equivalent Privacy (WEP)

There is a lot of misconception surrounding WEP, so let's clear that up right away. WEP is not, nor was it ever meant to be, a security algorithm. WEP was never designed to protect your data from script kiddies or from more intelligent attackers who want to discover your secrets. WEP is not designed to repel; it simply makes sure that you are not less secure because you are not keeping your data in a wire. The problem occurs when people see the word "encryption" and make assumptions. WEP *is* designed to make up for the inherent insecurity in wireless transmission, as compared to wired transmission. *WEP makes your data as secure as it would be on an unencrypted, wired Ethernet network.* That is all it is designed to do, period; now your misconceptions are gone and you can move on. WEP can be typically configured in three possible modes:

- No encryption mode

- 40-bit encryption

- 128-bit encryption

WEP is an optional, agreed-upon encryption standard that is configured before the wireless user's connection to the WAP. After it is configured on the both the WAP and the user's end, all communications sent through the air are encrypted, thereby providing a secure link that is reasonably difficult to break, although recently developed hacker tools are gaining ground on this front. A side benefit of using WEP is that users wanting to connect to a WAP using WEP must have it enabled previously on their machine and have the "passphrase" or "key" that is shared between the end user and access point.

Wired Equivalent Privacy (WEP) was intended to give wireless users the security equivalent of being on a wired network. With WEP turned on, when each packet is transmitted from one access point to a client device, each packet is first encrypted

by taking the packet's data and a secret 40-bit number and passing them both through a encryption algorithm called RC4. The resulting encrypted packet is then transmitted to the client device. When the client device receives the WEP encrypted packet, it uses the same 40-bit number to pass the encrypted data through RC4 algorithm backward, resulting in the client receiving the data. Of course this process occurs in reverse and a client device is transmitting data to an access point. The encryption key used in this example was 40-bit, but 128-bit is also supported and, given the misconceptions and flaws with WEP, it is recommended that you always use the 128-bit encryption because it is better than 40-bit.

WEP Limitations and Weaknesses

WEP protects the wireless traffic by combining the "secret" WEP key with a 24-bit number (Initialization Vector, or IV), randomly generated, to provide encryption services. The 24-bit IV is combined with either the 40-bit or 104-bit WEP pass phrase to give you a possible full 128 bits of encryption strength and protection—or does it? There are a few issues surrounding the flawed current implementation of WEP:

- WEP's first weakness is the straightforward numerical limitation of the 24-bit Initialization Vector (IV), which results in 16,777,216 (2^{24}) possible values. This might seem large, but you know from discussions in Chapter 4, "Security Protocols," that this number is deceiving. The problem with this small number is that eventually the values and thus the keys start repeating themselves; this is how attackers can crack the WEP key.

- The second weakness is that of the possible 16 million values, not all of them are good. For example, the number 1 would not be very good. If an attacker can use a tool to find the weak IV values, the WEP can be cracked.

- WEP's third weakness is the difference between the 64-bit and 128-bit encryption. Perception would indicate that the 128-bit should be twice as secure, right? Wrong. Both levels still use the same 24-bit IV, which has inherent weaknesses. Therefore, if you think going to 128-bit is more secure, in reality, you will gain absolutely no increase in the security of your network.

Of course, freely available tools can accomplish all these things and are ready for the attackers to download and use as discussed in the section, "Essentials First: Wireless Hacking Tools," later in the chapter. Using WEP is better than nothing; however, layering the security of any part of your network is the key to safety and security, as has been established in all earlier chapters. Extensible Authentication Protocol (EAP) is the next level of security and is discussed in the correspondingly titled section.

MAC Address Filtering

MAC address filtering is another way people have tried to secure their networks over and above the 802.11b standards. A network card's MAC address is a 12-digit hexadecimal number that is unique to each and every network card in the world. Because each wireless Ethernet card has its own individual MAC address, if you limit access to the AP to only those MAC addresses of authorized devices, you can easily shut out everyone who should not be on your network.

However, MAC Address filtering is not completely secure and, if you solely rely upon it, you will have a false sense of security. Consider the following:

- Someone will have to keep a database of the MAC address of every wireless device in your network. If there are only 10–20 devices, it is not a problem. However, if you must keep track of hundreds of MAC addresses, this will become a nightmare quickly.

- MAC addresses can be changed, so a determined attacker can use a wireless sniffer to figure out a MAC address that is allowed through and set his PC to match it to consider it valid. Note that encryption takes place at about Layer 2, so MAC addresses will still be visible to a packet sniffer.

Extensible Authentication Protocol (EAP)

802.1X is a standard regarding port level security that the IEEE ratified. This ratification was initially intended to standardize security on wired network ports, but

it was also found to be applicable to wireless networking. ***Extensible Authentication Protocol (EAP)*** is a Layer 2 (MAC address layer) security protocol that exists at the authentication stage of the security process and, coupled with the security measures discussed thus far, provides a third and final layer of security for your wireless network. Using 802.1X, when a device requests access to the AP, the following steps occur with EAP:

1. The access point requests authentication information from the client.

2. The user then supplies the requested authentication information.

3. AP then forwards the client supplied authentication information to a standard RADIUS server for authentication and authorization.

4. Upon authorization from the RADIUS server, the client is allowed to connect and transmit data.

The four commonly used EAP methods in use today are

- EAP-MD5

- EAP-Cisco Wireless (also known as LEAP)

- EAP-TLS

- EAP-TTLS

The following sections provide a quick overview of each EAP method.

EAP-MD5

EAP-MD5 relies on an MD5 hash of a username and password to pass authentication information to the RADIUS server. EAP-MD5 offers no key management or dynamic WEP key generation, thus requiring the use of static WEP keys. This version of EAP does have some limitations:

- Because there is no dynamic WEP key generation available, the added use of EAP provides no increased security over WEP. Attackers can still sniff your airborne traffic and decrypt the WEP key.

- EAP-MD5 does not provide for a means for the client device to ensure that it is transmitting to the proper access point. A client could erroneously transmit to a rogue access point.

Because EAP-MD5 offers no other features over the standard 802.1X, EAP-MD5 is considered the least secure of all the common EAP standards.

LEAP (EAP-Cisco)

EAP-Cisco Wireless, or LEAP as it is more commonly known, is a standard developed by Cisco in conjunction with the 802.1X standard and is the basis for much of the ratified version of EAP. Like EAP-MD5, LEAP accepts a username and password from the wireless device and transmits them to the RADIUS server for authentication. Cisco added additional support beyond what the standard required, resulting in several security benefits as follows:

- LEAP authenticates the client; one-time WEP keys are dynamically generated for each client connection. This means that every client on your wireless network is using a different dynamically generated WEP key that no one knows—not even the user.

- LEAP supports a RADIUS feature called session timeouts, which requires clients to log in again every few minutes. Fortunately, this is all handled without the user having to do anything. Couple this feature with dynamic WEP keys, and your WEP keys will change so often that attackers will not be able to determine the key in time.

- LEAP conducts mutual authentication from *client-to-access point* and *access point-to-client*; this stops attackers from introducing rogue access points into your network.

There is presently a single known limitation to running LEAP.

MS-CHAPv1 is used for both the client and access point authentication and is known to have vulnerabilities.

note
Not everyone has a RADIUS server that is ready to utilize LEAP; however, Cisco access points can be configured with a feature called local AAA Authentication on a per user basis. This allows the user database to reside in the AP instead of RADIUS and works well if you have only a limited number of users.

EAP-TLS

Microsoft developed EAP-TLS, which is outlined in RFC 2716. Instead of username/password combinations, EAP-TLS uses X.509 certificates to handle authentication. EAP-TLS relies on transport layer security to pass PKI information to EAP. Like LEAP, EAP-TLS offers the following:

- Dynamic one-time WEP key generation

- Mutual authentication

The drawbacks of EAP-TLS include the following:

- PKI is required to use EAP-TLS; however, most companies do not deploy PKI.

- Microsoft Active Directory with a certificate server can be used; however, change is difficult in this model.

- If you are using Open LDAP or Novell Directory Services, you need a RADIUS server; again, not everyone has immediate access to one.

- If you have implemented PKI using VeriSign certificates, all the fields required by EAP-TLS are not present.

Unless you are ready to follow the implementation of EAP-TLS exactly as Microsoft has laid it out, you should probably look for another method.

EAP-TTLS

Funk Software (http://www.funk.com/) pioneered EAP-TTLS as an alternative to EAP-TLS. The wireless access point still identifies itself to the client with a server certificate, but the users now send their credentials in username/password form. EAP-TTLS then passes the credentials in any number of administrator specified challenge-response mechanisms (PAP, CHAP, MS-CHAPv1, MS-CHAPv2, PAP/ Token Card, or EAP). The only challenges to EAP-TTLS are

- The slightly less secure than dual certificates of EAP-TLS

- The upcoming standard developed by Microsoft and Cisco that works exactly the same way—Protected EAP (PEAP)

Increasing Wireless Security

As discussed, there are some possible means of securing your wireless network beyond WEP. It is unlikely, however, that anyone has a RADIUS server ready and waiting to be used; therefore, you need to identify steps you can take immediately to increase the security of your wireless network. The attention on the pitfalls of wireless LANs has inspired some organizations to ban wireless LANs altogether. However, security-conscious organizations are fortifying their wireless LANs with a layered approach to security that includes the following:

- Putting the wireless network behind its own routed interface so you can shut off access to at a single choke point if necessary

- Discovery of rogue access points and potential associated vulnerabilities

- Physical and logical access point security to ensure that someone cannot walk up to an access point and alter its configuration without your knowledge

- Changing the SSID and then picking a random SSID that gives away nothing about your company or network

- Disabling active SSID broadcasting

- Rotating your broadcast keys every ten minutes or less

- Encryption and authentication, which might include a virtual private network over wireless

- Using 802.1X for key management and authentication

- Looking over the available EAP protocols and deciding which is right for your environment

- Setting the session to time out every ten minutes or less

- Establishing and enforcing wireless network security policies

- Implementing proactive security measures that include intrusion protection

As shown in Figure 8-6, these steps and recommendations can be illustrated as a phased approach, which enforces the concept of first knowing what the vulnerabilities are and moving forward from that point.

Figure 8-6   Stages of Securing Your Wireless Network

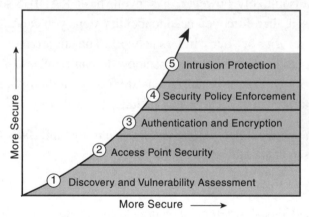

Essentials First: Wireless Hacking Tools

This section examines some of the tools that eliminate some of the threats discussed in the preceding sections. In theory, these tools were all designed to help network administrators take care of their networks, and they are still touted as such on each website. In reality, these are some of the same tools that attackers can and will use; thus, network administrators should also use them to ensure that their wireless networks are secure.

NetStumbler

Wireless networking is everywhere! That is not meant as hyperbole—it really is *everywhere*. Wireless technology uses radio waves to transmit data, so wireless packets are probably flowing in the air in front of you as you read this.

As everyone knows by now, where wireless packets flow, wireless access points are pumping them out (where there is smoke, there is fire). If only there was a way to find out whether any WAPs were nearby. Fortunately (and unfortunately), there is a way to discover just that.

A little piece of freeware called Net Stumbler is available on the Internet (found at: http://www.netstumbler.com/) that provides you with such secret pieces of information as the following:

- WAP's SSID (Service Set Identification, the unique name you can assign to your WAP)

- Signal strength of the discovered WAPs and whether the WAP is using WEP

What channel the WAP is transmitting on, and some other sneaky bits of information

 note
NetStumbler is also available for Apple computers in the form of an application known as MacStumbler (http://www.macstumbler.com).

You might have even seen NetStumbler make an appearance on the local evening news under the headline, "Wireless Security Threats: You Could Be Next!" or some other scary tagline. Figure 8-7 shows the NetStumbler interface.

Figure 8-7   NetStumbler Scanning

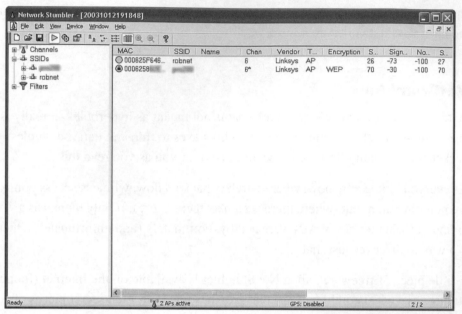

NetStumbler sends out a broadcast on all channels looking for a response. If your WAP is configured to respond to the broadcast (SSID broadcast "enabled" setting), NetStumbler logs that WAP and furnishes you with a "bing-bing" tone designating a target. A word of caution, however: NetStumbler can lock only onto 802.11b and some 802.11a-compliant WAPs.

The truth is that NetStumbler does not tell you much more than your wireless NIC's configuration interface. However, the trick is that NetStumbler tells you all the information you need about someone else's wireless network.

Most wireless NIC configuration programs allow you to perform a *site survey*, which sniffs around for other wireless access points that are configured to broadcast on the same channel as your NIC. If you happen to find a WAP with the default SSID (in this case, the default SSID of a Linksys WAP is "linksys") displayed, you can assume that you can connect to that WAP with little or no trouble.

One of the best features about NetStumbler is its capability to integrate laptop-based GPS units into its WAP discovery adventure. Imagine driving along with your trusty laptop on the passenger seat of your POV (privately owned vehicle) and hearing the pleasant "bing-bing" tones generated by NetStumbler as it happily sniffs out WAPs within transmitting distance. Every time that your laptop makes that sound, NetStumbler queries the attached GPS unit and records the coordinates of the WAP it found. Later, you can download the coordinates into mapping software and have a nice, little map printed out to show you where the WAPs were found. And who says technology doesn't make our lives just a wee bit more interesting?

The whole GPS issue aside, NetStumbler is not actually a hacking tool because the information it reveals is just a step above what your NIC can already help you find out. Tools like NetStumbler are more along the lines of a "reconnaissance" tool because they help you discover things that might not have been immediately obvious. One mission that NetStumbler has recently been assigned is that of Rogue AP detector.

Wireless Packet Sniffers

Sniffing packets can be both fun and profitable if you know how and what to sniff. Any network administrator can lay his hands on a packet sniffer in a matter of seconds and snag a couple of hundred packets before you can even read this paragraph. The contents of these packets can reveal network secrets that have been closely guarded. "Sniffing," or "snarffing" in the HaXoR world, is the process of intercepting and recording traffic that was never supposed to be seen by anyone other than the sender or receiver.

To the layman, the idea of "sniffing," "capturing," or "snagging" packets is an alien concept; therefore, the basics of the operation deserve some brief discussion:

1. Packets travel over an Ethernet connection from source to destination.

2. A NIC set to "promiscuous" mode can "listen in" on all local traffic.

3. A packet "sniffer" can see and record all this traffic.

4. A packet "sniffer" can also decode the packet and display neat things like the source MAC address, the destination MAC address, and the data payload contained in the packet.

5. Packets contain things like unencrypted Windows LanMan v.1 passwords, passwords sent in clear text, and other tasty things relished by hackers.

Now that you know about wired packet sniffers, you also need to meet their wireless cousins. How is this possible, you ask? Can I really capture wireless packet traffic? Could it be that easy? Do hackers know about this? The answers are, yes, yes, and *yes*.

Yes, hackers know about sniffing wireless connections, and they have made the most of it. Have you turned on a MAC filter on your WAP? Packet captures rat you out by telling the hacker the MAC address' source. It is easy to spoof a MAC address on your wireless NIC, especially with a program called SMAC, lovingly created by a group of guys at KLC Consulting. They make both a Win32 and Linux version of the software that virtually (as in not actually, but makes it appear so) changes your NIC's MAC address. If a hacker "sniffs" your wireless packets, he can decode the packets, read the MAC address of a machine listed in the WAP's MAC filter, plug that number in SMAC, and impersonate a machine that is authorized to use the WAP. It can do all this in less than one minute. That is correct—60 seconds. In the time it takes to dip a biscuit in gravy and eat it, a hacker can intrude on your network. But what if I am running WEP, you might ask? Read the following section and save your question for later (http://www.wildpackets.com/products/airopeek_nx).

AirSNORT

Now you understand more about the encryption used by WEP, how WEP does its thing, and how wireless is vulnerable. Things were going along swimmingly back in the year 2001 for the wireless world—until a piece of software called AirSNORT came along. The 802.11 protocol was under attack and that attack continues even today.

AirSNORT made its first widespread public appearance in the pages of *Wired* magazine on August 20, 2001. The concept of snagging packets and cracking the encryption protecting them was not a new concept; in fact, security experts had known of WEP's weaknesses for quite a while. The AirSNORT software was merely the hacker's "combo meal" that put the capture and the cracker in one easy to use application. The downside to AirSNORT was that it ran only on Linux (and still does today), which did not have nearly the level of acceptance that it does today.

The people who invented AirSNORT were interviewed at the time of release and professed that it was not written with the intention of it becoming a staple in the hacker toy box; rather, it was intended to be a proof of concept tool that demonstrated the inherent weakness of WEP.

It is estimated that AirSNORT needs to capture only five or six million packets and chew on them for as little as a minute, or as long as a couple of hours, before it can chew through the encryption and reveal the WEP key. Those time estimates were unbelievable in 2001. Can you imagine how much faster today's 2- and 3-gigahertz machines can mow through the same amount of data? Can you say s-e-c-o-n-d-s? From an attacker's point of view, the downside of this is that it can take a long time to gather the millions of packets necessary—but once they do....

As if this were not bad news enough for would-be wireless warriors, another piece of software called WEPcrack popped on the radar screen at the same. WEPcrack did roughly the same job as AirSNORT, but it was not as far along in the development phase. You can find AirSNORT at: http://airsnort.shmoo.com/.

note
Other wireless tools such as KisMET and KisMAC, which are wireless AP locators and include support for GPS location and positioning, can be used to create maps of all known, open wireless access points in a city.

Chapter Summary

This chapter has hopefully shed some light on the technology that drives wireless and the first steps for beginning to secure a wireless network. There are a variety of areas surrounding wireless that you should be concerned about; however, there are clear, layered steps that can be applied to secure a wireless network with minimal impact to users. Of utmost importance are the steps you take today to increase security that will not hamper or affect the security of your wireless network. The chapter concluded with a discussion of the *freely* available tools relating to attacking and securing wireless networks. Attackers commonly use these tools; more importantly, however, those who are looking to find flaws in their wireless network security *should* use them to patch them up and prevent easy attacks.

Chapter Review Questions

1. How are the terms 802.11 and Wi-Fi used? In what ways are they different or similar?

2. What are the five benefits to organizations that would provide reasons for them to implement a wireless network?

3. WarDriving is the most common means of searching for wireless networks. What is needed to conduct a WarDrive, and why is it so useful for attackers?

4. What is one type of freely available wireless packet sniffers?

5. Are wireless networks vulnerable to the same types of denial of service attacks as wired network? Are they vulnerable to any additional attacks that wired networks are not?

6. What are the four types of EAP available for use?

What You Will Learn

By the end of this chapter, you should know and be able to explain the following:

- ✔ The essentials of Intrusion Detection and why is it necessary even if you have a firewall

- ✔ The difference between a Network Intrusion Detection System (NIDS) and a Host Intrusion Detection System (HIDS)

- ✔ How an IDS detects intrusions (that is, attacks) and the potential ways a response can occur

- ✔ Some of the potential IDS solutions that are available today

Being able to answer these key questions will allow you to understand the characteristics and importance of Intrusion Detection in your network's overall security. By the time you finish this book, you will have a solid appreciation for network security, its issues, how it works, and why it is important.

CHAPTER 9

Intrusion Detection and Honeypots

The difference between 'involvement' and 'commitment' is like an eggs-and-ham breakfast: the chicken was 'involved'—the pig was 'committed.' — Author unknown

The machines have taken over the world. Check into it if you want, but the truth is that they have taken over, and we are simply providing the power to run them. We exist as some kind of power cell and nothing more. (Pretty weird so far, huh?)

Does this sound like some kind of nightmare, or perhaps the plot of a high-end science-fiction movie? Take a moment and decide whether the guy in the trench coat and sunglasses is telling you the truth. Are you ready to cross through the looking glass and really see what's going on? Are you ready to give up 24 hours of cable TV, media propaganda, chocolate milk, and video games? You decide if you want the truth. *You can't handle the truth!* Or can you?

You wake up and find yourself surrounded by a glass cocoon filled with sticky fluid and discover that you have probes plugged into your spinal cord. Could this story get any worse?

It can, and it does. You start unplugging the probes one by one. Before you completely realize where you really are, creepy spider machines start hovering around you and checking you out (don't you hate it when that happens?) and smacking you around.

And then…, and then…. Go ahead and turn the lights back on; yes, you over there by the light switch—flip the switch. We need to stop for a moment and discuss what in the world, if anything, all of this has to do with a chapter on Intrusion Detection Systems and Honeypots.

Although it is partially "borrowed" from a popular movie, this story gives you a sneak peek at the basic premise of how an *Intrusion Detection System (IDS)* works. IDSs function on three basic premises:

- Where to watch

- What to watch for

- What to do

The first premise, "where to watch," tells the IDS the logical location it will be monitoring for something to happen. Our little story has you as the "where to watch" portion. The evil machine empire has instructed the creepy spider machines to monitor you and make sure that you do not wake up.

The second premise, "what to watch for," tells the IDS conditions for which it is supposed to be looking for to raise an alarm or some other kind of action. In this case, the creepy spiders were programmed to look for you to wake up and unplug the probes. Back in the old days, all it took was someone waking up to get the creepy spiders going. Things really have changed, haven't they?

The third premise, "what to do," is the action the IDS has been told to take when a situation meets certain parameters. The creepy spiders were programmed to fly up to your pod and smack you around if you happen to wake up and start monkeying around with your sleep chamber.

Let's put all the spiders and sci-fi stuff aside for a minute and take a look at a real-world example of an IDS in action:

1. You install an IDS to watch the Internet connection and those trying to get into your network through your firewall.

2. You tell the IDS what types of hacks and attacks to look for based on their packet and connection type and what activities these might generate.

3. You tell the IDS to page you and send you an e-mail when one of these attacks occurs.

4. Uber Haxor comes knocking on your door with a port scan (can't be too uber or too much of a haxor, starting off with something that obvious) that scans the first 1000 TCP ports.

5. The IDS sees the sequential connection attempts to all these ports, checks its database, and sees that this behavior matches the profile you entered that tells it how to recognize a port scan.

6. It attempts to e-mail you and page you at the same time.

7. Suddenly, the port scans increase, and they also come from another source.

8. The IDS also notifies you of this attempt.

Now you have your IDS configured properly; it sits and watches your network 24 hours a day, ready to alert you at the first sign of any funny business.

Sounds pretty cool so far, doesn't it? Has anyone spotted the flaw in the whole IDS operating principle?

First, the IDS can watch only one interface at a time.

Secondly, the IDS watches only for conditions that you tell it about. If it has not been programmed to watch for the "double-reverse twinkie" attack, it will not let you know if one does occur.

Finally, an IDS can actually become an ally to hackers. Impossible, you say? How many times do you still run right out of the house and check your car when you hear the factory-installed alarm go off in the middle of the night? The same "crying wolf" situation can occur with an IDS. If your pager starts filling up with messages sent by the IDS, you start filtering out what you believe to be "false positives;" this could lead to you missing the pages that could really mean something.

The secret to configuring and deploying an IDS is "tweaking." You must deploy the IDS in a lab first, see what normal traffic causes the IDS to alert, and then start "turning down the squelch"—that is, decreasing the IDS's sensitivity to these conditions. You can also resist the urge to alert on everything that occurs. Most people want to be notified of every little "burp" that takes place, but this is not realistic. IDSs are not perfect, and they generate false positives from time to time. Let's take a real-world look at the essentials behind Intrusion Detection.

Essentials First: Intrusion Detection

Networks of all sizes are designed to enable the sharing of information, and only rarely is security a part of that design. Many businesses are leveraging IP-based networks, such as the Internet, to bring remote offices, mobile workers, and business partners into their trusted internal network environments. The Internet is continuously growing and connecting more and more places; as it becomes increasingly reliable, companies can redefine how corporate applications function. The clearest example is how almost everything is becoming based on HTML. Although this enables businesses to have broader interaction with customers, streamline operations, reduce costs, and increase revenues, it also comes at a price and with risks.

note

Cisco NID supports 802.1q trunking and can thus be set up to monitor multiple VLANs per single interface. Keep in mind to not over burden the sensor. This means that, if it is a Cisco NID, a NID can monitor more than one interface at a time.

The very reach and openness that makes the Internet such a powerful business tool also makes it a tremendous liability. Simply put, the Internet was designed to connect and share, not to secure and protect. The websites and portals that welcome remote sites, mobile users, customers, and business partners into the trusted internal network might also be welcoming attackers who would misappropriate network resources for personal gain. As discussed in Chapter 8, "Wireless Security," the growth of wireless networks is compounding this problem.

The question becomes this: How are these mission-critical communications protected from an inherently insecure medium such as the Internet? This book has covered various means of increasing the security of these resources by adding layers of protection. The most common layers of security in a network are an Internet router prescreening packet and a stateful firewall. However, your organization has both a web and e-mail server that must be accessible from the Internet to function. You cannot block this traffic because your business depends on it. We also know that, as the Internet has grown, so have the sophistication of the attacks; however, the knowledge level required to conduct these attacks has decreased, as shown in Figure 9-1.

Figure 9-1   Attack Sophistication and Attacks

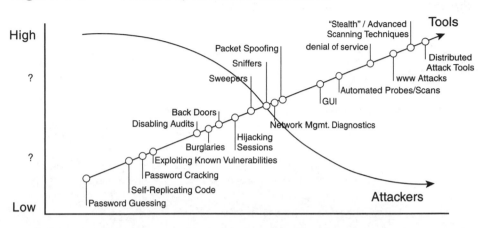

Neither the router nor the firewall can tell you if that WWW packet actually contains an attack or a customer; unfortunately, many people have placed their trust in these devices, which can fall short in the detection arena. Perhaps your organization has a talented system administrator who is trusted to "secure and lock down" business-critical servers or implement thorough security policies and procedures. None of the security solutions discussed so far address the need to *detect attacks or intrusion attempts!*

In Internet terms, Intrusion Detection is rather young; research began in the 1980s with the efforts and writing of Anderson and Denning. In the 1980s, the government first began using basic IDS functionality on what was then still the ARPANET. Late in the 1980s, members of the Haystack Project formed Haystack Labs as a commercial venture into developing host-based intrusion detection. Network-Based Intrusion Detection followed in the 1990s with Todd Heberlein leading the charge. By then, several organizations were developing IDS tools, Haystack Labs, SAIC; the United States Air Force developed ASIM (automated security measurement system), and the team that developed this solution formed the Wheel Group in 1994, as shown in Figure 9-2.

Figure 9-2   IDS Development Timeline

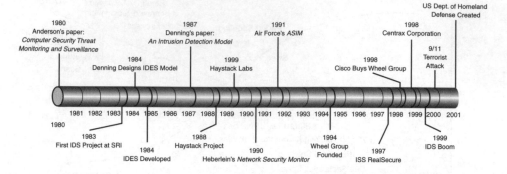

This is relevant to the discussion because, in 1994, Cisco purchased the Wheel Group; this acquisition formed the core of the IDS and security services.

note

If you are interested in obtaining a more detailed look at the history of IDS, I recommend the following article:

http://www.securityfocus.com/infocus/1514

Whether an attacker's motive is intellectual challenge, espionage, political, financial, or even just to make trouble, your network will face an attack. Not only is it common sense to monitor these attacks, but in many cases, it is also a business imperative. Starting in the early 1990s, new products began to appear to deal with this aspect of network security: *Intrusion Detection Systems (IDS)*. An IDS is like an alarm system for your network. The network is protected, but without the IDS (alarm), you would never know whether an attacker was trying to gain entry. The goal of Intrusion Detection is to monitor network assets to detect unusual behavior, inappropriate activity, and attacks, or stop the attack (intrusion) and even provide information to prosecute the attacker.

IDS can be deployed in a variety of locations within a network to further increase an organization's security and protection. In general, two basic forms of IDS are used today: *network-based and host-based IDS*. Both types of sensors offer different techniques for detecting and deferring malicious activity, and both should be deployed to provide the most effective enhancement to a layered defense strategy:

■ *Network-Based Intrusion Detection System (NIDS)* reside directly on the network and watch all the traffic that traverses the network. NIDS are effective at both watching for inbound/outbound traffic flows and traffic between hosts on or between local network segments. NIDS are typically deployed in front of *and* behind firewalls and VPN gateways to measure the effectiveness of those security devices and interact with them to add more depth to the network's security.

■ *Host-Based Intrusion Detection System (HIDS)* are specialized software applications that are installed on a computer (typically a server) to watch all inbound and outbound communication traffic to and from that server and to monitor the file system for changes. HIDS are extremely effective on mission-critical, Internet-accessible application servers, such as web or e-mail servers, because they can watch the applications at its source to protect them.

NIDS and HIDS should be deployed together to provide a truly effective layered defense with visibility into and control of an organization's communications. IDSs also provide organizations a check-and-balance on the effectiveness of their security systems and the overall effectiveness of their security dollars. The next section discusses the overall capabilities of an IDS.

IDS Functional Overview

IDS systems that are available on the market today promise a plethora of feature sets and capabilities. In evaluating an IDS for your organization, the following capabilities should generally be the focus, beyond traditional event logging:

■ **Event correlation**—When an IDS is deployed in a busy network with multiple IDS, the ability to correlate events (attacks) is crucial to ensuring that your network is secure. Consider that an attack could span multiple segments as one host is compromised and then used to attack another, and so on. Without proper event correlation, this attack could cause great confusion and lead to many hours of wasted resources attempting to isolate the cause

of the outage. Event correlation allows the IDS administrator to quickly track down and relate events that occur across multiple sensors that are deployed in different subnets, or perhaps in different geographical locations and over extended periods of time.

■ **Centralized sensor management**—Having an IDS be able to correlate events is important, and having all the IDS managed via centralized management is just as critical. In the real world, every device (server, router, firewall) creates logs; however, they are rarely checked, let alone reviewed. Therefore, having a centralized management platform that allows for event correlation and response control over multiple sensors and the ability to run detailed reports on your network's security is crucial for success.

■ **Customizable signatures and thresholds**—Company or business-specific applications, software upgrades, new operating systems, viruses, and intelligent hackers are always looking for and discovering new vulnerabilities. There is always a delay from when a new vulnerability is discovered and IDS developers release a new signature that detects the attack that is used to exploit the vulnerability. Therefore, an IDS must allow administrators the ability to create attack signatures to deal with any eventuality.

■ **Elimination of false positives**—Just like every operating system (such as Windows) that comes with all the features enabled, so do IDS devices. In other words, they are overly sensitive out of the box and provide a lot of false positives, thereby resulting in FUD (fear, uncertainty, and doubt) about your network security. You can understand, then, that every good IDS must have the capability to eliminate false positives. Caution, however—only eliminate if you are sure and, if you are sure, wait 24 hours.

■ **Standards-based implementation**—An important aspect of deploying any technology is choosing an implementation that is standards-based. Many vendors create products that perform wonderful security services, but few are interoperable or provide the framework for future implementations. IDS is no exception to this rule, and few standards currently exist. Because the most important aspect of integrating IDS and managing it are its reporting capabilities, a standard has emerged based on the Common Vulnerabilities and Exposures (CVE) database. The CVE database both classifies and groups vulnerabilities into an easily referenced system. CVE compatibility is important for IDS because it provides reporting capabilities that far surpass the typical cryptic reporting historically found in IDS. By integrating CVE-compatible IDSs, organizations can use other CVE-compatible tools, such as Vulnerability Assessment (VA) tools, to further enhance the accuracy and criticality of event reporting. CVE has become widely adopted and will continue to be a standard method of reporting and classifying network security events (http://cve.mitre.org/cve/).

- **Intrusion Prevention functionality**—Intrusion Prevention is essentially the ability to actively respond to and prevent intrusions and unwanted traffic. The term "Intrusion Prevention" has recently been the subject of much confusion and is often marketed as a competing technology to Intrusion Detection. However, the reverse is true: In today's market, an IDS must support the capability to actively respond to suspected threats.

- **Signature matching**—Monitors all traffic traversing a network and then matches each packet or series of packets with known attack patterns (signatures). The IDS then responds either passively or actively to that event. The response can vary from generating an SNMP alarm, crafting an e-mail alert, or actively stopping the attacker from being able to complete the attack (also referred to as Intrusion Prevention).

- **Anomaly detection**—Allows an IDS to establish a baseline of normal traffic patterns and information flows, and then respond whenever the normal thresholds are exceeded (for example, if a new protocol is detected on a network). Anomaly Detection becomes most effective when it's coupled with Protocol Decoding, whereby the IDS knows what normal behavior is expected within certain protocols and responds if abnormal commands or requests are detected.

There is a common misconception about IDSs and the fact that they can monitor everything; this is just not true. Having an IDS as a layer in your overall security plan is a good idea. However, depending on it as a one-stop solution is a bad idea.

Network Intrusion Detection System (NIDS)

Network Intrusion Detection System (NIDs) sit and "capture" all the packets on the network segment to which they are connected. This reading is similar to a packet sniffer; however, the differences appear after the packets are captured or sniffed. NIDSs are built on the wiretap concept and can be implemented in a couple of different ways. These methods have been developed to deal with the prevalence of LAN switches and how they operate to isolate traffic. An IDS must see as much of the network traffic as possible to be effective. The different NIDS implementation methods are as follows:

- *Inline wiretap*—This method of capturing packets places a physical *tap* in between (that is, inline between) two network devices. The NIDS would be plugged into this tap.

- *Port mirroring*—Depending on the switch you are using, port mirroring, also known as port spanning, is perhaps a more flexible solution. This technique tells the switch to send copies of every packet that, for example, is to be sent to the port your firewall is plugged into to another port. The NIDS is connected to this mirrored port.

After the NIDS reads the packets, the packets are analyzed in a variety of ways, depending on the NIDS you are using. Some NIDSs look for a fingerprint match by comparing the packet to the attack signatures it has in its database, while others look for unusual packet activity that could indicate that an attack is in progress. One of the benefits of a NIDS is that, once installed, they are unobtrusive and stealthy.

There are some issues relating to scalability and timeliness that the IDS industry is still trying to overcome. NIDSs have had some trouble scaling as network speeds have increased, and with Gigabit Ethernet making inroads to networks of all sizes, it will not be long before 10 Gigabit speeds will be used. Of course, NIDSs want to capture every single packet and analyze its contents; this makes these new speeds a bottleneck that has not yet been completely solved. In addition, the updating of attack signatures is not yet close to being where it should be to detect the latest attacks. It is clear that IDS vendors and how they update signatures are still a far cry from the timeliness the anti-virus community has achieved.

note

Recently, however, Cisco released a module for its Catalyst 6000 switch that incorporates network Intrusion Detection directly into the switch that allows for increased accuracy when capturing packets.

NIDS deployment is entirely based on the existing network design and architecture that is in place at each location. The more network segments a network has usually determines the number and placement of NIDSs.

Traditional NIDS placement allows them to be the most effective on the network perimeter, such as on both sides of the firewall (internal and external), near the dialup server, and on links to business partner networks. This placement allows an organization to measure the real effectiveness of its pre-screening routers and firewalls. These links tend to be low bandwidth (T1 speeds) such that an IDS can keep up with the traffic. This provides a good measure of checks and balances and is ideal for the security-aware organization, where application servers behind the firewall are accessible to the public Internet. Another high-value point is the corporate WAN backbone. A frequent problem is hacking from "remote" areas of the network into the main corporate network. Because WAN links tend to be low bandwidth, NIDS can be extremely beneficial.

Security best practice says that, when considering an IDS solution, both internal and external NIDSs should be used. This allows the NIDSs to monitor attacks from the Internet and internal threats. It might seem a bit odd to have two NIDSs; however, remember that statistically, the majority of attacks come from internal sources. Neglecting either location reduces the effectiveness of the IDS solution and greatly decreases your network's security.

Host Intrusion Detection System (HIDS)

Host Intrusion Detection Systems (HIDS) monitor, detect, and respond to user and system activity and attacks on a given host. In contrast to NIDSs, HIDSs are installed on the host (for example, the web or e-mail server) to be monitored. HIDS monitors the host's audit and event logs, whereas a NIDS monitors packets. Rather than trying to identify packets contents versus attack signatures, the HIDS approach attempts to identify known patterns of local or remote users doing things they should not be doing.

note

NIDSs deal with TCP/IP packets transmitted from host to host over a network, while HIDSs are concerned with what occurs on the hosts themselves by monitoring usage and log activity. A NIDS is like a parking lot attendant who watches *all* the cars coming and going out of the garage, while a HIDS is more like an attendant who watches the one space in which you park inside the garage.

HIDS acts much like anti-virus software (however, they are not a replacement for it) with extended capabilities that greatly increase the level of security that can be provided. HIDS is best suited to combat security threats against hosts because of their capability to monitor and respond to specific user actions and file accesses on the server. The majority of computer threats come from within organizations, from many different sources such as disgruntled employees or corporate spies. HIDSs monitor servers by providing information regarding the following:

- Intrusion attempts or successes and suspicious behavior by authorized users.

- Scans of the host to ensure that they conform to accepted security practices such as having all the latest patches and not having unnecessary services running.

- Audit policy management and centralization, supply of data forensics, statistical analysis and evidentiary support, and, in certain instances, some measure of access control. More robust tools typically provide these functions.

The deployment of HIDS is fairly straightforward; it is an application that resides on a server that watches for file system changes, registry changes, open ports, running applications, and all traffic originating to and from the host on which it resides. Server farms are often placed on their own network and application servers are strong candidates for HIDS.

Where multiple hosts are concerned, HIDS should be configured to report to a centralized management console to provide event correlation and enterprise-wide reporting. Typical candidates for HIDS deployments are web servers, file servers, or any application server that provides network communication resources to the public Internet.

How Are Intrusions Detected?

Every IDS vendor (of which there are several) has *buzzwords* of every type to inflict FUD on the explanation of how an IDS performs its job. This seems counter productive because each vendor wants to sell, but alas, the world is a fickle place and security is full of snake oil! This section takes a high-level look at the methods any good IDS should use.

An IDS has a special implementation of TCP/IP that allows it to gather the packets and then reassemble them for analysis. It is not enough to simply sniff the packets; an IDS must examine them. They do this in several ways, as discussed in the following sections.

Communication Stream Reassembly

An IDS has the capability to reconstruct a stream of packets into the communication session and thus analyze what is actually happening. This process is crucial because it allows the IDS to piece together events and provide proper event correlation back to the management station. This becomes even more critical since studies have found that a core cause of network worms are when field employees take laptops to client networks, get them infected, and then bring them back to the corporate network. Even worse is when employees establish a VPN tunnel into the company and, at times, bypass the security checks for worms. The main reason is that the employee "carries" his PC past the firewall into his office, plugs it in, and logs into the corporate network with an infected PC. *Ouch*! It is a good idea to have HIDS on laptops to prevent this from happening.

Protocol Analysis

Attacks use methods of altering the underlying protocol information to be successful. For example, the *Ping of Death* is successful because it alters the packet size and, through protocol verification, this would be detected. An IDS has a verification system that can flag invalid packets; this can include valid packets that are severely fragment, which again proves that communication stream reassembly is important.

An important aspect of protocol verification is that of application verification, where the IDS detects inappropriate application, protocol behavior. For example, the WinNuke attack uses NetBIOS (a valid protocol) but adds out-of-band information, which is valid but is only used to attack a host.

Anomaly Detection

Anomaly detection is similar to the training of SPAM filters because a period of learning by an IDS allows it to determine normal baseline levels of activity. Of course, *normal* is different for every network. The thought behind this approach is to measure a baseline of statistics such as file activity, user logins, CPU utilization, disk activity, and so on. After the baseline is established, IDS is used to detect statistical anomalies.

For example, assume that you are monitoring activity and your IDS begins to note that, early every morning, many of the hosts on your network become very active. You might not immediately know what is going on, but you are alerted that you should investigate.

Signature/Pattern Matching

Signature/pattern matching is the most common method of detecting attacks, and it means that the IDS must be able to recognize every attack technique to be effective. An IDS has large databases with thousands of signatures that allow for the IDS to match attack signatures or patterns.

For example, many IDSs are used to monitor abuse, such as a user visiting pornography or gambling websites while at work. Detecting that kind of misuse is based on keyword; however, consider a different scenario in which someone is using ICMP to scan and map out your network. Packets contain certain signatures that can be matched, as demonstrated in Figure 9-3.

Figure 9-3   Enterasys IDS Detection Screen

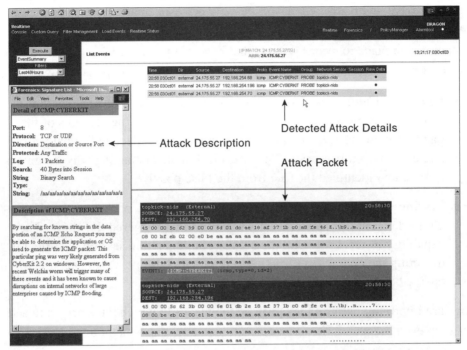

This type of attack detection takes place at a more granular level than protocol analysis or anomaly detection. As a result, specific events are identified that, for example, indicate that a compromise has occurred. One of the most frequently matched patterns is when an attacker ensures that he has achieved root permissions on a host. The host replies that root access was achieved in a packet that will be sent to the attacker and that can be analyzed for the word root. This is a greatly simplified example, but it demonstrates what an IDS looks for (that is, matches).

Log Analysis

IDSs have the capability to receive log messages from multiple devices and audit these logs for related security events. For example, an NIDS can simply log all the application layer protocols that are used on a machine. Downstream event log systems

(WinNT Event, UNIX Syslog, SNMP TRAPS, and so on) can then correlate these extended events with other events on the network. Log analysis not only means having the capability to correlate Syslogs and other events, but also to have a mechanism in place to record packets that have triggered the IDS to raise the alarm. Some of these additional useful mechanism functions are as follows:

- **Capture offending packets**—The IDS sensor captures the packet that caused the event/alarm to be triggered. This provides the contents of the packet for analysis. An IDS can be configured to collect additional packets and even the entire session. This is critical in understanding why a signature tripped and identified the true from the false positive.

- **Session reconstruction**—Often, an IDS alarms on a packet, perhaps a single packet, but that packet is only the event that triggered the alarm. The capability of reconstructing the entire communication session is critical in detecting the entire attack and helps eliminate false positives because you have a better picture of what has occurred.

Logs are important because they provide the means to which the alarm is raised when an event happens. The next step is to combine these methods to increase your network's security.

Combining Methods

Attackers continually modify and improve their abilities, thereby making them increasingly difficult to detect. To combat this, IDS continues to evolve, becoming smarter and better at detection by combining the methods they use to detect intrusions.

For example, an IDS might have the capability to combine the methods of signature-based pattern matching, protocol analysis, and anomaly detection. This ability to use multi-method attack detection is another example of the ever-evolving way in which IDSs continue to grow.

Intrusion Prevention

Intrusion Prevention Systems (IPSs) prevent an attack from being successful at the earliest possible moment. IPS works with an IDS, and vendors have combined the two technologies to make an IPS-capable IDS. Two techniques are used to prevent an attack:

- *Sniping*—Allows the IDS to terminate a suspected attack through the use of a TCP Reset packet or ICMP unreachable message.

- *Shunning*—Allows the IDS to automatically configure your pre-screening router or firewall to deny traffic based on what it has detected and therefore shunning the connection. As IDS becomes more advanced, this shunning is evolving into a new term, *blocking*, where an IDS contacts a router or firewall and creates an access control list (ACL) to block the attacking IP address.

caution

Shunning requires a lot of tuning to make it work effectively. Incorrect configuration or lack of IDS management when shunning is involved leads to a denial of service (DoS) to your network. Suppose an attacker knows or has determined that you are running an IDS that is configured to shun. The attacker could create thousands of packets that he knows will cause your IDS to shun the source IP address. The DoS occurs when the attacker sets that source IP address from the range of IP addresses assigned to Earthlink or perhaps AOL. This means that your e-commerce site could not allow anyone from either ISP to connect! You must carefully define what events trigger a shun, and for how long.

IPS Responses and Actions

As discussed so far, an IDS can take several actions to prevent detected intrusions. The most proactive ways include sniping and shunning. The IDS can handle sniping; however, shunning requires the assistance of other devices. However, IDS

sensors should report back to a central console that, in turn, also generates some responses if so configured. Following are some actions that an IDS can generate in response to an attack:

- **Reconfigure firewall/router**—An IDS with a shun enabled can configure the firewall to filter out the intruder's IP address. However, the intruder can still attack from other addresses. Checkpoint firewalls support a Suspicious Activity Monitoring Protocol (SAMP) for configuring firewalls. Checkpoint has its OPSEC standard for reconfiguring firewalls to block the offending IP address.

- **Send an SNMP trap**—Configure the IDS to send an SNMP trap datagram to a management console like HP OpenView, Tivoli, Cabletron Spectrum, and so on.

- **Generate log**—An IDS can log to Windows event log, Syslog server, pager, or even send an e-mail.

note
Perhaps the best response to an attack that I have heard of included several of the aspects from the preceding list, which was then supplemented by the playing of a sound file: "Do you want to play Global Thermonuclear War?"

Remember my caution, however; only allow the IDS to proactively change your other network devices *after* an extended period of manual monitoring and extensive tuning. IDS is a developing field, and IPS is even younger (only a couple of years).

IDS Products

Many IDS systems exist, and a lot of confusion surrounds them because there is little in the way of standards with regards to how they operate. It is difficult to provide a direct comparison between products because terminology, meanings, features, and functionality have not matured to a level at which an effective comparison can occur. However, many products are based on the work done by the open source community efforts in the IDS arena. The foremost of these products is Snort.

Snort!

Snort! Snort! Snort!

Don't worry—the snorting that you are hearing is not coming from some sort of weird beast; it is coming from an open source IDS developed by the folks over at http://www.Snort.Org. Here is a description of "Snort," quoted on the website:

> Snort is an open source network Intrusion Detection System, capable of performing real-time traffic analysis and packet logging on IP networks. It can perform protocol analysis, content searching/matching, and can be used to detect a variety of attacks and probes, such as buffer overflows, stealth port scans, CGI attacks, SMB probes, OS fingerprinting attempts, and much more.
>
> Snort uses a flexible rules language to describe traffic that it should collect or pass, as well as a detection engine that utilizes a modular plugin architecture. Snort has a real-time alerting capability as well, incorporating alerting mechanisms for syslog, a user specified file, a UNIX socket, or WinPopup messages to Windows clients using Samba's smbclient.
>
> Snort has three primary uses. It can be used as a straight packet sniffer like tcpdump(1), a packet logger (useful for network traffic debugging, etc.), or as a full blown network Intrusion Detection System.

Before you get too excited by the graphical interface you see in Figure 9-4, that is not part of the Snort IDS software package; it is a GUI interface developed by a group of people at Engage Security (http://www.engagesecurity.com).

The Snort application itself is a command-line application that is extremely well written, albeit sometimes difficult to configure and monitor. As shown in Figure 9-4, the IDScenter GUI front-end allows users to have a graphical configuration and monitoring interface.

Figure 9-4   IDS Center Main Snort Configuration Screen

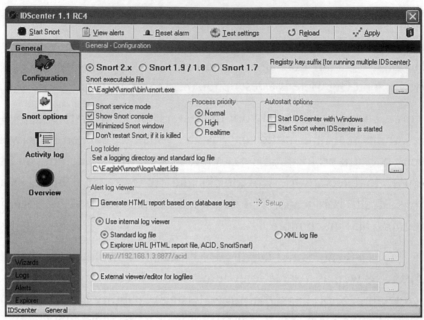

Figure 9-5 gives you an idea of the basic configuration options that can be set for Snort operation. This screen in IDS Center is crucial for beginning the inevitable tweaking that must occur.

Figure 9-6 shows the method users have for selecting the intrusion or attack profiles that Snort will be required to look for and how to notify customers. In addition, Figure 9-6 shows the alerting options that can be set when situations that require administrative attention occur.

Figure 9-5   **IDS Center Snort Rule Configuration Page**

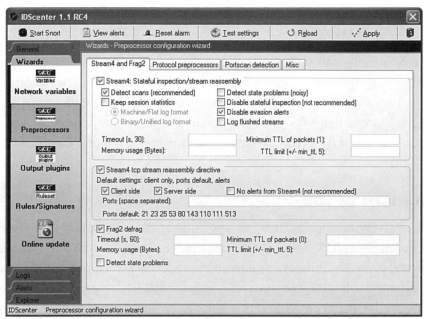

Figure 9-6   **IDS Center Notification**

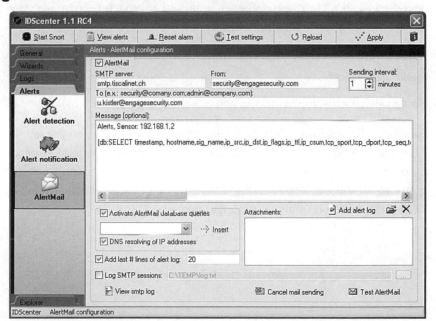

You might already know about Snort if you are familiar with Linux or other *nix operating systems, but what you might not know is that the IDS Center software is Win32-based, as is the version of Snort that it manages.

Created by people who really want Snort to work under Windows, a handful of Win32 Snort installation packages are available on the Internet. The majority of these packages work well, but a few of them need additional development cycles. Also keep in mind that, after you configure and deploy a Snort machine, you will not be able to use it for anything else after you engage the monitoring functions.

Limitations of IDS

Still an evolving technology, IDS has some manageable limitations given its over-riding benefits. An IDS should always be deployed in addition to pre-screening routers and firewalls. Primary systems such as firewalls, encryption, and authentication are rock solid. Bugs or misconfiguration often lead to problems in these devices, but the underlying concepts are proven and accurate. Regardless, some of the limitations are as follows:

- **HIDS versus NIDS debate**—This should never be a debate; both are needed and should work together in a unified approach to increase your network's security as they play different roles.

- **Attack patterns**—IDS products are not always updated with the latest attack signatures.

- **False positives**—Normal traffic can cause false positives.

- **Resource limitations**—NIDSs sit at centralized locations on the network. They must be able to keep up with, analyze, and store information generated by potentially thousands of machines. NIDS must emulate the combined entity of all the machines sending traffic through its segment. Obviously, it cannot do this thoroughly, and it must take short cuts.

note
When buying an IDS, ask the vendor how many packets per second the system can handle. Many vendors try to tell you how many bits per second, but per-packet is the real performance bottleneck. Virtually all vendors can handle 100-Mbps traffic using 1500-byte sized packets; few can handle 100-Mbps traffic using 60-byte packets. This might seem counter-intuitive, but consider that an IDS simply has to look at a 1500-byte packet and then make a decision, versus doing the same for many 60-byte packets that require the same level of inspection. Doing so definitely impacts performance.

For performance stats of Cisco IDS options, see the following URL:

http://www.cisco.com/univercd/cc/td/doc/pcat/nerg.htm#xtocid4

- **Long term state**—A classic problem is "slow scans," in which the attacker scans the system very slowly. The IDS cannot store that much information over that long of a time period, so is cannot match the data together.

- **Sensor blindness**—IDSs are built on regular computers that do not have any special capabilities; thus, it is possible to saturate the link to which they are connected and blind them, thereby causing them to drop packets they should have been recording. For example, the open source port-scanning tool *nmap* includes a feature known as *decoy scans*, which causes nmap to send hundreds of scans using spoofed IP addresses. It therefore becomes an improbable task for the administrator to discover which of the IP addresses was real and which was one of the decoy addresses. These two scenarios retain forensics data, however. If the attacker is suspected, the data is still there to find. Another attack is to fill up event storage.

- **Storage limitations**—When an attacker is trying to blind the IDS sensor, she might have the dual purpose of filling up the sensor database or hard drive. This causes the sensor to delete events or stop recording events.

- **Denial of service**—An IDS is extremely complicated because it has an entire TCP/IP implementation running. As a result, IDS can be susceptible to attacks. Attackers can often download the same IDS their targets use free of charge, and then experiment to find packets that will disable the IDS. During the attack, the intruder then disables the IDS and continues the attack undetected.

■ **Fragmentation**—The act of breaking up large packets into multiple smaller packets. The receiving TCP/IP stack then reassembles the packets and their data. Most IDSs do not have the ability to reassemble IP packets. Simple tools exist that can automatically fragment attacks to evade IDS.

note

Fragmenting the IP packets in the middle of the TCP header has long been used to evade firewall port filtering. Some industrial grade NIDSs can reassemble traffic. Also, some firewalls can "normalize" traffic by forcing reassembly before passing the traffic through to the other end. IDS sensors have monitor ports (the sniffing port) that have no IP address assigned to them and are therefore not susceptible to DoS attacks. A management interface that has an IP address assigned to it should be placed in a VLAN and isolated from normal network access.

■ **Pattern evasion/change**—Many simple NIDSs rely on "pattern matching." Attack scripts have well-known patterns, so simply compiling a database of the known attack scripts provides pretty good detection; however, it can easily be evaded by simply changing the attack script and thus rendering the IDS pattern match useless.

■ **IDS "evaluation" tools**—A variety of tools are freely available to *test* the accuracy and usefulness of an IDS. The two most commonly used are "snot" and "Stick." These tools create thousands of attacks to see whether the IDS will sense them. An attacker can use these tools to hide their attacks or to potentially blind the IDS.

These limitations do not mean that the uses of IDS are invalid or somehow lessened. Hacking is so pervasive and attack tools so readily available that it is astounding what an IDS will detect. Properly maintained and managed, IDS dramatically improves the security of any network. However, one of the key fundamental points of properly using an IDS has been saved for the end of this section.

A security policy is crucial to the successful use of an IDS. You might ask, "But why do I need another policy and process to follow? They are such a burden!" It cannot be emphasized enough that the assets your security measures are designed to protect have value, and not ensuring that *everyone* involved in protecting them follows the same standards would be a grave mistake. One cowboy can ruin it for everyone.

Essentials First: Honeypots

You are probably wondering what is Winnie the Pooh and his predilection with honey doing in a book about network security.

Until this point, this book has not discussed taking the fight to the attackers, and that is what this section does by covering Honeypots. A *Honeypot* is a highly flexible computer system on the Internet that is customized to be a security tool and is expressly set up to attract and "trap" people who attempt to penetrate other people's computer systems through probes, scans, and intrusions. This target audience includes the hacker, cracker, and script kiddie, regardless of their location in the world.

Honeypots do not fix a single security problem—how bizarre is that? Instead, they are used for misdirection, prevention, detection, and information gathering by being closely monitored and designed to *look like something they are not* for the attackers to hack into. Conceptually, this means that a Honeypot should not be used for production because its value lies in being probed, attacked, or compromised. When I first heard of a Honeypot, I was confused as to *why* in the world would you want such a device on your network? It seems to me that having a computer designed to let attackers hack into would not serve much of a purpose. Honeypots, in fact, serve several crucial purposes:

- Honeypots distract attackers from more valuable resources on your network, thus allowing the protection of your resources by distracting attackers to devices that they presume are real.

- Honeypots provide early warning about new attacks and intrusion attempts. IDS can generate false positives, whereas those who are likely to intend harm access only a Honeypot because it is nonproduction.

- Honeypots allow for in-depth examination of an attacker's activities during and after the exploitation of a Honeypot. This might seem like something only someone involved in research might do, but think about what you can learn. You can use this education to ensure that the real security resources on your network are configured/patched correctly.

- Perhaps the most interesting benefit of Honeypots is CYA, or cover your assets. Honeypots have the unique ability to *show* that your network security design is effective.

- To know your enemy is another reason why Honeypots exist. It is not enough to know that attackers are out there; everyone knows this—just turn on the evening news. What is important, however, is determining their techniques and methods. After you have an attacker profile, you can defend against further exploits.

note
Lance Spitzner, an expert on Honeypot systems, documents them in a series of articles entitled "Know Your Enemy" as a part of the Honeypot Project (http://www.honeypot.net). He describes how to track attackers through the system to gain sufficient information about how they operate in these articles.

Clearly the problem of false positives discussed in the IDS section is not a real issue with Honeypots. Specifically, if an attack happens to a Honeypot that is just a passive device, you will know it. This really means that detection of attacks is really no longer much of an issue, is it? In the real world, you often see Honeypots deployed on a Demilitarized Zone (DMZ); however, the Honeypot is not listed in DNS, WINS, or registered, nor is it linked to a production machine in any way. If the Honeypot begins to get scanned from hosts within the DMZ, that tells you something. What if the Honeypot is inside the network and it gets attacked? These placements of Honeypots are passive in that they are waiting for someone to attack them.

This chapter covers Honeypots to demonstrate that, just as an active device such as IDS has a role in securing your network, so does a passive device such as Honeypot, which does not have the same limitations as an IDS.

The design and intent of Honeypots fall into two categories:

- **Research Honeypots**—Complex to deploy and maintain and primarily used by research, military, or government organizations.

- **Production Honeypots**—Used by organizations that are concerned with the security of their networks; we focus on these. A production Honeypot is typically deployed with a certain goal or intent in mind.

note

There is currently some question as to the legality of Honeypots and whether they fall under the banner of "wire-tapping" devices. As silly as that sounds, the FBI and other law-enforcement agencies are still battling over this question.

In addition to these two broad categories of Honeypots, Honeypots can also be classified by their function, as follows:

- **Port monitors**—A rather straightforward type of device, these Honeypots listen on ports that are targeted by attackers. By design, they respond to port scans, thus letting the attacker attempt to connect. These types of Honeypots log on connection attempts on a port.

- **Deception systems**—Take the next step from just monitoring a port and deceive attackers by interacting with them as a real system would. This means that, instead of just replying on TCP port 110 like an e-mail server configured for POP3, a deceptive Honeypot responds as if it were a real mail server. Deception systems do not implement every aspect of a mail server; rather, they implement just enough to make it sweet as honey to an attacker.

note

The three most commonly attacked servers on the Internet are unpatched systems that run older versions of Linux (Red Hat 5.0), Solaris 2.6, and Microsoft IIS 4.0. Therefore, as part of your Honeypot plan, you might want to set up one or all three of these operating systems as Honeypots.

- **Multi-deception systems**—Increasing yet another level are the more advanced Honeypots that not only allow for multiple services that can be emulated, but can also simulate different operating systems. One of the most commonly used tools for this purpose is Specter, which can be found at http://www.specter.com/.

note

Additional aspects of Honeypots can be explored where there are entire systems dedicated as Honeypots. Then, the detection is taken a step further through the use of an IDS when Honeypots are in use. One of the best resources for Honeypots can be found online at http://www.honeypots.net/honeypots/links.

You can also download a freeware Honeypot for Win32 machines called, of all things, "Honey Potter" from http://honeypott4.tripod.com/.

It is a basic piece of software (it is free, after all) that provides an introduction to Honeypots.

Honeypot Design Strategies

Perhaps the clearest and most present danger is that when your Honeypot is working correctly, it detects attackers coming after your network and its resources. In practice, this means that you already have a criminal in some part of your network. As a result, a few items must be taken to ensure the security of the network.

Use a firewall! Yes, a firewall—even though the Honeypot is designed to let attackers in, still use a firewall to ensure that they do not get too suspicious. Create a rule set that allows basic Internet functionality out from the Honeypot back to the Internet. Experts recommend that you should allow all inbound traffic to reach the Honeypot, but only allow FTP, ICMP, and DNS outbound.

The way you are going to see an attacker's activities is through various logs and through the actual Honeypot logs. Failure to ensure that these are working will make your life = difficult and basically nullify your entire motivation for setting up a Honeypot.

note
Some people feel that capturing criminals in this manner is something that should be considered a form of entrapment. This is a misconception because Honeypots are not active lures—they do not advertise themselves. A Honeypot is not stumble in any way into by any legitimate user, and a good user would never root kit you.

Honeypot Limitations

Although a Honeypot has many benefits, it also has the following limitations:

- If the system does indeed get hacked, it can be used as a stepping-stone to further compromise the network.

- Honeypots add complexity. In security, complexity is bad because it leads to increased exposure to exploits.

- Honeypots must be maintained, just like any other networking equipment/ services.

Chapter Summary

This chapter introduces two of the newest available security-related technologies—Intrusion Detection and Intrusion Prevention. This chapter began by exploring the two fundamental types of IDS: host-based that run on servers, and network-based IDS that run on a network. This chapter also covered the basic operation of an IDS and concluded by covering Honeypots.

Chapter Review Questions

1. When and who were the first to develop a commercial IDS?

2. What are the two types of IDS, and should they be deployed together or separately?

3. Define and discuss NIDSs. How and where are they effective in a network?

4. Define and discuss HIDSs. How and where are they effective in a network?

5. When is anomaly detection the most effective and why?

6. Which Intrusion Detection methodology also verifies application behavior?

7. List and define each of the two techniques an IDS can employ to prevent an attack.

8. List the three most important IDS limitations, in your opinion, and explain why you choose them.

9. Honeypots distract attackers from more valuable resources. True or false?

What You Will Learn

By the end of this chapter, you should know and be able to explain the following:

- ✔ The fundamental types of attacks that your network might experience

- ✔ How to conduct or contract a security assessment of your network's security

- ✔ How to use the results from a security scan and vulnerability assessment to better secure your network

- ✔ How to conduct or contract a penetration test of your network's security

Being able to answer these key questions will allow you to understand the overall characteristics and importance of network security. By the time you finish this book, you will have a solid appreciation for network security, its issues, how it works, and why it is important.

CHAPTER 10

Tools of the Trade

The happy people are those who are producing something; the bored people are those who are consuming much and producing nothing.— William Ralph Inge

The HaXor that stole Christmas…what a great way to start this tools-of-the-trade chapter.

Every holiday season all over the world, people experience an OOBE, otherwise known as an "out of box experience." OOBE is an acronym that refers to the excitement and wonderment that many people enjoy when they open the box their new computer comes in. The smell of the new plastic, the tactile sensation of the new keyboard, the sound that a new PC makes when you boot it up for the first time, all the sights and sounds that come with getting your brand new, shiny SuperComp 2000 Mini-tower PC with 1 full gigabit megabytes of super duper speedy RAM and the 78-gigabyte triple IDE hard drive, otherwise known as an Apple G5—or so I have heard.

As you might imagine, this scene plays out in many households throughout the world every time the Christmas season rolls around. The previous year's PC is relegated to being the de facto "family" computer—the one that never gets its hard drive defragged or patched and consequently takes three days to boot up.

This year's PC is going to little Johnnie (or Joanne, to be politically correct) because he is a freshman in high school now and is required to turn in top-notch reports for biology and chemistry and whatever other classes require report writing on a computing platform 150 times more powerful than the computers on the Space Shuttle and NORAD combined.

Besides, little Johnnie/Joanne needs something pretty powerful for playing all those online games that are available via the brand spanking new broadband connection you got last month when you were planning ahead for the big box under the tree! And, of course, the computer will be up in their room to make doing their homework less of a chore and more of an individual accomplishment, achieved in their combination bedroom and office. Perhaps they might even have received a laptop; that broadband modem has wireless, so you can use it when you need to work, too.

Take a moment to get a few things crystal clear. First, teenage children do not need a computer that is capable of breaking RC5 encryption in less than two days; we already have several government agencies that are capable of doing just that, and they really do not like the additional competition. Secondly, the words "You've got mail" will not be heard through the speakers of the super computer in question when it gets connected to an unsupervised broadband connection that has download speeds rivaling a T1. You can expect to hear the sounds of heavy metal, rap, and whatever other kinds of music they can download via MP3s.

Regardless of whatever story your little high-school sophomore tells you, if they are in any kind of computer science course at school (as more than 80 percent of them are), they are striving for one goal: to be crowned "Uber Haxor" (pronounced oober hacksor) by their little felonious classmates. That's right, your little baby that used to eat peas and carrots with their toes is but a few mouse-clicks away from being brought up on charges under the U.S.A. Patriot Act, and the shiny new PC you bought for Christmas is the high-tech hotrod that might end up getting them an extended stay at the "grey bar" motel. How many of the attacks, techniques, and tools discussed in this book cost money? Not many, and those that do have cracks available in the Internet.

The combination of intelligence and a burgeoning contempt for authority in any form (teenager) can make a state-of-the-art computing device a dangerous thing if it ends up in the wrong hands. Now, you might be saying to yourself, "my child would never do anything like that. I've brought him up to respect authority and have taught them the difference between right and wrong." All this might be 100 percent correct, but in educating the little tyke, you might have forgotten that the Internet is still as wild and wooly as the west was in the 1800s.

Surfing the Internet is a common occurrence for children who have grown up in the last 10 years, and the morality of the Internet is still in its infancy. At last count (and some people have actually counted), thousands of websites are dedicated to hacking, cracking, and computer crime. Finding information on how to write viruses is easier and more fun than locating a recipe for double fudge brownies.

Broadband Internet access has created a culture of anonymity that has never existed before for children seeking ways to rebel and embarrass their parents for grounding them or taking away the car keys. E-mail, websites, and chat rooms have empowered children to explore the boundaries of society in an instant and exploit the weakness of that very society on a whim when they determine that society has treated them badly.

Even at this point, you might still be convinced of your child's enduring innocence and good intentions when it comes to behaving responsibly with regard to Internet usage. You might be correct in maintaining your belief; but then again, if you had asked the attacker's mother who was recently in the news if her son was capable of these kinds of acts, she probably would have denied that her son was capable of executing the attacks, and we know how that story turned out.

This chapter discusses the security tools that attackers use so readers can understand what they are up against. The chapter then examines the tools available to identify weaknesses in your network and the anatomy of a security audit, which is a crucial piece to ensure that your network is secure.

Essentials First: Vulnerability Analysis

This section looks at some of the tools that are freely available to attackers. The fundamental truth this section teaches is that *the bad guys have good tools*. Previous chapters touched on many of the specific attack tools; however, attackers have a broad toolset with which they can launch multilevel attacks against your network. When an attacker gains a foothold in one aspect of your network, it is then leveraged to exploit another aspect of your network.

Attackers, for example, can, do, and will take advantage of weak authentication and authorization, improper allocations, poor security implementation, shared privileges among users/applications, or even poor employee security habits to gain unauthorized access to critical network resources.

Throughout this book, you have seen that there are many ways to allow even the best security procedures and technologies to be circumvented. To understand how this is done, you must spend some time understanding the exact methods and tools the attackers use. Perhaps it is exciting to see an attacker's tools; however, if *any* network resource is your responsibility, you better ensure that you are using these tools to assess your network's security. It is extremely important that you use these tools on behalf of your network so that vulnerabilities can be detected and found before an attacker uses them against you. You can count on these tools being used in your network—the decision you have to make is *who is going to use them first?*

Fundamental Attacks

Leading edge security technologies, policies, and procedures can quickly have their effectiveness nullified if those who are responsible for network security do not understand the methodology and tools that will be used against your network. This chapter discusses some of the methodologies and various tools that attackers use, how they operate, and the tools and techniques you can use protect your network resources against these hacker tools.

Even the best security technologies and procedures can be rapidly nullified unless you know the precise methods and tools being employed against you. Therefore, it is crucial to be able to identify the various tools of the hacker trade, how they operate, and what kinds of protections thwart these attacks. This includes a thorough knowledge of the common tools and techniques discussed in the sections that follow.

IP Spoofing/Session Hijacking

This type of attack occurs when an attacker creates a packet with a different IP address to gain entry to a system. This attack exploits trust relationships by allowing the attacker to assume a trusted host's identity. For this attack to be successful, the attacker must determine the "patterns of trust" for the target host—that is, for example, the range of IP addresses that the host trusts. After the attacker determines the pattern of trust, he can move onto the next step of the attack by either compromising the host or disabling it in some manner. These types of attacks are often used as the first step in the overall attack strategy.

note

Because the attacker has spoofed an IP address (that is, made it up so the target trusts it—the address could be a local LAN address, whereas the attacker is not local) the attacker might not see the response from the target. This means that the attacker is blind to their success, and is why this is usually a first step. It is common to blindly exploit a vulnerability in this matter and, after the host is compromised, move to the next step.

IP Spoofing/Session Hijacking Tools

A variety of tools accomplish exploitation through IP spoofing/session hijacking:

- **Dsniff**—A collection of tools for network auditing and penetration testing specifically known as Dsniff, filesnarf, mailsnarf, msgsnarf, urlsnarf, and webspy passively monitor a network for interesting data (passwords, e-mail, files, and so on). arp spoof, dns spoof, and macof facilitate the interception of network traffic.

- **Hunt**—A program for intruding into a connection, watching it, and resetting it. Hunt was an outgrowth of similar products like Juggernaut, but it has several features that cannot be found in these products.

- **Ettercap**—A powerful Apple OS X- and UNIX-based program employing a text-mode GUI, easy enough to be used by "script kiddies." All operations are automated, and the target computers are chosen from a scrollable list of hosts detected on the LAN. Ettercap can perform four methods of sniffing: IP, MAC, ARP, and public ARP. It also automates a variety of other tools.

Prevention

Of course, preventing these kinds of attacks is as important as understanding them and the tools that are used. Virtual private networks (VPNs) are effective against IP spoofing because a VPN encrypts the original IP addresses as they are transmitted across the network. If either the data or the source address prove to be tampered with, the packet is deleted. This prevents an attacker from penetrating a system without access to the VPN encryption keys.

Packet Sniffers

These tools gather packets being transmitted past the point where the sniffer is connected to on a network. Sniffers generally come either software-based (for PCs/PDAs) or hardware-based (on a dedicated computer). Using sophisticated network sniffers that can decode data from packets across all layers of the OSI model, attackers can steal usernames and passwords and use that information to launch further attacks. In general, attackers can use sniffers by compromising the corporation's physical security—say, walking into the office and plugging a laptop into the network. With the growing use of wireless networks, someone in the parking lot with a wireless device can access the network. By using sniffers, attackers can obtain valuable information about usernames and passwords across public or private networks—in particular, from applications such as FTP, Telnet, and others that send passwords in the clear. Protocols such as SMTP, IMAP, and POP3 are used for remote access to e-mail applications via simple username and password authentication techniques and are especially susceptible to sniffer attacks. Because users tend to reuse passwords across multiple applications and platforms, attackers can potentially use the acquired information to obtain access to other resources on the network, where their confidentiality could be compromised.

Denial of Service (DoS) Attacks

Also known as *Distributed Denial of Service (DDoS)*, Packetstorming, Tribal Flooding, and the other DDoS attack methods used to overload networks by making so many requests that regular traffic is slowed or completely interrupted have existed for some time—not only in theory, but also in practice. A "regular" denial of service (DoS) attack does not involve breaking into the target; rather, the attacker's goal is to simply overload the target (router or web server) with so much fake traffic that it cannot cope.

When the target is unable to cope, genuine users are unable to connect and are therefore "denied service." A *distributed denial of service* (DDoS) attack generates the false traffic from multiple hosts across the Internet. A DDoS attack uses multiple computers throughout the network that it has previously infected with a ***DDoS Daemon*** (program); these computers are then known as ***zombie computers***.

note

A DDoS daemon is a specialized computer program that was designed for use in controlling and coordinating a DDoS attack. As of this writing, there are four known programs: Tribal Village (TFN), TFN2K, Trinoo, and Stacheldraht, which is German for "Barbwire." You can learn more about these programs by visiting the following URLs:

http://staff.washington.edu/dittrich/misc/trinoo.analysis

http://staff.washington.edu/dittrich/misc/tfn.analysis

http://staff.washington.edu/dittrich/misc/stacheldraht.analysis

These zombie computers all work together as a ***zombie network*** to send out bogus connection messages, thereby increasing the amount of open connections with which the target must deal. This prevents legitimate users from accessing the services being offered. DoS attacks are easy to implement and can cause significant damage, thereby disrupting a server or network's operation and effectively disconnecting them from the Internet. A DoS attack can be conducted using various bogus connection techniques. For example, a SYN flooding attack uses fictitious, half-open TCP connection requests that exhaust the resources of the targeted system. DoS attacks exploit weaknesses in the architecture of the system that is under attack; as we just saw, capacity limitations are one example. In some cases, DoS attacks exploit the weaknesses of many common Internet protocols, such as the Internet Control Message Protocol (ICMP). For example, some DoS attacks send

large number of ICMP echo (ping) packets to a broadcast address. These packets being sent use a spoofed source IP address of the potential target. The replies coming back to the target can cripple it. These types of attacks are called smurf attacks.

A *smurf attack* is a type of DoS attack that exploits the use of the Internet Control Message Protocol (ICMP, a.k.a. PING) and the IP's network and broadcast addresses. A smurf attack's purpose is to disable a target host or network by consuming all of its resources; aside from this, it causes no permanent damage. Every IP subnet has two special addresses:

- The network address, which is the first address in the subnet

- The network broadcast address, which is the last address in the subnet range

The IP network address serves as the identity address of a given subnet in the IP routing table. The IP broadcast address was devised as a method for sending information to all the hosts in a given subnet. Most IP implementations respond to messages with the network or broadcast address as the source address. This support is known as "directed broadcast." This feature is also data used for legitimate purposes.

ICMP/Ping Attack

A ping-based attack uses the characteristics of ICMP to the attacker's benefit. The compromised hosts are directed to attack the designated target via a continuous stream of ping packets. This causes an incredible number of ping requests coming from thousands of compromised hosts to begin impacting the host. This is certainly an unwelcome scenario, but the attacker has also altered the ICMP Packet [ICMP echo request]. Each packet does *not* contain the compromised host's source address; instead, each packet's source address is the *target's* address (that is, the source and destination address are the targets). The target system then transmits a response [ICMP echo reply] to each packet, which is destined to itself, thus causing traffic to increase exponentially until the target crashes because of its inability to handle such a high volume of traffic. To take this further, imagine if a broadcast was allowed onto a LAN with the target's source address. The real caveat implicit in this attack is that the traffic appears completely normal and is typically allowed into any network and through firewalls, and so on. You can see this attack in action with a properly positioned sniffer or probe.

SYN Flood Attack

In TCP/IP, a three-way handshake occurs whenever a client attempts to connect to a service, such as FTP or HTTP. The three-way handshake is defined as follows:

1. The client sends a packet with the SYN (synchronization) flag in the TCP header set to the service.

2. The service responds with a SYN-ACK (synchronization-acknowledgment).

3. The client sends a handshake to the service(a SYN-ACK transaction) and the session is considered established so data begins to flow.

note

Richard Stevens (*TCP/IP Illustrated*, p. 231) explains the format of the SYN packets and is an excellent resource for those wishing to understand the details of TCP/IP.

A SYN flood attack is when the client does not respond to the service's SYN-ACK, thereby tying up the service until it times out. In this type of attack, the client never responds because the client's source address is forged (spoofed). The attacker's goal is to send SYN packets to the service faster than it takes for the service to timeout waiting for the client's SYN-ACK response. This causes the service to become so busy acknowledging the SYNs and waiting for the client that it cannot answer requests for service from legitimate users and therefore denies them service.

Preventing DoS Attacks

You might be wondering how can you defend against denial of service (DoS) attacks. This is perhaps one of the most difficult attacks to defend against because many of the attacks come in the form of traffic that would be considered a normal occurrence on your network. Perhaps one of the most common defenses is to rate

limit certain types of traffic. For example, you might want to allow **ping** (IMCP); however, too much of it could be considered a DoS attack, so you would rate limit ICMP. In contrast, you must carefully watch other types of traffic. Perhaps limiting HTTP (web) traffic to your Internet e-commerce site would be a mistake! Again, the depends rule strikes fear into your IT staff when considering how to defend against a DoS attack.

Man-in-the-Middle Attacks

In this form of assault, the attacker places himself in the middle of a communication flow between two hosts: usually, a server and a client. The attacker then intercepts messages transmitted between the two hosts. The attacker can look for a variety of things. Perhaps he wants to see how much money is in your bank account, your password to the fantasy football website, or even block the connection. The interesting part and point of concern here is that if the attacker does not alter anything, you will not know that the packets are being intercepted by an attacker in the middle!

Network sniffers, or Ettercap (http://ettercap.sourceforge.net/), are often used to accomplish this type of attack. You will also find that man-in-the-middle attacks can be used to reconstruct public cryptic keys. This discussion is beyond the scope of this text; however, protecting passwords and keys is always a good idea in case you need another reason for a password policy.

ARP Spoofing

ARP spoofing is one way in which a man-in-the-middle attack can be successful if executed on either a wired or wireless LAN. The process of updating a target computer's ARP cache with forged entry is referred to as "ARP poisoning." This technique involves the attacker constructing forged a ARP request and reply packets to change the Layer 2 Ethernet MAC address to one of their choosing. By the attacker sending forged ARP replies, a target computer could be convinced to send frames destined for Host B to instead go to the attacker's computer first so they can be recorded and read. When done properly, Host A has no idea that this ARP redirection took place, as shown in Figure 10-1.

Figure 10-1   Man in the Middle: ARP Spoofing

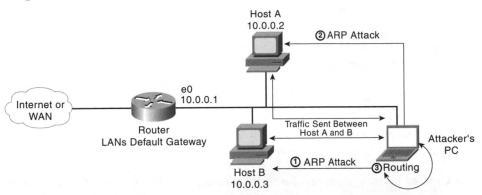

Role of IP Spoofing in Man in The Middle Attacks

IP spoofing plays an important role in man-in-the-middle attacks. In IP spoofing, an attacker compromises or disabled a trusted host. The attacker then sends IP packets with the source address of the disabled trusted host to the target, effectively masquerading as the trusted host to gain access to or disable the target host.

Back Doors

A back door, or trapdoor, is a secret way of gaining access to a program, operating system, BIOS, or network service. You often see these types of back doors in computer games where a certain phrase or key combination provides you unlimited money, power, health, and so on. Back-door entry to resources can be accidentally or intentionally opened by users or by design; consider the following examples:

- Deliberately placed by system developers to allow quick access during development and not turned off before release.

- Placed by employees to facilitate performance of their duties because the 'proper procedure' made them think that it made their jobs harder, so there must be a smarter and easier way. Users might not be as technical as your IT staff, and often they find back doors because they do not have a preconceived notion of how something should work.

- Normal part of standard 'default' operating system installs that have not been eliminated by "OS hardening," such as retaining default user logon ID and password combinations. Again, vendors do not want technical support calls, so they make it as easy and open as possible. This means that your IT staff must review and harden every server!

- Placed by disgruntled employees to allow access after termination. In many cases, an employee suspects that the loss of his job is coming. This makes him angry and feel unappreciated, so he wants to ensure that he can strike back as necessary when the time comes.

- Created by the execution of malicious code, such as viruses or a Trojan horse that takes advantage of a vulnerability in an operating system or application.

As discussed previously, these attacks and tools are the most common types of vulnerabilities used by attackers. Understanding them will better allow you to understand the tools and techniques discussed in the following section.

Miscellaneous Attacks

This section provides an overview of some of the more unusual and unique attacks.

Land Attacks

A land attack is an IP spoof-based attack where the source and destination address are the same. This attack crashes some TCP/IP implementations that do not know how to handle the packet. This is a rarity in terms of appearance in the real world, but is a standard signature on ISS, NFR, Dragon, and Cisco Net Ranger and IDS-IOS.

Xmas Tree Attack

In an Xmas tree attack, a TCP packet sent to any known service port sets all the code flags (URG, ACK, PSH, RST, SYN, and FIN). An alternative version of this attack is a TCP packet without any flags set. Both cases are the result of packet craft and do not exist in the "wild."

Teardrop Attack

The teardrop attack uses fragmented UDP packets. The first fragment is fine, but the second packet overwrites part of the first fragmented packet. This results in a memory error, and the system crashes.

Ping Pong Attack

There are two variations on the ping pong attack:

- A flood of spoofed packets to the echo service (UDP/TCP port 7), which is a simple service that echoes back any data sent to it.

- Sending a spoofed UDP message that appears to be from the chargen service port to the echo (UDP port7) service on another system. The chargen service responds to any packet sent to the service port with a 72-byte random character string. After the spoofed connection is established, the echo port sends traffic to the chargen port and a loop develops.

Both variations consume CPU resources; enough attacks cause the system to becomes CPU-bound and crash.

Ping of Death

Like teardrop, this attack exploits IP's fragmentation capability. The attack host sends an ICMP with a packet size that exceeds the maximum IP datagram size of 65,535 bytes. The attacked system waits until all the fragments are delivered, and then reassembles the packet; this results in a buffer overflow that crashes the system.

SYN Flood (Half-Open Attack)

Each TCP open (SYN) request requires a server to reserve resources to support the connection. The attack works by flooding a service with SYN requests from spoofed IP addresses (routable or unroutable addresses work). The server then acknowledges the SYN requests and responds with SYN-ACKs. These are never responded to because sources of the SYN requests never made the request. Depending on the system, the connection timer can allow between one to three minutes before reclaiming the allocated resources. The actual expected response

to SYN-ACK is a few milliseconds. With a steady stream of SYN requests, the server's connection queue can be filled with incomplete connections that block out legitimate user requests.

Firewalking

Many people consider firewalls immune to attacks or standard techniques that allow attackers to figure out their rule sets in order to bypass them. That belief was true for a while; however, new techniques are always being developed and, in this context, *firewalking* is a concept that allows the attacker to send specially crafted packets *through a firewall* to determine what ports and services are permitted through the firewall. An attacker with this knowledge can make their port scans *hidden* and thus map your network through your firewall.

Firewalking works because IP packets contain a field that prevents them from being sent around a network forever. This field is known as the Time-To-Live (TTL). When this field reaches zero, the packet is discarded. In firewalking, this field is set to a value that will allow the packet to get beyond the firewall and then be dropped by a host or device after the firewall. What allows this to happen is that the TTL value is one of the first things checked and, if its value is zero, a device sends back a packet acknowledging that it is being dropped without the original packet ever really being processed.

The following section discusses security assessments and penetration tests and the value they bring to securing your network.

Security Assessments and Penetration Testing

Companies with security offerings these days often have a *security assessment* as their first step in assisting a client in securing their network. A security assessment is an excellent first step for an organization that is concerned with understanding the extent of the security on their network (and its effectiveness). A *strongly recommended* practice is that individuals outside of your organization perform security assessments on a yearly basis. This provides an objective and honest evaluation of your security, and because vulnerabilities are always being discovered, your network would be evaluated often enough to understand its effectiveness. A variety of available types of security assessments exist:

- Internal vulnerability and penetration assessment

- External vulnerability and penetration assessment

- Physical security assessment

Before arranging a security assessment of any sort, you should learn more about the processes and procedures that the vendor is going to use. Because too many security service companies exist out there to risk your company's security without some due diligence, you should review the following paragraph:

> *Understand the plan for the security assessment. If not planned and understood, assessing the actual network vulnerabilities can cause havoc in your network. There must be a legal agreement on the scope of the testing and the extent to which it will go; this protects both parties. Finally, it is important to define the success criteria of an assessment so that both parties understand what is to be accomplished.*

The following sections examine the recommended approach that you should take and the benefits to the security of your network for each type of assessment.

Internal Vulnerability and Penetration Assessment

According to a recent study by the FBI, internal users and processes account for over 60 percent of network security threats in today's enterprises. These threats are a result of improper configuration of network devices, lack of effective security procedures, and outdated and unpatched software. Security consultants should be able to identify these threats to determine your network's level of risk to intentional or accidental threats.

Today's organizations find it difficult to stay up-to-date on the numerous new vulnerabilities found each day in operating systems and applications. Security consultants should be aware of the latest vulnerabilities and help you assess the state of your internal network security mechanisms. They should also be able to recommend corrective steps for moving forward with your organization's security goals.

Assessment Methodology

Internal network security assessments must be performed onsite at your location and focus on internal security risks associated with policies, procedures, and networked hosts and applications. At a minimum, a security consultant should perform the following work:

- Gather customer-provided network information, if applicable.

- Gather and document publicly available network information for your review so you can understand what an attacker would know.

- Perform network mapping techniques to determine the topology and physical design of your network.

- Network application probing and scanning.

- OS fingerprinting and vulnerability detection to expose vulnerable hosts.

- Identification of traffic patterns and flows to compare with expected normal business expectations.

- Detect any potentially weak user authentication systems such as users who never change passwords, or insecure wireless networks.

- Vulnerability analysis using public, private, and custom tools.

- Manually verify all detected vulnerabilities to ensure that false positives are not reported.

- Observe internal security practices and policies throughout your network.

- Analyze findings and report analysis along with specific recommendations for moving forward.

The end result of an internal risk assessment should be a document that contains the assessment methodology, the work performed, and details gathered on every system, including the high-risk systems found vulnerable to attack, and detailed lists of vulnerabilities. The assessment results document provides a clearer picture of your network architecture and security risks. The document should also contain the results of all work performed and conclusions from each test phase regarding the remediation required and the relative priority of these recommendations. Of course, this document must also include recommendations for mitigating detected network security risks in a cost-effective manner.

External Penetration and Vulnerability Assessment

As traditional business systems become more distributed among an organization's geographically disperse locations, the risk of external attacks increases. These risks are further exaggerated by improper router and firewall configuration and insecure, outdated, or improperly configured web-based applications.

Today's small and medium-sized businesses find it difficult to stay up-to-date on the numerous new vulnerabilities found each day in operating systems and applications. Granite Systems (www.granitesystems.com) world-class network design consultants are aware of the latest vulnerabilities. They can help you assess the state of your current perimeter defense mechanisms and recommend steps for moving forward with your organization's security awareness.

Assessment Methodology

External Penetration and Vulnerability Assessments are performed against your network at places where it interacts with the outside world. This could be through connections to the Internet, wireless, phone systems, and other remote access locations. The intent of this type of security assessment is to determine where and how your network is vulnerable to external attacks.

In many cases, an External Assessment and an Internal Security Assessment look at the same types of things. The difference is the point of view and, in this case, it

is from the outside trying to look in to see what can be discovered. The following list examines the work that should be done for an External Penetration and Vulnerability Assessment:

- Gather customer-provided network information, if applicable.

- Gather and document publicly available network information for your review so you can understand what an attacker would know.

- Perform stealthy network mapping techniques to determine your network's topology and physical design and to see if these simulated attacks can be detected.

- Network application probing and scanning.

- Firewalking, war dialing, and war driving, as needed.

- OS fingerprinting and vulnerability detection to expose vulnerable hosts.

- Identification of traffic patterns and flows to compare with expected normal business expectations.

- Detect any potentially weak user authentication systems such as users who never change passwords or unsecure wireless networks.

- Vulnerability analysis using public, private, and custom tools.

- Manually verify all detected vulnerabilities to ensure that false positives are not reported.

- Analyze findings and report analysis along with specific recommendations for moving forward.

The end result of an external penetration and vulnerability assessment is a document that contains the same level and type of information as an internal assessment, except from an external point of view. Although this chapter examines internal and external assessments separately, these assessments are best performed together in the real world. They will then allow a clearer picture of your network's security, end-to-end.

Physical Security Assessment

This book focuses on the *logical* security of networks, which is only part of the coverage that this type of assessment provides. Many assets are physical in nature and can be harmed through cruder and perhaps simpler methods than we have discussed. For example, are your IT resources kept in a room with overhead water-based sprinklers? If so, that is not physically secure because microchips and water do not mix. A simple denial of service would be to trigger the fire alarm in your building and let the water do the rest. I hope your tape backups are protected from water damage and that they are current....

Although this is a digital age, today's IT systems still depend on physical hardware and reside in physical locations. Without the use of proper physical security mechanisms, all other security measures in place can be defeated. As the sensitivity of an organization's information increases, physical security takes a more important role. What good is it to have the latest firewall, IDS, and VPNs if you leave the door open to your equipment?

Physical security controls can be either deterrent or detective in nature and are designed to limit your organization's exposure to physical threats. A physical security risk assessment can help your organization design and implement cost-effective physical security measures to deter would-be attackers, monitor suspicious activities, and ultimately protect your valuable corporate resources from tampering, compromise, or destruction.

Assessment Methodology

A Physical Security Assessment must be performed onsite at your location and focus on physical security measures and internal practices of a physical nature that are in place to protect your network resources. A Physical Security Assessment should entail the following:

- Observe external building access points and safeguards in place.

- Observe physical safeguards in place, such as closed-circuit cameras, badge access, and visitor sign-in practices.

- Review physical protection mechanisms for IT resources, but also paper records.

- Determine physical safeguards in place for securing IT equipment, such as restricted access to computing environment, floppy-drive locks, redundant power sources, and protected data communication channels.

- Observe employee habits as it relates to physical security.

- Observe the physical disposal methods of critical data; do you recall dumpster diving?

- Make recommendations for securing your IT resources from physical security breaches.

- Understand the backup procedures and storage of critical data.

- Examine vendor and visitor access policies (if they exist) to determine how unknown individuals are handled.

The end result of a physical risk assessment is a document that contains the methodology followed, the work performed, the results of the work performed, and recommendations for mitigating detecting physical security risks in a cost-effective manner.

Many of these assessments cannot be automated to any great degree, so you must open your network and its resources to a trusted outside organization. When selecting this organization, you should request the following:

- Review of industry standard certifications to ensure that there is at least a measurable level of competence associated with those who are assessing your network.

- Contact several references of the company you are thinking about using and make sure that the references are relevant to the services you need performed.

- Ask for and review sample assessments. This can be difficult to do because assessments usually contain sensitive customer data, but any company that is committed to providing security services should have the ability to show you a sanitized version.

- Set expectations and deliverables clearly in the agreement to proceed/contract and so forth, thereby protecting yourself and the vendor's employees. Clear communication can solve 99 percent of the world's problems.

- Ask the security company to walk you through the assessment process before they come out to your location. If they cannot recite the process from memory, chances are they have either not been in business very long, or the person you are speaking with is not a field technician.

Miscellaneous Assessments

Other types of assessments that are related to security in some ways should be mentioned for possible consideration:

- **Procedural risk assessment**—This assessment allows security professionals to review your security policies and procedures to ensure that they conform to best practices. Chapter 2, "Security Policies and Responses," discussed policies and procedures of this nature.

- **Disaster recovery**—Where your organization is based in an area of the world that is susceptible to tornados, hurricanes, earthquakes, lightning strikes, floods, fire, or some combination of these, the need for a plan of recovering your network infrastructure and critical data becomes more important with every passing day. The influence and persuasiveness of IT is ever-increasing.

- **Information handling security assessment for banks and medical offices**—With new legislation regarding the security of financial and medical records (HIPPA for medical and Gramm-Leach-Bliley Act for financial) coming out each year, professions tasked with maintaining these types of records are being held to increasingly higher data security standards, or face jail time.

Assessment Providers

A simple Google search on security assessments reveals over 400,000 hits, and this number will continue to grow. Some companies, such as the following, are worth mentioning as excellent providers of assessments services:

- **Cisco Secure Consulting Services**—Provides enterprise customers with comprehensive security analysis of large-scale, distributed client networks externally from the perspective of an outside hacker and internally from the perspective of a disgruntled employee or contractor according to their website. You can learn more at http://www.cisco.com/go/securityconsulting.

- **INRGI**—Provides customized security solutions and assessments for customers of all sizes with a specialization in ensuring that business focus drives the security solution versus the more common occurrence of IT driving business. You can learn more at http://www.inrgi.netindex_security.html.

- **Aegis Security**—Provides contract security work and web design: http://www.aegis-security.com/.

- **Granite Systems**—Provides assessments of all types to understand, design, and recommend the proper solution. Granite Systems hold the distinction of the three in that they offer Managed Security and Network Services to further support any organization's needs. You can learn more at http://www.granitesystems.net.

The following section begins looking at the assessment and vulnerability tools that are available to automate the search for security risks.

Vulnerability Scanners

When hackers want to breach your systems, they typically look for well-known security flaws and bugs to attack and exploit, some of the most common of which have been discussed in earlier chapters of this book. A true attack, which has the end goal of penetrating and controlling the target system, relies on the attacker gathering the most accurate and comprehensive view of an organization's security. As the attacker evaluates the network, he exploits vulnerabilities to determine precisely how to get control of valuable information assets.

Attacking vulnerabilities used to be a time-intensive procedure that required a lot of knowledge on the part of the attacker. Today, however, automated tools have changed all of that. Almost gone are the days of having to figure out the publicly available exploit codes and maintaining them all in order to be effective.

You might be wondering if I am talking about the role of attackers and commiserating with them about how hard it is to control the data. Or perhaps I am talking about how network administrators are faced with such a daunting task. In fact, I am talking about both, and the point is that this is no longer the biggest concern. Today, attacks have been scripted and published, and companies have formed to automate the detection of attacks and exploit vulnerabilities. This section looks at the most comprehensive of these tools that, included with the individual tools covered elsewhere in this book, should provide you with excellent resources to detect vulnerabilities and begin correcting them.

Features and Benefits of Vulnerability Scanners

Applications that perform security scan and vulnerability assessments do the scanning and calculations in the background. Frankly, the focus here is not in *how* vulnerabilities are detected, but on *what* is vulnerable. The value of these scanning tools can be summarized in the following four categories:

- **Scan and detection accuracy**—Scans and reported vulnerabilities must be accurate with minimal false positives—defined as normal activity or configuration that the system *mistakenly* reports as malicious. The opposite also holds true then; there can be no false negatives—defined as malicious activity that is not detected.

- **Documentation and support**—Must be clear, concise, well written, and easy to understand (like this book). This includes reporting documentation and application operation so users can figure out how to make the application work and see the documented findings in the report.

- **Reporting**—The most important aspect of a vulnerability scanner is when you need to know the next steps after a vulnerability has been detected (that is, what was detected and how to fix it); thus, a report must be customizable, useful and accurate.

- **Vulnerability updates**—New vulnerabilities are constantly being released and, with today's technology, every system should have a way to update itself automatically.

The following section looks at three of the most popular vulnerability scanners that are currently on the market.

Nessus

Nessus is to vulnerability detection what Snort is to IDS: an open source solution supported by a community of Internet volunteers. You can learn more about Nessus at http://www.nessus.com.

In Their Own Words

The following section is a direct quote from the Nessus web page on how it describes its product:

> The "Nessus" Project aims to provide to the Internet community a free, powerful, up-to-date and easy to use remote security scanner.
>
> A security scanner is software, which will audit remotely a given network and determine whether bad guys (a.k.a. 'crackers') may break into it, or misuse it in some way.
>
> Unlike many other security scanners, Nessus does not take anything for granted. That is, it will not consider that a given service is running on a fixed port - that is, if you run your web server on port 1234, Nessus will detect it and test its security. It will not make its security tests regarding the version number of the remote services, but will really attempt to exploit the vulnerability.

Nessus is very fast, reliable and has a modular architecture that allows you to fit it to your needs.

Scan and Detection Accuracy

Scans and reported vulnerabilities must be accurate, with minimal false positives—defined as normal activity or configuration that the system *mistakenly* reports as malicious. The opposite also then holds true; there can be no false negatives—defined as malicious activity that is not detected.

Nessus has good capabilities to detect vulnerabilities and is accurate in the vulnerabilities it detects and finds. Being an open source project, Nessus is constantly being watched, tested, studied, and improved upon. With so much visibility, this product has become configurable for those with the knowledge to understand its underpinnings. Figure 10-2 shows the Nessus setup screen and its flexibility, strength, and many possible options.

Documentation and Support

Documentation must be clear, concise, well written, and easy to understand. This includes reporting documentation and application operation so users can figure out how to make the application work and see the documented findings in the report.

Nessus documentation is excellent, average, and very poor. If you are trying to install Nessus on an Apple laptop or for the first time, some excellent resources can help you get Nessus running with minimal stress.

When you are trying to determine how Nessus functions or what it can do as part of its standard documentation, you are going to have to deal with the fact that what little is written has been done by programmers. Ever try and read a Linux MAN page? If you have, you know what I mean—it is not for beginners.

From a technical support perspective, because Nessus is not a company, there is no formal technical support number, and the website is basic. However, a mailing list has many of the core Nessus programmers, and they can be helpful.

Figure 10-2   Nessus Vulnerability Scanner Setup Screen

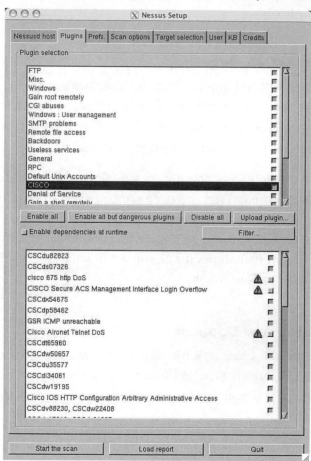

Reporting

The most important aspect of a vulnerability scanner is when you need to know the next steps after a vulnerability has been detected (that is, what was detected and how to fix it); thus a report must be customizable, useful, and accurate.

Nessus creates reports in a variety of formats, the most useful being HTML. These reports are fully hyperlinked with complete analysis of the vulnerabilities detected, their level of risk to your network, and with great, pretty pictures that can visualize the vulnerabilities. On a downside, the reports are UNIX-centric and full of contextual and grammatical errors, not something that you can share without serious editing. The information is accurate, just not as polished as a commercial product.

Vulnerability Updates

New vulnerabilities are constantly being released and, with today's technology, every system should have a way to update itself automatically.

Nessus is kept up-to-date via scripting that can be automated to ensure that it has the latest signatures. Although Nessus does not run on Windows, it does have a Windows client that allows connections to Nessus servers so scans can be run remotely.

Nessus is a good vulnerability scanner that has exceptional functionality as a result of its open source status. There are some excellent resources available for Nessus. Other related links can be found at the following URLs:

http://www.securityprojects.org/nessuswx/

http://list.nessus.org/

Nessus is freely available for download and requires no purchase because it is open source software. This means that it is an excellent solution for network administrators that will not cost their organization any money. However, this also means that the old computer sitting in the corner of your neighborhood attacker can be loaded with Linux (free) and Nessus (also free). Then, the vulnerability scanning, which is also free, will commence against your network.

Retina

Retina is eEye's premiere security scanner that leads their suite of security products. eEye offers several products that focus on securing the Microsoft product line. You can learn more about Retina at http://www.eeye.com.

In Their Own Words

The following section is a direct quote from the eEye corporate web page on how they describe their vulnerability scanner, Retina:

> Created by eEye Digital Security, Retina Network Security Scanner is recognized as the #1 rated network vulnerability assessment scanner by Network World magazine. Retina sets the standard in terms of speed, ease of use, reporting, non-intrusiveness and advanced vulnerability detection capabilities.
>
> Retina can scan every machine on your network, including a variety of operating system platforms (e.g. Apple, Windows, UNIX, Linux), networked devices (e.g. switches, firewalls, routers, etc.), databases and third-party or custom applications, all in record time. After scanning, Retina delivers a comprehensive report that details all vulnerabilities and appropriate corrective actions and fixes.
>
> eEye is a recognized digital security research powerhouse. As a result, Retina incorporates the most comprehensive and up-to-date vulnerabilities database -- automatically downloaded at the beginning of every Retina session. In addition to scanning against the most complete database of known vulnerabilities, customers can write their own customized audits. Furthermore, Retina's unique, artificial intelligence option (CHAM) can be used for extensive testing and detection of previously unknown security issues within your network.

Scan and Detection Accuracy

Scans and reported vulnerabilities must be accurate with minimal false positives—defined as normal activity or configuration that the system *mistakenly* reports as malicious. The opposite also holds true, then; there can be no false negatives—defined as malicious activity that is not detected.

Retina has an excellent presentation interface for the execution of scans; it is intuitive and comes with a variety of other tools so it can be used for more than just a vulnerability scanner. One of the best features that Retina provides is the easy customization, scheduling, and penetration audit customization. What sets Retina apart is the capability to create scanning policies with different scans for different devices. For example, you can scan Internet servers differently than employee PCs. Figure 10-3 shows an example of targeting a specific device in Retina.

Figure 10-3   Selecting a Target Range in Retina

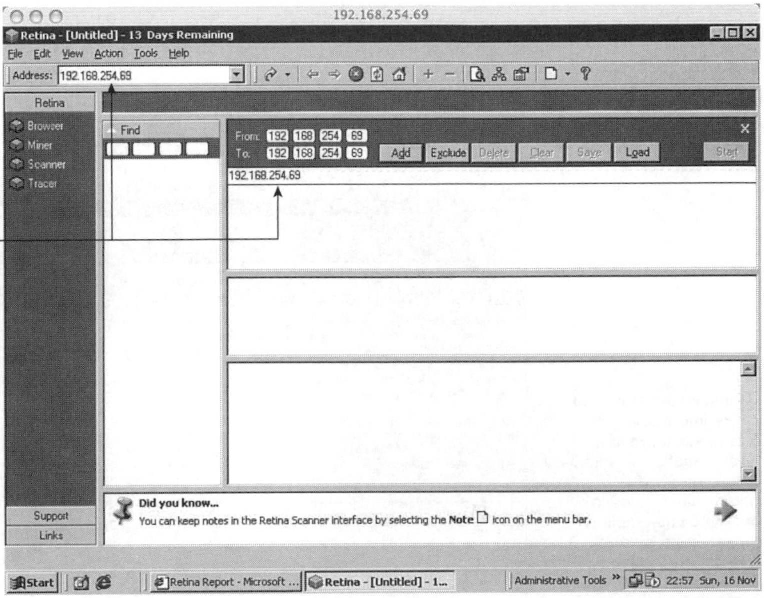

Retina allows for the user to select single host IP addresses or entire subnets to be scanned for vulnerabilities by the parameters placed in the indicated fields. In this case, a single host is targeted.

Documentation and Support

Documentation must be clear, concise, well written, and easy to understand (like this book). This includes reporting documentation and application operation so users can figure out how to make the application work and see the documented findings in the report.

Retina documentation is included in the Windows help file and appears to be complete, answering many of the questions a typical user would have. It does not contain many in-depth how-to's, but it provides enough examples that their lack is not a hindrance. A web-based form that is submitted to the eEye technical support team only provides support options for users.

Reporting

The most important aspect of a vulnerability scanner is when you need to know the next steps after a vulnerability has been detected (that is, what was detected and how to fix it); thus, a report must be customizable, useful, and accurate. Figure 10-4 shows the summary of vulnerabilities after Retina completes its scan of your network.

Figure 10-4   Vulnerability Summary by Risk Level

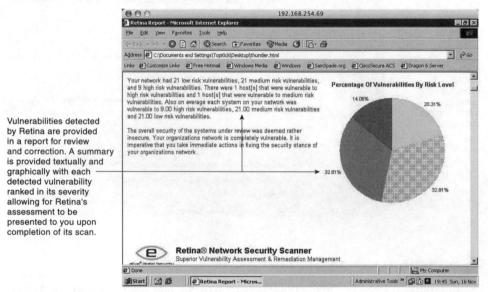

Like Nessus, Retina provides an overview of the detected vulnerability along with links to additional information and corrective actions, such as a Microsoft HotFix. Figure 10-5 shows specific detected vulnerability information, what the risk is and where to find the manufacturers fix.

Figure 10-5 Vulnerabilities Details

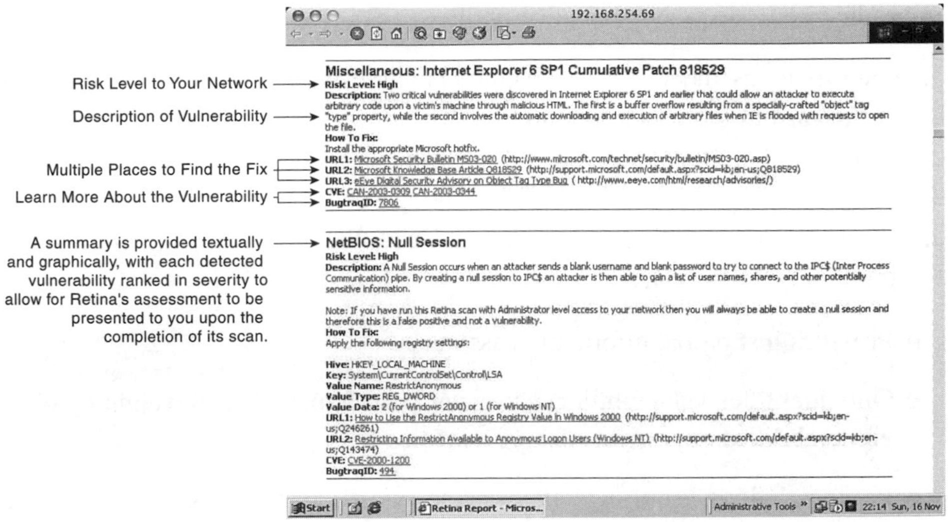
192.168.254.69
Risk Level to Your Network
Description of Vulnerability
Multiple Places to Find the Fix
Learn More About the Vulnerability
A summary is provided textually and graphically, with each detected vulnerability ranked in severity to allow for Retina's assessment to be presented to you upon the completion of its scan.
Miscellaneous: Internet Explorer 6 SP1 Cumulative Patch 818529
NetBIOS: Null Session

Vulnerability Updates

New vulnerabilities are constantly being released and, with today's technology, every system should have a means of updating itself automatically.

Retina is exceptional is this regard; it can be configured not only to update its list of vulnerabilities, but also the application itself. Curiously, the open source movement has missed the boat on that feature. Retina takes a bit of getting used to, and it is an effective vulnerability scanner.

Penetration Testing Products

Vulnerability identification, detection, and prioritization are all assessment functions. You can only classify a product as penetration testing if it actually exploits a given vulnerability. Vulnerability assessment and penetration testing complement each other. They do very different things, so they must be two separate categories.

This "confusion" is often encountered during the sales process. Penetration testing product picks up where the vulnerability scans leave off.

Vulnerability assessment does an adequate job of providing the tester with a snapshot of the current network configuration. Unfortunately, this snapshot does not address the implication of a successful intrusion to organizational assets. It only relates what the vulnerabilities are; it does not probe deeper to reveal what happens when the vulnerabilities are exploited. The following details the limitations of vulnerability assessments and scanners:

- Provides just partial information assurance

- Only identifies vulnerabilities; does not provide meaningful weighting of vulnerabilities or prioritization of remedies

- Produces a long list of potential weaknesses, often including numerous false positives

- Does not demonstrate what information assets can be compromised

- Cannot simulate real-world attacks

- Does not exploit trust relationships between network components, nor demonstrate the implications of a successful attack

Core security is roaring into the security penetration testing marketplace with its exploit product, Core Impact! Yes, *exploit* product (they run applications in the product). Core Impact actually does not detect a vulnerability; rather, it exploits a vulnerability and installs an *agent on the targeted server.* This agent then allows you to escalate attacks and own the target machine. Core Impact product eliminates the annoying and embarrassing occurrence of false positives. Although the following section discusses at length how Core Impact achieves this, you can learn more about Core Impact at http://www.coresecurity.com.

In Their Own Words

The following section is a direct quote from the Core Security web page describing their product:

> CORE IMPACT is the first comprehensive penetration testing solution for assessing specific information security threats to an organization. The product is designed to replace expensive, inconsistent manual penetration testing with a professional, state-of-the-art automated penetration testing product. CORE IMPACT goes beyond vulnerability scanners by enabling real-world attacks on IT assets and presenting analysis of information security risks in one comprehensive application.

Scan and Detection Accuracy

Scans and reported vulnerabilities must be accurate, with minimal false positives—defined as normal activity or configuration that the system *mistakenly* reports as malicious. The opposite also holds true, then; there can be no false negatives—defined as malicious activity that is not detected. Impact, however, does not actually scan for vulnerabilities; in fact, only limited scanning is possible with this product—in scanning mode, simple port scanning and target operating system detection. As you will see, this OS detection is a nice capability because it makes taking advantage of an exploit easier to accomplish! Why, though, are we talking about a product that does not detect my *potential* vulnerabilities? Impact eliminates false positives and actually allows you to compromise a host and proceed as if you were an attacker, thereby taking the analysis of vulnerability detection to a whole new level.

Documentation

Documentation must be clear, concise, well written, and easy to understand. This includes reporting documentation and application operation so that users can figure out how to make the application work and see the documented findings in the report.

Core Impact provides a variety of excellent reports that log every action of the application during its function, scanning, and compromising of hosts throughout your network. Impact can generate two types of reports:

- **Findings report**—A report that enumerates all the discovered hosts and their found vulnerabilities

- **History report**—An exhaustive report of all the activities performed by the auditor using Impact

Normally, these reports are standard type reports that you would expect. What makes them unique, however, is that Impact allows them to be customized and printed according to the level of detail you want to present. For example, the report given to an organization's executive team should differ greatly from the report presented to the IT staff. Impact allows this level of customization.

Documentation and Support

The most important aspect of a vulnerability scanner is when you need to know the next steps after a vulnerability has been detected (that is, what was detected and how to fix it). Therefore, a report must be customizable, useful, and accurate.

When learning new software or applications, I find that it is important that the product has a good documentation and support. This allows users to learn on their time versus other methods, such as training or scheduled web seminars (which I'm not a big fan of).

Vulnerability Updates

New vulnerabilities are constantly being released, and with today's technology, every system should have a way of updating itself automatically.

Impact allows for easy updating of the attack modules through a single click of a button. Core Security is committed to making the product grow and evolve so they have an aggressive development schedule. You will not find every possible vulnerability within Core Impact; however, there are also continual updates in this regard. It is a challenge to determine exactly which vulnerabilities become modules and, so far, observations have shown that good choices and options that rather limited; however, they are growing quickly.

Core Impact In Action

This section discusses how Core Impact actually exploits a vulnerability and installs a special, undetectable piece of software known as an *agent* on the target machine. This agent allows you to control the targeted server. The level of control depends on the vulnerability the agent has exploited. For example, in the figures that follow, the exploit taken advantage of allows full control of the targeted server. In Figure 10-6, you can see that Core Impact is targeting the MSRPC DCOM vulnerability against a Windows 2000 Professional laptop that runs SP3 with the corresponding agent deployed.

After the agent is deployed on the server, you can determine the level of access you have gained by exploiting this vulnerability. As shown in Figure 10-7, the agent has been successfully deployed. Right-clicking the deployed agent displays a list of possible available options.

Figure 10-6   Core Impact Agent Deployed

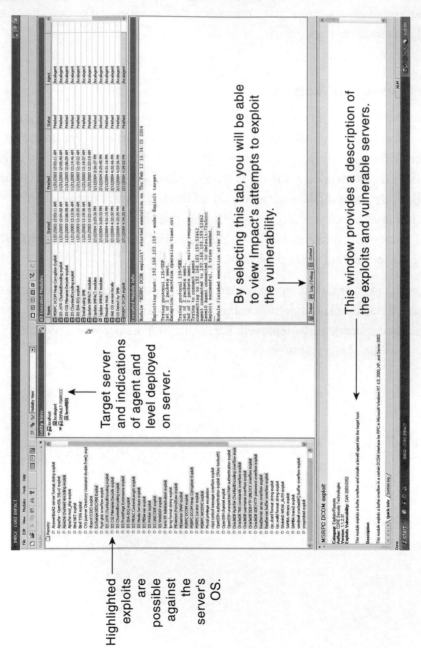

Figure 10-7   Agent Options

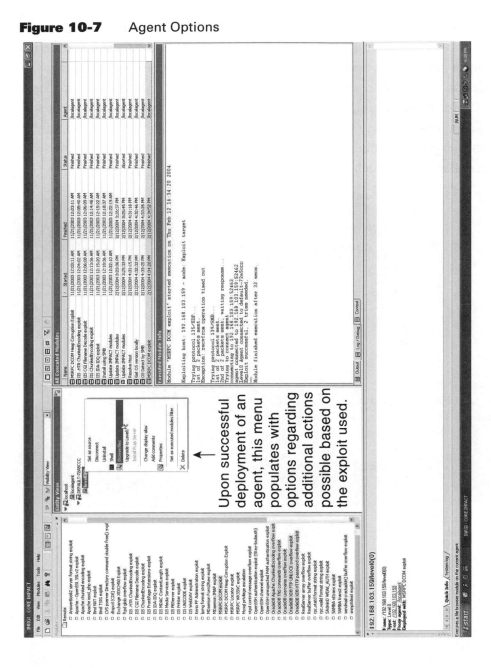

One of the scariest things about the possibilities in this scenario is that this agent allows you to browse all the files on the server on which the agent is installed. As shown in Figure 10-8, the agent can provide you with access to the most sensitive files on the exploited server. Specifically, you can upload, download, and manipulate files at your whim. Agents are not detectable when running on an exploited system; however, they are present and provide you with the capability to truly test whether your systems are vulnerable to exploits that might have been detected by a similar product, such as Nessus or Retina.

Figure 10-8 Browsing Files

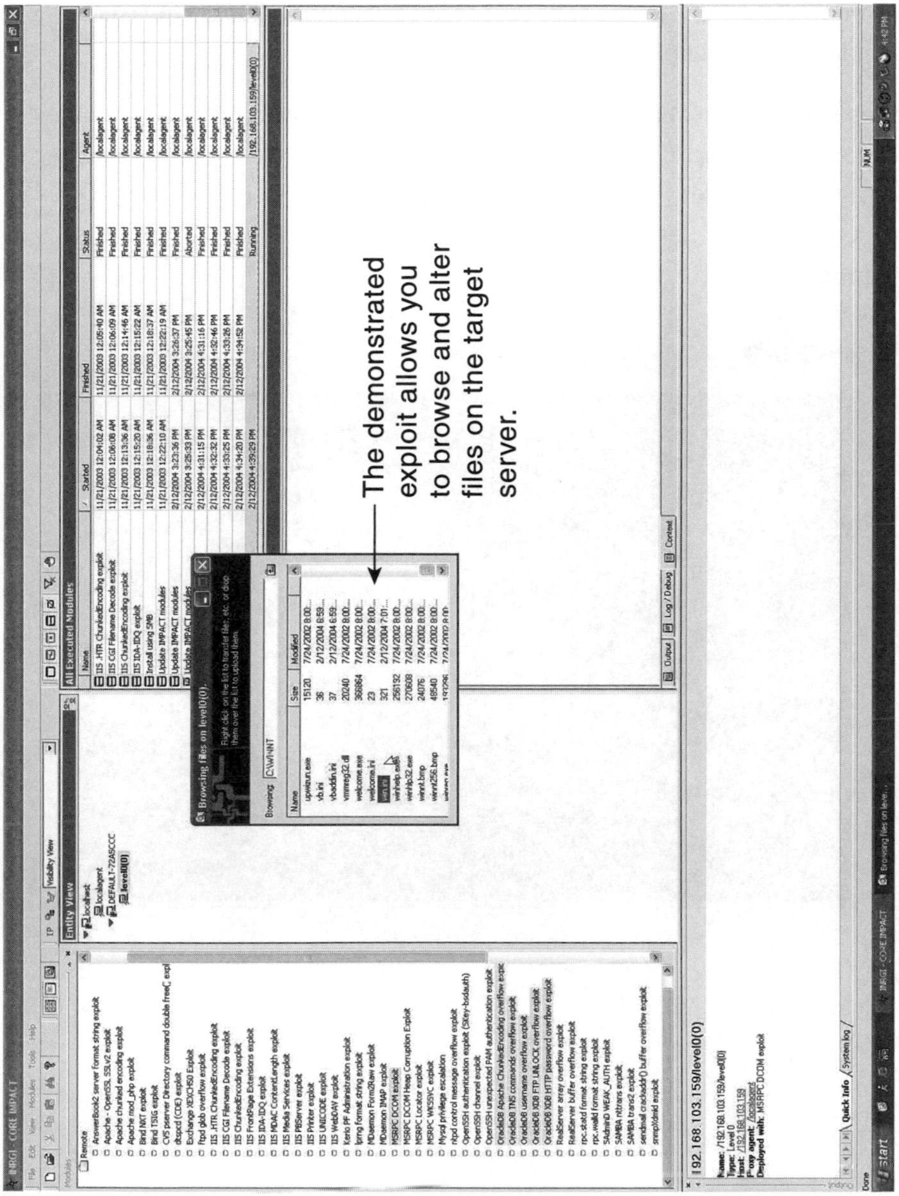

The demonstrated exploit allows you to browse and alter files on the target server.

The last point to cover is the mini-shell. Figure 10-9 shows the shell screen and the available options. As you can see, uploading, downloading, and executing files is simple once an agent is deployed.

It is also possible to deploy additional agents against other servers when you find the weak link. In the example, it is possible to leverage that access gained against other internal devices. The interesting and disturbing part here is that, if these attacks were in fact detected, they would appear to be coming from the compromised machine!

Figure 10-9   Mini-Shell

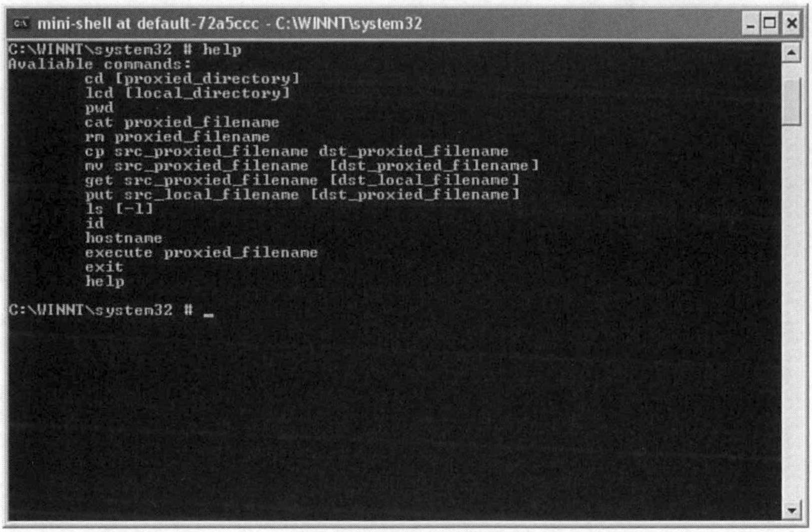

```
mini-shell at default-72a5ccc - C:\WINNT\system32                    _ □ ×
C:\WINNT\system32 # help
Available commands:
        cd [proxied_directory]
        lcd [local_directory]
        pwd
        cat proxied_filename
        rm proxied_filename
        cp src_proxied_filename dst_proxied_filename
        mv src_proxied_filename [dst_proxied_filename]
        get src_proxied_filename [dst_local_filename]
        put src_local_filename [dst_proxied_filename]
        ls [-l]
        id
        hostname
        execute proxied_filename
        exit
        help

C:\WINNT\system32 # _
```

Chapter Summary

This final chapter covered several additional new vulnerabilities and described how they are used to attack systems. Understanding these common attacks is crucial for understanding what the rest of the chapter is explaining. Security assessments and penetration testing are effective tools that, if used correctly, allow your network to be evaluated by qualified engineers who deploy the proper security analysis tools to find the vulnerabilities. A good security assessment, however, covers more than just the logical vulnerabilities in your network. The remainder of this chapter was dedicated to the various security scanning tools that are available, some of which are free open source solutions.

Chapter Review Questions

1. The freely available tool known as Ettercap can perform what four types of packet sniffing?

2. Define what a DDoS is and how it functions.

3. Identify and explain three reasons that can result in a back door exploit being present on a system.

4. Define the concept of firewalking.

5. Where should an external penetration and vulnerability assessment performed in your network?

6. When considering vulnerability scanners, why are a program's ability to conduct an accurate scan crucial?

Answers to Chapter Review Questions

Chapter 1

1. What is a target of opportunity?

   Answer: A target of opportunity is one in which a vulnerability has been detected by an attacker, who decides to try an exploit because the target has allowed them to find it.

2. What is a target of choice?

   Answer: A target of choice occurs when an attacker chooses you as a target. His reason is irrelevant because this is a mental commitment on the part of the attacker.

3. What is the purpose of footprinting?

   Answer: Footprinting is the process an attacker takes to understand a target's network and associated systems. This is a continuous process that is used throughout all planned attacks, and in which attackers are looking to gain as much information about the target as possible.

4. Which of the following are ways by which an attacker can gain access?

   a. Operating system attacks

   b. Application attacks

   c. Misconfiguration attacks

   d. Script attacks

   e. All of the above

   Answer: E. All of the above.

5. List four of the Network Security Organizations.

Answer:

CERT

SANS

SCORE

Security Focus

ICAT

Center for Internet Security

6. Briefly explain why it is important for an attacker to cover his tracks.

Answer: Presuming that an attacker has compromised a system, the ability to remove the forensic evidence of his actions (in other words, cover his tracks) allows the attacker to utilize the compromised system at his leisure if the system administrator never knows they have been compromised.

7. Social engineering can be damaging without an overt attack ever happening. Explain why.

Answer: The purpose of social engineering is to trick a person into believing that the attacker is someone else and thereby allowing that person to believe that the attacker is entitled to sensitive information.

8. What kind of information might be found if an attacker dumpster dives at your place of work?

Answer: Perhaps there might be financial reports, customer lists, human resource information, or other sensitive data. The point here is to never "simply throw out" information that might have value.

9. DNS information gained through WHOIS is used for what kind of reconnaissance?

Answer: WHOIS information is used for passive reconnaissance.

10. What two free reconnaissance tools are available with most versions of the Windows operating system?

Answer: Nbtstat and net view.

Chapter 2

1. How important is it to involve other departments and employees in the crafting of security policies?

   Answer: Involving your fellow employees is crucial to a policy's success. Their involvement allows everyone to understand and support the company's commitment to security.

2. True or false: It is a well-known fact that users circumvent security policies that are too restrictive. Explain your answer.

   Answer: Absolutely true. The tighter you create your security policies, the harder it is for users to function effectively. Therefore, you must balance security and productivity.

3. What are three things that you should keep in mind when writing or reviewing a security policy?

   Answer:

   Determine who gets access to each area of your network

   Determine what they can access and how

   Balance trust between people and resources

   Allow access based on the level of trust for users and resources

   Use resources to ensure that trust is not violated

4. Why is it important to include an enforcement section in every security policy?

   Answer: The enforcement section defines the penalty for failure to follow the policy. Dismissal is typically the most severe penalty, but in a few cases, criminal prosecution should be listed as an option.

5. An Acceptable Use Policy defines what kind of expectations for users?

   Answer: An AUP defines the systems that are to be used for business purposes that serve the interests of the company, our clients, and our customers.

6. When and under what circumstances should you reveal your password to someone?

   Answer: No one in a company should ever ask for your password; in the event of a technical difficulty, it will reset the password. Never reveal your password to anyone and, if asked, report the request to corporate security immediately.

7. Which of the following sample passwords would be considered effective when checked against the corporate password policy?

   a. wolfpack

   b. thomas67

   c. simonisnot4

   d. sJ8Dtt&efs

   e. Missing$4u

   Answer: D is clearly the correct answer because it has all the proper characteristics of a secure password as outlined in the password policy.

8. Define VPN and the role it can play within a company's network infrastructure.

   Answer: A network is constructed using a public network such as the Internet to connect systems to a main site, typically the headquarters. VPNs use encryption mechanisms to protect data that is transmitted across the Internet. Additional protections are put in place to ensure that only authorized users or devices can connect via a VPN.

9. VPNs support a technology called split tunneling: define this technology and explain whether it should be used in a network?

   Answer: Split-tunneling is a method of configuring a VPN, and it is either on or off. Essentially, if split-tunneling is on, users are allowed to connect to the corporate network and the Internet simultaneously. This presents a danger to the corporate network's security because an attacker was to take control of the computer creating a VPN to the corporate network; then the attacker can also gain access to the companies' network via the VPN.

10. How frequently should security policies be updated or reviewed?

    Answer: Ensure that your policies are updated annually, if not sooner, to reflect the changes of the past year.

Chapter 3

1. What are the six security design concepts you should consider when looking at the security technologies for securing your network?

   Answer: Layered security, controlling access, role specific security, user awareness, monitoring, and keeping systems patched.

2. What rule is always implicitly present at the end of every packet filter?

   Answer: Deny all packets.

3. When a device is performing stateful packet inspection what characteristics in a packet's header are inspected, and why are they important?

   Answer: Firewalls perform stateful packet inspection and monitor the IP header information to track the status of a connection.

4. What are some limitations of stateful packet inspection?

   Answer: SPI cannot inspection/track every type of packet; for example, ICMP and UDP are not stateful.

5. Define the differences between public and private IP addresses.

   Answer: Private addresses are for internal, non-Internet use. Public addresses are those used on the Internet.

6. Compare and contrast the three different version of NAT and identify which of them is the most commonly used.

   Answer: Static, dynamic, and overloading. Refer to the bulleted list in the section, "Network Address Translation (NAT)" in Chapter 3 for a full comparison. Overloading is the most commonly used form of NAT.

7. What are the two types of proxy firewalls?

   Answer: Standard and dynamic firewalls.

8. Why is content filtering so important to networking?

   Answer: Content filtering protects a company by restricting harmful websites.

9. What is the potential value of PKI to securing a network and e-commerce?

   Answer: Seamless global security.

10. AAA provides security for what aspect of a network?

    Answer: Network devices.

11. Search the Internet and find three potential vendors that can offer an effective RADIUS solution. Describe what features about each are beneficial.

    Answer: Cisco ACS and Funk Steel belted radius are two vendor-specific RADIUS solutions.

Chapter 4

1. How long, in bits, is the DES key?

   Answer: 56 bits.

2. In 3DES, the same key is used to encrypt at each of the three stages: True or false?

   Answer: True.

3. Define a hash in your own words.

   Answer: By way of an analogy, a hash is a grinder that takes something recognizable, like beef or pork, hashes it, and ends up with something unique that is based on the original. In this case, it is hamburger or sausage.

4. What is used to create a digital signature?

   Answer: A hash.

5. Define authentication and provide an example.

   Answer: Authentication is the process of identifying an individual or device based on the correct username/password combination.

6. Define authorization and provide an example.

   Answer: Authorization defines what individuals are allowed to access; have they been authenticated?

7. A hash check occurs at what point in the operation of MD5?

Answer: When using a one-way hash operation like MD5, you can compare a calculated message digest against the received message digest to verify that the message has not been tampered with. This comparison is called a **hash check**.

8. Of the security protocols covered in this chapter, which of them use generic routing encapsulation (GRE)?

Answer: PPTP and L2TP.

9. Describe several security benefits of L2TP.

Answer: Refer to the bulleted list in Chapter 4 under the "Benefits of L2TP" Section.

10. What are the three core SSH capabilities?

Answer: Secure command shell, secure file transfer, and secure port forwarding.

Chapter 5

1. Who needs a firewall?

Answer: Everyone connected to the Internet or with IT resources to protect needs a firewall. Depending on a router and ACLs is an incomplete solution in layering your network's defense.

2. Why do I need a firewall?

Answer: A firewall provides protection for your network resources through technologies such as SPI, which is not possible with any other device.

3. Do I need a firewall?

Answer: Yes, yes, yes you need a firewall!

4. How is a firewall an extension of a security policy?

Answer: A firewall's rules reflect the network security policy that your organization has as expressed in a written security policy.

5. What is the name of the table in a firewall that tracks connections?

Answer: State table.

6. What fundamental does a DMZ fulfill?

Answer: The DMZ protects Internet accessible servers and services.

7. What are four benefits of a DMZ?

Answer: Auditing of DMZ traffic, locating an Intrusion Detection System (IDS) on the DMZ, limiting routing updates between three interfaces, and locating DNS on the DMZ.

8. Can firewalls enforce password policies or prevent misuse of passwords by users?

Answer: No, they cannot.

Chapter 6

1. Because every company that connects to the Internet has a router, should you deploy security on those routers?

Answer: Definitely! You have the router and this book, and you need to protect your network; use the knowledge presented here to go out and start some packet screening at the router. Layered security is best!

2. What is the value of edge routers being used as choke points, and how effective can they be in increasing your network's security?

Answer: The value of edge routers being configured as choke points is that they can prevent access to specific devices and applications in a performance-friendly way. This increase in security is typically provided through the use of standard and extended access control lists that can address traffic concerns at Layers 2, 3, and 4 of the OSI reference model.

3. What technology is at the heart of Cisco's Firewall Feature Set IOS?

Answer: At the heart of Cisco's Firewall Feature Set IOS is Context-Based Access Control (CBAC). CBAC is a stateful packet inspection engine that extends the router's filtering capability to the application layer (Layer 7) of the OSI reference model.

4. How does the firewall feature set employ dynamic filtering of packets using ACLs?

Answer: CBAC allows return path filtering for TCP, UDP, and ICMP that creates dynamic stateful entries based on the bidirectional communication sessions in the filtering of access lists when a conversation is first established. CBAC allows these to be created provided there are permit statements in extended access lists that are unique; this eliminates the need to leave any statically open ports. In other words CBAC, opens ports dynamically only when traffic matches an ACL. The ports that are opened dynamically are limited in lifespan (the duration of the conversation) and only to specific to hosts, thus limiting the opportunity for external attacks.

5. Can the Cisco IOS IDS have multiple points of packet inspection?

Answer: Of course you can have multiple points of packet inspection in the form of ACLs. The only requirement of the FFS and CBAC is that the filtering must occur after the inspection. Having the FFS determine access based on conversation direction maintains the ability for the router to still function primarily as a router.

6. Temporary access control lists have timers associated with them. Define how they function based on protocol (ICMP, UDP, and TCP)?

Answer: ICMP and UDP sessions are removed based on configurable inactivity timers. TCP sessions are removed five seconds after the exchange of FIN packets. In the event of an RST packet, the session is terminated and corresponding ACL entries are removed immediately.

7. What is the difference between atomic and compound signatures?

Answer: Atomic signatures are concerned with attacks directed to single hosts, while compound signatures look at attacks that are directed to groups of machines.

8. What happens when an attacker uses chargen and echo together? How would you stop this from being able to occur in a Cisco router?

   Answer: Pointing the "chargen" service at the "echo" service creates a loop that causes an enormous amount of traffic to be generated and eventually overwhelms the router's CPU and RAM resources; therefore, this provides the makings of a very serious denial-of-service attack (DoS). The easiest way to prevent this kind of attack is to disable these services on the router. The commands to do so are **no tcp-small-servers** that disables echo, chargen, discard and daytime; and **no udp-small-servers**, which disables echo, chargen, and discard.

Chapter 7

1. Is it possible to have unencrypted VPNs?

   Answer: Yes; in that case, other protocols are used to handle the encryption.

2. What are the three types of VPNs?

   Answer: Site-to-site, extranet, and remote.

3. Select three VPN features and benefits and explain how your organization can directly benefit from each.

   Answer: VPNs are secure, encrypt traffic, and can be used to link sites securely over the Internet.

4. VPN Concentrators are designed for many users—explain how many and when they should be used.

   Answer: VPN concentrators are built to handle the requirements of VPNs and are available in models that are suitable for everything from small businesses with up to 100 remote-access users to large organizations with up to 10,000 simultaneous remote users.

5. Does the VPN Client Software for PCs support Apple's powerful new operating system, MAX OS X?

   Answer: Yes.

6. When does split tunneling occur?

Answer: Split tunneling occurs when a remote VPN user or site is allowed to access a public network (the Internet) at the same time that he accesses the private VPN network, without placing the public network traffic inside the tunnel first.

7. In relation to a datastream, what role does authentication play in securing it?

Answer: Authentication establishes the integrity of the data stream and ensures that it is not tampered with in transit. It also provides confirmation about data stream origin.

8. When tunneling data in IPSec, what are the three protocols that play a role in process?

Answer: GRE, IPSec, and ISAKMP.

9. In site-to-site VPNs, what are the two different encapsulating protocols and what are the differences between the two?

Answer: In site-to-site VPNs, the encapsulating protocol is usually IPSec or generic routing encapsulation (GRE). GRE includes information about what type of packet you are encapsulating and about the connection between the client and server. The difference depends on the level of security needed for the connection, with IPSec being more secure and GRE having greater functionality. IPSec can tunnel and encrypt IP packets, while GRE can tunnel IP and non-IP packets. When you need to send non-IP packets (such as IPX) over the tunnel, IPSec and GRE should be used together.

10. Name three of the benefits of IKE.

Answer:

Eliminates the need to manually specify all the IPSec security parameters at both peers.

Allows you specify a lifetime for the IPSec SAs.

Allows encryption keys to change during IPSec sessions.

Allows IPSec to provide antireplay services.

Enables CA support for a manageable, scalable IPSec implementation.

Allows dynamic authentication of peers.

Chapter 8

1. How are the terms 802.11 and Wi-Fi used? In what ways are they different or similar?

   Answer: These terms describe the IEEE wireless standard and are used interchangeably. Wi-Fi is the buzzword associated with the 802.11 standard.

2. What are the five benefits to organizations that would provide reasons for them to implement a wireless network?

   Answer:

   Attractive Price—Deploying a wireless LAN can be cheaper than a wired LAN because you do not have the needs for wires; just hook up an access point and it can provide service to multiple computers.

   Mobility—Boost user productivity with the convenience of allowing them to wirelessly connect to the network from any point within range of an access point.

   Rapid and Flexible Deployment—Quickly extend a wired network with the ease of attaching an access point to a high-speed network connection.

   Application Agnostic—As an extension of the wired network, wireless LANs work with all existing applications.

   Performance—Wireless LAN offers a high-speed connection that, while equal to Ethernet, is quickly passing it in speed.

3. WarDriving is the most common means of searching for wireless networks. What is needed to conduct a WarDrive, and why is it so useful for attackers?

   Answer: Ideally, an attacker conducting a WarDrive would need a program to detect wireless networks such as Net or Mac Stumbler installed on a Laptop. They can gain additional information through the use of a GPS device and an antenna.

4. What is one type of freely available wireless packet sniffers?

   Answer: Ethereal.

5. Are wireless networks vulnerable to the same types of denial of service attacks as wired network? Are they vulnerable to any additional attacks that wired networks are not?

    Answer: Yes, and they are also susceptible to attacks that interfere with radio signals, such as jamming, because wireless networks are based on radio signals.

6. What are the four types of EAP available for use?

    Answer: Following are the four commonly used EAP methods in use today:

    - EAP-MD5

    - EAP-Cisco Wireless (also known as LEAP)

    - EAP-TLS

    - EAP-TTLS

Chapter 9

1. When and who were the first to develop a commercial IDS?

    Answer: Late in the 1980's, members of the Haystack Project formed Haystack Labs as a commercial venture into developing Host-based Intrusion Detection.

2. What are the two types of IDS, and should they be deployed together or separately?

    Answer: In general, two basic forms of IDS are in use today: *Network-based and Host-based IDS.* Both types of sensors offer different techniques for detecting and deferring malicious activity, and both should be deployed in correlation to provide the most effective enhancement to a layered defense strategy.

3. Define and discuss NIDS and the how and where they are effective in a network.

   Answer: Network-Based Intrusion Detection Sensors, or NIDSs, reside directly on the network and watch all traffic traversing the network. NIDSs are effective at both watching for inbound/outbound traffic flows and traffic between hosts on or between local network segments. NIDSs are typically deployed in front of *and* behind firewalls and VPN gateways to measure the effectiveness of those security devices, and to interact with them in order to add more depth to the security of your network.

4. Define and discuss HIDSs and the how and where they are effective in a network.

   Answer: Host-Based Intrusion Detection Sensors, or HIDSs, are specialized software applications that are installed on a computer (typically a server) to watch all inbound and outbound communication traffic to and from that server and monitor the file system for changes. HIDSs are extremely effective on mission critical, Internet-accessible application servers such as web or e-mail servers because they can watch the applications at its source to protect them.

5. When is anomaly detection the most effective and why?

   Answer: Anomaly detection becomes most effective when coupled with protocol decoding, whereby the IDS knows what normal behavior is expected within certain protocols and responds if abnormal commands or requests are detected.

6. Which Intrusion Detection methodology also verifies application behavior?

   Answer: Protocol analysis.

7. List and define each of the two techniques an IDS can employ to prevent an attack.

   Answer:

   Sniping—Allows the IDS to terminate a suspected attack through the use of a TCP reset packet or ICMP unreachable message.

   Shunning—Allows the IDS to automatically configure your prescreening router or firewall to deny traffic based on what it has detected, thus shunning the connection.

8. List the three most important IDS limitations, in your opinion, and explain why you choose them.

   Answer: Answer will spur classroom discussion.

9. Honeypots distract attackers from more valuable resources. True or false?

   Answer: True.

Chapter 10

1. The freely available tool known as Ettercap can perform what four types of packet sniffing?

   Answer: Ettercap can perform four methods of sniffing: IP, MAC, ARP, and Public ARP.

2. Define what a DDoS is and how it functions.

   Answer: A distributed denial-of-service attack generates the false traffic from multiple hosts across the Internet. A distributed denial of service (DDoS) attack uses multiple computers throughout the network that it has previously infected with a DDoS Daemon (program); these computers are then known as zombie computers.

3. Identify and explain three reasons that can result in a back door exploit being present on a system.

   Answer:

   1. Deliberately placed by system developers to allow quick access during development and not turned off before release.

   2. Placed by employees to facilitate performance of their duties because the "proper procedure" made them think that it made their jobs more difficult, so there must be a smarter and easier way. Users might not be as technical as your IT staff, and often they find back doors because they do not have a preconceived notion of how something should work.

3. Normal part of standard "default" operating system installs that have not been eliminated by "OS hardening," such as retaining default user logon ID and password combinations. Again, here we see that vendors do not want technical support calls, so they make it as easy and open as possible. This means that your IT staff must review and harden every server.

4. Placed by disgruntled employees to allow access after termination. In many cases, an employee suspects that he is going to loss his job. This makes him feel angry and unappreciated, so he wants to ensure that he can strike back as needed when the time comes.

5. Created by the execution of malicious code, such as viruses or a Trojan horse that takes advantage of an operating system or application's vulnerability.

4. Define the concept of firewalking.

Answer: Firewalking is concept and tool that allows the attacker to send specially crafted packets through a firewall to determine what ports and services are permitted through the firewall. An attacker with this knowledge can make his port scans hidden and thus map your network through your firewall.

5. Where should an external penetration and vulnerability assessment performed in your network?

Answer: External Penetration and Vulnerability Assessments are performed against your network at places where it interacts with the outside world.

6. When considering vulnerability scanners, why are a program's ability to conduct an accurate scan crucial?

Answer: Scan and Detection Accuracy—Scans and reported vulnerabilities must be accurate with minimal false positives—defined as normal activity or configuration that the system mistakenly reports as malicious. The opposite also holds true, then; there can be no false negatives—defined as malicious activity that is not detected.

Glossary

3DES (Triple Data Encryption Standard)   A modification of the original DES algorithm that uses three separate keys when running its encryption algorithm and associated computations. Through the use of three separate keys, the key length was effectively increased from 8 characters to 24 characters, resulting in 168 bits-worth of encryption strength.

802.11b   A family of specifications created by the Institute of Electrical and Electronics Engineers (IEEE) for wireless, Ethernet local-area networks (LANs) in 2.4 gigahertz bandwidth space.

802.11g   A new IEEE high-speed wireless standard that allows users to transmit data at rates of up to 54 Mbps—nearly five times faster than 802.11b technology.

AAA (authentication, authorization, and accounting)   Pronounced "triple A," this technology is designed to verify a user's identification, ensure that the user is authorized to make a given request, and collect information about the user transaction.

ACLs (access control lists)   The method used to configure and deploy packet filters on Cisco routers. The two main types of ACLs are standard and extended ACLs; standard ACLs filter on IP address, and extended ACLs look further into a packet header if so configured.

active reconnaissance   After a hacker has sufficient information about a target's network, this phase usually begins through passive reconnaissance. The hacker begins taking some risks as he more actively scans and probes a target's network. A hacker actively tries to determine the operating system, the services running, and where the routers and firewalls might be.

ad-hoc   A wireless LAN (WLAN) mode of operation, also known as peer-to-peer wireless networking, in which several wireless computers need to transmit files to each other. This mode of operation is also known as Independent Basic Service Set (IBSS). You can think of ad-hoc as being able to happen without the use of an access point. Each computer can communicate directly with all the other wireless-enabled computers. They can share files and printers this way, but they are unable to access wired LAN resources unless one of the computers acts as a bridge to the wired LAN using special software. (This is called "bridging.")

AH (Authentication Header)   Provides authentication and antireplay services (optional). AH provides services to limited portions of the IP header and extended header but does not provide for encryption of the data by applying a one-way hash to create a message digest of the packet. AH is embedded in the data that is to be protected (a full IP datagram, for example). AH can be used either by itself or with Encryption Service Payload (ESP). Refer to RFC 2402. This protocol has largely been superseded by ESP and is considered deprecated.

application level firewall   A type of firewall that provides the most secure data connections because they can examine every layer in the TCP/IP model of the communication process. To achieve this level of protection, these firewalls—also known as proxies—actually mediate and control connections by intercepting each connection and inspecting it. If the proxy determines that the connection is allowed, it opens a second connection to the server from itself, on behalf of the original host.

associating   In a wireless LAN, the process that establishes communication between a wireless client and a wireless access point.

attack signature   An attack signature details the patterns of misuse in network traffic (packets) that indicate that an attacker is attempting to gain entry into the protected network by using an attack, such as denial of service attempts or the execution of illegal commands during an FTP session.

authentication   One of the functions of the IPSec framework. Authentication establishes the integrity of the data stream and ensures that it is not tampered with in transit. It also provides confirmation about data stream origin. The process of identifying an individual or device based on the correct username/password combination. Authentication does not determine what an individual is allowed to access, but merely that they are who they claim to be. Authorization defines what access an individual is allowed to have—assuming that they have been authenticated, of course!

bit bucket   A lighthearted term meaning trash or garbage can. When saying that a packet is thrown in the bit bucket, this really means that the router, firewall, or proxy has chosen to discard the packet and ultimately all data is just bits (1s and 0s).

CA (Certificate Authority)   A third-party entity that is responsible for issuing and revoking certificates. Each device that has its own certificate and public key of the CA can authenticate every other device within a given CA's domain. This term is also applied to server software that provides these services.

CBAC (Context-Based Access Control)   A stateful packet inspection (SPI) engine that extends the router's filtering capability to the application layer (Layer 7) of the OSI reference model. This is accomplished using CBAC-based access lists CBAC as the heart of the Firewall Feature Set that tracks TCP, ICMP (as of Cisco IOS Software Release 12.2.15T), and UDP-based application packet flows between hosts on either side of the firewall (router), thus performing SPI.

CHAP (Challenge Handshake Authentication Protocol)   A type of authentication in which the client and server know the password. The password is never sent between the devices; instead, MD5 is run on the password and the resulting hash is sent. The receiving device runs MD5 on its password and compares the hashes; if they match, the connection is allowed. By transmitting only the hash, the password cannot be reverse-engineered.

choke point   Refers to a single point in which everything tries to either enter or leave your network.

choke point router   A router that is the single point from which the entire Internet gains access to your network. The router, then, is also a single point of failure.

content filtering   A collection of security solutions designed to monitor and filter content from the Internet, chat rooms, instant messaging, e-mail, e-mail attachments, web browsers, and other applications served over the Internet.

crypto map   A Cisco IOS Software configuration entity that performs two primary functions: (1) selects data flows that need security processing and (2) defines the policy for these flows and the crypto peer to which traffic needs to go. A crypto map is applied to an interface. The concept of a crypto map was introduced in classic crypto but was expanded for IPSec.

CVE   A list of standardized names for vulnerabilities and other information security exposures, CVE aims to standardize the names for all publicly known vulnerabilities and security exposures. A dictionary, *not* a database, the goal of CVE is to make it easier to share data across separate vulnerability databases and security tools. While CVE might make it easier to search for information in other databases, CVE should not be considered a vulnerability database on its own merit. CVE's content is a result of a collaborative effort of the CVE Editorial Board. The Editorial Board includes representatives from numerous security-related organizations such as security tool vendors, academic institutions, the government, and other prominent security experts. The MITRE Corporation maintains CVE and moderates Editorial Board discussions.

DDoS (Distributed Denial of Service)   A type of attack wherein the target site (server or router) receives packets (ICMP, PING, or TCP SYN) that appears to be normal traffic. In reality, this traffic is not normal; the target site is actually flooded with these false packets, which prevent legitimate traffic from accessing the site and thus deny service to real users. In recent days, these attacks have become distributed in nature as computers throughout the World Wide Web join together to attack a site.

DDoS Daemon   A specialized computer program that was designed for use in controlling and coordinating a DDoS attack. As of this writing, there are four known programs: Tribal Village (TFN), TFN2K, Trinoo, and Stacheldraht (which is German for "barbed wire").

DES (Data Encryption Standard)   A standard cryptographic algorithm developed by the U.S. National Bureau of Standards and modified from the IBM Lucifer algorithm.

Diffie-Hellman algorithm   The first public-key algorithm, which is used in IKE negotiations to allow two peers to agree on a shared secret by generating the key for use.

digital signature   A technological means by which you can guarantee that the individual sending the message really is who he claims to be.

DMZ (Demilitarized Zone)   An interface added to a network device that acts as a buffer to protect Internet-accessible servers and services within a network.

downstream liability   This latest entry into the realm of network security is concerned with the fact that, authorized or not, someone is using a system from Company A to attack Company Z; when Company Z investigates this attack, they find that the attack is coming from Company A. The question becomes, who is liable? To further this point, consider what might happen if these two companies are competitors and the attack succeeds?

dumpster diving   **1.** The practice of sifting refuse from an office or technical installation to extract confidential data, especially security-compromising information. ('dumpster' is an Americanism for what is called a 'skip' elsewhere). Back in AT&T's monopoly days, before paper shredders became common office equipment, phone phreaks used to organize regular dumpster runs against phone company plants and offices. Discarded and damaged copies of AT&T internal manuals taught them a great deal. The technique is still rumored to be a favorite of crackers who operate against careless targets. **2.** The practice of raiding the dumpsters behind buildings where producers or consumers of high-tech equipment are located with the expectation (usually justified) of finding discarded but still-valuable equipment to be nursed back to health in some hacker's den. Experienced dumpster divers frequently accumulate basements full of moldering (but still potentially useful) stuff. (http://www.phonelosers.org)

Dynamic NAT   Provides for mapping a private IP address to a public IP address from a group of registered IP addresses. In this type of NAT, there is a one-to-one relationship in the mapping from private to public. For example, if your PC was assigned an internal IP address of 10.0.0.2 and your coworker was 10.0.0.3, each of you would be assigned a public IP address at the firewall via NAT as your traffic went to the Internet.

EAP (Extensible Authentication Protocol)   A Layer 2 (MAC address layer) security protocol that exists at the authentication stage of the security process for a wireless network.

encryption   A means of achieving data security by translating it using a key (password). Encryption prevents the password or key from being easily readable in the configuration file.

ESP (Encapsulated Security Protocol)   A security protocol that provides data confidentiality and protection with optional authentication and replay-detection services. ESP completely encapsulates user data. It can be used either by itself or in conjunction with AH. ESP runs using the TCP protocol on ports 50 and 51 and is documented in RFC 2406.

Extranet VPNs   A type of VPN that allows secure connections with business partners, suppliers and customers for the purpose of e-commerce. Extranet VPNs are an extension of intranet VPNs with the addition of firewalls to protect the internal network.

firewalking   A concept and tool that enables an attacker to send specially crafted packets through a firewall to determine what ports and services are permitted through the firewall. An attacker with this knowledge can make their port scans hidden and thus map your network through your firewall.

firewall   A networking device deployed at the point where private network resources connect to the public Internet and protect networked computers from hostile actions that could compromise internal computers, thereby resulting in data corruption or a denial of service to authorized users. Firewalls can be dedicated hardware devices or specialized software. Before the term "firewall" was used for a component of a computer network, it described a wall that was designed to contain a fire. A brick-and-mortar firewall is designed to contain a fire in one part of a building and thus prevent it from spreading to another part of the building. Any fire that can erupt inside a building stops at the firewall and does not spread to other parts of the building. Therefore, a network firewall will hopefully stop any attack.

GRE (generic routing encapsulation)   A method of encapsulating any network layer protocol over any other network layer protocol. The general specification is described in RFC 1701, and RFC 1702 defines the encapsulation of IP packets using IP. In general, GRE encapsulates a packet called the payload packet, and another protocol called the delivery protocol forwards it to its destination.

hash   Basically a grinder that takes something recognizable, such as beef or pork (metaphorically speaking), hashes it, and ends up with something based on the original, but unique—in this case, hamburger or sausage.

hashcheck   A comparison method used when using a one-way hash operation like MD5. A hashcheck is the comparison of a calculated message digest against the received message digest to verify that the message has not been tampered with.

HIDS (Host-based Intrusion Detection Sensors)   Specialized software applications that are installed on a computer (typically a server) and that watch all inbound and outbound communication traffic to and from that server and monitor the file system for changes. HIDS are extremely effective on mission-critical Internet accessible application servers such as web or e-mail servers because they can watch the application at its source to protect it.

Honeypot   A highly flexible computer system on the Internet that is customized to be a security tool and is expressly set up to attract and "trap" people who attempt to penetrate other people's computer systems through probes, scans, and intrusions.

IDS (Intrusion Detection System)   A security service that monitors and analyzes system events for the purpose of finding (and providing real-time or near real-time warning of) attempts to access system resources in an unauthorized manner.

IKE (Internet Key Exchange)   A security association (SA) that provides negotiation, peer authentication, key management, and key exchange. As a bidirectional protocol, IKE provides a secure communication channel between two devices that is used to negotiate an encryption algorithm, a hash algorithm, an authentication method, and any relevant group information. It uses key exchange based on Diffie-Hellman algorithms, and network administrators can closely tie IKE with policy management systems.

Infrastructure   A wireless LAN (WLAN) mode of operation that requires the use of a Basic Service Set (BSS) that is a wireless access point. The access point is required to allow for wireless computers to connect not only to each other, but also to a wired network. Most corporate WLANs operate in Infrastructure mode because they require access to the wired LAN to use services such as printers and file servers.

inline wiretap   A method of capturing packets by placing a physical *tap* in between (that is, inline between) two network devices. Plugged into this tap would be the Network-based Intrusion Detection Sensor (NIDS).

integrity   A method that ensures that the packet the receiving party receives has not been altered during transmission. This is achieved via the use of a one-way hash algorithm.

intrusion detection   Intrusion detection involves the ongoing monitoring of network traffic by looking at each packet for potential misuse or policy violations. Intrusion detection matches network traffic against lists of attack signatures to look for patterns of misuse.

IPS (Intrusion Prevention Systems)   Systems designed to prevent an attack from being successful at the earliest possible moment. IPS work in conjunction with an Intrusion Detection System (IDS).

IPSec SA (IPSec Security Association)   IPSec SA is unidirectional and thus requires that separate IPSec SAs be established in each direction. IPSec SA is a two-phase, three-modes procedure. In phase 1, two modes can be used—*main mode* and *aggressive mode*. In phase 2, the only mode available is called *quick mode*. The end user has no control over which mode is chosen; rather, the selection is automatic and depends on the configuration parameters set up by both peers.

ISAMKP (Internet Security Association and Key Management Protocol)
A framework that defines the mechanics of implementing a key exchange protocol and negotiating a security policy. ISAKMP is used for secure exchanges of both SA parameters and private keys between peers in an IPSec environment, as well as key creation and management.

L2F (Layer Two Forwarding)   A tunneling protocol developed by Cisco Systems. L2F is similar to the PPTP protocol developed by Microsoft in that it enables organizations to set up virtual private networks (VPNs) that use the Internet backbone to move connect distant sites.

L2TP (Layer Two Tunneling Protocol)   An extension of the Point-to-Point Tunneling Protocol (PPTP) that is documented in RFC 2661 and is used to enable the operation of a virtual private network (VPN) over the Internet. RFC 3193 defines using L2TP over a secure IPSec transport. In this approach, L2TP packets are exchanged over User Datagram Protocol (UDP) port 1701. IPSec Encapsulating Security Payload (ESP) protects UDP payload to ensure secure communication. Cisco and Microsoft agreed to merge their respective L2TP, consequently adopting the best features of two other tunneling protocols: PPTP from Microsoft and Layer 2 Forwarding (L2F) from Cisco Systems.

LAC (L2TP access concentrator)   An L2TP device to which the client directly connects and whereby PPP frames are tunneled to the L2TP network server (LNS). The LAC needs to only implement the media over which L2TP operates to pass traffic to one or more LNS. It might tunnel any protocol carried within PPP.

layered security   A network design concept that implements security consistently at as many points as possible throughout a network. This design concept combats the weaknesses of a network with just a single point of defense.

least access   When access is granted, this principle requires that it is done in as limited a manner as possible, while still allowing the purpose such a connection was granted to be accomplished. In a more functional definition, if access was granted so a user can FTP to a specific server, that is all that she should be allowed to do; therefore, she has the least access possible.

LNS (L2TP network server)   A termination point for an L2TP tunnel and access point where PPP frames are processed and passed to higher layer protocols. The LNS operates on any platform that is capable of PPP termination, and both Cisco and Microsoft have solutions. The LNS handles the server side of the L2TP protocol.

MD5 (Message Digest 5)   Developed in 1994 by Rivest, MD5 is a one-way hash algorithm that takes any length of data and produces a 128-bit nonreversible fingerprint known as a hash. MD5 is officially described in RFC 1321. This output hash/fingerprint cannot be reverse engineered to determine the data that was used to produce it. Functionally, this means that it is impossible to derive the original file contents from the MD5; this is why they call it one-way.

NAT (Network Address Translation)   An IP address mechanism deployed and implemented on a device (firewall, router, or computer) that sits between an internal network using private IP addresses and the Internet, which uses public IP addresses. The device performing the *Address Translation* from private to public is usually a firewall and, to a lesser extent, a router. The device performing NAT usually sits with one part connected to the internal network and another part connected to the Internet (or some external network).

NIDS (Network-based Intrusion Detection Sensor)   An IDS that resides directly on the network and watches all traffic traversing the network. NIDS are effective at both watching for inbound/outbound traffic flows, and traffic between hosts on or between local network segments. NIDS are typically deployed in front of *and* behind firewalls and VPN gateways to measure the effectiveness of those security devices and to interact with them to add more depth to your network's security.

NMAP ("Network Mapper") An open source utility for network exploration or security auditing. Although it works fine against single hosts, NMAP was designed to rapidly scan large networks. It uses raw IP packets in novel ways to determine what hosts are available on the network, what services (ports) they are offering, what operating system (and OS version) they are running, what type of packet filters/firewalls are in use, and dozens of other characteristics. NMAP runs on most types of computers, and both console and graphical versions are available. NMAP is free software that is available with full source code under the terms of the GNU GPL. (http://www.insecure.org)

OAKLEY A key exchange protocol that defines how to acquire authenticated key information. The basic mechanism for OAKLEY is the Diffie-Hellman key exchange algorithm. You can find the standard in RFC 2412, *The OAKLEY Key Determination Protocol*.

open key authentication An authentication method used during the associating phase between a wireless client and a wireless access point. This default authentication method is considered the easiest to use, although it provides no security whatsoever.

overloading A form of dynamic Network Address Translation (NAT) that provides for the translation of multiple private IP addresses to a single public IP address by using different TCP ports. Known also as PAT (Port Address Translation) or single address NAT, this type of NAT is the most commonly used because it serves large numbers of users at once.

packet filtering One of the oldest and most common types of packet inspection technologies available, packet filtering begins by inspecting the contents of a packet to determine whether the contents match the criteria based on a predetermined set of applied rules. If the packet contents match these rules, the packet is allowed. The packet is dropped if the contents do not match the rules of the preset packet filtering rules.

packet sniffer   An application that enables the user to capture all packets going out over a single or multiple Ethernet connection for later inspection. These "sniffer" applications grab the packet, analyze it, and reveal the data payload contained within. The theft of an authorized user's identity poses one of the greatest threats caused by a packet sniffer.

PAP (Password Authentication Protocol)   An authentication protocol that could be used and, because of its poor encryption, it has been considered deprecated. PAP uses "clear text" during the authentication process so, in my opinion, offers "no" encryption.

passive reconnaissance   Steps a hacker takes to learn more about a potential target through means that do not alert the target to what is occurring. Examples include dumpster diving, visual observation of companies buildings, observing and eavesdropping on employees, packet sniffer (usually easy to do if target has wireless improperly deployed), and researching the target through commonplace tools on the Internet such as nslookup.

PKI (Public Key Infrastructure)   An evolving security technology that will eventually become an IETF standard. The goal of PKI is to provide a foundation for a system that will support a variety of security services, such as data integrity, data confidentiality, and nonrepudiation. PKI will provide through a combination of hardware, software, procedures, and policies so users can communicate and securely exchange information regardless of location.

POLP (Policy of Least Privilege)   A network security practice where access decisions are based on the concept of "block everything and allow only what is needed to conduct business." This is the default action of Cisco firewalls.

port mirroring   Also known as port spanning, depending on the switch you are using, this technique tells the switch to send copies of every packet that (for example) are to be sent to the port your firewall is plugged into to another port. The Network-Based Intrusion Detection Sensor (NIDS) is connected to this mirrored port.

PPTP (Point-to-Point Tunneling Protocol)   A protocol (set of communication rules) that allows corporations to extend their own corporate network through private "tunnels" over the public Internet. Effectively, a corporation uses a wide-area network (WAN) as a single large local area network. A company no longer needs to lease its own lines for wide-area communication, but it can securely use the public networks. This kind of interconnection is known as a virtual private network (VPN).

proxy   See application level firewall.

RADIUS (Remote Authentication Dial-In User Service)   A client-server based system that secures a Cisco network against intruders. RADIUS is a protocol that is implemented in Cisco IOS Software that sends authentication requests to a RADIUS server. A RADIUS server is a device that has the RADIUS daemon or application installed. RADIUS must be used with AAA to enable the authentication, authorization, and accounting of remote users.

remote access VPN   A type of VPN that allows individual dialup users to connect to a central site across the Internet or other public network service in a secure way. This type of VPN is a user-to-LAN connection that allows employees that have a need to connect to the corporate LAN from the field. Their systems use special VPN Client software that enables a secure link between themselves and the corporate LAN. Typically, a corporation that wishes to set up a large remote access VPN provides some form of Internet dialup account to its users using an ISP. The tele-commuters can then dial a toll free number to reach the Internet and use their VPN client software to access the corporate network. A good example of a company that needs a remote access VPN would be a large firm with hundreds of sales people in the field. Remote access VPNs are sometimes referred to as soft (as in software-based) VPNs, virtual private dialup networks (VPDN), or dial VPNs. Users pay a low "fixed cost" to a local ISP using a local call and therefore no long distance fees.

Rogue APs   Deployed wireless access points (WAPs) that have not been officially authorized for use within a company by its IT department. Rogue APs can leave a company's network vulnerable to attacks.

RSA   A public key cryptographic algorithm (named after its inventors, Rivest, Shamir, and Adleman) with a variable key length. RSA's main weakness is that it is significantly slow to compute compared to popular secret-key algorithms, such as DES. Cisco's IKE implementation uses a Diffie-Hellman exchange to get the secret keys. This exchange can be authenticated with RSA (or preshared keys). With the Diffie-Hellman exchange, the DES key never crosses the network (not even in encrypted form), which is not the case with the RSA encrypt and sign technique. RSA is not public domain, and it must be licensed.

script kiddie (sometimes spelled kiddy)   Coined by the more sophisticated hackers of computer security systems, a derogative term for the more immature, but unfortunately often just as dangerous exploiter of security lapses on the Internet.

security protocol   A secure procedure for regulating data transmission between computers.

shared key authentication   An authentication method used during the associating phase between a wireless client and a wireless access point. When the access point is set to shared key authentication, an access point is transmitted a challenge key after a client device associates with the access point. The client device encrypts the challenge key using WEP and returns it to the access point. The client device is allowed to transmit if the proper WEP encryption is used.

shunning   An attack prevention technique that allows the IDS to automatically configure your prescreening router or firewall to deny traffic based on what it has detected, thereby shunning the connection. As Intrusion Detection Systems (IDS) become more advanced; this shunning is evolving into a new term—*blocking*— where an IDS contacts a router or firewall and creates an access control list (ACL) to block the attacking IP address.

site survey   A process by which someone deploying a wireless LAN can detect (among other things) other wireless access points that are configured to broadcast on the same channel as the intended deployed NIC.

Site-to-Site VPNs   A type of VPN used to extend a company's existing LAN to other buildings and sites through use of dedicated equipment so that remote employees at these locations can utilize the same network services. These types of VPNs are considered actively connected at all times. Site-to-Site VPNs are sometimes referred to as hard (as in hardware-based) VPNs, Intranet, or LAN-to-LAN VPNs.

smurf attack   A type of denial of service (DoS) attack that exploits the use of the Internet Control Message Protocol (ICMP, a.k.a. PING) and IP's network and broadcast addresses. A smurf attack's purpose is to disable a target host or network by consuming all of its resources; aside from this, it causes no permanent damage.

sniping   An attack prevention technique that allows the Intrusion Detection System (IDS) to terminate a suspected attack using a TCP Reset packet or an ICMP unreachable message.

social engineering   A term used to define hacking techniques whose goal is to fool people into revealing passwords or other potentially sensitive information that compromises a target system's security. Classic social engineering scams include phoning up a target that has the required information and posing as a field service technician or a fellow employee with an urgent problem.

SPI (Stateful Packet Inspection)   An advanced technique of packet inspection usually implemented in a firewall so TCP/IP connections can be more closely inspected.

split tunneling   A method by which a remote VPN user or site is allowed to access a public network (the Internet) at the same time that he accesses the private VPN without placing the public network traffic inside the tunnel first.

SSID (Service Set Identifier)   A 32-bit character that identifies a wireless network. By default, the header of the wireless packet's broadcast includes the SSID from a wireless access point (WAP) every 10 milliseconds. The SSID differentiates one WLAN from another; therefore, all access points and all devices attempting to connect to a specific WLAN must use the same SSID. A device is not permitted to join the wireless network unless it can provide the unique SSID. It is strongly recommended that WAPs have the broadcasting of their SSID disabled.

SSL (Secure Socket Layer)   A certificate-generating protocol whereby a web browser confirms the validity of the SSL certificate and proceeds to communicate in a secure mode with the server so you can complete a secure web-based transaction.

static NAT   Provides for mapping a private IP address to a public IP address on a one-to-one basis. Particularly useful when a device needs to be accessible from outside the network—for example, if your web server has an internal IP address of 10.0.0.1 and it needs to be accessible from the Internet—it is your web server after all! NAT must be statically configured to allow users who go to a public IP address to always be translated to 10.0.0.1. The use of static NAT is quite common for devices like web servers that always need to be accessible from the Internet.

syslog (System Message Logging)   Syslog provides a means for the system and its running processes to report various types of system state information. There are three classes of system state data: error, informational, and debug. Cisco IOS Software provides an extensive system message and error reporting facility. In fact, IOS uses more than 500 service identifiers known as "facilities" to categorize system state data for error and event message reporting. System logging data is an important resource in diagnosing problems in general and, when sued by the Firewall Feature Set, it allows for the reporting of events.

TACACS (Terminal Access Controller Access Control System)   A client/server-based system that secures a Cisco network against intruders. Three methods of TACACS exist: TACACS, extended TACACS, and TACACS+. All three methods authenticate users and deny access to users who do not have a valid username and password.

TCP/IP Model   A functional protocol model similar to the OSI reference model and consisting of five layers.

VPN (virtual private network)   A network constructed using a public network, such as the Internet, to connect systems to a main site, typically the headquarters. VPNs use encryption mechanisms to protect data that is transmitted across the Internet. Additional protections are also put in place to ensure that only authorized users or devices can connect via a VPN.

VPN-aware firewall This type of firewall either has special software that understands VPNs or dedicated hardware that allows for the encryption/decryption of user data.

VPN Concentrator A dedicated hardware device whose only role in a network is to allow VPNs to connect to it, thereby allowing users access to other network resources.

vulnerability scanning A proactive process that scans systems to determine whether they can be exploited using software that seeks out known security flaws in software.

WapChalking Variant of WarChalking set up by the Wireless Access Point Sharing Community, an informal group whose code of conduct forbids the use of wireless access points without permission. The group uses the WarChalking marks as an invitation to wireless users to join its community. In WapChalking terms, the two half-moon open node mark means that a wireless access device is currently indicating factory default settings and is thus easily detected.

WarChalking The practice of marking a series of symbols on sidewalks and walls to indicate nearby wireless access. This way, other computer users can open their laptops and wirelessly connect to the Internet for free. WarChalking was inspired by the practice of hobos during the Great Depression of using chalk marks to indicate which homes were friendly.

WarDialing An early form of hacking involving dialing random numbers in hopes of finding a modem attached to a computer.

WarDriving The act of driving around in a vehicle to look for unsecured wireless networks. Part of the appeal here is that you can now use GPS systems that are connected to your laptop, which are then powered by your car. This makes the act of WarDriving accurate and potentially rewarding for people looking for an unsecured wireless network because they can cover a much larger area with a vehicle than by simply walking.

WarFlying (a.k.a. WarStorming)   The act of searching for unsecured wireless networks while flying in an airplane. This act was first recorded in Perth, Australia.

WarSpamming   The act of sending spam after hijacking an unsecured connection to a wireless LAN.

WEP (Wired Equivalent Privacy)   A method intended to give wireless users the security equivalent to being on a wired network. With WEP turned on, when a packet is transmitted from one access point to a client device, the packet is first encrypted by taking the packet's data and a secret 40-bit number and passing them both through an encryption algorithm called RC4. The resulting encrypted packet is then transmitted to the client device. When the client device receives the WEP encrypted packet, it uses the same 40-bit number to pass the encrypted data through RC4 algorithm backward, resulting in the client receiving the data. Of course, this process occurs in reverse, and a client device is transmitting data to an access point.

Wi-Fi (Wireless Fidelity)   The commonly used term to describe 802.11 wireless networks. Wi-Fi also refers to certification by the Wi-Fi Alliance, an international nonprofit association of 802.11 product vendors. 802.11 products that receive Wi-Fi certification have been tested and found to be interoperable with other certified products.

wireless networking   A term referring to radio technology that enables two or more computers to communicate using standard network protocols such as IP but without cables.

zombie computer   A computer, typically Windows-based, that has been compromised and, without the knowledge of its owner, has had a DDoS Program installed that will control the generation of packets toward the intended victim. Zombie Computers are also known as agents because they respond to commands from other systems.

zombie network   A term used in a DDoS attack that describes the linking of multiple zombie computers into a "virtual" distributed network, allowing the hacker to coordinate their operation to initiate a DDoS against a target. The installation of one of the four commonly acknowledged DDoS programs—TFN, TFN2K, Trinoo, and Stacheldraht—is key in this network.

INDEX

J-K

Java applet blocking, 201
Jones, Matt, 28

keepalives (TCP), enabling, 216
key IDS functions, 327–329

L

L2F (Layer 2 Forwarding), 140
L2TP (Layer 2 Tunneling
Protocol), 139
   benefits of, 141
   LAC, 142
   network architecture, 142
   operation, 142–143
   versus PPTP, 140–141
L2TP Network Server (L2TP
Network Server), 140
LAC (L2TP Access
Concentrator), 140–142
land Attack, 40
land attacks, 364
layered security, 86
LEAP, 309
legality of WarDriving, 292
liability, downstream, 34

limitations
   of ACLs, 95
   of choke routers, 196
   of content filtering, 111
   of FFS, 213–214
   of firewalls, 184–185
   of IPS, 342–343, 345
   of NAT, 103–104
   of PKI, 114–115
   of proxy firewalls, 107–108
   of PPTP, 138–139
   of SSH, 152–153
   of WEP, 306
line vty command, 227
local authentication, TACACS+, 218
lock and key dynamic ACLs, 199
log analysis, 336
log messages, time stamping, 216
logging
   console logging, 218
   enabling, 217
   NetFlow, 225
   Syslog, 225
login sessions, SSH, 145
   authentication ciphers, 150
   limitations of, 152–153
   operation, 149–151
   port forwarding, 151
   versus Telnet, 146–149

S

X-Y-Z

CISCO SYSTEMS

Cisco Press

3 STEPS TO LEARNING

STEP 1　　　　　**STEP 2**　　　　　**STEP 3**

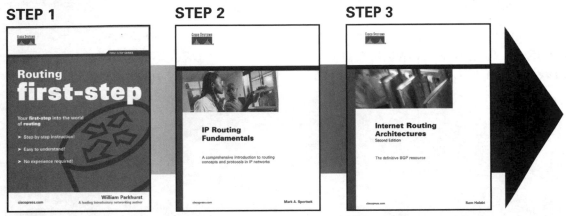

First-Step　　　**Fundamentals**　　　**Networking Technology Guides**

STEP 1　**First-Step**—Benefit from easy-to-grasp explanations. No experience required!

STEP 2　**Fundamentals**—Understand the purpose, application, and management of technology.

STEP 3　**Networking Technology Guides**—Gain the knowledge to master the challenge of the network.

NETWORK BUSINESS SERIES

The Network Business series helps professionals tackle the business issues surrounding the network. Whether you are a seasoned IT professional or a business manager with minimal technical expertise, this series will help you understand the business case for technologies.

Justify Your Network Investment.

Look for Cisco Press titles at your favorite bookseller today.

Visit **www.ciscopress.com/series** for details on each of these book series.

DISCUSS
NETWORKING PRODUCTS AND TECHNOLOGIES WITH CISCO EXPERTS AND NETWORKING PROFESSIONALS WORLDWIDE

**VISIT NETWORKING PROFESSIONALS
A CISCO ONLINE COMMUNITY
WWW.CISCO.COM/GO/DISCUSS**

CISCO SYSTEMS

THIS IS THE POWER OF THE NETWORK. now.